ROLAND PENROSE

THE FRIENDLY SURREALIST

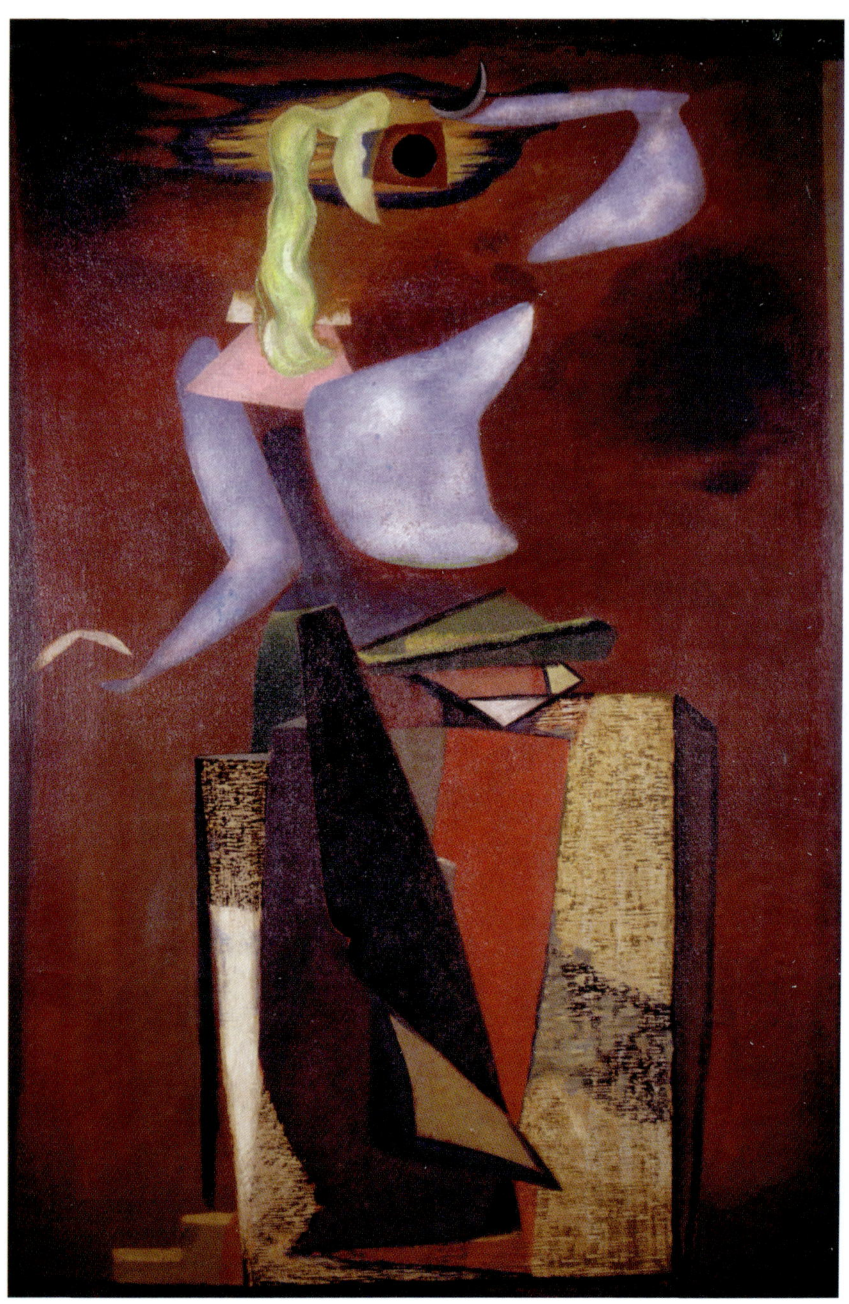

Abstract Composition, 1946, Oil on Panel. Collection Ami Bouhassane

ROLAND PENROSE
THE FRIENDLY SURREALIST

A Memoir by
Antony Penrose

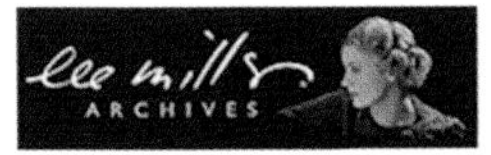

Colophon 2020

FIRST EDITION: Prestel Verlag Munich • London • New York 2001
REVISED AND EXTENDED EDITION: Lee Miller Archives, UK 2020

Farleys House and Gallery Ltd are the managing agents of the Lee Miller Archives
Farleys House, Muddles Green, East Sussex, BN8 6HW, England
www.leemiller.co.uk

A catalogue record of this book is available from the British Library
ISBN: 978 0953 23 8958

Designed by Unicorn Publishing Group and the Lee Miller Archives
Printed by Unicorn Publishing Group

CONTENTS

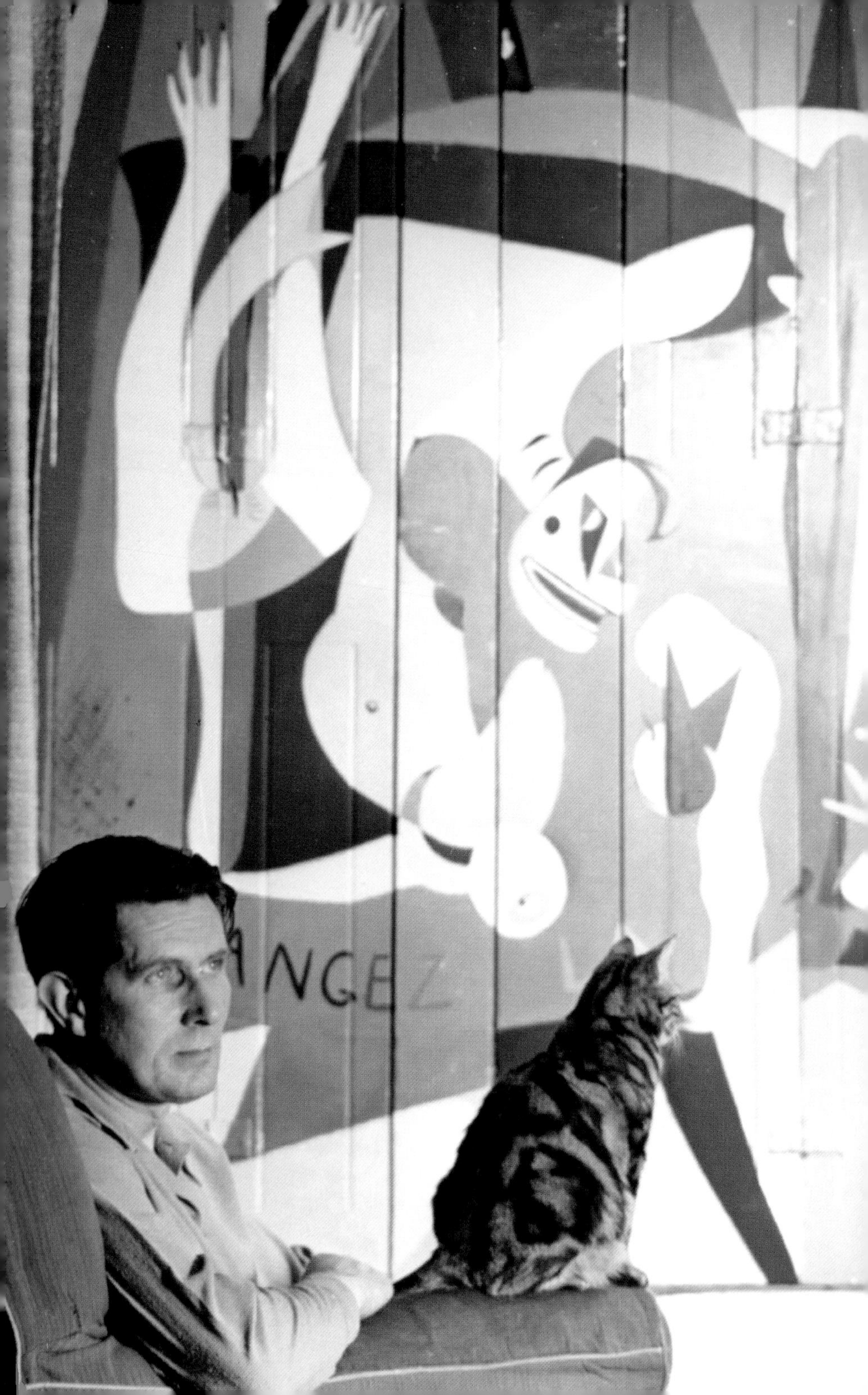
ANGEZ

FOREWORD

George Melly

If the friends and acquaintances of your youth become famous and remain of interest today, and especially if they are dead, you yourself become fascinating through association, a living example of the person questioned by Robert Browning in Memorabilia:

> *'Ah did you once see Shelley plain?*
> *And did he stop and speak to you…?'*

In this category Antony Penrose certainly qualifies. As a child he played with Picasso and took for granted the visits to his father's farm of Max Ernst, Miró, Man Ray and many others. This book could in fact have got by on gossip and anecdote, and there's plenty of that, but it's only the icing on a rich, many-layered cake.

It describes, for example, a typical English case: the young anarchic rebel who metamorphoses into a landed country gent – from Surrealist to Sir Roland. In Penrose's case, however, it didn't affect his wonderful eye; there was no parallel shift from Miró to Munnings. What's more, his position within the Establishment allowed him to manipulate within the then rather stuffy art world. Without Roland's generosity, the Tate Modern for one would have been much the poorer.

Although he quarrelled with it off and on in later years, the Institute of Contemporary Art in London was his most significant achievement. It

OPPOSITE: Roland Penrose, painter and collector, Downshire Hill, London, England 1940

helped stimulate much of what has proved significant in British post-war art, not always to Roland's taste. All this, and with admirable objectivity, Antony describes exactly. Nor must it be forgotten how good-mannered and charming Roland was. This too leaps off the page.

What Surrealism did for Penrose – among other things – was to release him sexually from his inhibiting Quaker background. He comes across, however (and here Antony is extremely open) as a complicated masochist, his love-making usually involving a set of police handcuffs. In particular his second wife Lee Miller, great beauty, photographer, tragic drunk and the subject of Antony's previous book, treated him like a doormat. Of course he loved her to distraction.

The final and deepest level of this remarkable book is how Antony himself learnt to love and understand his often impossible parents. The odds were against him, especially in Lee's case. But Antony is a real farmer now, the harvest is safely gathered in – *and* he played with Picasso.

For Roz

My beloved fellow traveller

PREFACE

Roland's Surrealist gift of friendship has never been more apparent to me than in my encounters with his friends. Many I already knew from their visits to Farley Farm, but until writing this memoir, others were only names. Some were completely unknown to me, but as soon as it was known I was researching about Roland or Valentine, doors were opened to me with a generosity of spirit inspired by their affections for Roland or their admiration for his work. There is a whole story in my quest for Roland, but I have to condense it into a few brief lines, wholly inadequate to convey my gratitude to all who helped me.

This book would not have been possible without the work of Michael Sweeney, who over ten years archived all of Roland's books and papers which are now in the Roland Penrose Archive at the Scottish National Gallery of Modern Art, Edinburgh. He then took a further three years to amass the notes and interviews that form the database for this book, which is now part of the Roland Penrose Archive. My warmest thanks to Ann Simpson, Liz Ficken and Jane Furness of the Scottish National Gallery of Modern Art Library for their patience and professionalism during the many weeks I spent crouched in their archive. Michael's research work was funded by The Elephant Trust, and I am particularly indebted to the original Elephants, the Chairman Lord Hutchinson, and John Bodley, Joanna Drew, John Golding, Julie Lawson and Antony Forwood for their encouragement and tenacious support. The enthusiam of the new Elephants chaired by Joanna Drew, with Nikos Stangos, Sarah Whitfield, Dawn Ades, and Richard Wentworth as trustees, continues in the best tradition.

I am deeply indebted to Carole Callow and Arabella Hayes at the Lee Miller Archives, who cheerfully undertook the massive task of printing the many photographs by Roland, Lee and others from which many of the illustrations have been selected. The photographs also provided information about many topics, particularly the Balkan and Egyptian travels and Roland's collection.

I am very grateful to people from other archives and collections for their help: Joanna Drew and the Arts Council Archive; Jennifer Booth and Adrian Glew, Tate Archive; Chris Webster and Jennifer Stuart-Smith, Tate Publishing; Charlotte Lorimer, The Bridgeman Art Library; Rosa Maria Malet, Fundació Joan Miró; Anne Baldassari, Museé Picasso; Jenny Ramakalawon, The British Museum; James Kilvington, National Portrait Gallery; Toby Whatley, Ferens Art Gallery, Hull; Vicky Isley, Southampton Art Gallery; The Getty Research Institute, Los Angeles; James Mayor and the Mayor Gallery Archive; Andrew Murray, Andrew Murray Archive; Lee Gruver, Penn State University; Malcolm Davis, The Brotherton Library, University of Leeds; Alice Beckley and Martin Davis, The Henry Moore Foundation; Melanie Clore, Phillipe Garnier and Lavinia Calza, Sotheby's; and Mary Shackleton, Religious Society of Friends in Ireland. Harriet Mackay of The National Trust, 2 Willow Road, and Paula Arnold of The National Trust, Peckover House, and their staff generously assisted me, and I am also grateful to the Wisbech Society and Christina Swaine, biographer of the Peckover family. My thanks to Neil Hamilton for his researches on Oxhey Grange, and to Norbert Lynton and Anthony Van Laast for the information they gave me. Major Robert Priestley kindly provided information about General Montgomery. Dr Jeffrey and Ruth Sherwin gave me details of their collection, and Jeff Towns contributed information on Dylan Thomas.

I am most grateful to Françoise Gilot for the generosity of spirit she showed in talking to me about the painful events surrounding the publication of this book. Mylene Bresson kindly answered my questions about Robert Bresson's films, and Christo Georgadidis helped me decode *The Road Is Wider Than Long* during an unforgettable journey around Greece. I will always remember with gratitude and affection Baudoin

Jannink, the owner of Le Pouy and Monique Soulyarol, the owner of Villa Les Mimosas for the warmth of their hospitality.

Henri and Elvira Faget de Cassaigne, as dedicated historians of the Gers and relatives of Valentine, gave me an invaluable insight into her early life and her family, greatly assisted by her relatives Marie-Gilberte and Jacques Devise, and Gisèle Aimon, Georgiana Coleville and Whitney Chadwick both contributed valuable understandings of Valentine's work. Gwendoline Wells translated Valentine's letters with particular sensitivity.

Michel Remy was wonderfully generous with his knowledge of British Surrealism, and my thanks to David and Judy Gascoyne, George Melly, Conroy Maddox and Simon Watson-Taylor, who were there at the time. I am very grateful to the many people who gave interviews to Michael Sweeney, in particular Robert Short, Bill Turnbull, Kenneth Armitage and David Sylvester. Thanks also to Rosemarie Scherman for her generous and continued support.

Patsy Murray encouraged me throughout, helping me recall events and the spirit of Roland at Farleys. Thanks also to Georgina (neé Murray) and David Erskine, Peter Braden, Terry O'Brien, John and Cynthia Thompson, Joanna Drew, Julie and Alastair Lawson, David Sylvester, Daniella Kochavi, Anthony van Laast and Ron and Frances Geesin for rekindling so many memories. In Hampstead Diana Uhlman, her daughter Caroline Compton, Margaret Gardiner, and Richard and Deborah Klein helped me recreate the Downshire Hill years.

The Penrose family is spread across the world, and I have greatly enjoyed the renewal of contact this project has brought. A thank you to Annie Penrose, Gerry Penrose, Sam Penrose, Professor Oliver Penrose, Sir Roger Penrose, Dominic Penrose, James Penrose, Edward Penrose, Joan Jenkins, Gwen Penrose, John Penrose, and Dr Shirley Hodgeson for the much-valued help you have all given.

I will always be grateful to my readers Christopher Johnstone, Sue Butler, Patsy Murray and Roz Penrose for their insightful and constructive criticism. At the Scottish National Gallery of Modern Art Richard Calvocoressi and Keith Harley have been unfailing in their help and enthusiasm for this memoir and for their major exhibitions of works by Roland and Lee. My gratitude goes to Janis Adams, Head of the Publications Department for enabling this work to originally be published by Prestel, where I want to thank Philippa Hurd most sincerely for her sensitive and constructive editing.

I am very grateful to everyone on the farm and in my other various enterprises who have tolerated my neglect of them, thus freeing me to concentrate on this book. Finally, I could not have completed this task without the help of my friends and most especially my family, Ami and Salim Bouhassane, Eliza, Genevieve, Joshua and above all Roz, for her deep understanding and for cheering me on in the dark moments.

ANTONY PENROSE

PROLOGUE

'Let me quote you a little saying of Apollinaire's: 'One will never grasp reality once and for all; the truth will always be new.' That's it, isn't it?'

Roland Penrose[1]

On the morning Roland died, the first person to ring up was Henry Moore. His strong, kind voice with a trace of a Yorkshire accent warmed me. Did I know Roland was one of the best friends he had ever had? Did I know the first big sculpture he ever sold was to Roland, and that gave him money and confidence when he needed it most? 'He helped me, and a lot of other people, he was one of the most important people in the development of modern art in this country,' said Henry, 'he was a good man.'

Letters flooded in from all parts of the world, heartfelt and personal. Bill Hayter wrote:

> 'We met seldom in these last years but our friendship never lapsed – so that I cannot adjust to the idea that we shall meet no more, merely far off. His greatest contribution was the talent he had for bringing people together in creative action with unfailing patience and kindness. You have a whole life before you while mine is nearly done but the privilege of knowing such a man as your father is something we shall always remember with gratitude. We shall not see his like again.'[2]

The obituaries recorded his achievements in the world of art. None spoke of the precious things we knew, such as his plantations of poplar trees, sweet chestnut and Scots pine, now grown tall, the secret places in the woods he frequented where the ceps grew and the rare orchid known as the twae blade flourished, or the fat Labrador dog who still waited patiently. No one could write of how much I missed the smell of his cigars, the scuff of his leather slippers on the brick floors or his unashamedly tuneless whistle when he was happy. Suzanna and I scattered Roland's ashes in his beloved garden at Farleys. We made sure some fell on those of Lee and of Valentine.

The show at the Gardner Arts Centre, University of Sussex, opened ten days after he died.[3] It was the first time the work of Lee and Roland had ever been exhibited together.

On 22 October we hired the ICA for an evening and invited everyone we could think of to *Roland's Party*. The two cinemas ran a continuous programme of films associated with Roland, including *L'Age d'Or.* In the theatre, Ron Geesin elevated the music of the banjo, milk churns and piano to unprecedented heights. Anthony Van Laast and Micha Begesse performed *Three Piece Suite*, a witty high camp duet in underpants and sequins. Two young dancers, Cherie Gillespie and Oke Wambu, performed a tenderly erotic pas de deux that would have thrilled Roland to the core. The flamenco guitarist Juan Martin played the accompaniment to a silent film entitled *Guernica* that I made and dedicated to Roland, and followed with works from his album *Picasso Portraits*.

About five hundred people from all walks of life jostled and talked. Roland was remembered with love and affection, and in a surreal way he was more present than if he had been there in person. Indeed he truly was and remains *Surréalist dans l'amitié.*

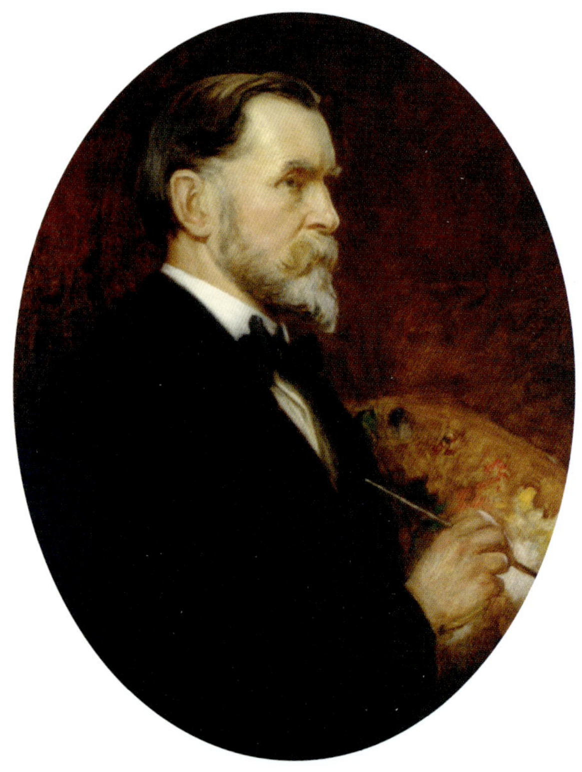

Self-portrait, *c.* 1893. Oil on canvas by James Doyle Penrose

1

1900-19

'As the Twig is Bent, Thus the Tree shall Grow'

Anon.

The oilskin-clad figure seen habitually stumping round Farley Farm, rain or shine, seemed indistinguishable from any other Sussex farmer. Stick in hand, battered trilby jammed on his head and an amiable fat Labrador trotting at his heels, he belonged in his surroundings as surely as the gnarled oaks in the hedgerows. The mist of rain might fog his heavy-rimmed spectacles, but nothing would dull the piercing blue of the eyes, protected by craggy eyebrows and distorted by the spectacle lenses so they appeared to study the world from a distance. As he walked, he scrutinised intensely every detail of the land like a farmer whose profession relied on acute observation.

In the summer the farmer disguise was less convincing. The oilskin might give way to an un-farmerish boldly striped blue and white shirt and later in the season he might be seen carrying home a basket full of cêpe, a most un-English partiality. Judged by local standards, those who accompanied him on his walks were often decidedly weird and he conversed freely with them in a language recognisable by his gesticulations as French. Some of his visitors had recognisable names – he had taken Picasso into the village pub and Man Ray had been seen on television so he was known to be important.

He had two wives living together in the same house and many tales were repeated of strange goings on. This was not entirely surprising behaviour for someone who was said to have been at the centre of avant-garde art, but those who visited were always made welcome with warmth and impeccable English old-world manners. Inside the old farmhouse visitors found comfortable but frayed furniture and walls painted pink, brick red, yellow or sky blue from which hung one of the world's major private collections of modern art. For some it was a bewildering experience.

From time to time his picture would appear in the newspaper linked to important events in the art world, usually connected with the Tate Gallery or the Institute of Contemporary Art. He had been honoured with a CBE and a knighthood. He was clearly famous for something; but in Muddles Green he seemed more interested in his cows, hearing the call of a rare bird in the woods, or studying the lore of the Long Man of Wilmington.[1]

These were but small outward signs of the many paradoxes surrounding Roland Penrose, the man who was born into a family of strict Victorian Quakers, who vowed to live the life of a hedonist, yet who became utterly dedicated to advancing the careers of others. He was a member of the Surrealist movement who became a figure of the establishment and saw the art that was incubated in the heat of subversive protest enshrined in the world's most prestigious museums.

My own Roland Penrose was a completely different person to the Roland Penrose that other people knew. He was my father, but later in life I could never bring myself to call him Dad or Daddy and I assiduously avoided referring to him as 'my father', which led to some interesting verbal contortions when talking about him to others. Among friends and family I mostly called him 'The Old Man', a term which held the grudging respect that might be afforded a sea captain.

As a child I was aware that Roland Penrose had many faces. His disguises enabled him to blend with his surroundings like a chameleon, yet although I had not the words to express it, I instinctively knew he was the same person underneath. Not surprisingly he was a Libra and he made a success of weighing and balancing the disparate and sometimes apparently irreconcilable elements of his life.

It baffled me that given the delights of the farm he should want to go to London at all, but when he was not overseas he would leave on a Monday afternoon and return on Friday afternoon, regular as clockwork. He would make puns about his desire to 'make week-ends meet' and stay permanently in the country, but in truth he needed a balance between the earthiness of the farm and the sophistication of the city.

As I grew up I became aware of his many contradictory aspects and on the whole failed to understand how he made sense of them himself. The paradoxes of his life would have been easy for him if he had been superficial or dishonest, but he was a genuine person with great honesty and empathy for others. I believe he would go to any lengths to avoid hurting another person, yet he had a darker side and was seemingly unaware of how badly some of his actions hurt those closest to him. After he died I could say I knew him well, I loved him dearly, but I understood him hardly at all. That is the way he wanted it to be, but years after his death I find myself still searching for revelations about what constituted his relentless inner drive.

The date of his birth was 14 October 1900 and with his Surrealist love of the serendipitous quality of chance he was fond of pointing out the day was the 834th anniversary of the Battle of Hastings.

In a television interview in his seventy-fifth year he unexpectedly talked of the 'inner light' which was the background to the deepest level of his conscience.[2] Later in a radio interview, he said; *'Certainly I don't think I would ever have become a Surrealist in the ardent way I did if I hadn't been born a Quaker. My parents on both sides were very strict and puritanical Quakers'.*[3]

His autobiography that he modestly titled *Scrap Book* begins:

> *'I was born in a cloud smelling strongly of oil paint, honest banking and piety'.*[4]

Roland's father, James Doyle Penrose 2nd was a moderately successful portrait painter, whose work turned to historical or religious themes following his marriage to Josephine, the daughter of Lord Peckover the wealthy East Anglian banker. The pince-nez severity of his mother Josephine's upbringing by her maiden aunts had done nothing to prepare her for motherhood. Her first pregnancy was a terrifying ordeal that ended with her locking herself in the bathroom at the onset of labour and refusing to allow anyone to come near her. She survived, but the child was born dead. It is hard to understand why, but

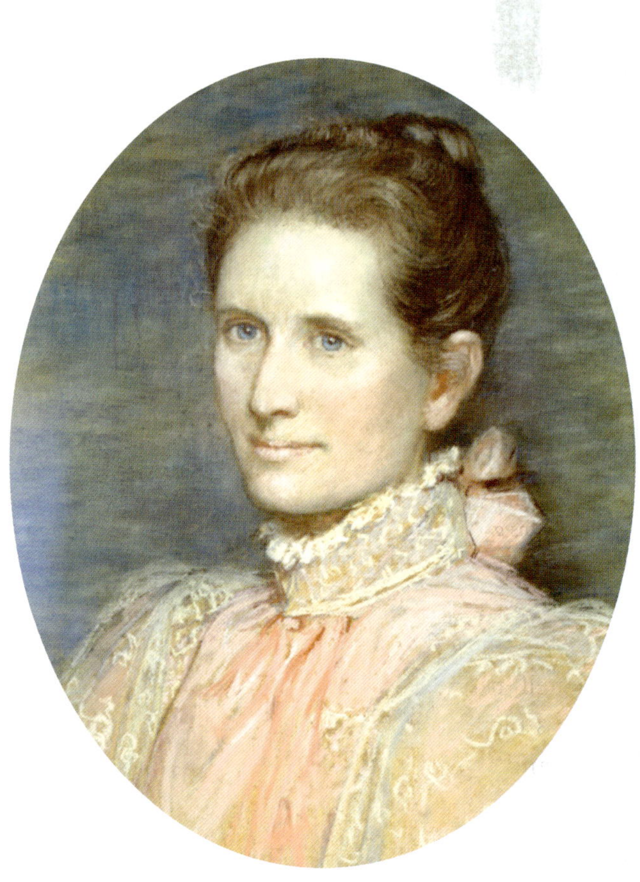

Josephine Penrose, about the time of her wedding in 1893, chalk on paper, by James Doyle Penrose

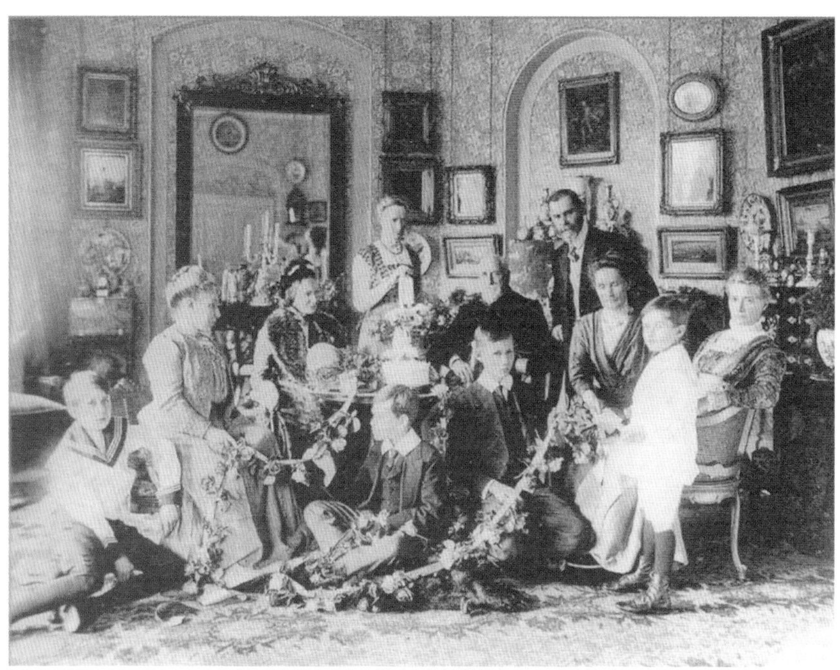

Alexander Peckover on his eightieth birthday, presented with a ribbon of eighty roses and a telegram, 1910. Left to right, in front: Roland, his brothers Lionel, Alec and Beacus. Left to right, behind: Roland's great aunts Algerina and Priscilla Hanna, his aunt Alexandrina, his grandfather Lord Peckover, his parents James Doyle and Josephine Penrose, and his aunt Anna Jane. Photographer unknown.

she allowed herself to become pregnant again, this time successfully carrying Roland's older brother Alexander (Alec). He was born four years before Roland in 1896, followed by Lionel in 1898 and finally Bernard, known as Beacus, was born in 1903. Josephine found her maternal duties conflicted with her charitable work, so she engaged a Norland-trained nurse to care for the children.

In 1908 the family moved from London to Oxhey Grange, a vast Victorian country house standing in an estate of 110 acres near Watford. Nearly all parents try to protect their children from harmful influences and the Penroses were more successful than most. While the boys were growing up in those golden years before World War I when Queen Victoria's values still ruled, the parents managed to create an environment for the children prescribed by the boundary of their estate that must have come close to their ideal world.

In this context much more than just the landscape of mock Tudor gables and rhododendrons was un-real. Roland's parents' insistence on the value of unworldliness created a separate reality within which great efforts were made to exclude the many things that they considered immoral or otherwise harmful. In many ways the boys were to find the estate a prison, albeit with plush-velvet-covered bars. The web of parental constraints gave the boys much to rebel against and whenever Roland spoke of his childhood it was easy to feel his resentment against the cocooning that surrounded him.

Morning prayers with father, James Doyle Penrose, the second, reading from the Bible with his stumbling diction, evening prayers, Meetings on Sunday in the corrugated iron meeting house in Watford, Monthly Meetings at Jordans Meeting House and frequent prayer meetings at Oxhey itself. The unshakeable routine was interspersed garden parties at the rate of two or three a week in the summer for the missionaries or Temperance Society supporters. Overseas visitors included a delegation from China who received a special plea from Josephine to conduct the affairs of their country peacefully and must have taken a curious impression of England with them on their return.

In the face of their unremittingly pious routine the brothers banded together in an alliance. Alexander took an authoritative role and was the most compliant with his parent's wishes. Lionel demonstrated right from the start that he had the most formidable intelligence and curiosity about everything. To begin with this was limited to dissecting his clockwork toys and dead animals in the kitchen. This later brought him into conflict with his mother when, following a dissection of his own existence, he announced that he no longer believed in God. It is a measure of the good lady's compassion that she forgave him for what must have been a deeply wounding cut.

Roland in his early years was a dreamer. His schooling was moderately successful, but he always had to struggle with his lessons, as the temptation to escape into the world of daydreams overcame him all too frequently. When my own school report indicated similar tendencies, he confessed he too would allow his mind to slip free and wander miles away enjoying untrammelled delights of fantasy. He would imagine himself with the ability to fly, winging through the branches of the oak woods, perhaps in the company of a nightingale whose nest the gamekeeper had shown him. On other days he might become a badger, or become part of some exotic scene illustrated in the pages of one of the books in his Grandfather's library. The tedium of schooldays and Meetings alike could be made bearable through these mental escapes.

The youngest brother Bernard was always the mascot of the nursery. Early on he was nicknamed Beacus after a character in a children story called Baby Beak and the sobriquet stuck for life. Beacus's intelligence took a less conventional form. His record at school was dismal and led to grave disappointments among the parents. At the age of about 14 he confided in Roland that he firmly believed he was some kind of monkey, unsuited to the life to which he had been born. Roland understood him well. They were both romantics.

The alliance between Beacus and Roland was not entirely without its tensions. One day in the garden Beacus decided he wanted to dig a canal through Roland's newly planted vegetable patch. After a moment's deliberation Roland's conciliatory side got the better of him and he reluctantly agreed. This infuriated Beacus who really wanted a fight, so he took a swipe at Roland with his spade, gashing his brother's head quite severely. Beacus was punished by being sent to bed in a darkened room with no food, leaving Roland with a bandaged head and confused thoughts. To the end of his days Roland never fully understood that confrontation couldn't always be resolved with conciliation and kindness.

In his turn Roland followed Alec and Lionel to Quaker boarding schools. First to a prep school near Malvern called The Downs, then to Leighton Park School near Reading. Both Alexander and Algernon Peckover, Roland's maternal grandfather and great grandfather had supported this school and by 1916 they were honoured by the naming of a Peckover Hall. The grandparent's financial control that governed the boy's home must have seemed inescapable.

The greatest moments of personal freedom in Roland's life came on his visits to his uncles' farm Beechcroft, near Cowbeech, in Sussex. Roland's grandfather had set up James Doyle's brothers Arthur and Henry (Harry) with a small farm near Herstmonceux. They had become successful farmers, expanding over the years to take in several other properties in the area and becoming well known for their skills at growing peaches under glass. Harry had bought the grassland farm a few miles away at Cowbeech.

In his early teens Roland would make the train journey by himself, arriving at Hailsham station where one of the family would meet him with a pony and trap. Harry and his wife Annie lived on the farm and raised their three boys. Their traditional Seventeenth century house nestled among farm buildings beside a windmill with sweeping views across the Weald. The whole family was Quaker, but their ties to the land made them refreshingly forthright and earthy. Roland enjoyed helping where he could on the farm, pitching sheaves and gathering hay. He readily perceived the difference between the integrity of a working farm and Oxhey Grange, the artificial estate of a landed gentleman. Roland the dreamer wanted his dreams to have a shade of reality and his days at Cowbeech fostered a love of the land and of East Sussex in particular that stayed with him for his whole life and later found expression in his love for his own Farley Farm.

The family holidays, by complete contrast were as routinely prescribed as the rest of life and centred on Grandfather and the aunts. A month in the summer and a fortnight at Christmas would be spent at Grandfather Peckover's home, Bank House in Wisbech and then an Easter holiday on the Isle of Wight in the thatched Hillside boarding-house at Ventnor overlooking the English Channel. With Grandfather presiding, the entourage of the two spinster aunts Alexa and Anna Jane, Nanny Ellis and the Penroses would travel by rail to Portsmouth. The train halted at the end of a wooden jetty with the sea surging underneath and the party boarded a paddle steamer ferry tied up along side.

Mornings at the Hillside boarding-house began with the voice of Grandfather Peckover booming up the stairs with the command 'Monkeys, monkeys, on parade!' The first boy to arrive was termed 'Wonderful Quick Monkey', the next 'Quick Monkey', then 'Slow Monkey' and at last 'Wonderful Slow Monkey'. Lionel made graphs with the boy's names and recorded their classifications. Beacus recalled that his name habitually meandered along the path of the Wonderful Slow Monkey.

In the evenings back at the boarding-house the aunts carefully averted their gaze as the servant brought Baron Peckover his glass of milk. Both they and the rest of the family knew full well that it contained about one third whisky, but no one dared say a thing as the slightest criticism of Grandfather was impermissible. At Bank House, in defiance of his family's commitment to the Temperance League, he kept a cellar well stocked with fine wines. He regularly used to enjoy wine or champagne, with a glass of port after dinner. Roland told me that on these occasions he kissed his grandfather good night with more than his usual enthusiasm, as he could sample the taste of port or champagne from the droplets caught in the old man's beard.

Night time at Bank House was at times a cause for further excitement for the boys who experienced the strange phenomena of collective dreaming. Nightly they were visited by a troupe of fantastically attired black musicians who paraded before them dancing wildly and playing an indescribable dirge. The performances were made all the more fascinating because all music except hymns was forbidden, together with other worldly pleasures such as dancing, billiards, card playing, horse racing and drinking wine. The boys named the apparitions 'The Derwe Band' and there was no doubt among them that they were real people whose adventures were eagerly discussed and compared the following morning.[5]

The main pleasure pursued on any holiday was drawing and painting and most of the family participated with pencil sketches and watercolours while James Doyle usually chose to paint landscapes in oil. Roland and Lionel became the most proficient artists among the boys, but for Lionel his very real talent for drawing was rapidly eclipsed by his passion for science. Few examples of work from Roland's youth remain, but those that have survived show him steadily developing his technique. There is the usual exuberance to be hoped for in a child's drawing, but none of the leaps of imagination he came to live for. Unexpectedly it was the highly restrictive atmosphere of Bank House that triggered his understanding of the fantastic possibilities art can hold.

In his autobiography Roland described the library:

> The smell of cedar-lined drawers and the stare of glass-fronted cabinets teeming with this precious paraphernalia were haunting. The locked cases contained careful arrangements of innumerable curiosities drawn up like royalty at the saluting base; mummies, coins, walking-sticks, bottles of water from the Jordan, watches, rhino horns, specimens of the smallest in the word or the largest of unlikely objects, all meticulously preserved, dusted and dominated by my grandfather's commanding voice booming incessantly at the young, 'keep off dirty paws.' … the quality of the library built up over many years by this revered white-bearded patriarch was of a high order. 'The four folios of Shakespeare,' he would declare with authority, 'are its cornerstones.' Splendidly illuminated manuscripts – 'pure gold,' his daughters would whisper over our shoulders – a collection of rare bibles and incunabula gave the collection an international reputation.[6]

Amid the stultifying splendour of this collection were books that contained images and concepts so powerful that they were to cause Roland to begin challenging the influences of his upbringing and start the process of his escape. Hidden away on the bottom shelf of the library he discovered facsimiles of *Songs of Innocence* (1789) and *Songs of Experience* (1794) by the Romantic poet and artist William Blake and *Night Thoughts* (1797) by Edward Young, illustrated by Blake. Roland was inspired by Blake's exquisite illustrations. God and his angels mixed freely with serpents, monsters and beautiful nymphs in scenes of fantasy that revealed the elements of terror, pathos and delight with a fascinating disregard for rationality.

The spirit of Romanticism appealed directly to the romance already in Roland's heart. Here he found vitality, towering passions and temptations. There were female nudes that carried hints of a forbidden sexual freedom to tantalise him further. Every illustration celebrated the profound mystery and power of imagination, giving the irrational and the visionary the importance it deserved, an antidote to the stiff reserve of his father's art. For Roland it must have been like finding a cool spring of water in a parched desert. Surrealism, although as a movement still twenty years away for him, was born in his soul. The inexorable tick of the clock in the silence of Sunday Meetings would now be bearable as Blake's unearthly visions paraded through his mind. From this moment he entertained thoughts of becoming an artist or a poet, living in seclusion in the Irish countryside.

The year was 1916 and the incomprehensible madness of World War I made the lifestyle of a hermit still more seductive. Roland's cynicism about the validity of religion was confirmed by the inefficacy of his parent's fervent prayers for peace. What was the point of all this piety when hundreds of thousands of young men like him were being slaughtered in mud and filth to gratify the power-lust of a few? The parents themselves, although despondent at the lack of answer to their prayers,[7] rallied to their Quaker belief in freedom from earthly authority and redoubled their efforts in opposing conscription. They actively supported the No Conscription Fellowship and James Doyle and Alec helped to set up a local branch at Watford, to assist people applying to the local tribunals for exemption as Conscientious Objectors. The tremendous social pressure in favour of enlistment must have brought them some severe opprobrium, but their Quaker traditions accustomed them to the holding of controversial views in a dignified manner.

The tribunals were invariably severe, but Quakers stood a slightly better chance than most and both Alec and Lionel in his turn were classed as Conscientious Objectors and given exemption from combatant service. Alec was still obliged to serve but as a non-combatant so he joined the Friends Ambulance Unit (F.A.U.) as an orderly. His training at Jordans involved visits to Oxhey Grange where his parents accommodated part of the training. In April 1915 he was posted to France on an F.A.U. ambulance train, taking the wounded from the casualty clearing stations in Flanders to hospital. For the next two-and-a-half years he coped with an endless stream of terribly mangled people in appalling circumstances. The trains frequently came under attack from bombs and shells. In July 1917, after an accident that left him with facial burns, he was invalided home a nervous wreck, suffering from severe shell-shock. The trauma affected him for life. Lionel joined the F.A.U. in June 1918 and although exposed to similar ordeals he came through with less sinister effects. Like Alec, he refused to discuss the experience, but his drawings give us some understanding of the events.

Despite the nightmare Alec and Lionel had suffered, Roland felt they had at least experienced something important of the real world and privately feared the war might be over before he could become involved in what he described as *this fascinating horror.*[8] Seeking to make himself eligible for the F.A.U. he went to Beechcroft Farm and persuaded Uncle Arthur to teach him to drive the farm lorry. This new-found skill allowed him to enrol for training three months ahead of his call-up date.

Roland joined the F.A.U. in August 1918, passed his First Aid exam and shortly before his eighteenth birthday left England on a secondment to the First British Red Cross Ambulance Unit for Italy. The Italians, allied with the British and latterly the Americans were fighting the combined forces of the Austrians and Germans who, the year before, had defeated the Italians at Caporetto and occupied the country as far south as the Piave River. The Italian ambulance units suffered severe staff shortages due to the Allied offensive on the Western Front and were glad of whatever manpower they could get. The volunteers in the Red Cross units were organised on a more personal basis than the F.A.U. and only a few members were Quakers or Conscientious Objectors but all were outstandingly committed, many giving their services unpaid.

Roland made his way overland through France, arriving in Padua during the first few days of the October combined Italian and British offensive. He was fortunate in joining G.M. Trevelyan's unit serving with the 11th Italian Army Corps on the right wing of the Piave front.

The fighting was swift and effective and within a few days the Austrian retreat became a rout, culminating in their surrender on 4th November. The front moved forward with such speed that the ambulances were held up on the south side of the Piave River until the bridges could be repaired sufficiently to allow them to cross. In the brief time this took, the fighting had nearly died away, but a different and unexpected problem confronted the Red Cross teams. There were more than 100,000 liberated Italian prisoners, half starved and dying at the rate of two to three hundred a day. The civilian population had suffered grievously under the Austrian occupation and many peasants were starving and homeless. Instead of ferrying wounded, the ambulances were deployed to distribute food whilst the medical staff took over the hospitals and got them running again.

The Unit ran about thirty-five Talbot and Ford ambulances staffed by a wide variety of men, many of who were artists, musicians or writers. The Talbots were big and hard to drive on the winding mountain roads that were better suited to the smaller Fords. Roland was assigned to a Ford but his service as a driver ended quickly. In a state of extreme fatigue he turned a small brass valve the wrong way. It was the oil-feed to the engine which, deprived of its lifeblood, immediately became a casualty itself. Roland was demoted to tasks of less critical importance.

The official demob for the unit was on 31st December, but by Christmas most of them were back at their base in Monselice at the Seventeenth century Villa Trieste in a romantic location near to the Eugenean Hills. This part of Italy was famous for its associations with Shelley and Petrarch's home at Acqua. The celebrations were monumental and were the only part of the war that Roland related to me in detail. He told of how amid the partying he tasted his first glass of wine. 'Oh so this is wine,' he exclaimed – 'it is marvellous – I will drink nothing else!' This was one totalitarian pledge he came close to keeping.

Part of the celebrations at Villa Trieste was a cabaret that included a local girl who danced most alluringly. Roland was overcome with embarrassment and turned to his neighbour begging, 'Oh please don't let her take off any more of her clothes!' Further educational experiences followed. One morning Roland found himself perching precariously beside his commanding officer on a plank over the pit that served as their latrine. 'The Italian diet is a marvellous thing,' grunted Trevelyan, 'pasta to bind you up and red wine to counter the effect. Everything in its true proportion – it is the mark of an ancient civilisation.'

In *Scrap Book* Roland makes only a passing reference to the squalor and misery of the war although he recounts seeing roads strewn with rotting corpses, which he contrasts with the lyrical beauty of the plains of Venezia.[9] Even in his brief war he glimpsed aspects of its extreme horror and in particular witnessed the dreadful sufferings of the civilians and starving prisoners. In common with many, his experience, although relatively minor, could simply not be related. The paradigm of the British stiff upper lip ruled supreme and besides, how could he bring such tales of suffering to the comfortable drawing-rooms of his family without offending their genteel sensibilities?

The chaos of war had given Roland a new understanding of life; he wrote *'the blinkers of my sheltered education fell from my eyes'*.[10] His metamorphosis had begun. The evil of war had come to him inextricably mixed with the romantic wonders and beauty of Italy. Out of this bewildering confusion he sensed the beginnings of a new era; one where life would be governed by more liberal principles and art would be ever-present as a vibrant force for freedom. He began to see art as the salvation of the world – an alternative to prayer for the betterment of mankind through communication and enlightenment. Art was something to be lived with total conviction. However the basic principles of his Quaker upbringing were to remain beneath the surface as solid foundations. His belief in honesty, egalitarianism, patronage and the strength of the Inner Light were to survive many compromises, but from this moment on he moved steadily outwards on his own path.

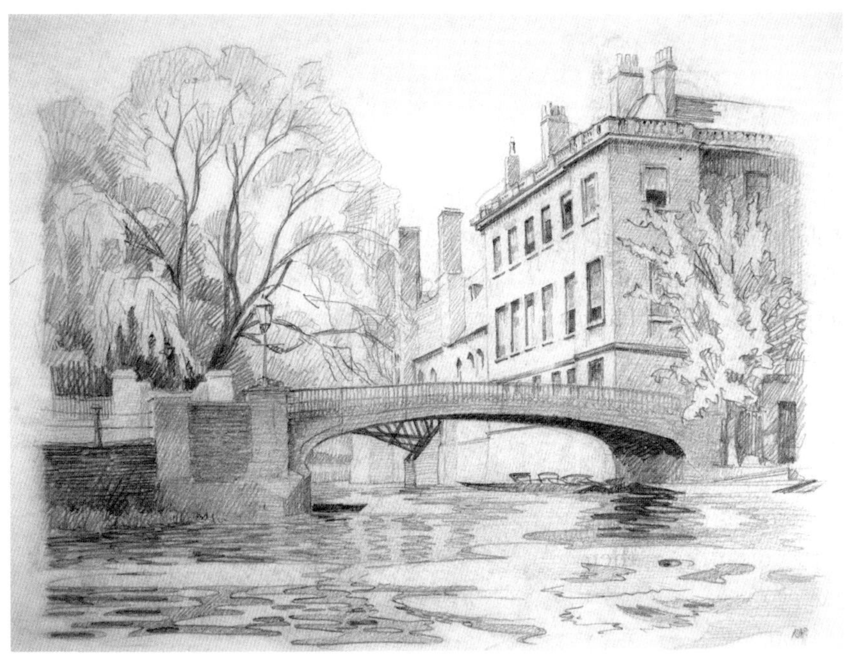

Queens College, Cambridge, England *c.*1920, graphite on paper.

2 1919-23
Cambridge to Paris

'Pour se rincer l'oeil.
Moïse Kisling

On 18 January 1919, only ten days after returning from his war service, Roland arrived at Queens' College Cambridge as part of a vast intake of returned servicemen. Roland had wanted to study art, but his parents desperately wanted him to follow his brothers to University, so he elected to read architecture, in which Queens' had recently initiated a degree course. Fortunately, he was not to be alone; Lionel went up to St John's College on the same day and Alec had arrived at King's College a few days earlier. Lionel's course was Moral Sciences, which was a combination of mathematics, logic, psychology and philosophy with Bertrand Russell as professor of mathematical logic. After attending a lecture on Freud's theory of dreams Lionel became fascinated by psychology.[1]

Young men with the experience of war were less inclined than their predecessors to blindly accept the restraints placed on their lives by Cambridge's traditional atmosphere and rigid customs and Roland and Lionel soon discovered that life around Alec in King's College with its more liberal atmosphere was preferable. Here dons and undergraduates lunched at the same tables and compulsory attendance at chapel had been abandoned.

In their youth the brothers had developed an enjoyment of theatre. The strict Quaker censure of the former generation against worldly entertainment had relaxed enough to allow reverence for the works of

Shakespeare. The boys parleyed this into approval for their own dramatic efforts, for example a play titled *The Amateur Squire* written by Alec and performed for the household in 1916. All three brothers enrolled in the Marlowe Dramatic Society, dominated by King's students. It was unusual for students who were not from King's to have acting roles, but in time both Roland and Lionel were given parts.

Backstage in the Penrose household, another drama had been brewing for some time. Alec's war experiences had left him badly traumatised. While recuperating at Beechcroft Farm he caused a scandal by falling in love with Annie, the wife of his cousin Harry. Her portrait, attributed to James Doyle Penrose, shows her as a warm, attractive person with the kindness to comfort a shattered young man half her age. The affair rocked the family and Alec was packed off back to Oxhey Grange in disgrace. Annie was soon to die of cancer.

To forestall further embarrassment, Alec's parents quickly found him a suitable future wife. Bertha Baker was beautiful and vivacious and came from a highly respectable Quaker family. Alec took to her straight away and the match caused James Doyle and Josephine to breathe a sigh of relief. The wedding took place at Jordans Meeting House on 24 March 1919 in the spring vacation. After a honeymoon, the couple settled into rooms in Cambridge and soon Bertha was occupied with their first baby. The one problem thus solved for the sake of decency was to create a host of far greater crises in the years to come. With the wedding over, the parents left on holiday, glowing with the knowledge that they had done the right thing in settling the boy down. Roland, now quite the driver, drove them in their newly acquired car to the Isle of Wight for their traditional pursuits of sketching and boating.

In Cambridge, Roland had rapidly discovered that the university in general suffered from a remarkable lack of interest in the visual arts. This general absence of artistic stimulation would have been unbearable for Roland and but for the intervention of Alec he might have quit. Through Alec he made contact with what he described as 'a few heaven-sent eccentrics' and the foremost among these was Mansfield ('Manny') Forbes. Roland recalled visiting his rooms that were waist deep in books and persuading him to talk for hours on his latest discoveries among the French modern artists such as Cézanne and the sculptor Gaudier-Brzeska.[2]

It was, however, Maynard Keynes and his associates that were to be of greater importance to Roland. By the time Roland met him early in 1920 he was thirty-seven, had resigned from his post in the HM Treasury and was teaching at Cambridge. His book *The Economic Consequences of Peace* was a best-seller, but he was not yet the famous economist he later became. On Sunday evenings Keynes often gave a small dinner party for undergraduates, (his economics students had a separate evening)[3] and Roland described his attendance at one;

> One Sunday evening I was embarrassed to find myself the first to arrive in the well-ordered rooms of Maynard Keynes, made impressive by the large quantities of books on economics and philosophy such as I knew I would be incapable of reading. My respect for the great man, whose face always suggested to me wisdom and the cunning of a fox, was greatly intensified by the presence on his walls of pictures by Cézanne, Matisse and the first cubist paintings of Braque and Picasso I had ever seen. Maynard, who could be both formidable and immensely kind, started the conversation at once by asking me how I had got on with a paper I was to read to an embryonic art club on William Blake. 'Well, it's all over', I said enigmatically. 'Good', was the enthusiastic answer. 'It's a wonderful feeling, isn't it, just like getting rid of an enormous turd!' He could not have expressed my feelings more candidly and concisely, putting me happily at ease for the rest of the evening.[4]

It was an exciting time for Roland to enter the charmed circle of Keynes and his friends. Although Keynes himself lacked the fine-tuned knowledge of art to build a collection unaided, he was wise enough to allow himself to be guided in his acquisitions by people he respected; Duncan Grant and other Bloomsbury friends such as the art critic Clive Bell and his wife Vanessa, who knew Picasso before the war, had all been influential.

The Bloomsbury group was a loose association of extraordinarily talented artists and writers, who came to public prominence just before, during and after the war. Many of them, such as Roger Fry, Lytton Strachey, Virginia Woolf, Keynes and others closely associated with Bloomsbury such as E. M. Forster, were to become key figures in English literature and philosophy. Influenced especially by Cambridge philosopher G. E. Moore, they held a confirmed belief in the importance of openness, truth, pacifism and the right to have personal freedom and liberal sexual attitudes. Many of them had a passion for French art and the French way of life, perceiving that the climate on the far side of the Channel was more attractive both intellectually and in terms of sunshine. It is hard to be a romantic pleasure seeker in England where it is wet and cold so much of the time.

Duncan Grant, who was by then established as a British Post-Impressionist painter and designer, had first decorated Keynes's rooms with murals during 1910 and 1911. Roland was probably there when Grant and Vanessa Bell were replacing the original mural with new works showing the essential components of Keynes's life; Science, Political Economy, Music, Classics, Law, Mathematics, Philosophy and History.[5]

Grant's cousin was Lytton Strachey, the biographer and critic who had just achieved considerable notoriety with his book *Eminent Victorians,* a work which tilted at the figures held up by the establishment as role models for young men like Roland.

Each year only a few undergraduates were elected to the Apostles, a highly select debating society. Alec and Lionel became Apostles, but not Roland. It is probable that he was active in a similar but less select society called The Heretics. Their agenda was oriented more towards philosophy, religion and the arts with talks given by Roger Fry and Clive Bell. Law 4 of The Heretics required the rejection of all authority in religious questions, a deeply held Quaker tenet, but one which in this context may have caused Roland some confusion as he used his faith's own principle to reject the faith itself. As he became further drawn into Cambridge philosophy the inevitable conflict it brought about with his upbringing greatly encouraged him to continue challenging and discarding the outmoded beliefs of the old ways.

Despite Roland's later complaints that Cambridge held an indifferent attitude to art, it must have been a period of seminal importance for him. Although the excitement of the modern art scene could only be felt in the distant rumblings from Paris, Zurich and Munich, in Cambridge he was with people who stimulated his dreams and partly formed ideas of artistic and personal freedom. The paintings by Cézanne and the Cubist Picassos hanging on Keynes's wall represented a germ of the passion for modern art that was to later grip Roland and transform him irrevocably. They embodied a whole realm of new possibilities that built on Roland's love of Romanticism and fostered his rebellion against the staid constraints of works such as his father's. At this stage the germ could only be nourished by information from books and from luminaries such as Roger Fry, a friend of Keynes. It is possible Fry may have influenced Roland's first ever purchase of a work of art; he bought a Gauguin drawing for £15, but he got so hard up a year later he sold it for £16.[6]

Fry had organised two Post-Impressionist exhibitions in London. The first in 1910 featured Cézanne, Gauguin, Van Gogh and Manet, the latter being the only one whose name had achieved some recognition with the British public. The show which Fry titled 'Manet and the Post-Impressionists' coined the term Post-Impressionist and was followed two years later with his 'Second Post-Impressionist' exhibition. Works by Picasso, including some of his Cubist paintings, as well as Matisse,

Derain and Vlaminck were hung alongside a British section including works by Bloomsbury artists.

It was the British public's first real taste of the modern art that had flourished in Europe for more than a decade and the exhibitions caused a sensation. Record crowds attended and Fry was attacked in the press as a sensationalist, lampooned and accused of charlatanism. The backlash caused him to be socially ostracised by those who respected him as an established critic and writer on Old Masters.[7] For Fry the reward of satisfaction came from the younger generation of British artists who were impressed with the shows and his promotion of European painters continued unabated. Roland was too young to be part of these battles, but the whiff of gunpowder drifted down the wind to tantalise his senses.

Early in 1919 Fry took a studio in Camden where Picasso and Derain visited him. In return Fry visited Picasso regularly in Paris and this and other contacts no doubt provided much material for his immensely influential book *Vision and Design,* published in November 1920. In the book, which contained an essay on African art, Fry attacked the idea that the classical is the only valid art tradition and stressed the importance of form in art, rather than the classical objective of creating an imitation of nature. Form could be line or colour and when reduced to shapes of Cubist purity it offered an escape from the constraints of representational art.

Roland's father felt personally attacked by Fry and his ideas. Apart from the threat to his chosen art form, he had after all vigorously supported missionary societies who brought back tribal art from Africa and India to show the civilised world how desperately these primitive people needed the refinement of Victorian culture. He could not believe someone was seriously proposing that what he saw only as ghastly distortions were as equally valid forms of expression as his own canvases and the fact that Roger Fry came from a highly respected Quaker family, compounded the heresy to a point beyond his comprehension. Others, whose taste has proved more enduring, took a different view.

Cambridge students found Fry friendly and approachable. His enthusiasms could be exhausting for his friends and his willingness to promote others whom he saw as more talented than he often led him into situations where people took advantage of him. Fry had had to overcome his puritan background but still retained a puritan streak.[8] Uncannily, Clive Bell's description of Fry in his book *Close Friends* closely resembles Roland's character and it is not surprising that Fry was soon to become a pivotal influence in his life.

It seems that Keynes was the start of Roland's gradual introduction to the Bloomsbury group and his subsequent visits to their country home at Charleston near Firle in East Sussex, the modest farmhouse shared by Duncan Grant and Vanessa Bell and a gathering place for their Bloomsbury friends. Roland and I revisited Charleston Farmhouse in the late 1970s during its restoration and he recalled being present when Duncan Grant was painting the mural around the fireplace in his studio. 'Rather too modelled, don't you think?' Duncan had inquired, indicating the two blancmange-like nudes. Roland told me he was too fond of Grant to say he hated the style and considered it lacking in force.

After Cambridge all four brothers became regular fringe associates of the Bloomsbury group, attracted by their liberal views and sexuality as much as by their intellectual principles. Alec, living in London, was a regular at the literary soirées in Leonard and Virginia Woolf's house in Tavistock Square. Lionel and in turn his wife Margaret were both particularly welcomed as the group found his studies in psychology interesting. Beacus in years to come was to have an affair with the artist Dora Carrington that ended badly for them both. And Roland was to remain friends with Duncan Grant, the novelist David ('Bunny') Garnett and Roger Fry for the rest of their lives. Roland however never became an aficionado of the Bloomsbury style and many years later he would fail to understand the near deification accorded to some of the Bloomsbury painting and literature. But all this was many years ahead.

At Cambridge the Marlowe Dramatic Society continued to be the focus for Roland's attentions and he was chosen to act in the March 1920 production of Webster's *The White Devil*, directed by the lecturer John Sheppard. The following year Sheppard, who had the reputation for coaxing excellence from amateurs, presented the triennial University production of the Greek trilogy *The Oresteia*, with music conducted by the soon-to-be-famous choir master, Bernard Ord. Alec took charge of the costumes and scenery assisted by Roland, who also had a part as a guard. Later in the year Roland had a part in *Arden of Faversham*, but more importantly was responsible for the set design and construction. His painting was appreciated by his contemporaries, some of whom invited him to decorate their rooms with murals. On the staircase of Corpus Christi College he painted two giant beasts with the bodies of cattle, griffins' paws and heads surmounted by a single vast horn; they are in violent combat, the arm of one forcing the horned head of its adversary to the ground. Roland recalled; '*Figures came struggling out of darkness, symbolic but with that urgent yet forbidden aspect of sex, still too incomprehensible and dangerous for me to admit except in naïvely veiled appearances*'.[9]

In keeping with the accepted policy of excluding women from drama productions, the role of Electra in *The Oresteia* had been taken by a freshman named George ('Dadie') Rylands. Rylands had been asked to come up to King's from Eton early to take the part and his combination of good looks and outstanding talent made him the toast of undergraduate theatre.[10] He was to be Roland's first love. More than seventy years later Rylands recalled; '*It was a full love affair, it was sexual. We were really very attracted to each other and close friends*'. He remembered Roland as being sensitive and having beautiful manners … '*modest and not at all egotistical – a completely sympathetic person*'.[11] These attributes must have been exceptional in the ego-dominated world of drama production. Rylands's acting career at Cambridge went from strength to strength and he took the part of Alice, the murderess in the production of *Arden of Faversham* with Roland. He later became a highly respected English don at King's and an important influence in British theatre.[12]

The relationship prospered for the year, with their shared interest in theatre being a source of delight. It is not surprising that homosexuality was widely and openly accepted among undergraduates. A young man's upbringing of that period seems to have been calculated to instil in him fear and bewilderment about women, something that the sugar-coated dominance of Roland's mother did little to counter. Perhaps it was as an alternative to this hot house environment that Roland took up cross-country running. He distinguished himself with a Blue, an award given to those chosen represent the University in their sport. Nothing gave relief from family ties however and Roland's mother was a regular visitor to see her boys in their plays.

As his Cambridge days neared their end, Roland's desire to escape from his family in particular and English society in general grew unbearable. His studies of modern painters had convinced him that Paris was the place where the cutting edge of art and the excitement of an unfettered life style could be found. In the summer of 1920 he had travelled down the Rhône valley to Avignon, Arles and Nimes and in 1922 he visited Munich.

His later recollections show that it was in France that he found a sense of personal freedom and delight in the beauty of the country. He loved the severing of roots that travel brings, for ever after referring to the feeling by its French term – *dépaysé.* He felt that by crossing to France he had changed his skin. It was the start of a romance with that country and a feeling of emotional liberation that he remained hooked on for the rest of his life. His initial visit enlarged the first chinks in the rigid armour of his upbringing. The sunlight of Provence streamed through these chinks, piercing the gloom of his spirit and lighting sharp profiles in thoughts tangled by years of inner conflict. The distant stirrings of the Dada movement also reached Roland though the scorn poured on the artists and their art by the press, further strengthening his desire for wider horizons.[13]

Academic studying took second place to the excitements of the March

1922 Marlowe Dramatic Society production of *Troilus & Cressida*, with the distinguished cast including Rylands as Diomedes and Roland as Calchas. It was designed by Alec Penrose and produced by Frank Birch, who later took the play to the Everyman Theatre in Hampstead, where the female parts were taken by actresses.[14]

Theatre was not the only drama in Alec's life. Bertha had taken too lively an interest in some of Alec's student friends and one explosive encounter spilled out into the street with Alec yelling threats of horse-whipping at the back of Bertha's fleeing lover. The drama of the event was greater than its efficacy and Bertha became pregnant by Scanes Spicer, a fellow King's undergraduate and Apostle.[15]

Amid all the excitement Roland must have worked hard for his degree. On 17 June he graduated B.A., with a First in Architecture. At the close of the *Troilus & Cressida* production he returned to Oxhey Grange and then went to Cornwall with Beacus for a holiday. Roland had made a previous visit with Lionel, but it was with Beacus that he was to find the deep spiritual link they both had with Cornwall. Their romantic yearnings fed on the remoteness of the area, which appealed to them, its crumbling tin mines and mansions hinting at recently passed glories super imposed on the far greater mysteries of long-vanished older civilisations. For Roland a dolmen in a windswept field or an old weathered granite wayside cross was an eloquent and moving sight that he could commune with. A few years later Beacus was to buy a farm near Helston and later a succession of properties near Truro, where Roland was a regular visitor.

At Oxhey Grange, James Doyle eagerly awaited his son's return, anticipating that Roland would join an architectural practice and make steady progress in his career. His hopes were shattered. Roland announced that he wanted to go to France and study painting and furthermore he had shown his work to Roger Fry who had greatly encouraged him and provided the address of a decent hotel and an introduction to Othon Friesz, an art teacher. James Doyle was devastated. Roger Fry was still his *bête noire* and now the dangerous charlatan who had introduced Post-Impressionism into London had visited his corrupting influence upon Roland.[16] It was a serious blow. Alec's behaviour had stretched the family tolerance to breaking point. Lionel no one could understand because his intelligence and eccentricity placed him on another plane. Beacus had run away to sea on a sailing ship. And now Roland, the son most like his father and for whom great hopes of a 'sensible' career had been entertained had with one stroke ruined the long process he had been put through in preparation for a successful entry into English middle-class society.[17] It is a great tribute to the old man's forbearance that he and Josephine finally gave Roland their approval and an allowance of £300 a year, but they did extract a promise that Roland should avoid the kind of studios which used nude female models.

Within a few days, Roland was aboard a cross-channel ferry and thence to his cheap hotel. '*The alluring sparkle of Paris in winter involved me by day and night. I was absorbed in museums, art galleries, dealers, marché aux puces, le Jardin des Plantes while it was light and the glamour of Pigalle and Montparnasse after dark....*'[18] It would have been easy for Roland to become side-tracked by the easy life and this first heady taste of total freedom. The high value of the pound against the French franc would have allowed him to live in comfortable indolence on his allowance, but he burned to become a painter and he attended his art classes at l'Académie Othon Friesz regularly. Friesz was on the down-swing of an erstwhile promising career. The former affiliate of Fauvism had abandoned the brisk brightly coloured brush strokes characteristic of the style and turned to more easily acceptable works. The Académie itself was a sham with Friesz turning up to teach only when he felt like it. Roland soon left for the studio of André Lhote.

Roland found an immediate rapport with Lhote whose ability as a teacher he admired, although later in the light of further experience he deprecated the value of Lhote's own work. For Roland the most valuable aspect of Lhote's teaching was his great enthusiasm for the works of Braque and Picasso, the co-inventors of Cubism. Lhote also had a strong interest in one of their seminal sources – African art. It is probable that Roland's deep fascination with Cubism stems from this encounter. Here at last he was able to lay to rest the tenets of figurative painting from his father's studio.

The Cubist style, with its transformation of form into strong rhythmical patches of colour was to endure as an influence in Roland's own work. The inclusion in Cubist paintings of ready-made texture and colour in the form of pieces of wallpaper, labels and newsprint etc. remained an inspiration to Roland that found expression in the 1930s with his use of picture postcard collages within his paintings. He was still working on further developments of this style in the last months of his life sixty years later.

Even more important than the excitement of the studio was the re-birth of Roland himself. The most important agent of this process was Yanko Varda, a young Greek painter from Smyrna in Turkey, whom Roland met during his first few weeks in Paris. Varda had the classic Greek attributes of good looks, charm, intelligence and bold opportunism. He spoke his own kind of English and fluent French and was entirely familiar with some of the rougher areas of Paris where he lived in a small pungent-smelling shack in the outskirts. Varda's painting, executed in the confines of his one small room, distinctly showed the influence of Cubism. Roland had found another brother who was about to initiate him to the world of many glorious hedonistic delights while expanding the horizons of his passion for art.

Varda was well known as a voracious womaniser with a string of adoring young girls always in tow. An ex-lover was later to write of him that he '*had a satyr's eyes … virginity to him was a fruit to be eaten*'.[19] Roland, encouraged by his friend's rampant adventures, was beginning to experience his own stirrings in that direction;

> I had some difficulty in adjusting myself to the spectacular heterosexual society of Montparnasse. I had got to know Kisling, a very amiable Polish painter who had a retinue of saucy girls as models. He took great pleasure in transforming them with oil paint and canvas into peachy nudes that sold well. I was encouraged by him to come up to his studio as often as I liked 'pour se rincer l'oeil.' As our intimacy grew I found the courage to ask Kisling if he had ever had a boyfriend. 'Mais bien sûr,' was his cheerful reply, 'quand j'étais jeune j'ai tout essayé – les trous du cul aussi bien que les cons', a revelation which conclusively released me from my past and the torments of a conventional puritan conscience.[20]

In truth, the release from the past that Roland related to me was not quite so straightforward. Although Roland was finding women attractive, he was much tormented by guilt from his earlier homosexual relationships that he feared might in some way prevent him from enjoying girls. He felt there was no alternative but to experiment and try to shed the burden of his heterosexual virginity. Briefed in detail by Varda and fortified by cognac, he went to a brothel carefully selected by his friend who handed him over to an experienced but gentle girl. When the great moment had finally passed successfully, Roland was so overcome with relief that he convulsed into paroxysms of laughter. The girl was greatly alarmed and tried to calm him, but his attempts to explain in his inadequate French only triggered further hysterics. Finally he became dimly aware of photographs being thrust under his nose – artless but formally posed pictures of small children swam before his eyes. It seemed he was being confronted by the inevitable consequence of heterosexual sex, as the girl sought to distract him with photographs of her many children who were being taken care of by their grandmother in the country. This part of the lesson was not lost on Roland, who although he seldom allowed the possibility of consequence to interfere with enjoyment, became very careful about contraception.

One of Varda's Greek friends was a successful wood-engraver named Galanis who habitually held a tea party at five o'clock every Sunday at his house in the rue Cortot in Montmartre. On the first occasion Roland went there with Varda he met a quiet man in his early forties with the friendly face of an honest workman, a man of great intensity and kindly disposition whose work Roland had long admired. It was Georges Braque. Roland recalled;

> I was at once captivated by the imposing presence of a man who could spend a good half hour completely absorbed in contemplation of a mere photo of Goya's *Naked Maja*. Never before had such concentration on a painting seemed possible and Braque's example alone did much to encourage superficial good taste and academic standards to float rapidly away and to be replaced by a passionate dedication to the arts.[21]

He later returned to the theme in an interview; *'The intensity of his concentration was something new. It removed painting from being the amusing pass time that it had been before in my life'*.[22]

Braque was probably quite unaware of the turning point he had triggered in Roland and his friendly attitude to the rather gauche young Englishman who hardly spoke French was typical of his modesty. The Braque family had been a prosperous firm of house painters in Le Havre and both his father and grandfather had been amateur painters. Braque's work frequently contained artisan's techniques such as mock wood-grain or marble and Roland was immediately attracted to this technique of deception. In a roundabout fashion it was a way of borrowing from his father's academic realist style and subverting the style in the process – deeply satisfying for Roland. The illusion of the reality of wood becoming a realistic element in an abstract composition was the kind of conundrum that appealed to him. His interest in changing the meaning of things in this way presaged his fascination with the *objet trouvé* of Surrealism, the movement that unknown to him was incubating somewhere across town like a clutch of reptile's eggs buried in the fertile decaying matter of the Dada movement.

Unsurprisingly Varda had a strongly avant-garde taste in literature. The life and work of the rebellious gun-running poet Rimbaud appealed to him, as did the sagas of Baudelaire and the *Ubu* series of anarchic satirical farces by Alfred Jarry. All this Varda shared with Roland, who responded in kind by elucidating *Alice in Wonderland,* which was soon to become adopted as Surrealist literature. Roland introduced him to Herman Melville's *Moby Dick* which appealed to Varda's craving for adventure and broader horizons that was soon to find gratification.

By the summer of 1923 Roland's life in cheap rented accommodation had begun to pale and he allowed Varda to persuade him that living beside the Mediterranean would be much more fun. They boarded the overcrowded express to Marseille, standing for most of the eighteen-hour journey. Then they journeyed 10 miles further east to Cassis-sur-Mer, a small fishing village tucked in beside a bay flanked by steep rocky cliffs, known among artists for its fine but severe scenery and pellucid light.

They cast about until half way up the narrow Chemin de Saint Joseph that leads from the town up to the heights of Le Cap de Canaille they found Villa Les Mimosas. The small two-storied house of ochre stucco has a square tower at one corner that gives it a similarity to an Italian church. A high wall excludes it from the road and affords seclusion to the long narrow garden. The elevation gives superb views of the valley and the town of Cassis beyond. Roland bought it straightaway for 35,000 francs from M. Joseph Jacquet, *entrepreneur maçon* and it became their home for the next year and a half.

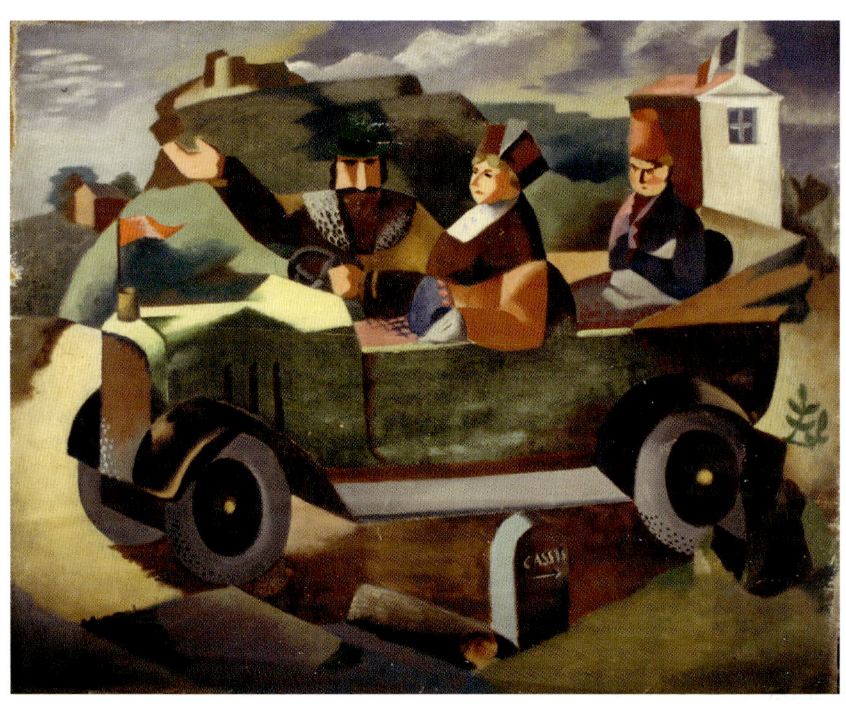

The Road to Cassis, 1924, Oil on Canvas

3 1924-31
Cassis and Paris

'Penrose est Surréaliste dans l'amité.'
André Breton

Nearly half a century after his arrival in Cassis, Roland helped me build my workshop in the garden at Farley Farm. He designed the simple lean-to structure on paper as I watched, moving doors, windows and whole walls with ease at the stroke of a pencil. During the week while he was in London I dug foundations and mixed concrete and eagerly awaited his return with further instructions. As the walls rose he talked about how he and Varda built his studio at the bottom of the garden at Villa Les Mimosas. This was also a simple lean-to, roofed with the traditional orange curved *tuiles de Marseille*. A loft spanned part of the interior and two big north-facing windows in the tallest wall gave all the light they needed for painting and a superb view of the craggy summit of La Couronne de Charlemagne rearing up behind the house. They did all the work themselves and Varda, who was better at scavenging than building, had cunningly expropriated most of their materials.

Seeking respite from their labours they wandered down to the port and feasted on shellfish. The vendor had kept the crustaceans fresh by dashing buckets of sea water over them at regular intervals and since the town sewers emptied into the harbour it was not surprising both Varda and Roland were stricken with acute dysentery. It was a nasty moment, as typhoid was also a possibility. They both recovered, but the building programme was set back a few weeks.

When my workshop was finished, Roland surveyed it with obvious satisfaction. 'You can't just move in – you must invite all the local girls round for a party first', he said, 'that is what Varda and I did!' As a spotty teenager I was too shy to follow suit.

Roland and Varda's party must have been a success and they soon formed a circle of friends around them. Varda was an unparalleled tutor in womanising. They bought a small lateen-rigged fishing boat named *Lou Cat* and Varda insisted on taking his girlfriends out in impossibly rough weather as their terror of the violently pitching boat made them cling to him like limpets. Although he never mentioned anyone in particular it was clear that Roland experienced his own share of the delights afforded by the local ladies.

In Roland's day, during the sunshine interval between the wars, Cassis was an isolated fishing port perched on the edge of two small, connected bays. The ruins of a medieval castle overlooked the Hotel Cendrillon and the huddled streets of houses built of stuccoed limestone. The hotel was yet to become popular with tourists, but there were already the beginnings of a multi-national artist's colony, which over the next decade, with further arrivals from England, expanded to become a virtual Bloomsbury on the Mediterranean. Virginia Woolf would comment *'A delicious life, with a great deal of wine … and the society of curious derelict English people, who have no money and live like lizards in crannies, sometimes keeping a few fowl or breeding spaniels'.*[1]

I wonder what comment Virginia Woolf would have made about Josephine and James Doyle Penrose, who in their spirit of hardened European travellers visited Villa Les Mimosas several times. The occasion of their first visit was in October 1923. All evidence of parties and girls was carefully removed and Roland told me that when they arrived they expressed their delight with the house and all his arrangements. Dinner, cooked by Elise Anghilanti, a local woman Roland had engaged as housekeeper, was served without a trace of wine and all retired to bed. At first light of dawn the next morning Roland was surprised to see his mother walking in the garden. Thinking she was enjoying the romance of the Provençal dawn he left her to it, enquiring at breakfast if she had enjoyed the light. '*Dear boy*', she replied '*I have to tell thee I was so troubled by the fleas in thy mattress I could not stay in bed*'. Appropriately the mattresses had come from the local *marché aux puces* and were infested. Roland burned them in the garden, the released springs skyrocketing amid showers of sparks.

One of the first friends Roland made was an English eccentric named Peter Teed, a kind but shrewd retired Colonel of the Bengal Lancers. Teed had left his wife behind in India and bought the estate of Fontcreuse a mile up the valley from Cassis. There he settled with his lady friend and supplemented his army pension by making a very pleasant light white wine. Teed had an unexpected liking for artists and intellectuals and Roland was a frequent visitor to his small *château* at Fontcreuse, probably lending a hand with the *vendange*, a community event among the ex-patriots.

Roland gained his learning most readily by relating directly to more experienced people whom he admired and Varda proved a wise choice. When the two were not building or chasing girls, they settled down to paint. Roland's work from this period shows strong tonality and bold brush work that relates to his interest in cubism and the influence of André Lhote. The appearance of *trompe-l'œil* wood surfaces show ideas borrowed from Braque, but at this stage of his life Roland took nothing too seriously. *The Road To Cassis* may refer to his parent's visit and the later *Boat Bath* gives a playful taste of Surrealist perceptions. Boats return as a sexual theme through Roland's work. Varda's work which, unsurprisingly, has female figures as a dominant theme, also shows the influence of Cubism which he blended with the folk art of his own country. His technique of reducing form to strongly defined monochrome areas lent itself well to his passion for making mosaics of shaped fragments of mirror embedded in painted cement.

Varda's enthusiasm for the work of Picasso had always excited Roland

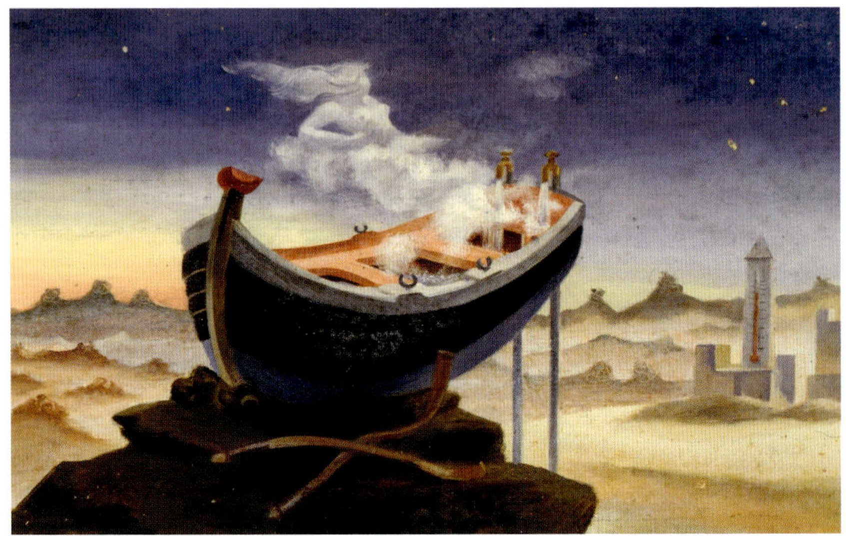

Boat Bath, 1937, Oil on Canvas.

and now he introduced Roland to the work of the Surrealist poets Paul Eluard and André Breton. Roland's command of French was not up to deciphering Breton's texts, but Varda filled the gaps and at once Roland felt a deep affinity with the work. Here was a pathway to the acceptance and understanding of dreams and eroticism; the raw sexual power engendered by Provence, its freedom and its beautiful women united with the intellectual constructs of Surrealism. Breton's ideas on the centrality of chance, the significance of dreams and the illogical and the rejection of religion, the family and bourgeois society in general provided a key for Roland to accept himself in his new role as a hedonist.

The Surrealists' attitude to sex and women also suited him well. Free love was part of their creed and women were valued for their beauty and their ability to inspire, rather than for their intellect or their ability to create. The men regarded those women who did achieve recognition for their work as something of a threat, cherishing instead the ideal they had created of the *femme-enfant*, the dependent child-woman. She was epitomised as a woman innocent of worldly ways whose arcane femininity was emphasised by her deep contact with nature and a refusal to be bound by convention. Irrationality and in-utility in the *femme-enfant* were valued as mystic attributes. These qualities provided poetic and erotic inspiration and conveniently the *femme-enfant* avoided any challenge to the creative supremacy the men so jealously protected.

By this time Roland had discarded so much of his old life that the moment was right to espouse new beliefs and he found them in Surrealism. For Roland Surrealism was far more than an interesting art movement, it was a way of life. His Quaker upbringing had ingrained in him the conviction of holding dissident views in the face of persecution, a preparation that paradoxically was to help him feel at home among the iconoclasts.

In spite of the stirrings of the Surrealist undercurrent, it is easy to imagine Roland painting happily in Cassis-sur-Mer for the rest of his days, content to be a little-known affiliate of Surrealism. But there was part of his puritan side that would not be suppressed and it whispered subconsciously to him that puritans must work, strive and suffer pain for their reward of pleasure; it gave a tinge of discomfort to his indolent pleasures. The puritan in him was soon to be gratified.

One hot summer's afternoon the jangling of the bell by the iron gate that opened on to *Chemin de Saint Joseph* announced the confluence of two lives that were to be entwined for the next fifty-five years. '*On opening it I found myself face to face with a girl of great beauty dressed in a conventional well-tailored black suit and carrying an elegant cane. Her appearance was unexpected and incongruous, a thunderbolt falling out of a serenely blue sky*'.[2] Thus Roland described his meeting with the Surrealist poet Valentine Boué, an extreme embodiment of both pain and pleasure in his life. This chance encounter was due to Valentine's search for a literary critic who was staying with Roland and Varda at Villa Les Mimosas.

The perfection of Valentine's oval face would have sent Modigliani into raptures. Framed by her rich dark hair, her face contained a

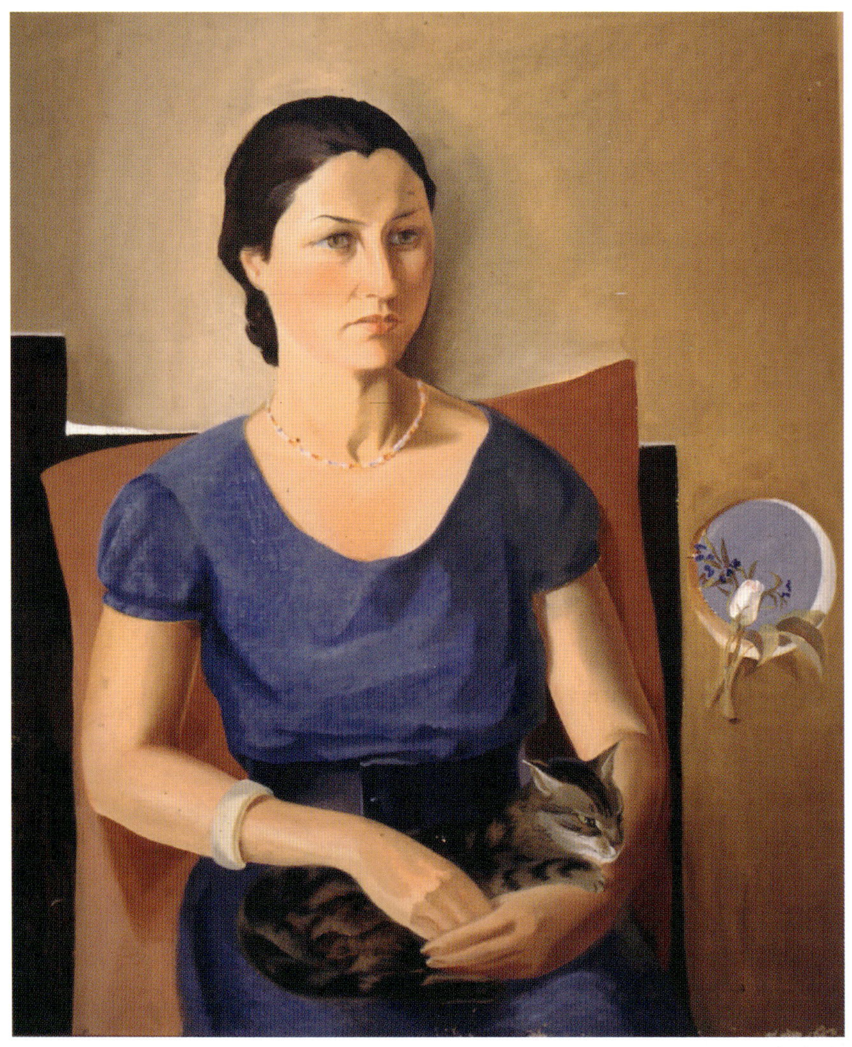

Valentine with Cat, *c*.1932, Oil on Canvas

mysterious beauty, quite indefinable except to say she held an air of inaccessibility that made her seem to be a manifestation from another world, a world of enchantment and powerful feminine magic. Her magic was far more profound than the power of seduction suggested by her beauty. She had an arcane connection to the primordial elements of female creativity; she understood the secrets of the stars, the ways of animals and the intimate lives of plants. Astrological charts were her street maps and her Tarot cards gave her insights of the future. The planes of place and time held no firm attachment for her. She was a spirit woman, not wholly present or comfortable in the exquisite body she had chosen for her stay in this world.

Many around her were intimidated by her intensity and her habit of sudden irrational tirades against the things she disapproved of, which was in effect anything banal or modern. Roland was captivated by her. He had found his perfect *femme-enfant* with predominant qualities of irrationality, in-utility and above all, rebellion. It is, I feel, also true to say that Valentine was in the grip of some undefined mental or hormonal disorder. The well-spring of Valentine's poetry stemmed from her regular excursions to somewhere way beyond the edge of rationality and as this became apparent to Roland it only caused him to love her more. He was a man who loved ideals and she was his poetic muse, embodying the antithesis of all bourgeois qualities, female or otherwise.

She was also unattainable. It was impossible to connect intimately with a mind that worked in such an obscure and irrational fashion, but that is what Roland wanted at the time. He shunned emotional involvement in the form of what he always referred to as sentimentality. The family propensity for nauseating drawing room mawkishness about fluffy cats and their general denial of emotion caused him to redefine love as an intellectual exercise and Valentine gave him plenty. They loved each other passionately in their strange esoteric way, but their life together was fraught with conflict. With characteristic irrationality, innocent words or deeds would provoke Valentine's greatest moments of wrath and some of Roland's friends avoided the couple rather than risk a gratuitous burst of her vituperation.

Sexual difficulties must have added to their emotional tension. Valentine's vagina was obstructed in a way that would not allow Roland to penetrate her. He told me that after much agonising Valentine overcame her understandable reluctance and they sought medical advice from a respected gynaecologist. The specialist gently told them that Valentine was indeed very small; *'You could not admit even this'*, he said, waving a silver pencil in the air, adding emphatically *'I am really sorry, there is absolutely nothing that can be done'*.

'It did not matter', Roland later told me, *'for a couple as much in love as we were there were no limits to the ways we could enjoy each other'*. It was a brave response, but in the long term Valentine's condition took its toll on the relationship.

At the outset Roland found in Valentine a passionate and willing lover who delighted him in every way, greatly helping him to assuage the pain of his youth, although some traits remained buried beyond even her reach. Referring to himself in the third person, Roland recalled an incident one afternoon in the forests on the slopes of L'Etoile Noir, a mountain that stands above Cap de Canaille to the south-east of Cassis;

> RP suffered from an obsessive desire to make sure that the object of his desire would never escape him and vanish from his horizon. In his most lucid moments he attributed this to the vague horror of being snatched from his mother's breasts and handed to a wet nurse of whom he had only a vaporous memory. He longed to make sure of his girl, his love and possess her in an imperative manner which would not offend her but assure him that she would not slip from his grasp and his uncontrollable desire for his mother's breasts. High up in the pine forests of Cap de Canaille he bound his first love Valentine naked to a pine tree. She seemed honoured, even excited by this sylvan and unexpected ritual, but angry afterwards because the resin stuck to her tender skin.[3]

Despite this experience, Valentine stayed at Villa Les Mimosas for long periods and apart from anything else, Roland's command of the French language improved dramatically. He referred to his method of learning as *l'école horizontal* and his graduation triumph came when he found himself dreaming in French. His new ease with the language allowed Roland's circle of friends to expand and a group of young poets, all friends of Valentine, were frequent visitors to the villa from nearby Marseille.

In due course Roland visited Valentine's home in the delightfully named town of Condom-sur-Baïse in the Ger and found her father was marvellously antithetical to his own. Colonel Maxime Boué, retired after his military career, was living apart from his wife Suzanne who remained in the old family home of La Selisse. The couple endured frequent separations. Suzanne was deeply pious, calm and distanced herself from worldly things. Being such a devout Catholic, she would not consider giving her husband a divorce, so they remained shackled together in permanent hell. Colonel Boué, in contrast to his wife was highly choleric and authoritarian, known for his violent irrational outbursts.

Henri Faget de Cassaigne, who knew the family well, told me that although he had great affection for Le Colonel, he was impossible to live with.

> He was a little mad, he had an extreme originality. He was not like others, he had imagination, – it ran in the Boué family. He had a brother called Gilbert who wrote poetry and marvellous letters like Proust. Le Colonel's father who was mayor of Condom gave him many radical socialist ideas, including his intolerance of the church, which caused him much conflict with his wife. Valentine was devoted to her father and whenever he left her mother, Valentine would go too. She fought incessantly with her mother. The house was full of combat and Valentine was brought up in an atmosphere of continuous tension.[4]

Both Roland and Valentine were escapees from highly bourgeois families that suffered from extreme religiosity. Their mothers were exceedingly pious and their fathers were rebellious – Roland's in an indirect way as he knew where his bread and butter came from and Valentine's with an almost brutal frankness. Both fathers inherited a vein of poetry in their make-up and they both used the arts as their means of escape.

Perhaps by way of light relief from his eternal round of quarrels, Le Colonel was given to inventing. Among his best creations was his *bicyclette à voile.* He attached a square-rigged sail to a mast mounted on the handlebars of his bike, with an ingenious system of ropes and pulleys to give tension to the canvas. On a suitable day, blessed with a steady northerly breeze, he left Condom heading for the neighbouring town of Valence. Despite a few spills, he made the eight kilometres in great style. Then disaster struck. '*Cochon de moine!*' he railed at the sky, the bike and the bystanders on discovering that nothing he could do would make his contraption beat to windward. Always a patient strategist, the old Colonel took a room at the inn and waited for the wind to change.

Roland always adored eccentric people and he and Colonel Boué developed a strong affection for each other. In October Roland and Valentine were married in Condom. It was a modest ceremony at which Valentine astonished the locals by wearing a sari. A small but lively gathering followed at Colonel Boué's home. That night, Le Colonel flung open the door to the spare room. He had lashed two large single beds together and decorated their enormous expanse with drapes. '*Voila!*' he declared with satisfaction, '*quel champ de manœvre!*'.

The couple's reception in England was less ebullient. Although I am sure there was no lack of courtesy in James and Josephine's welcoming of Valentine, it is easy to imagine how desperately stifled she must have felt in that household, like a meadowlark expected to behave like a budgerigar. Valentine spoke very little English and although no stranger to the repressed ways of the bourgeois, the complexity of the rules and the boredom of the company made a deadly combination.

Bertha, who was having an affair with Clive Bell at the time, wrote of a visit to Oxhey Grange;

> I am so suffocated with ennui that I can hardly bring myself to write any sort of letter let alone a sort of love letter. It's dreadful at this place where there is no one intelligent to speak to, no subject one can discuss if there were, except the weather & missionaries and where one can't even read, because the books one wants to read are generally taboo ... Alec has been away all this week most mysteriously & I am full of hopes that he is conducting a really successful affair....[5]

James and Josephine must have felt they were under siege by the avant-garde. Lionel returned from Vienna with a copy of Arthur Schnitzler's *La Ronde,* a cycle of ten dramatic dialogues graphically depicting the heartlessness of men and women driven by lust. His mother approached him on his return after a few days away.

'*I am very sorry Lionel*', she said, '*but I burned thy book which thee brought back from Vienna. I had to burn it*'.[6]

We will never know how much of it she read before consigning it to the flames, but any part she sampled might have been made unbearably poignant by the suspicion that her husband was having an affair with one of his models.

The marriage between Roland and Valentine was first ratified at the Registry Office in Watford and then afterwards at Jordan's Meeting House. It was 21 December 1925, the winter solstice and longest night of the year as Roland fondly recalled, although it is hard to imagine how they achieved much erotic delight in the atmosphere of Oxhey Grange. Valentine sought relief from the oppressive atmosphere in long and solitary walks through the rain soaked woods and Roland responded to his bride's torment by emotionally withdrawing. This well-established technique worked effectively for him, but gave him a lack of empathy for the feelings of others. I suspect that by now Valentine had realised that she would never have all of Roland to herself – then at Oxhey Grange or at anytime in the future. '*He has a life inside and no one can get in there. No, no no!*'[7] she stated many years later with a vehemence that showed time had done nothing to ameliorate her feelings.

Back in Cassis, they slipped gratefully into an interlude of blissful indolence with old friends, of whom some like Galarnis were delighted to visit from Paris and a few Bloomsbury visitors. Valentine resumed her writing and three of her poems were published in the August edition of *Les Cahiers du Sud* edited by Jean Ballard. They rarely broke away from their pleasant isolation, except for visits to their respective parents, including another Christmas at Oxhey Grange in 1926. This proved sufficiently fraught that they resolved not to repeat it the following year.

Reasoning they could escape from Christmas festivities by going to an Islamic country, they accepted an invitation from Roland's Cambridge friend Bonamy Dobrée and his wife, also called Valentine, to spend Christmas in Cairo. Dobrée, who was professor of English at the University of Cairo was like many ex-patriots more than usually enthusiastic in his observance of his own traditional customs. He delightedly welcomed Roland and Valentine with the news they were just in time to help decorate the tree that had arrived that morning. Christmas rolled on inexorably with turkey, plum pudding and all the trimmings faultlessly presented by uniformed servants.

Among Dobrée's friends was a quiet, highly intelligent man called Aziz Eloui Bey, who apart from numerous other business interests, was a high ranking official on the Egyptian Railway Company and lived in a house on Gezira Island that would have looked more at home in Henley-on-Thames. He was married to Nimet, a woman of Circassian descent who was later to become celebrated as one of the great beauties of the epoch. Aziz was a man of great charm and entertained Roland and Valentine with wonderful traditional tales in the style of *The Arabian Nights*. Roland had good reason to reflect on the convolutions of these stories when he found himself back in this same house ten years later.

Back in Cassis Roland found that whilst Valentine could stand heat and cold with apparent indifference, wind, or even a draught through a keyhole drove her to distraction. The mistral, a cold wind that blows relentlessly from the *Alpes Maretimes* for weeks at a time, was more than she could bear. Roland noted; *'It provides the most exquisite cloud formations like angels' wings, a brilliant crystal-clear sun and sky and a wicked knife blade of wind that stabs you in the back and cuts into every shadow'*.[8] The delight of their rock-bound valley had paled, so they went to Paris in search of a studio apartment, leaving Varda to fill Villa Les Mimosas with his ladies.

Hearing that Ernst was likely to vacate his studio, they set off to find it in the Rue Tourlaque, which in effect connects the living with the dead on its course between the Cimetière de Montmatre and the night-spots of the Moulin de la Galette. Ernst opened the door and Roland was instantly enchanted by this gaunt man with prematurely white hair and piercing blue eyes set in an aquiline face. Ernst had the appearance of a Horus-like bird-messenger. Straightaway Roland knew he had crossed the threshold into a new world where imagination migrated from the poet's domain of the written word and now confronted the onlooker from the powerful and mysterious canvases piled high around the walls. Dreams had been captured and made permanently visible in ways that defied rational interpretation and demanded that the viewer delve deep into his own subconscious. A picture that immediately caught Roland's eye was a large white canvas hung high on the wall. At the top, beautifully calligraphed in a style that reminded Roland of the lettering on Spanish peasant carts were the lines *Photo; ceci est la couleur de mes rêves* [Photo; this is the colour of my dreams]. The colour of the painter's dream was a splash of the same pure vivid blue that was to recur time and again in Roland's own works and the walls of his houses. Some years later Roland discovered that the work on the studio wall was by Ernst's Spanish Catalan friend Joan Miró who lived next door.

The previous year Ernst had published a collection of his frottage drawings titled *Histoire Naturelle* and these he showed to Roland who was astounded. '*It was like waking in another country*', he said and he was not going to rest until he found out for himself how to get back there. The immediate rapport between Roland and Ernst strengthened into one of Roland's deepest friendships and was heightened by the close association that formed between Valentine and Ernst's wife, Marie-Berthe Aurenche.

The studio however was not in an area where they wanted to live. They turned their attention to the more village-like atmosphere of the Left Bank and found what they were looking for in Saint-Germain-des-Prés on the first floor of an elegant eighteenth-century building at 8 Rue des Saints-Pères on the corner of the Rue Verneuil. The apartments are centred round a courtyard entered through an archway closed to the street by vast double wooden doors, tall enough to reach the third floor, wide enough to admit carriages and with the concierge's apartment on the left. The lofty proportions of the building and its calm, protective atmosphere produces an echo of Bank House, in Wisbech. Inside the tall windows made the rooms light and airy. Their love of provincial furniture softened the big city formality and Roland's early acquisitions of paintings by Ernst and others added to the bohemian atmosphere. The happiness of Roland and Valentine was enhanced still further when Ernst and Marie-Berthe moved close by.

At the north end of the street the roof of the Louvre, only a short walk across the Pont du Carrousel, appears above the tops of the trees lining the Left Bank of the Seine. A walk in the opposite direction would have taken Roland to Place Saint-Germain-des-Prés and the Café Flore. Here in 1919 the poet Guillaume Apollinaire had introduced the poet Philippe Soupault to André Breton with the words '*You will become friends*'. They did and, with the collaboration of Louis Aragon, that same year, they founded the Surrealist review *Littérature*. The next year, Breton and Soupault went on to publish *Les Champs Magnétiques,* a collection of automatic writing, to be followed in 1924 by Breton's

Manifeste du Surréalisme and *Les Pas Perdus*.

These texts, that had penetrated as far as Cassis and awakened Roland's senses, finally drew him to their place of origin. It was to be a while before Roland made the acquaintance of Breton and his followers and became accepted by them but until his meeting with Ernst he had yet to enter their charmed circle.

The next few months were a flurry of activity as they settled in to the apartment and swung into Paris life. Valentine who had been educated in Paris felt quite at home and investigated courses at the Louvre and Sanskrit classes at the Sorbonne. Roland, possibly following an introduction by Ernst, had his first one-man show in June at the Galerie Van Leer, two blocks away on the Rue de Seine. Van Leer, a Dutchman, formerly an importer of cotton goods, had taken advantage of the boom in the art market to follow his passion for dealing in paintings by artists of the School of Paris, including Utrillo, Modigliani, Derain and Vlaminck. The gallery prospered with exhibitions of Dufy, Pascin, Marquet and in 1926, Van Leer held Ernst's first big Paris show which was a success.[9] Sadly, Roland kept no records of the paintings he sold and nothing remains to tell us how well his exhibition fared.

Despite his recent success, Ernst and Marie-Berthe were still too hard up to afford a holiday, so with characteristic generosity Roland invited them to Provence for the summer. He rented La Noblesse, a vast slab-sided Provençal *mas* among the vineyards of La Cadière d'Azur five kilometres inland from Bandol and the two couples arrived there in July. The *mas* was only twenty kilometres from Cassis, but it seems that Roland recognised Villa Les Mimosas would be too small for them all and preferred the medieval romance of the rat-and bat-infested *mas.*

Roland was later to say of Ernst; '*He was really the person who taught me more about how to paint, the actual techniques of painting that he had invented himself and there was no sort of privacy about that, he was not jealous of his own inventions*'.[10] One of Ernst's hallmarks was a technique called *frottage*, through which he picked up the grain of wood or other low relief surface textures by rubbing paper pressed against it with graphite or wax crayon. Frottage was to dominate Roland's works on paper for the next year or so as he explored its possibilities in ingenious ways. He also learned *grattage*, the process in reverse where the paint is scraped off the canvas as it is pressed against the textured surface to reveal a negative of its texture.

Collage was Ernst's passion and it was to emerge as the strongest influence on Roland's later works. At this time the proliferation of photolithographic printing was still decades away and most of the readily accessible published images were monochrome engravings, routinely done to high standards. Thus the images Ernst seized from diverse sources such as sales catalogues, magazines and advertising all had a homogenous style, so when skilfully cut and pasted to form the wildly impossible scenes his imagination created, they presented a cohesive image. At first glance it is often difficult to believe the picture is a composite. Both Roland and Valentine became highly accomplished collagists.

Ernst also adopted the Surrealist concept of the *objet trouvé* that

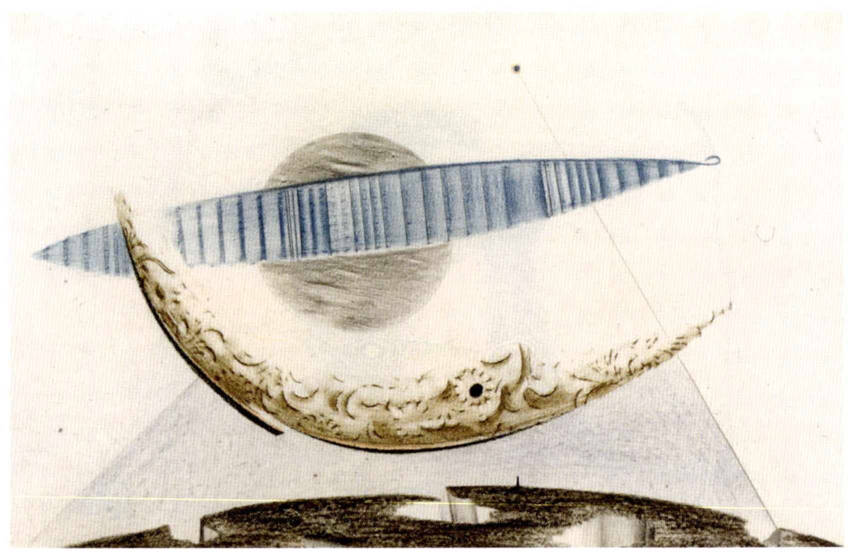

Eclipse of the Pyramid, 1929, Frottage

appealed to Roland greatly. Any 'found item' could be elevated to the status of a work of art in its own right and become an *objet trouvé* simply by bestowing on it the importance of a title or a placement unconnected to any hierarchy of value or taste. To someone whose home was a mass of revered Victorian curious, this new importance for items ranging from a wind-eroded pebble from the desert to Marcel Duchamp's *Fountain*, a urinal signed 'R. Mutt', must have been refreshingly subversive.

Under Ernst's guidance Roland's own style was freed from rational control and buried feelings and images quickly found their way into his work. He was always a person who found it hard to work in isolation and these summer months must have been among the most formative of his artistic life.

Ernst's generosity extended beyond painting and from him Roland became familiar with the intricate theories behind the Surrealist movement. The main protagonists of Surrealism, Breton, Eluard, Tzara, Tanguy, Masson, Miró, Man Ray, Buñuel and Dalí were all well known to Ernst and he brought their work to life for Roland, preparing the way for him to number them among his friends in times to come.

Roland's work from this period experiments with a greater degree of abstraction than before. *Conversation between Rock and Flower* suggests to me a reference to Valentine and himself. The profile of her torso is unmistakable, growing up out of a solid mass like a tree stump which is undercut, suggesting her roots have limited contact with the earth. She has two faces hinting at the duality of her temperament. One is witch like and ugly. The other, facing the rock is calm and ethereal. The rock has an agonised face and is peering nervously from inside its hard shell, apprehensively guessing how long it will be before the calm face switches to an angry storm. From a hole in its top a sprig of foliage resembling olive leaves protrudes, possibly intended as a peace offering to the animated flower. A stick leans against the rock, perhaps a biblical reference to when Moses struck a rock to produce water. Water is often the metaphor for emotion and the rock's expression suggests there is

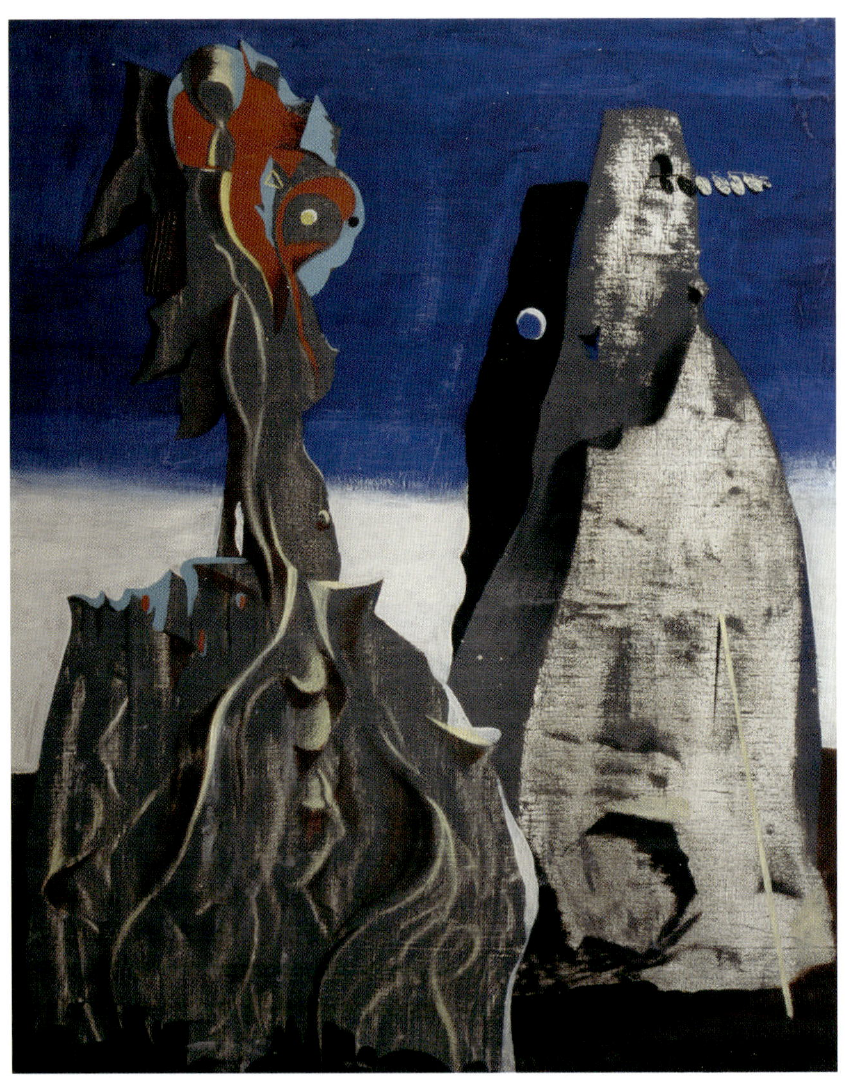

Conversation Between Rock and Flower, 1928, Oil on Canvas

enough pent up inside it to produce a flood. The brushwork on the rock shows a frottage technique were Roland picked up the texture of the bare canvas by lightly rubbing on dry colour.

Roland's summer of 1928 was probably one of the most innocent and lyrical periods of his life. His gentle but firm assertion of his independence from his parents helped his relationship with Valentine to flower and in the company of Ernst he was filled with excitement for his own work and the ways of the Surrealists. Valentine and Marie-Berthe loved and understood each other in a way that gave them an alliance against the powerful friendship of Roland and Ernst. Although Ernst and Valentine disliked each other, the tensions between them were yet to flare seriously. In a photograph taken by Roland, Ernst faces the camera, his boxing gloves heightening his already aggressive stance. Slightly behind him Valentine faces forwards hesitantly, her arm linked through that of Marie-Berthe who presents her back. The two women appear equally divided between staying and going and this was soon to become their reality. In the meantime the summer passed blissfully amid the delights of the Provençal countryside and coast.

The following winter Roland and Valentine travelled via Switzerland to Venice where they took a ship for Alexandria, arriving in early December. The Dobrées were in England, so Roland rented a small house close to the Sphinx. The intention was to spend many days sitting at the feet of the Spanish guru Count Galarza de Santa Clara, a mystic scholar they had met on their previous visit. Valentine became strongly drawn to his insistence that meditation and retreat was the key to perfecting an inner harmony and the exclusion of all other influences.

Roland, while having a strong affection and respect for his severe looking teacher, could not bear to isolate himself from the vibrancy of the world that so excited him. Outside the whitewashed walls life surged through the streets. The fecundity of the Nile brought smells, sounds and colours that drew him irresistibly. The contrast between the sterile aridity of the desert and the life-giving force bestowed by water in

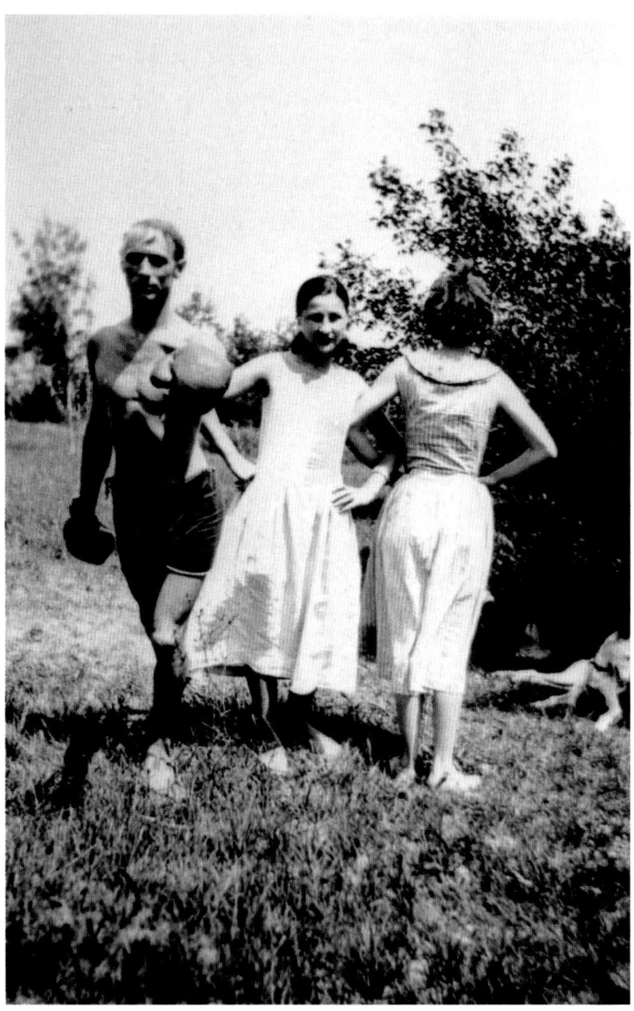

Max Ernst, Valentine Penrose and Marie Berthe, La Noblesse, La Cadière-d'Azur, France 1928

the irrigated plots, the disparity between the rich and the poor and the unimaginable antiquity of the civilisation fired Roland's passions and demanded a full-blooded response.

Working with enthusiasm, he produced a series of delicate dream-like frottages and water colours. The pyramids, the planets and the mysteries of the open landscapes of the deserts appear, referred to in elegant abstract forms. There is an assured touch that brings lightness to the compositions and heightens their mystery.

Roland and Valentine travelled back from Egypt via the Middle East and Greece, arriving in Paris in March. Following Ernst's introduction, Roland became connected to the Surrealists, who soon regarded him as one of their number. Roland recalled;

> Breton was very impressive to begin with and extremely polite, going out of his way to be polite to any newcomer. Of course one met chiefly in cafés where the Surrealist group would gather either at Saint-Germain-des-Prés or in Montmartre. He would be surrounded by people like Tanguy and a great many painters and poets too and would dominate the conversation, but not aggressively. He would encourage other people to come into the conversation, but one felt his presence there was very important. ... He spoke perfect French, very polished and was like that in his manners too. His politeness was of the highest eighteenth-century French style. ... He was always well dressed. In fact all the Surrealists were pretty well dressed. I remember one of them coming to London not very long ago and going to some opening – I think it was at the ICA – and saying 'If the Surrealists had dressed like this, it would have been a scandal!'[11] Paul Eluard was a very loveable person, a man also one felt, of authority. But [he had] a great deal of warmth, much more so than Breton. Breton was polite, but not warm. Eluard was highly spontaneous and a very pleasant person to know and to meet and talk to and get ideas from.[12]

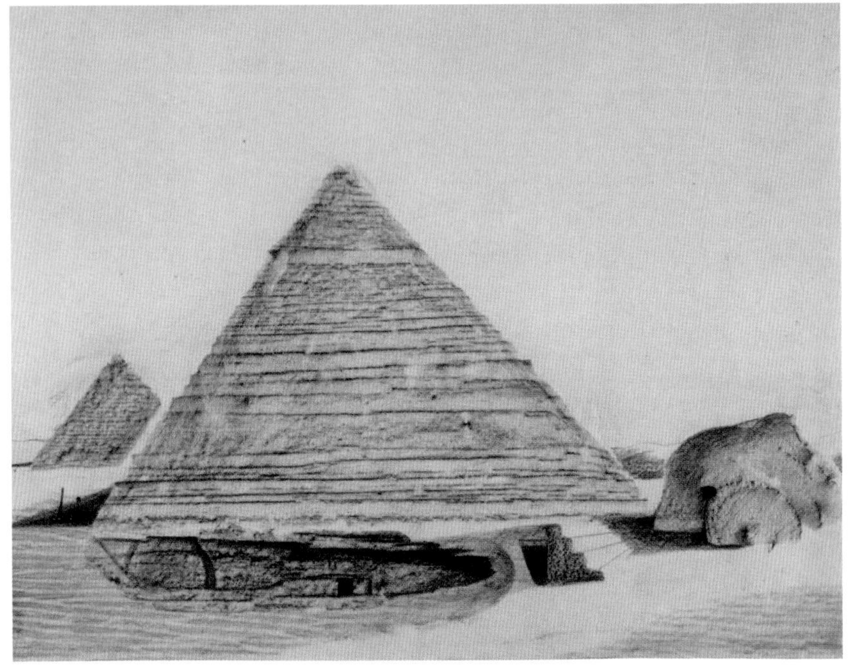

Egyptian Pyramid, 1928 Frottage

Breton declared '*Penrose est Surréaliste dans l'amitié*', but it was Eluard who became Roland's closest friend. Roland amused Eluard with his knowledge of Lewis Carroll, Edward Lear, Jonathan Swift and James Joyce – Roland's Irish antecedents helping to associate him with the latter two. The Surrealists admired the way a conventional event like a tea party was subverted by the Mad Hatter's irrationalities in *Alice's Adventures in Wonderland.* Lear's 'nonsense verse' made perfect sense to them, Swift tilted at civil authority and Joyce's stream-of-consciousness narrative satisfied their delight in the spontaneous connection to the subconscious, running close to their own passion for automatic writing.

Valentine's work was becoming acclaimed among the Surrealists. Nearly fifty years later Roy Edwards wrote in the preface to his translation of her poems;

> Breton admired her utterly personal intransigence; she secured and retained ... the devotion of Paul Eluard; her other friends de toujours included René Char, Robert Desnos and Guy Lévis Mano.... The homage of Max Ernst, Pablo Picasso, Wolfgang Paalen, Joan Miró, Man Ray, Antoni Tàpies, Roland Penrose and Eileen Agar is more obviously evidenced by the engravings, lithographs, paintings, drawings and photographs here reproduced.[13]

In March 1930 Ernst came to Roland in a state of high excitement. The Vicomte and Vicomtesse de Noailles, already redoubtable patrons of the Surrealists had funded Buñuel's film *L'Age d'Or* to the tune of one million francs. Roland was the only Surrealist in Paris they knew who owned a dinner jacket; would he appear in the film as an extra, they asked? Roland accepted and Valentine, who despite her disapproval of films also appears in the same ball room sequence.

The scene, filmed at Billancourt Studios has Roland in white tie and tuxedo standing stiffly in a ballroom with Marie-Berthe and other players. Ernst himself starred as a brigand and the film contained, for its time, the most iconoclastic scenes ever screened. Its public release attracted the attention of various fascist organisations that rioted and sacked the cinema, destroying Surrealist paintings and photos displayed in the foyer. A week later *L'Age d'Or* was banned by the French Government and the print seized.[14]

Roland was suddenly summoned home during the production. His mother had died after a brief illness. Towards the end of his own life he told me, in a way that conveyed his dismay at his own feelings, that he had not felt a real sense of loss at her death. Perhaps her affection and compassion were so strongly directed outside of her family that it was difficult for him to feel the loss of someone whose love he had only experienced from a distance.

Roland's father was now infirm and in his senility was paying unrestrained attention to any woman that came near him. Under Alec's firm guidance the boys packed James Doyle off to a nursing home in Bognor Regis where he could be wheeled about on the promenade in a wicker Bath chair by a male nurse. He was never to return to Oxhey Grange, where, for the last time the furniture had been covered with dust sheets.

Roland's inheritance from his father's estate allowed for some changes. Varda had moved on, so Roland and Valentine decided to sell Villa Les Mimosas and to look for a property in her native Gascony. Through Valentine's contacts in the area they found, standing alone on a hilltop near Auch, the ancient, nearly derelict Château le Pouy, which they bought on 26 November 1930. The austere isolation was exactly what Valentine wanted. For Roland, his love of Valentine, combined with his love of old buildings fired his enthusiasm to restore what amounted to a ruin into a palace for her.

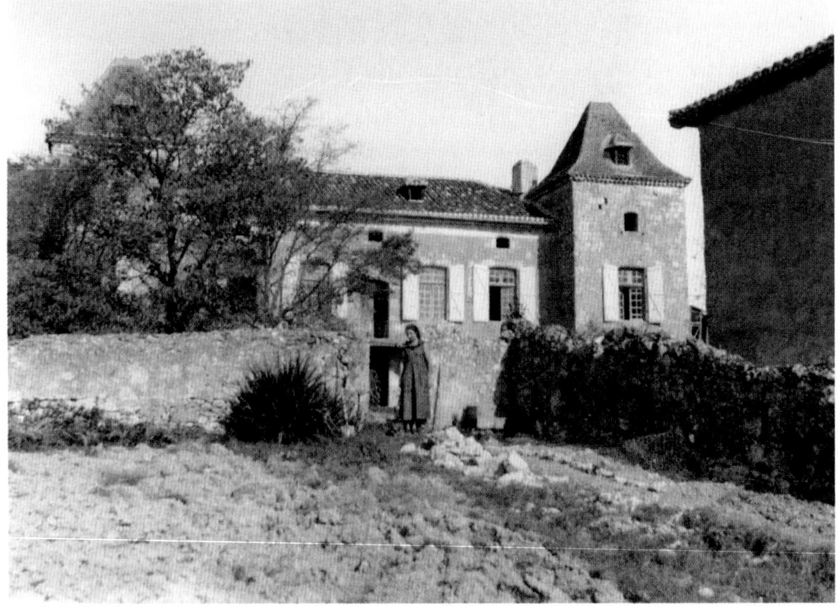

Valentine Penrose, Château le Pouy, d'Antras, Canton de Jegun, Gers, France *c.*1931

To begin with, Valentine loved the place and Roland described how she would revert to her underlying persona of a benign witch. He would awake to find her returning to bed at dawn, naked and dew-soaked, having been watching a family of badgers among the rocks and black oaks.[15]

Roland painted her seated in a chair, looking implacably stern, holding a tabby cat on her lap. The cat's ears are back and its lips twist in a snarl. I commented to Roland on its apparent desire to escape. He told me it was impossibly wild and would let no one near it except Valentine who adored it in spite of its frequent displays of ferociously evil temper. I wondered if he had included the cat in the painting as Valentine's alter ego.

The rugged beauty of the Pyrenees lay a hundred kilometres to the south. Roland and Valentine ascended to the treeless crags from the leafy valleys of the foothills. A hike recalled with particular fondness took them over the pass by Col de la Pierre Saint Martin to the Spanish side in a white-out that forced them to shelter in a flea-infested stone hut with some Basque shepherds. In the remote villages, Roland was delighted to discover the peasant custom for carving anthropomorphic, erotic or pagan signs on the lintels of their buildings.

They carried a tent made of pale yellow unbleached Egyptian cotton. It had a flysheet, bamboo poles with brass ferrules and must have been the top of the range in its day. Roland gave it to me and I used it for many years. I pitched it in the woods on the farm and tried in my imagination to transform Sussex into the Hautes-Pyrénées, because the adventures Roland had there sounded so good.

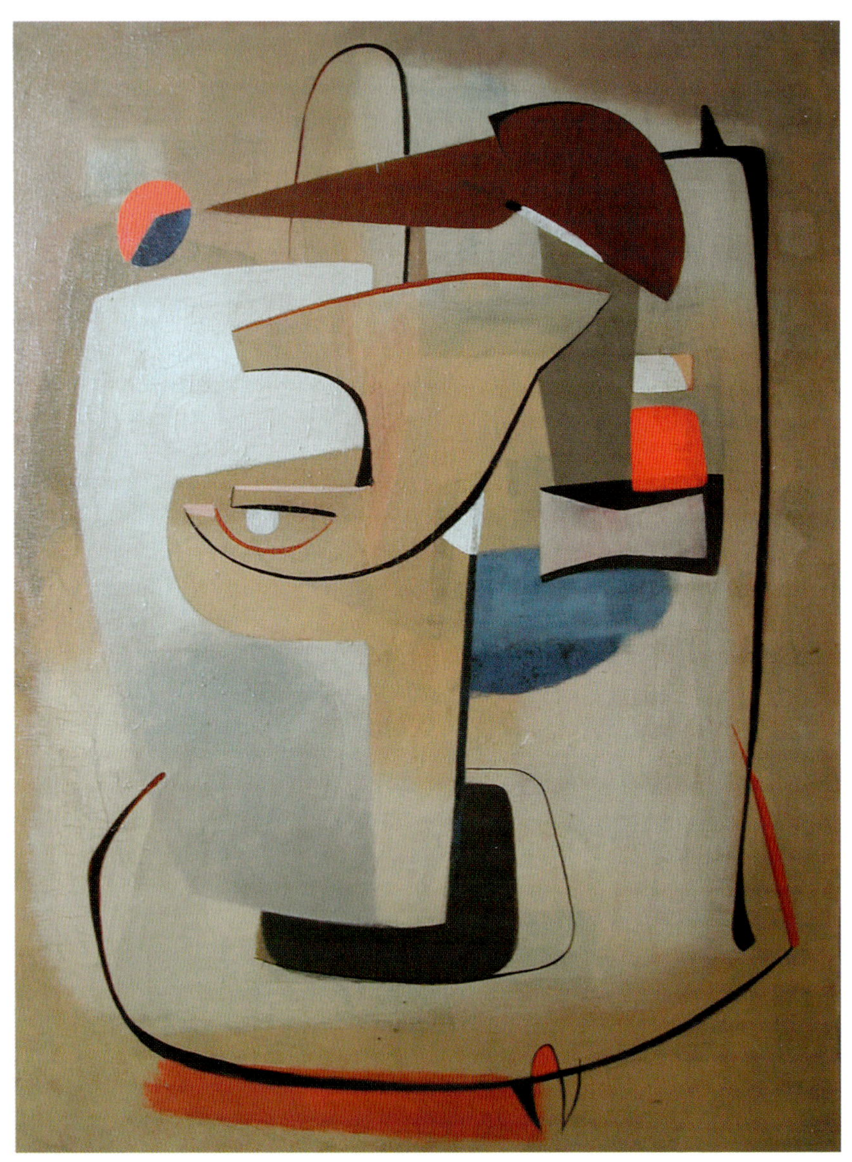

Oasis, 1936, Oil on canvas

4 1932-35
Le Ménage Surréaliste

'One should take the trouble to practice poetry.'
André Breton

I had not planned to arrive in Bombay (now Mumbai) by sea. With my chums Bozourg and Dom, I had set off from England in a Land Rover six months earlier with the intention of driving to Australia. We arrived in Islamabad, Pakistan on 4 December 1971, the day the long threatened India–Pakistan war really got going. Aged Hawker Hunter jets screeched overhead through black puffs of flak, dropping bombs that shook the city. Police and self-appointed air-raid wardens herded the population to and fro in the crowded streets, promoting hysteria with the incessant blowing of their whistles. All the Embassies except the British had evacuated and we found our Ambassador having tea with his family on the lawn of the Residence. '*I should just stick around old boy*', he said, '*it will all be over in a day or so*'. We tried, but the next morning we had to admit our nerves were not strong enough. We backtracked across Afghanistan and Iran and eventually boarded the *MV Dumra* at Khorramshah, bound for Bombay.

Roland wrote regularly, addressing his letters poste restante in towns along our route, recounting events of the farm and the art world. It was not until recently when I read his letters to Alec that I realised I had unknowingly retraced some of his journey of 1932 in my own Indian adventures. The *Dumra*'s approach to Bombay followed the course of the Italian liner, the *Conte Rosso*, which had conveyed Roland and Valentine to the same spot forty years previously. We watched from the ship's rail, just as they must have done and saw the massive jumble of Bombay loom out of the leaden haze. After the open ocean the air felt like treacle, too viscous to stir the patched sails of the dhows plodding across the bay. Our serene and pampered world encased by the Dumra's steel sides edged closer to the wharf and the thought of leaving her protection gave me a sudden convulsion of fear. The grey lattice jibs of the cranes threatened like siege engines manned by the seething mob below. Thousands of faces stared up at us, dark faces peering from a mass of grubby white cotton punctuated by vivid splashes of colour from the women's saris. As I stood there with a full stomach, money in my pocket and my Land Rover in the ship's hold I knew I was rich beyond the dreams of all who looked back at me. It was a guilty, shaming feeling.

Roland and Valentine travelled first class and on arrival were met by an aged servant, Poushana Butler, who was to be their discreet and devoted companion for the next four months. Roland's Cambridge friend Bill Edgerton had made the appointment and had briefed Roland on the expected demeanour of an Englishman in India. Roland wrote to Alec;

> I am told that I must treat him like a dog and that any kindness towards him would neither improve his opinion of me nor mine of him. This may be true but the work of screwing oneself up to becoming one of a conquering race among slaves is at first tiring and afterwards fills one with astonishment at one's own callousness. When I meet the young hopes of British commerce who take all this for granted and without being any more offensive than you of I in England accept their role of undisputed tyrant with gusto, I feel hopelessly un-English.[1]

To begin with this racial self-consciousness stood firmly in the way of Roland's connection to India. The seductive power of its mysteries took a while to penetrate his Englishness. His early letters carry a defensive cynicism, but gradually the barriers began to dissolve.

Without Valentine, Roland might not have escaped from the formality of the British Raj. She insisted on seeking people with a spiritual or theological interest. Before leaving Bombay, a Parsee who had a French wife took them to see the Towers of Silence, where the adherents of the Parsee religion lay out their dead for the vultures to devour. The elements of earth, fire and water are considered too holy to be contaminated by the disposal of dead bodies and Roland wrote;

> the work is left to those who really enjoy it. You are not allowed to see inside the towers, which are low hollow drums, but you can see the vultures all right, sitting round the top like so many profiteers waiting for the next comer. Even the rain which washes down the bones into the hole in the centre is drained off and carefully filtered through charcoal so that its purity shall not be contaminated by Parsee dust. I don't know how much good Parsees do during their lives but at any rate great care is taken that dead Parsees shall not err.[2]

They made the journey to the old Portuguese colony of Goa by sea, arriving amid fusillades of firecrackers celebrating the feast of St Francis Xavier, the first Jesuit missionary. Observing a mass in one of the churches of Old Goa, Roland commented on St Francis;

> He has entered long ago into the Pantheon of Indian Gods for those who remain Hindu and has become a god unique for those who have been converted. …there was really no difference in spite of the tiger skin plush caps and the mantillas and that St Francis Xavier was enshrined instead of Shiva – man makes his religion and not religion the man…. The cloisters each enclose a garden of oriental flowers and tropical plants, which are watered from the centre by a fountain and shaded by banana trees. The perfume

> and seclusion of these gardens and their overgrown state and their decayed look makes them by far the most beautiful and romantic that I have yet seen.[3]

The romantic atmosphere was not to be savoured long; Christmas with Bill Edgerton in Indore beckoned and they moved on again by steamer south to Mangalore and then inland by car to Hassan, crossing the Western Ghats. Dense clouds of butterflies of all imaginable colours swarmed in the jungle. Rows of ox-carts were laid up by day on the edge of the road to avoid the heat. On the Deccan plateau Roland found the landscape more like the plains of France, with the unbroken flatness of the rice fields irrigated from vast man made tanks storing the monsoon rain; '*They get one crop a year and the peasants remain as poor and shrivelled as cockroaches*'.[4]

They covered the 700 miles to Indore by rail.

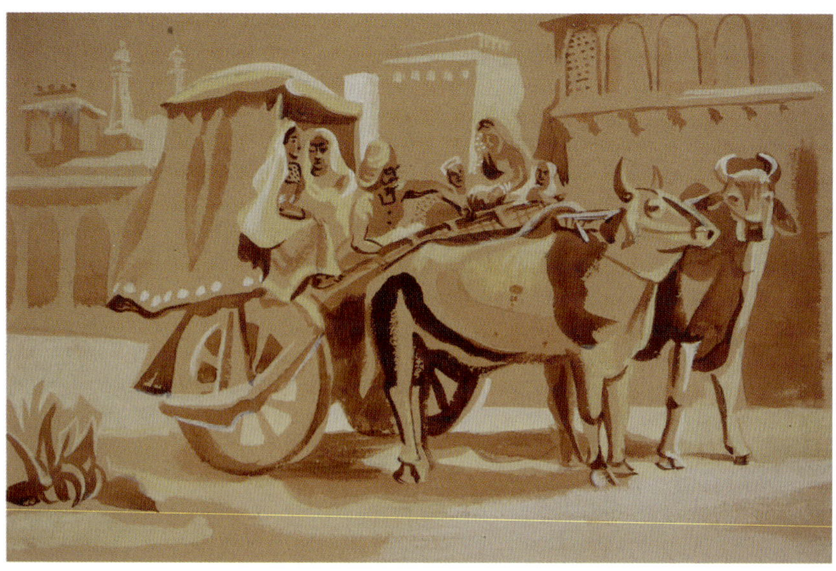

Ox Cart in India, 1933, Watercolour

> Billy met us at the station with a superb white turbaned, red and gold coated servant who made us feel at once that we had moved into the proximity of princes and Viceroys. He lives in a charming airy bungalow in the Residency with pleasant gardens kept green by the unceasing toil of gardeners in white turbans and women covered with bracelets, who scratch and sweep and water. The result is a garden with green lawns in spite of months of drought and roses, canas and all sorts of strange Indian flowers.[5]

William le B Edgerton was an official in the Central Indian Agency and Roland and Valentine found themselves honoured guests of one of the rulers of the country. They were treated royally, swimming in the pool, dining on peacock (not very succulent) and being taken to watch the young Maharaja play tennis. The Maharaja invited them to his Christmas party, but they had already accepted an invitation to the party at the British Residence. On the way to the Residence they encountered a splendid elephant with her face and forequarters painted with bright orange and blue patterns topped with a golden howdah and attended by gold and red-liveried servants. He was heading for the Maharaja's party as Father Christmas's designated transport. The party with music, dancers, acrobats and fireworks began at eight a.m. in a whirl of colour and sound that continued for twenty-four hours.

The Governor General of Central India presided over a party that resembled a lamentation. The twelve guests could talk of nothing but the coming duck shoot. Then afterwards charades of the most gloomily respectable type were organised. The strains of music drifting on the wind punctuated by the iridescent flashes of fireworks served to deepen Roland's dejection. He wrote;

> No one from the beginning of the evening to its weary end said or did anything of the slightest interest. In India there is a decided opinion that Indians should not penetrate into clubs or see the

> Englishman enjoying himself in his own way – perhaps this is just as well.[6]

At a subsequent visit to the Maharaja there was much talk of shooting tigers and panthers by staking out a calf with floodlights to strip the predator of its mantle of darkness while the party waited, playing bridge in their comfortable pavilion. The trophies from many such slaughters were displayed in the Maharaja's palace. Roland noted that the Royal Taxidermist, bent on flattery, had over-stuffed the tigers to the point of what would be today described as morbid obesity.

By contrast a few days later they found that the Maharaja of Udaipur sent servants every day at dusk to a temple by the lake to feed the wild animals. Droves of creatures came through the arid vegetation raising a plume of dust – wild boar, hares, monkeys, peacocks, flying foxes and innumerable birds clustered round. Here and elsewhere Roland noted that '*all the animals were very punctual about getting up and going to bed … no dallying or overtime … they were exactly on time at their occupations*'.[7]

In Jaipur, a few days later, they visited the famous observatory built by Jai Singh II two hundred years earlier.

> In a large courtyard there lies scattered the strangest collection of shapes with marble facings very accurately graded with geometrical forms. These solid instruments were built for taking observations of the sun or stars and telling the exact time. The beautiful white curves and unfamiliar bird-like forms give one the impression of strange beings with their wings open waiting patiently to receive inspiration for which they have been destined. One is only surprised that having recorded their particular event they have not long ago taken leave and flown away.[8]

The harsh reality of Calcutta soon dampened Roland's romanticism. Grime and filth, degradation and poverty surrounded the factories. The

British nation, so prominent in the banning of slavery, condoned the slave-like treatment of its colonial workers. The elderly or infirm simply died on the street, a spur for the thousands of men and women who, driven to escape the fate of the unemployed, toiled endlessly at filthy, dangerous tasks in jute mills, foundries and other hell-holes. Roland was so appalled he was at times tempted to deny his nationality and pass himself off as an Irishman;

> Wherever the white man has settled in any numbers, the result is commercial horrors, else where the heathen live and die in superstition but at least they escape a blacker death.[9]

The seeds of his later anarchism were planted here in Calcutta. The attraction here was their guru Galarza, who had taken the professorship of Arabic Philosophy at the University. He lived alone in his room, scarcely venturing out, but received Roland and Valentine regularly twice a week for meditations and discussions of his philosophy. Roland was so enamoured that he made arrangements to prolong their stay and they rented a bungalow at Belur, five miles up the Hoogily River and a few yards from its banks. It was close by the Rama Krishna monastery, where Valentine took lessons in Sanskrit. Roland felt at peace there and wrote to Alec;

> I am able to draw. To begin with I have painted elephants, flowers and Indian girls on the whitewash walls and would like to repeat my efforts for Jerry's benefit when I get back home. While I paint, a monk intones the Sanskrit verses with the same heroic ring with which Grandpa used to chant 'Down fell the misbeliever'.[10]

Roland's watercolours from Belur show a complete departure from the abstraction of the Cairo frottages. Instead there is a series of bold representational works showing the scenes and people around him. They are forceful, with strong straightforward brushstrokes. He has returned to his pre-Ernst style, last seen in his watercolours from his early visits to Condom. It is as if Ernst's influence had never been and it seems to me that an important motivation for Roland's journey to India was a conscious attempt to determine whether his future lay with Valentine and a more spiritual life, or with the values of his Surrealist friends.

Ernst had painted Valentine's portrait in about 1928 and for many years it hung at Farleys Farm in the sitting room. Her face looks coldly past us, tight and angry-eyed. Immediately behind the image of her head is repeated, but her features are missing. Her hair caps a void of blue sky that fills the outline of her face, connecting through to the fathomless background behind the screen on which she appears to be mounted. Butterfly-like creatures cluster round the corner of the portrait and there are three glove-like motifs intruding into the otherwise clear space.

From my conversations in the late 1970s with Valentine about the symbolism in the work I felt that the gloves represented the gauntlets of repeated challenges. She did not like her portrait and she made it clear she had liked Ernst even less. She told me that in the apartment on the Rue des Saints-Pères she had once overheard Ernst talking to Eluard. Ernst was denigrating Roland's painting and saying he would never make it as an artist.

'*If he is so hopeless, then why do you encourage him?*' asked Eluard.

'*It is always good to have rich friends like Penrose*', came the cynical reply.

Echoes of bygone feuds caused Valentine to relish this story and it was true, Ernst could be very cruel to his friends and he enjoyed tormenting Valentine. He once related a story about a scientific experiment where a live seal was thrown into a cauldron of boiling water. She fainted into Roland's arms. I am sure Roland meant more to Ernst than a meal ticket and remembering them together in the last decades of their lives, I clearly recall their deep and genuine friendship. Perhaps on that day in the Rue des Saints-Pères it irked Ernst's pride that Roland virtually kept him alive by buying forty or more of his paintings during that period.

Valentine, however, never forgave or forgot the remark and despised

Ernst for exploiting Roland's generosity. The situation was compounded by her love for Marie-Berthe Ernst, a fellow *femme-enfant* who Roland considered to be seriously deranged. In the face of the complicated friendship of their husbands, the two women formed a strong alliance.

It seems that to Valentine the love of a woman was more deeply satisfying for her at every level. It was hardly surprising that this should be so and Roland had known she was lesbian when he married her. She was so intensely connected to the plane of female mysticism she had little use for physical intimacy with a man. She and Roland loved each other deeply, but the divergence of their paths gave rise to unbearable tensions.

Roland's determination to salvage his relationship with Valentine was, I think, marked by the purchase of Du Pouy and by the trip to India. He so wanted to please her, connect with her and make her happy. The attempt was doomed from the outset, for to please her meant subordinating too much of himself for any chance of success. Many years later when I was struggling with the break up of a long-term relationship, I said to him plaintively

'*I just want to please her – I want to make her happy*'.

'*You can never do that*', he replied, '*happiness is something she has to make for herself*'.

A sense of the absolute carried in his voice. I did not know then how much he knew.

On this trip not even the traditional art was of great interest to Roland. The Surrealists did not greatly admire Indian art, feeling it was the highly refined product of religion. They preferred instead the intense vitality and connection with the mysteries of the subconscious to be found in Oceanic and African works. So the trip went almost totally against Roland's interests, which perhaps accounts for some of the cynicism in his letters to Alec. They read like a diary, added to on an almost daily basis, but they give no hint about his relationship with Valentine.

Roland did write about his own spiritual odyssey following his visits to Galarza;

> Our long conversations with Galarza, which were the *raison d'être f*or our stay, cleared up a great many questions in which I was in doubt and have given me renewed energy to live this life which I now feel to be so well worth living since I have begun to understand it. … I begin to perceive that nearly all the insoluble questions which torment me are nasty bogies of one's own fabrication and one is so intent on admiring the complicated way in which one has contrived to sew them together that one fails to see their absurd nature.[11]

The adventure of spiritual discovery deepened. Ronald Nixon, one of Roland's friends at Cambridge had furthered his fascination with Indian religion and culture by taking the post of Professor of English at Lucknow University and had 'gone native' taking the name of Sri Krishna Prem. Roland sought him out;

> Found Nixon with his friends camping on the banks of the Ganges. Nixon has certainly gone the whole hog and accepted the Hindu religion with all it has, superficial and profound. … The English people who hear of it throw up their hands in horror and ask if he really wanted to go in for religion why didn't he do it decently and become a padre? … It is an extraordinary thing how little the English thinkers have tried to understand Indian thought in its deeper aspects. … (They are) too busy … with their own superiority. Trying to educate them with hockey, mechanics and Shelley … India is being cut adrift from her own culture. Nixon in his way is offering some slight atonement for the sins of his compatriots and he is respected and loved by everyone. He has no small courage in taking this path and the thoroughness with which he does it is amazing.[12]

Although Roland pretended to Alec to disapprove of the startlingly athletic eroticism of the carvings adorning the Black Pagoda at Karnak, he had fallen for the sensuality of the land. He noted the great beauty of the native women, particularly of the Santals, who resembled the carvings in having;

> the same faces and very round protruding breasts, slight waists and wide hips … fresh from some pre-Aryan past.[13]

Roland's erotic attachments were always a good barometer for his feeling in general and although he does not say as much to Alec in his letters, I feel he had in him at that moment the germ of an inclination to follow the example of Nixon. A life of chastity would not have appealed to him, but there was something seductive in the totality of the way Nixon and others lived. Echoes of the Quaker theme of gaining virtue by the renunciation of worldly things were not far away as he observed the way of life of the Fakirs and of the Jains. The latter had no possessions to give away but deliberately lay on vermin-infested mattresses in order to give their blood as an offering to the bugs. Sacrifice and commitment were understood and valued by him, but ahead of both of them comes choice and for Roland choice was bewilderingly complex.

They sailed from Bombay in early April aboard the fastest ship on the route, the *MN Victoria*, air-conditioned with a white, sleek hull like a battleship. She was bound for Genoa. The romantic twilight filled with the soft squeaking of the flying foxes in the fig trees, the pungent smell of burning cattle dung, along with the timeless, spiritual world of Nixon and Galarza spun out astern like the ship's wake and faded almost as fast. It only took Roland until Port Said to swing back into his English mode. He wrote;

> India has now become a piece of mental baggage, which must be put in a corner close at hand but not allowed to obstruct future action.[14]

They first went to Condom, where Valentine stayed and Roland continued straight on for Paris and then to London a week later on

2 March. It was the point of no return in the divergence of their paths. The schism of their religious and cultural aspirations was bad enough, but finally sexual difficulties began to matter to Roland and Valentine's bad temper and habitual disapproval of everything that lay outside her own preference made staying together unbearable for him.

On Roland's arrival in Paris, the genuine joy of his reunion with Ernst must have allayed any doubts about the friendship that Valentine had raised; 'Among the many things that interested him Ernst picked on the photos of the erotic sculptures of Karnak that greatly pleased him and insisted on having enlargements made. Even more important for his work were the wood blocks used in Rajputana for printing muslin. They were just the material he needed for frottage and in many canvases in the early thirties it is easy to see these designs emerging in the foreground of paintings such as *La Ville Entière* of which there are several versions and *Garden Airplane Traps* until finally they were lost during the war. The first of this series was *The Petrified City* painted when staying with Roland at Le Pouy.[15]

Ernst had an important project already awaiting Roland's attention. He had developed the themes from his previously published collage book titled *La Femme 100 Têtes* of 1929 into a more ambitious work, grouping series of collages into a sort of novel. The seven sections of the novel are named after the days of the week, the full title being *Une Semaine de Bonté, ou Les Sept Éléments Capitaux*. The second part of the title parodies the phrase *les sept péchés capitaux* – the seven deadly sins. Each day of the week represented one of his personally chosen fundamental elements, the first book being;

PREMIER CAHIER
DIMANCHE
ÉLÉMENT ;
LA BOUE
EXEMPLE ;
LE LION DE BELFORT

It occurs to me that the choice of *La Boue* [mud] for the Element might be a play on Valentine's maiden name Boué, as this book contains such disturbingly strident images of occultism and sadism. Against a background of anonymous locations, women appear in many of the collages as captives, bound as if for sacrifice. The victims in many cases are gagged, shot, tortured or beaten. They are terrified and ritually humiliated, elevated only to give pleasure to their monster masters. Ernst's treatment of the female image elsewhere in the work is less sadistic, but would still make a worthy subject for a psychiatrist's dissertation.

With his aquiline features and volatile reactions Ernst had some distinct bird-like qualities, so it is tempting to think the bird-headed men in *Wednesday*, the fourth book may refer to his inner feelings. The bird-headed creatures, which are usually male, are mostly on the run through the pages, pausing only to abduct or attack women. The last image in the collection is the spent figure of a woman drifting off into space, watched only by a pigeon.

Ernst's work was certainly at the visual forefront of the Surrealist revolution. His images articulated freakish fears and desires in a manner never achieved before. Roland was fascinated by this forceful expression of raw emotion and offered to fund its publication. *Une Semaine de Bonté,* five paperback *cahiers,* in a grey cardboard slipcover, was published in 1934 by *Editions Jeanne Bucher*, of Paris, creating something of a minor scandal. Roland must have known that it would never be a viable business venture, but he wanted to help Ernst's career. Valentine, deeply offended by the images of abused women, was furious with him.

She was incandescent with rage about Roland's next venture as a film producer. At least *Une Semaine de Bonté* was a book. Film, Valentine considered, was vain, frivolous and unforgivably modern. Through Ernst, Roland had met and become firm friends with Robert Bresson, who was seeking funding for his first film as a director, *Les Affaires Publiques.* Bresson and Roland formed a production company called Arc Films and through it Roland funded the entire movie for 230,500 francs, about £2,300 at the time. It was a burlesque fantasy about life in the legendary country of Crogandia where the most absurd events are entirely normal. The completed film vanished into obscurity after its first showing at the Cinéma Raspail in 1934, perhaps because the exhibitors were shy of avant-garde films after *L'Age d'Or.* Any chance of recouping Roland's capital also vanished, although this was not unexpected in a film made *entre amis*.

Although, since India, Roland and Valentine had lived apart most of the time, they still held the fervent wish that the other would change and all would then be well. Valentine's moods swung like a pendulum from great affection to irrational tirades directed at Roland or any of his friends unwise enough to visit her and she was tormented by headaches and a leaden fatigue that no amount of rest could relieve. Roland persisted in trying to find a solution, but he recognised they needed help and through Lionel, who had studied psychoanalysis in Vienna, he approached Jung. Valentine agreed to go with him to Zürich for a consultation, perhaps intrigued by Jung's interest in eastern religions.

Just as the arrangements were being finalised, Roland became seriously ill with a duodenal ulcer. He always claimed it was the rough red wines of the Ger, but I suspect emotional strain was the greater cause. He hastened to England for treatment, begging Valentine to go to Zürich alone. She refused, retorting that there was absolutely no point in her going, as it was clearly Roland who needed analysis.[16]

Alec and Frances welcomed Roland at their new home at Bradenham in Norfolk, where Alec had bought a large estate with a fine Georgian house. The best treatment available for the ulcer consisted of drinking pints of kaolin suspension mixed with chloroform and a strict diet that consisted mainly of porridge and a little boiled fish. Later he was to protest about Bradenham's '*blindly conventional … Bloomsbury atmosphere*'[17] but at the same time he was grateful for the shelter and caring.

Long stays at Bradenham were punctuated by visits to London to see doctors and on one of these visits he re-ignited a friendship with Julia, the niece of Lytton Strachey who had been married to the sculptor

Stephen Tomlin. She was witty, intelligent and accomplished as a writer having recently found success with her first novel *Cheerful Weather for the Wedding*. Roland found her attractive boyish figure enchanting, but best of all she offered light-hearted and amusing company. Roland was beginning to discover that there were women in the world who were bright, beautiful and not given to tormenting him. Although the affair was soon over, it helped to bring his troubled relationship with Valentine into sharp focus and on 8 November 1934, he wrote to her;

> Don't think I am writing this because of a new adventure – No, there is no one between us. It is that which permits me to see really clearly and to write with an absolute frankness. … It is from respect and the affection I have for you that I want to see your life take the path that I know from the bottom of your heart you want. I know above all there is an impediment in you, like me, to the right to affirming the desire for liberty. You have a future, a mission that you must not neglect. It needs courage I know, but don't let the hard things of the moment obstruct clearly seen objectives. When one has to do a painful operation, one does it because one sees beyond the suffering and I know you often said to me that you have not any doubt about your path. Your attitude this summer was the proof. I am of the opinion that we would do well to formalise our situation as soon as possible but I await your reply. If by chance you change your opinion about Switzerland I will wait longer to see the result.[18]

Valentine's generous reply was further dignified her by use of the formal *vous* instead of her usual intimate *tu*.

> My dearest Roland,
>
> When you find yourself in need of what love cannot give, of what no satisfaction can fulfil, of what art itself can only hint at, of what

> soothes all pain and gives meaning to every life, remember your only
>
> Valentine
>
> P.S. Do what seems right to you.[19]

It took a while for the shock to sink in and a month later, appalled at the enormity of what had happened to her life she arrived in London to try and effect reconciliation with Roland. She took a room at the Thackeray Hotel in Great Russell Street opposite the British Museum and wrote to Roland;

> Roland –
>
> Your letter is a masterpiece of cruelty; if you were truly yourself, you wouldn't be able to cause so much pain. But even that, it is for you that I offer it up, for you alone, who are still so dear to me.
>
> Why do you hate me? Yes, I find it normal that you should worry about me in your own way, because I know deep down that nothing consciously bad could come from you. I shall always believe in you, through everything. Write to me tomorrow, I beg you, or come to me.[20]

Roland was unmoved. It was characteristic that he would tolerate the most frightful abuse and adversity in pursuit of his dream, but up to a point. When that point was reached he would suddenly and irrevocably turn. Despite Valentine's entreaties, he remained absolutely resolved. He took a flat at 127 Rossmore Court on the southern edge of Regent's Park and there he began to paint again.

Valentine's face gazes at us in his 1934 *Portrait of a Leaf*, a gentle poetic Surrealist painting where her features are imbued with Indian overtones, but her eyes are impenetrable. She scrutinises us but we may not see into her depths. A profile on the side of her face indicates that

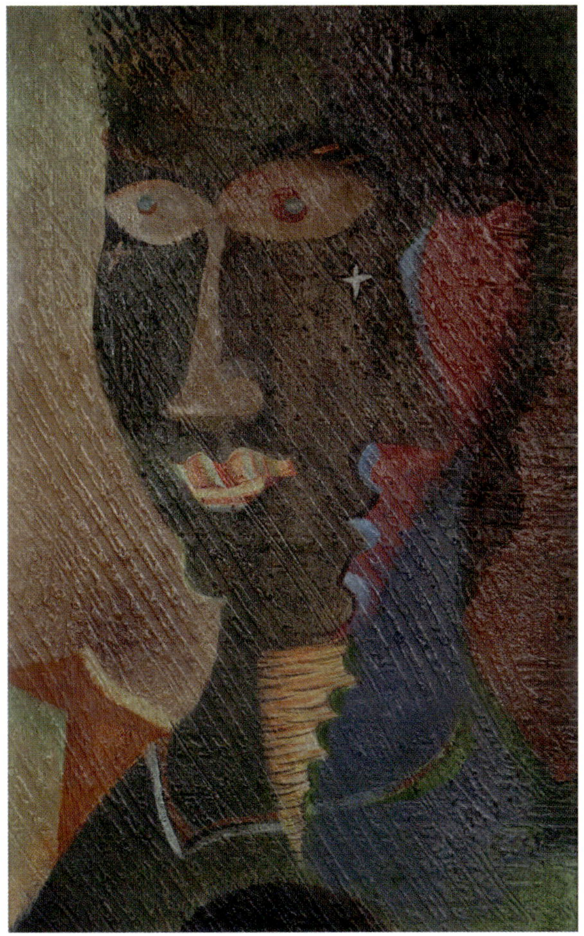

Portrait of a Leaf, 1934, Oil on Board

while we look into her eyes she is simultaneously looking sideways into another dimension and this is appropriate as Valentine was clairvoyant, using her Tarot cards to foretell the future.

Perhaps this painting was a stylistic postscript, as the following year Roland made an extreme change to an abstract style. In Paris he knew Jean Hélion, a French painter whose works were radically abstract at that time and who was a contributor to *Abstraction-Création; Art non-figuratif,* the journal of the *Abstraction-Création* movement that had adherents throughout Europe and in America. The Austrian Wolfgang Paalen, also part of the same movement, had become a close friend of Roland, who frequently stayed at Paalen's apartment when in Paris. Paalen's beautiful wife Alice Rahon, a Surrealist poet who later became a painter was one of the most important loves of Valentine's life. Paalen's portrait of Valentine from this period shows her tragically stricken and wasted.

The work of both Hélion and Paalen influenced Roland's new departure in search of a style to call his own. The style of his paintings refers to the work of both artists, where the forms are reduced to flat areas of colour and the abstraction is so extreme that in most of the works figurative references are only minimal. A composition of strange shapes crowds the canvas, like anonymous armoured creatures quietly but firmly manoeuvring for pole position. It was not Roland's intention that we should identify them or know their agenda. For me they suggest the ill-fitting elements of Roland's life, which he is trying to organise into some sort of harmony. The titles are uncompromising and the legend *Painting 1934* is un-helpfully applied to several canvases. Gradually a more enigmatic figurative slant appears in the paintings and the titles – *Armed Man* or *The Scales* – give us clues to decode their mystery.

It was Paalen who fostered Roland's interest in ethnographic art, selling him some small Oceanic artefacts. Roland, who as a child had been fascinated with the strange carvings brought home by his mother's missionary friends as evidence of dreadful heathen idolatry, eagerly bought items from his Surrealist friends and from the Charles Ratton Gallery in Paris, which was well known for dealing in ethnographic art. He was particularly affected by the exhibition of North American art of the Pacific North-West and bought a splendid mask from Vancouver Island. He reviewed the show for the British magazine *Axis,*[21] a quarterly magazine of abstract art founded in 1935, edited by Myfanwy Piper

Evans and John Piper. It was his first ever critical essay and his ability to convey passion and understanding for the work makes the piece thoroughly endearing. The beginning of a new form was set. Roland had become impassioned by a body of work, bought an example and shared his delight in the work and its creator by writing cogently about it.

For the first eight months of 1935 Roland stayed at Rossmore Court with occasional visits to Bradenham. He took a holiday in Six-Fours-Sur-Mer near Toulon, but he did not see Valentine, who was in Licq in the Pyrenees. He found Dr Glover, a psychoanalyst whom he visited regularly and his ulcer started to mend. Valentine wrote several times a week, unable to accept that the marriage was over. Her letters are filled with rambling details about things like the lameness in Roland's mare Brunette, a bird stealing fibre from the carpet in her room, or other day-to-day events related as if nothing had changed.

It was not until the end of October that Roland visited Valentine in Paris. She was staying at the Hotel Lutèce and he went to bid her farewell as she left for another long visit to India. They went to 8 rue de Varenne, the studio of the Hungarian photographer Rogi André (née Rozsi J. Klein) who was married to André Kertész. They posed for individual portraits in which the strain of their parting and of Roland's illness shows clearly in their faces.[22]

A few weeks later Valentine cabled from the liner *Strathmore*; '*ARRIVING BOMBAY GREATEST LOVE YOUR WIFE*'[23] and followed it by more letters and poems.

Roland replied;

> These interminable discussions by letter are really useless. If two people do not have need of each other, which is evident in our life together, they will not become attracted by discussion. I believe that rather than give up you are waiting for what I am not able to give you. … I am absolutely passionate about my work. That is why I cultivate it as much as possible, giving it the time it needs. With

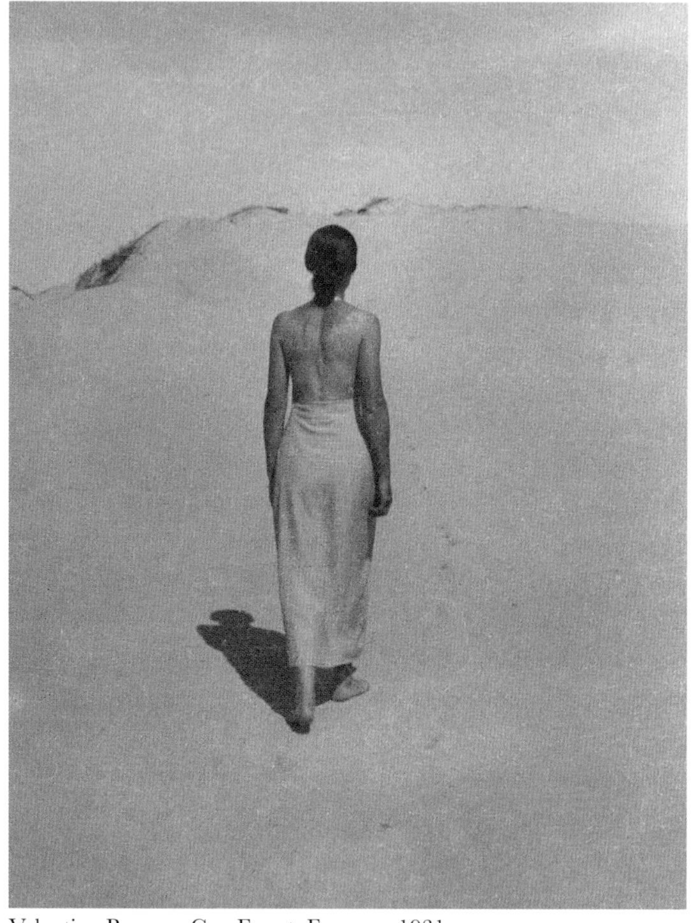

Valentine Penrose, Cap Ferrat, France *c.* 1931

> all my activity I have not the time to be unhappy. Moreover my personal unhappiness is character building.[24]

It was the end of their attempts to live as a couple. Six months earlier Le Pouy had been sold. Brunette and the other horses had been found new owners, likewise the numerous cats and dogs. Only the fleas remained to torment the new owner.

In their own ways they had both given of their best yet had been defeated by the very traits they adored in each other. It seldom seems like it at the time, but ends are always beginnings in disguise and as it happened they re-discovered each other in a new and far more loving relationship as if they were brother and sister. For the rest of her life Valentine was assured of Roland's support. Although protected from money worries, she lived frugally, as a kind of bohemian hermit. Her path soared off to the outer reaches of the stars, entwining on the way with mystic events that she recorded in her poems.

For Roland, chance, that element beloved of Surrealists, was just about to pitch him into an event that would open enough paths to fill an atlas. The catalyst was a gangling, painfully shy British poet.

In 1935, at just 17 years of age Gascoyne had been attracted to Paris by the work of the Surrealist poets he admired. He visited Eluard in his flat near the Gare du Nord. They became firm friends and Gascoyne was introduced to other poets and artists. The British printmaker and Surrealist associate William Hayter, who lived in Paris, introduced him to Breton and in no time he was an *habitué* at their current meeting place in the Café de la Place Blanche. The movement so inspired him he quickly researched and wrote a book *A Short Survey of Surrealism*, the first book on the subject published in England in November 1935 which was widely ignored. The much vaunted chance encounter of an umbrella and a sewing machine on a dissecting table,[25] although far more frequently quoted, was of far less impact on Surrealism in Britain than the chance encounter of Roland Penrose and Gascoyne. Gascoyne was walking in the Rue de Tournon with Eluard when they met Roland on one of his frequent visits to Paris. Roland recalled;

> We got talking and he said to me 'It is extraordinary, but in London they don't seem to know anything about the excitement that is going on here in Paris – why is that? Let's do something about it'. So I said 'Let's do something about it indeed'. So that my return to

> England was not a sort of retreat from France, but something very important that I felt I could do, with the help of David Gascoyne and all the other people I met such as Herbert Read, Henry Moore, Humphrey Jennings, Paul Nash when I came back to England.[26]

Their collaboration began that day and triggered events that remain enshrined in the history of Surrealism in Britain. Roland's umbrella would provide shelter for the fabric stitched by Gascoyne's sewing machine on the dissecting table of British art criticism.

5 1936-37 Surrealism in England

'So many love poems without an immediate object will, one fine day, bring lovers together.'
Paul Eluard, 1936

There is no way I will ever know for sure but I would take a sizeable bet that the late 1930s were the best years of Roland's life. He had returned to England freed from the limitations of his relationship with Valentine and with sufficient wealth from his parents' estate to give him tremendous scope. Old friends and new abounded; in particular Yanko Varda was in London, living at Durham Wharf close to the painter Julian Trevelyan and his first wife, Ursula Mommens, the potter.

1936 began with Roland's move into a pleasantly proportioned early nineteenth-century house at 21 Downshire Hill, Hampstead. The landscape painter Constable was said to have found the light superb when he used the upper rooms as a studio. Valentine, however, did not approve and wrote from her ashram in Pondicherry describing the area as a pseudo-rural suburb. Others considered the area to be rather *risqué*, populated by left wing people and weird artists who were regarded with some suspicion. Roland's near neighbours who were soon to become friends included the artists Barbara Hepworth, Paul Nash, Ben Nicholson, the writer Herbert Read and Henry Moore.[1]

Henry Moore, the son of a Yorkshire mining engineer, had a bluff straightforward nature that Roland grew to cherish, finding his combination of pragmatic strength excitingly mixed with soaring imagination and sensitivity. Moore was one of the first people Roland approached to further the idea he and Gascoyne were hatching for mounting a Surrealist exhibition in London. There were a few other artists and poets who had come to share Roland's interest through reading the works of Breton and Eluard or living in Paris for short periods but there was no organised form of the movement and it was virtually unknown to the public.

Herbert Read, editor of *Burlington Magazine* and known already as a critic and a poet, helped Roland contact people and form a group. Humphrey Jennings, the poet, painter and filmmaker was there keen to make film part of the event. Two other significant figures contributed; Paul Nash, known for his work as a war artist and for his dissatisfaction with the conventional values of British art and Hugh Sykes Davies, a Cambridge don and author of a novel *Petron* that presaged Surrealist prose in England.

Paul Nash had been the organiser of Unit One, a loose association of artists and architects, whose spokesman was Read. The group included Henry Moore, Barbara Hepworth, Ben Nicholson and Roland's old friend Tristram Hillier. It was dedicated to breaking away from traditional constraints and promoting modernism in all its forms including Surrealism.[2] Freddie Mayor, the director of the Mayor Gallery that was distinguished by its dedication to showing avant-garde painters, supported Unit One with an exhibition in 1934. Although Unit One disbanded soon after the show, it had successfully mounted a challenge to the established views on art and its spirit remained. This provided the impetus for Roland, Herbert Read and Gascoyne to form the group that organised the *International Surrealist Exhibition*, Britain's first important exhibition of Surrealist art and ultimately the foundation of the British Surrealist movement.

The first formal meeting of the organising committee was not until 6 April 1936[3], but Roland had excelled in preparing the groundwork. He loved going around meeting people, talking to them and gathering ideas. His enthusiasm was infectious, but more importantly, he was a natural diplomat. Roland's well-established friendship with Breton and Eluard won their wholehearted support for the project and he went to Paris at the end of February to discuss the arrangements. This particular trip however had more than one purpose. The magazine *Cahiers d'Art* had published a special triple issue on Picasso.[4] Roland found in it a reproduction of the painting titled *Nu sur la Plage* 'which seemed to contain magic of a kind I had never known before and to fill me with a longing to see and if possible own the original'.[5] As a shy Englishman who, despite his friendships with the French Surrealists, was still an outsider, I think Roland was overwhelmingly diffident about approaching Picasso and I wonder how he would have managed had it not been for the understanding of Eluard.

Eluard once declared that he was happy to be alive in this troubled time above all because he knew Picasso. Picasso was at this point at his closest to the Surrealists and he admired the rich imagery of Eluard's poems.[6] They collaborated on many projects, with Picasso illustrating several of Eluard's poems and celebrating the luminous beauty of Eluard's Alsatian wife, Nusch, in etchings and drawings.

Eluard took Roland to Picasso's studio in Rue La Boétie.[7] Encouraged by his friend, Roland summoned up the courage to ask Picasso if he could buy *Nu sur la Plage*. He had the luck to catch Picasso in a good mood because the response was '*Well, why not? But first you must see it, so we must go to Boisgeloup*'. Marcel the chauffeur was summoned and with Picasso's son Paulo, Eluard, Nusch and Cécile,[8] Picasso and Roland all packed into his spacious Hispano Suiza car for a fast and luxurious journey to Boisgeloup, a village near Gisors.

Everyone was in high spirits, greatly enhanced by a good lunch on the way. The car, packed with its ebullient passengers, swept into the courtyard of the small seventeenth-century château on the edge of the village. Picasso unlocked the front door to the well-proportioned grey stone building and the vast skull of a hippopotamus confronted the visitors from the centre of the hall. He led the way to an upstairs room where from the neatly stacked rows he selected without hesitation a small canvas of about 33 by 40 centimetres. Roland was astonished. The illustration in *Cahiers d'Art*, the hippopotamus skull and Picasso's personality had led him to expect that the painting would also be on a grand scale, but here instead was this diminutive-sized work. There was however, nothing small about the force contained in the picture.

The black form of the nude reclines with only the sensuous outline of her widespread legs visible, her anus being almost the exact centre of the canvas. The white shape of her vagina, surrounded with yellow rays is displaced to hover above her doubling as the sun but also it offers the suggestion of a portal through to another dimension. The erect fluke of an anchor seeks to penetrate either orifice. Juxtaposed over the accommodating black thighs is another female figure composed of hard-edged triangles, whose rigidity contrasts violently with the voluptuousness of the former as she lies diagonally across her. Her triangular face has two mean little eyes and the mouth doubles as a vaginal motif, but this time it signals danger, as it would seriously damage anything that entered. The white woman's breasts are two unsympathetic little groups of concentric circles. Her legs and arms are cold hard ribbons and her hands are reduced to small claws.

Roland, who was initially not fully aware of the anatomical features of the painting,[9] could not have found a work that explored and expounded more eloquently the duality he found in women. The irresistibly erotic inseparable from the dangers of rigid dominance, exemplified perhaps for Picasso by the contrast between the two women then prominent in Picasso's life, his wife Olga and mistress Marie-Thérèse. For both men I feel it signified their perpetual obsession with sex and their anger at the hold that it had over them.

The journey in the Hispano Suiza was the rite of initiation in Roland's passionate love for Picasso and his work. It was a love that, despite the cruellest tests Picasso could devise deeply enriched Roland's life and endured until the artist's death nearly forty years later. Jaime

Sabartès, Picasso's long-suffering secretary, was to remark; '*Ah, you too have caught the virus*', as Roland returned time and time again to brave the insults and torments that randomly occurred in Picasso's otherwise generous friendship.

The Belgian Surrealist painter René Magritte used to dress immaculately in a business suit every day and lived an outwardly conventional life and in his solid conventional style painted the bizarre fantasies of his dream scenes. So it was with the people who attended meetings to organise the Surrealist exhibition in the well-ordered comfort of Roland's front room at 21 Downshire Hill. The men in lounge suits and ties could have passed for the organising committee of the local cricket club. In the best traditions of guerrilla warfare nothing betrayed their true identity as revolutionaries plotting the end of the art world as it was then known.

These revolutionaries organised themselves assiduously. For the first meeting on 6 April the chairman was Rupert Lee, the former treasurer and secretary of the London Group; and Herbert Read, Paul Nash, Henry Moore and Hugh Sykes Davies attended. Man Ray, Humphrey Jennings, Gascoyne and Sheila Legge came to subsequent gatherings, as did William Hayter and McKnight Kauffer.

The selection of works from abroad was left mostly to Breton, Eluard, Mesens and Man Ray who were in contact with Surrealist artists across Europe. Roland, Nash and Read, on the other hand, had a more difficult task assembling works to represent Britain where there was no established group and few artists who could justifiably be called Surrealist.

In their eager search for work they were accused of inventing instant Surrealist artists all over England – some of who smartly de-invented themselves soon after the show. Eileen Agar wrote;

> The sudden attention took me by surprise. One day I was an artist exploring highly personal combinations of form and content and the next I was calmly informed I was a Surrealist.[10]

Maddox who, at Roland's request, came from Birmingham to meet him, recalled;

> I found it disturbing that Nash and Read had been going round the studios making Surrealists overnight. To some extent I think he [Roland] was too, but he picked artists who fitted Surrealism much better.[11]

At the time, Roland admitted to Maddox that there was a problem in making up the numbers.[12] Grumbling about the selection process persisted among the aged survivors of the event for more than fifty years, which proves if nothing else how well surrealists loved to hang on to a quarrel.

E.L.T. Mesens, a well-known figure among the Belgian Surrealists and a great friend and proponent of Magritte and Delvaux, chose the Belgian works. The French contingent threw a spectacular series of last minute-dramas due to a serious split between Eluard and Breton. Roland avoided taking sides and it was mainly Eluard's loyalty to Roland that kept the preparations on track. Roland funded the working capital of £200 for the exhibition and he certainly gave money to Eluard who, in return, lent generously from his own superb collection and worked unfailingly to secure loans from others.

Through his ex-wife, Gala, now living with Salvador Dalí, Eluard pleaded with the artist to lend more works. Dalí, who although no longer in favour with the Surrealists was considered too important to exclude, made it clear he was keeping his best works for his concurrent solo show at the Lefevre Gallery. Wishing to console Roland, Eluard pinned Dalí down to his commitment to giving a lecture at the exhibition, urging him to write to Roland at once, pleading '*C'est vraiment un garçon très gentil, très généreux, très bien*'.[13]

As the opening date of 11 June approached the work of the organising committee reached fever pitch and it was due to their wholehearted commitment that a bunch of dedicated amateurs carried the day. It was too early in the life of the British Surrealist Movement for any of their differences to have serious effect. On the hanging day, as if by magic, the loans from Europe appeared at the New Burlington Galleries, together with a fantastic assortment of ethnographic items and *objets trouvés.* Mesens arrived just as the hang was completed and demanded that it all be taken down and re-hung under his direction. He insisted on mixing works of different sizes and contrasting colours with no regard for chronology or grouping artist's works. The result was an exciting labyrinth of objects and paintings arranged in such a way that the viewer was obliged to engage with each piece individually.

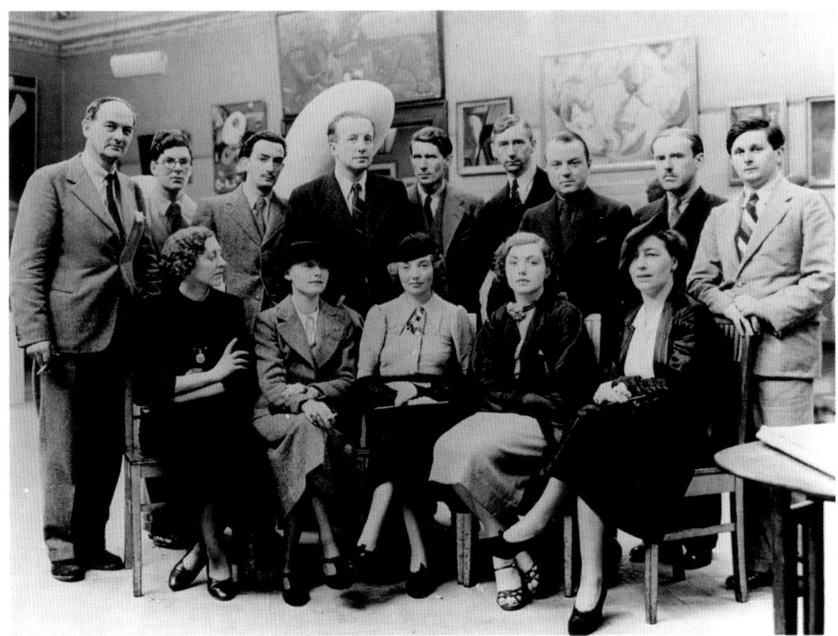

International Surrealist Exhibition, New Burlington Galleries, London 1936. Left to right, standing: Rupert Lee, David Gascoyne, Salvador Dali, Paul Eluard, Roland Penrose, Herbert Read, E.L.T. Mesens, George Reavey and Hugh Sykes Davies. Seated: Diana Brinton Lee, Nusch Eluard, Eileen Agar, Sheila Legge and an unidentified friend of Dali. Photographer unknown

Breton, dressed in a green suit, presided over the opening, attended by well over a thousand people on the hottest day of the year. Society notables, drawn to the show by the prospect of scandal and pornography, tried to avoid being noted at this risqué event. Altercations between the artists and the visitors and among the artists themselves abounded, adding to the excitement.

More than 400 paintings, drawings, sculptures and objects filled the gallery and if some prescient museum curator had bought the whole show it would have made an unrivalled Surrealist collection by today's standards. Arp, Bellmer, Brancusi, de Chirico, Dalí, Dominguez, Duchamp, Ernst, Giacometti, Klee, Magritte, Man Ray, Miró, Paalen, Picabia, Picasso, Tanguy and others represented the European Surrealists. Among the British field were Agar, Banting, Burra, Collins, Jennings, Richards, Maddox, Moore, Nash, Sutherland, Trevelyan, the New Zealander Len Lye and a painting with collage and an *objet* by Roland, as well as works by the mentally ill, which became known as Outsider Art. The British accounted for twenty-seven of the sixty-nine artists drawn from fourteen nationalities. The phantoms from the collective dreams of European Surrealism had arrived to celebrate the first cries at the birth of the movement in Britain. '*Do not judge this movement kindly,*' advised Read. '*It is not just another amusing stunt. It is defiant*'.[14]

The crowd sweated and jostled together. Dylan Thomas wandered round with a cup of knotted string asking people if they wanted it weak or strong and Meret Oppenheim's object, a fur-lined cup and saucer titled *Fur Breakfast*, further subverted the English tea ritual. Robert Melville, his brother John and Maddox arrived from Birmingham and pinned up a declaration that most of the English exhibitors were not worth calling Surrealists.[15]

The press immediately hooked onto the sensational value of the show and the critics piled on provocative comments that gave the Surrealists the extreme satisfaction of demonstrating they had found their mark with the bourgeois. The only critics who came out in favour of the show were John Betjeman and Cyril Connolly in the *Evening Standard*.[16]

A programme of lectures was organised, including Breton, Eluard and Dali. Dalí decided to give his lecture in a diving suit and Edward James, with whom he was staying, took him to Siebe & Gorman, the renowned makers of hard-hat diving suits. The technician took Dalí very seriously and inquired; '*Certainly sir and for what depths do you require this suit?*' To which Dalí replied; '*The depths of the subconscious!*' He arrived at the gallery like a bug-eyed monster from the deep with a jewelled dagger in his belt and Edward James's two Irish Wolfhounds on a leash. Edward James positioned himself close by the helmet to translate Dalí's muffled words from Catalan to English, but could hear so little that the speech became more than usually incoherent. What did become quickly recognisable were Dalí's shouts for help as he began to suffocate inside the helmet. The helmet, secured against the extreme pressures of the subconscious, could not be released. '*For heaven's sake go and get the spanner*,' Roland shouted in alarm to Gascoyne. The spanner was useless, but Edward James had been posing around with a billiard cue and that fitted neatly across the two brass pegs on the edge of the round porthole at the front of the helmet and gave them the leverage needed to unscrew it. Undoing it bought enough time to work out how to unscrew the helmet and save Dalí from becoming a more extreme event than even he had planned.[17]

Over one thousand people a day attended the show and when, after twenty-three days it closed, the committee found to their astonishment that they had made a substantial profit. The exhibition had planted the seeds of the British Surrealist movement, although the nature of the British people provided a harsh and infertile ground for the seeds' germination.

Desertions and later expulsions punctuated the rows, as political, artistic and cultural ideas simmered like a witch's brew. But the group hung on. With no Breton to lead and Roland diffident about being up front, Read became the main spokesman and the whole thing nearly died under the desiccating effect of his intellectualism. That the movement withstood the aridity of his and Hugh Sykes Davies' essays in the book *Surrealism*, which he edited soon after the exhibition, is a testament to its inherent resilience. The French means of controlling the beast within Surrealism was to try and nationalise it; the British tried to bore it to death – but it was too strong for them.

The close of the exhibition provided Roland with the opportunity for further purchases, among them Eileen Agar's *Quadriga*. Breton, who was desperately hard up, sold Roland his own *Object Poem* and the intense *papier collé* by Picasso titled *Tête*.

In the mean-time, Roland's work had changed direction again. The large sculpture Roland included in the Surrealist exhibition was titled *Captain Cook's Last Voyage*. This 'surrealist object' as Roland called it, featured the torso of a woman, painted with sinuous stripes of bright colours. She

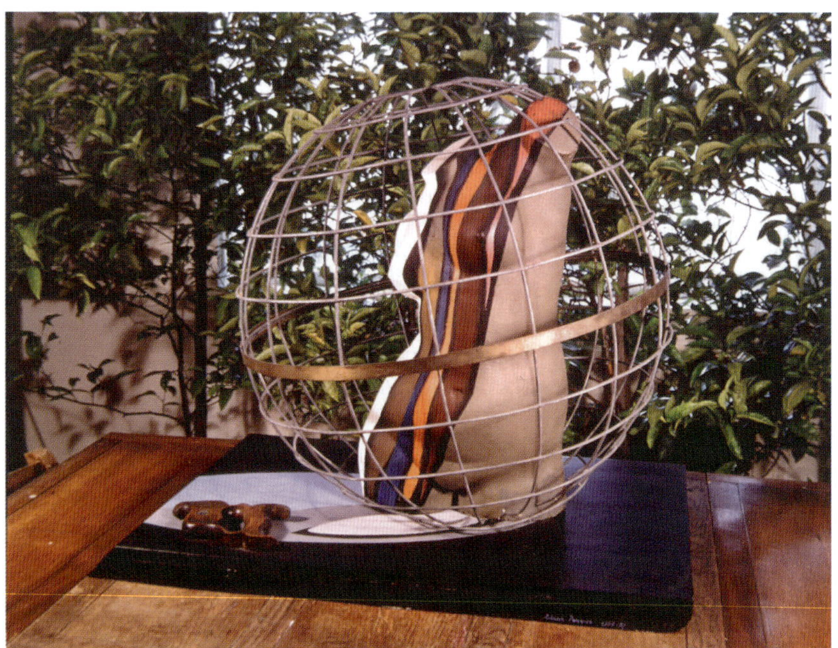

Captain Cook's Last Voyage, 1936, Mixed Media Object. Collection: Tate Modern

stands on a baseboard shaped in profile a little like a boat. The torso fills the volume of the wire globe that surrounds her, with the stump of her outstretched arm penetrating the surface near the Arctic Circle.

The globe, which he had specially made by an artisan, was lost in the war and the base disappeared. The torso and some good photographs remained and in the late 1960s Roland set about reconstructing the piece, asking me to remake the globe. I found a coil of heavy gauge wire in the barn and using the photographs as a guide I brazed rings together to make the lines of longitude and latitude. A brass strip around the equator concealed the join of the two halves that allowed the torso to be placed inside.

The completed work gave us both great satisfaction but I could not understand Roland's inspiration for his view of the dour and dutiful explorer from Whitby, although Cook had charted parts of the Pacific, that source of ethnological wonder for the Surrealists. '*This is at the heart of what we all seek*,' he said, indicating the luscious female curves that formed the core of the world. That was the closest I ever got to persuading him to venture an explanation for one of his works. His usual response was '*It is for you to make whatever you want of it*', thus pitching all questions of interpretation back to the questioner and affirming that every work of art is a transaction between the viewer and the artist.

Amid the news of the Spanish Civil War that had just begun, reports of left-wing extremists vandalising works of art and churches began to filter through. Roland was among those who sensed that the reports were Fascist propaganda designed to discredit the Spanish Republicans and he decided to go to Spain to see for himself with Christian and Yvonne Zervos, the writers and publishers of *Cahiers d'Art* and the Picasso *Catalogue Raisonné*.

To obtain safe conduct documents Roland and Valentine, with whom he was enjoying a rapprochement, became members of the Independent Labour Party, which had links with the Republican forces. Many young artists and writers had joined the republican forces and Roland was glad of finding a way to make his contribution in the role of a non-combatant.

For the Surrealists, art was an agent for social reform and politics were inseparable from their lives. Far from creating the united front they wished for, political arguments caused more divisions than anything else. The English group, despite these arguments, were soon active in direct political campaigns in the late 1930s, attacking the British Government's refusal to supply arms to the Republicans, a policy which effectively supported Franco's fascists.

During this time Valentine lived at 21 Downshire Hill. It was the beginning of the reconstruction of their friendship, but Gascoyne noted in his diary that he could see why she and Roland had such difficulties. He wrote;

> On Tuesday to lunch with Penrose, who has just returned from France with his wife Valentine; a rapt, dark, quiet woman with an occasional expression of bad temper, pre-occupied and seldom speaking unless she has something to say. A rather stuffy, frustrated afternoon, unremarkable. I never seem to be able to establish any communication in this house, with its soft carpets and lights and paintings ... We talked about Rimbaud and she grew enthusiastic. It is clear now why she cannot live with Roland for very long at a time. 'How well I understand Rimbaud', she said, 'and his hatred of perfection. That is what is the matter here' – she indicated the room with a vague gesture – 'all these pictures. I should like to take a piece of chalk and scribble on them all'. How Roland's *sens de correction* must exasperate her sometimes.[18]

Gascoyne, who was a Communist with strong political views, lacked the funds to go to Spain, but Roland helped him out so he could accompany them. They met up with Christian and Yvonne Zervos in Paris and then travelled on to Barcelona arriving on 23 October. An atmosphere of solidarity and optimism pervaded and the party was welcomed by officials from the Propaganda Ministry and installed in a hotel near the Plaza de Cataluña. The streets were packed with marchers and demonstrators all proclaiming their trade unions, including the newly formed Prostitutes' Union. Roland and Gascoyne were particularly drawn to the Anarchists and were disturbed to find how much they and the POUM [Worker's Party of Marxist Unification] were hated by the Communists. The divisions that were to contribute to the crippling of the Republican forces were already evident.

The party gathered sufficient material for Roland and Zervos to contribute a chapter on Art and the Present Crisis in Catalonia to the book *Catalan Art from the 9th to the 19th Century*, published the following year by Zervos. Seeking some photographs for publicity purposes he went to Robert Capa's apartment in Paris. Capa was away on an assignment, but his mother was there. She only spoke Hungarian and it was with great difficulty that Roland made it understood he wanted to see some of her son's war pictures. She found him a great sheaf of photographs and having selected the ones he wanted he managed to explain his wish to buy them. The old lady had no understanding of how much to charge, until acting on her instincts she shuffled off to the kitchen. She returned carrying a big pair of brass scales of the kind used on vegetable stalls in the market and proceeded to weigh out the photographs, all set to haggle over the price. The incident became a running gag between Roland and Capa, as whenever they met Capa would exclaim; '*Ha, here is the man who tried to buy my photographs by the kilo!*'

Back in England, Valentine could no longer face the tensions of life in London and left for India with Alice Paalen. In India the two women travelled together for nine months and stayed in Panuanaula at the Mirtola ashram at the foot of the Himalayas where Valentine resumed her studies of Sanskrit. They loved each other with an intensity that endured until Alice's death in Mexico in 1987 although they never saw each other again after their Indian adventure. Their tenderness surfaces in their poetry written long after the event.[19]

When, in 1938, the divorce that sealed the end of Roland and Valentine's marriage commenced, it was on the grounds of non-consummation. The expiation of his feelings for Valentine took the form of one of the key paintings of his career. *Winged Domino/Portrait of Valentine* was his farewell to her and his statement that although she would never again be his wife he would always love her.

Valentine's skin has become a cool, distant blue. The woodpeckers, one of which seems to whisper a secret in her ear and the dove perhaps refer to the abundant fauna of Le Pouy, with exotic moths and butterflies clustered round her lips and eyelids, searching for the sweetness of nectar. The thorns on the tangled stem of the single rose that adorns her neck threatens her tender flesh, ironically recalling the motto on the Penrose coat of arms, *Nulla Rosa Sine Spina* – No Rose Without A Thorn. The rose, a symbol of love, had proved as inseparable from its pain-inflicting thorns as love is from pain.

Ever since I can remember, the painting was a much-loved part of the collection at Farleys. I had always felt it to be a joyful image until after Valentine's death, when Roland offered, unprompted; '*I painted that when I knew she had gone for ever*'. In that moment, the melancholy of the blue came through to me, making palpable the intensity of his sadness both past and present.

For Roland the year unfolded with further commitments to the Spanish Republican cause and contributions to the Surrealist section of the Artists International Association exhibition *Unity of Artists for Peace, Democracy and Cultural Development* which opened in April 1937.

21 June of the same year found him staying with Ernst in Paris. It was a hot evening and Ernst invited Roland to go with him to a fancy-dress party, a *souper déguisé,* held in the home of the Rochas family. Monsieur Marcel Rochas was a wealthy businessman whose two fashionable daughters were taking advantage of the absence of their parents by holding a Surrealist ball in the family home at 66 Avenue d'Iéna.[20] Ernst dyed his white hair bright blue and went dressed in his brigand costume

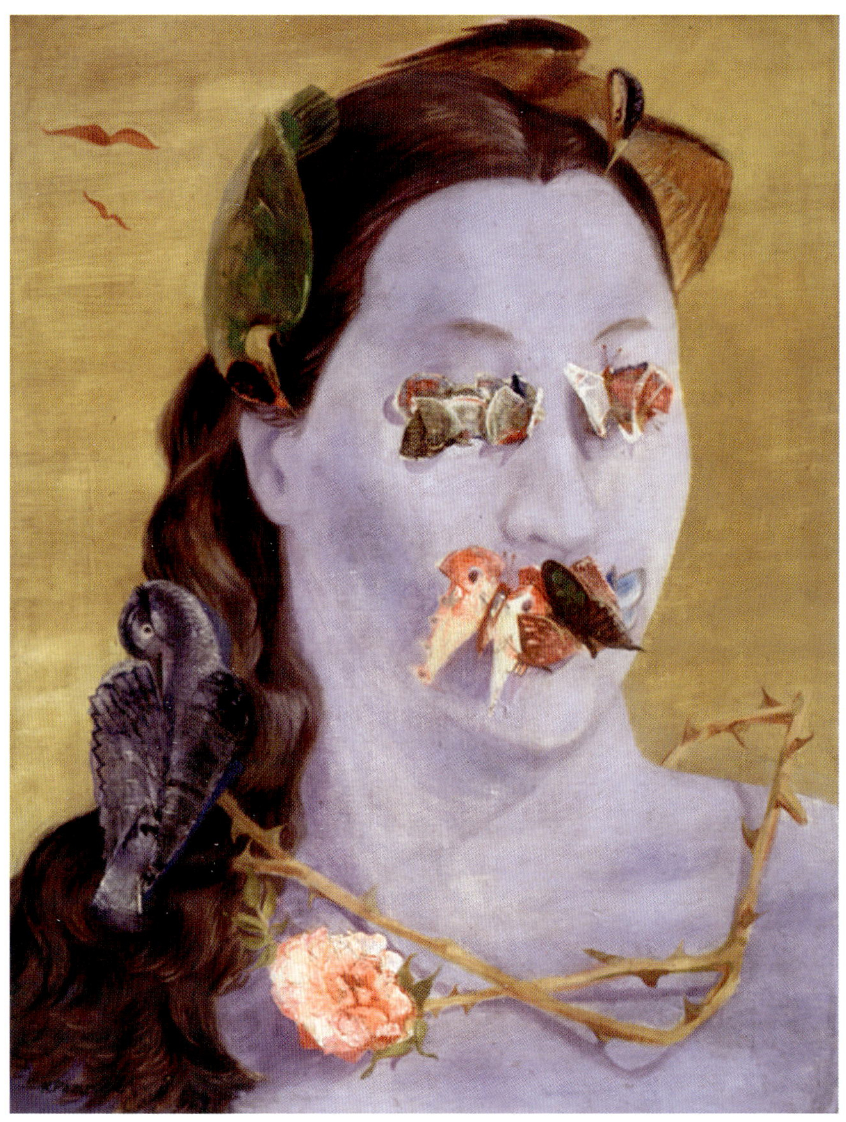

Winged Domino, 1938, Oil on Canvas, Private Collection England

from *L'Age d'Or*. Roland dyed his right hand and left foot blue and attired himself in a pair of Ernst's paint-encrusted trousers and a filthy old coat, an appearance that made a dramatic contrast with the elegant guests at the party.

Paul Eluard, Man Ray, Georges Bataille and Michel Leiris were there and Man Ray, in the true spirit of Surrealism, punched Eluard in the face. Eluard forgave him instantly, saying afterwards that it was only natural for a small man of courage to feel at some moment compelled to hit a man taller than himself. Beautiful women in all kinds of extravagant costumes abounded, including one who draped herself in nothing more than a few strands of ivy, presaging by a year Paul Delvaux's *L'Appelle de la Nuit*, a painting Roland was soon to own.

Despite these marvels, Roland could not take his eyes off one particular woman who was dressed in a simple dark blue robe. She had come as a guest of the American art dealer Julian Levy and although she seemed to know many people, there was a distance about her. She was there like an angel visiting a dream. Her soft blond hair held the faintest tint of green. Strong blue eyes gazed with warmth and confidence from a sun-tanned face. When she smiled she infused sunlight into the room and revealed a wide gap between her front teeth that in the overwhelming beauty of her face seemed another becoming feature. She was tall, athletic looking and wore her beauty with a casual ease. Bataille and Leiris said later they had never seen a more beautiful woman but it was Roland whom she totally captivated. For the second time in his life he felt as if he had been struck by lightning, the surrealists' prized *coup de foudre*.

A social earthquake, caused by Monsieur Rochas returning unexpectedly and ejecting his daughter's guests *en masse*, rapidly followed the lightning bolt. Roland barely had time to discover the name of his mysterious muse before he was bundled out of the door. He had met Lee Miller.

Roland had, by chance, already been enamoured with Lee's lips a year before he met her. One of the paintings in the *International Surrealist*

Exhibition that he had particularly admired was Man Ray's *L'Heure de l'Observatoire*, also known as *The Lovers.* When Man Ray's three-year love affair with Lee ended in 1932 he scaled up Lee's lips from a photograph and transferred them to the canvas. The lips float freely in a calm morning sky above the twin breast-like domes of the Observatoire de Montparnasse close to his studio. It was his expiation of a grief that had driven him to the very edge of suicide.

Ironically the birthplace of this Surrealist free spirit was Poughkeepsie, a small town in upstate New York on the Hudson River, where her father Theodore was an engineer at the de Laval Separator Company. Her Canadian mother, Florence, had been a nurse. Lee was the middle child, born in 1907. Her older brother, John, was to become an aviation pioneer and her younger brother Erik became chief photographer of the Lockheed Aircraft Corporation. The understanding of mechanical things and the challenge of danger were inherent in their childhood as Theodore encouraged them to build death-defying cable cars, railways that worked and catapults that fired snowballs hundreds of feet. Lee was an honorary boy capable of outsmarting and out-daring her brothers. She was a headstrong, wilful item of one, thrown out of every school in the Hudson Valley – the kind of girl who some mothers banned their daughters from associating with.

Whilst walking in Manhattan early in 1927 Lee was snatched to safety from the path of an oncoming car by Condé Nast, the publisher of *Vogue* and *Vanity Fair* magazines. He recognised Lee as having the face of the era, her bobbed hair and her *garçonne* appearance symbolising the new beginnings of female freedom. Within a few weeks her portrait by Georges Lepape was on the front cover of the March issue of *Vogue*. It was the start of a modelling career with the photographic greats of the day – Edward Steichen, Nickolas Murray and Arnold Genthe. Lee turned each of these sessions into a tutorial as she was more interested in what was going on behind the camera and Steichen in particular encouraged her, giving her an introduction to Man Ray. She went to

Paris and instantly became Man Ray's lover and pupil. Many of his best-known works are of Lee, the result of their artistic collaboration or in some cases their quarrels.

Lee objected to the way the Surrealist tenet of free love was biased in favour of the men who asserted they could have affairs whenever they wanted, but expected their women to be faithful. Lee met Man Ray on equal terms and the sparks flew because he became insanely jealous of her. Seeking to control her, he visually dismembered her body. He pasted her eye to the bob weight of a metronome for *Object to be Destroyed* (destroyed; re-made and re-titled in 1959 *Objet Indéstructible*) and sheared her head off for one of his most famous photographs which features patterns of shadows falling across her naked torso. Jean Cocteau followed suit when Lee, much to Man Ray's fury, took time out to star in Cocteau's film *Le Sang d'un Poète.* Cocteau turned her into an armless statue that is destroyed by a demented poet wielding a sledgehammer. But Lee defied her would-be captors and blithely had love affairs with whomever she chose. Her convictions of the individual's right to freedom were well in place before she came to Paris. She was a Surrealist before the movement had a name.

In 1929 Lee had an affair with Aziz Eloui Bey, a rich Egyptian businessman who was so smitten by Lee that he divorced his wife, Nimet who had become Lee's friend. Lee, however, was quite unprepared to marry anyone. She felt oppressed by people who wanted to possess her and the only way open to her was to return to New York. The night she left, Man Ray howled his grief from the Cimetière du Montparnasse under the window of her old studio. For some weeks, he had been carrying a pistol, announcing that he could not decide whether he should shoot Lee, Aziz or himself. In the early hours of the morning, with the model Jacqueline Goddard as his assistant, he photographed a self-portrait with the pistol in his hand, a rope round his neck and a bottle of poison at his elbow.

Man Ray remained fiercely hostile and grumbled about Lee from the day she left Paris. He had not expected to see her at the Rochas party –

she had only arrived in Paris that morning – and the sight of her moved him to forget the quarrels of the past. Amid the excitement they made peace.

In 1932 Lee had established her own studio in New York against all odds and became one of the city's foremost celebrity portrait photographers. But she was miserable doing the daily grind of portraits and advertising pack shots. In the heat of July, Aziz arrived unexpectedly and asked her to marry him. She agreed, was wed in New York, closed her studio and left for Cairo in the space of a few weeks.

She tried very hard to be a good wife to Aziz, learning to play golf and entertaining graciously. Eventually she sought relief from the triviality and the endless society gossip by making long-range expeditions into the desert, with a few well-chosen friends. Her viewfinder transformed villages, rock formations, monasteries, details of buildings and other snippets into some of the most powerful Surrealist images of her whole oeuvre.

After three years of Cairo not even desert travel was enough and Aziz, indulgent as always, sent her off on a trip to Paris with her maid Elda. The first night she was there, she attended the Rochas party. The next day, Ernst, who knew her well from her time with Man Ray, phoned to invite her to dinner to meet the shy Englishman she had fleetingly encountered the night before. The dinner was a fizz of excitement with the intense warmth and intimacy that comes from the most stimulating and agreeable of company. Lee enchanted everyone and Roland most of all. The next morning in his small room in the Hôtel de la Paix they awoke in each other's arms. So began a relationship that was torn by the most extreme tensions, yet forged by even stronger shared passions.

A few days later Roland left for London with Ernst to assist him with the mounting of his exhibition at the Mayor Gallery. He wrote to Lee; 'I have slept and woken at last from a dream – shall I ever dream again anything so marvellous?'[21] He enclosed the three hundred francs he had borrowed from her when he had evidently been so overwhelmed that his arrangements went to pieces and invited Lee to join him in Cornwall where he had rented Lambe Creek, his brother Beacus's beautiful Georgian house on the Truro River. The house stood at the edge of the tidal creek, sheltered by dense woodland yet open to the sun. It was just the sort of romantic setting that Roland adored and when, two days later, Lee arrived in the company of Paul and Nusch Eluard, with Man Ray and his new girlfriend from Guadeloupe Ady Fidelin, his joy must have been complete.

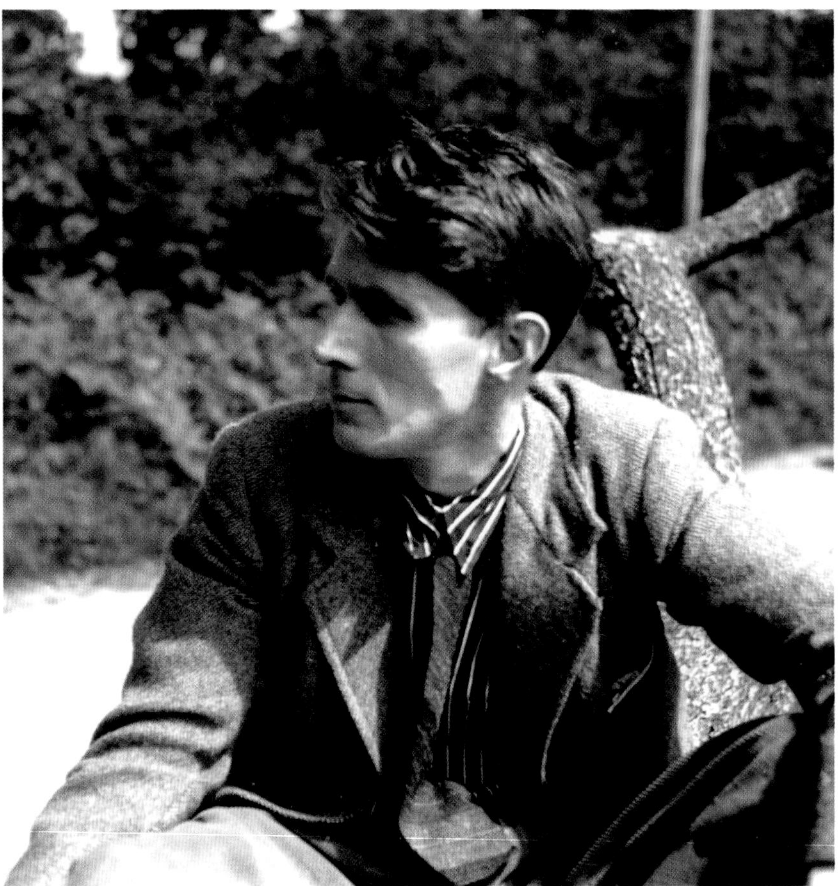

Roland Penrose, Lambe Creek, Cornwall, England 1937 by Lee Miller

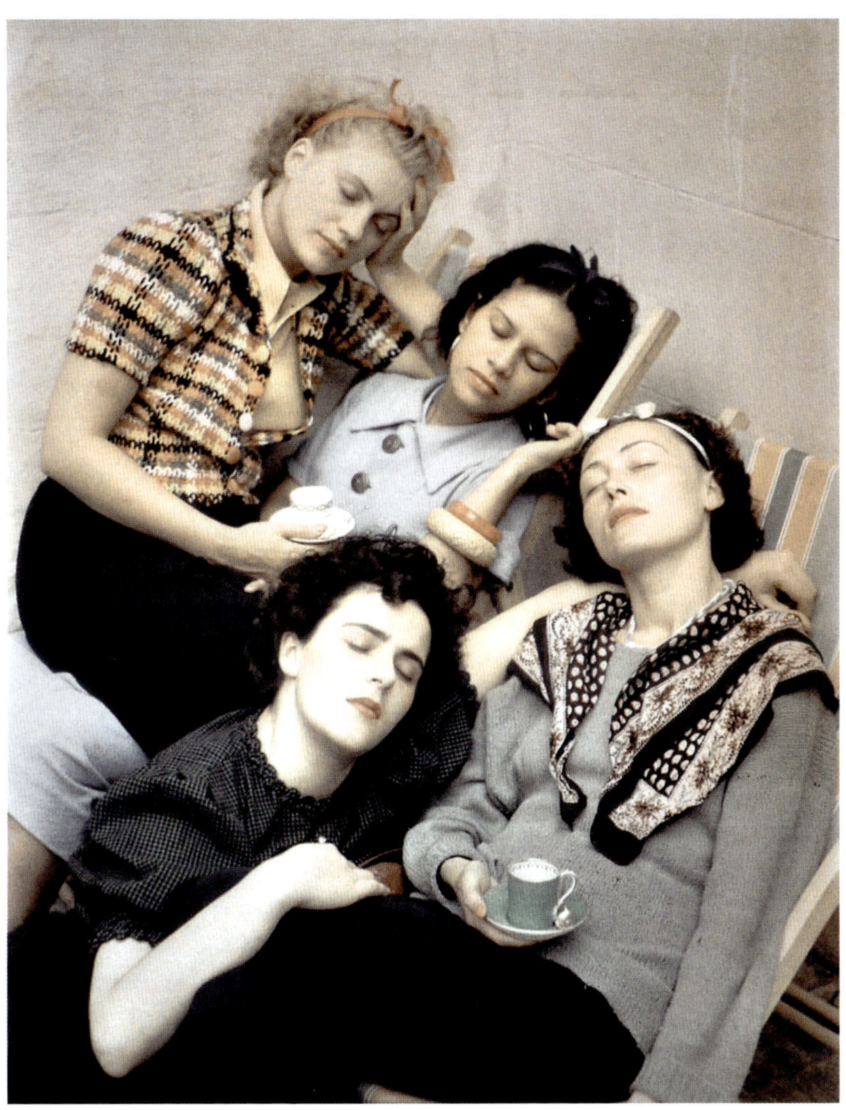

Four women asleep, Lee Miller, Leonora Carrington, Ady Fidelin and Nusch Eluard, Lambe Creek, Cornwall, England 1937

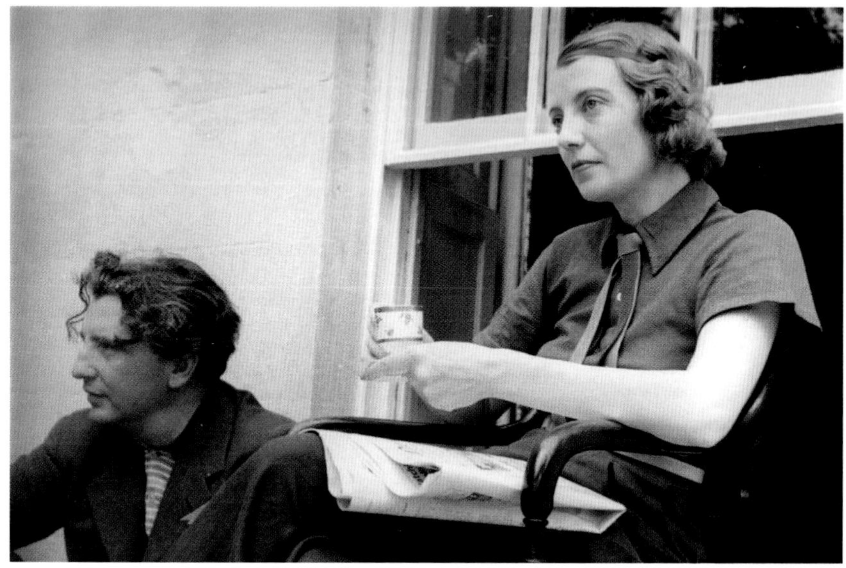

Joseph Bard and Eileen Agar, Lambe Creek, Cornwall, England 1937

Eileen Agar and her husband Joseph Bard arrived to stay and Moore and his wife Irina visited for a day. Ernst followed soon afterwards with Leonora Carrington, his lover since parting from Marie-Berthe who now devoted herself to praying for Ernst's salvation. Long indolent days were punctuated by frolicking in the mud of the creek; Ernst became the Old Man of the Sea, twisting fronds of seaweed into a wig and beard and Leonora posed for Lee's camera as his bare-breasted mermaid.

Eileen Agar wrote;

> It was a delightful Surrealist house party that July, with Roland taking the lead, ready to turn the slightest encounter into an orgy. I remember going off to watch Lee taking a bubble-bath, but there was not quite enough room in the tub for all of us ... The Surrealists were always supposed to be such immoral monsters, but I for one did not go to bed with everybody who asked me. When would I have had time to paint?[22]

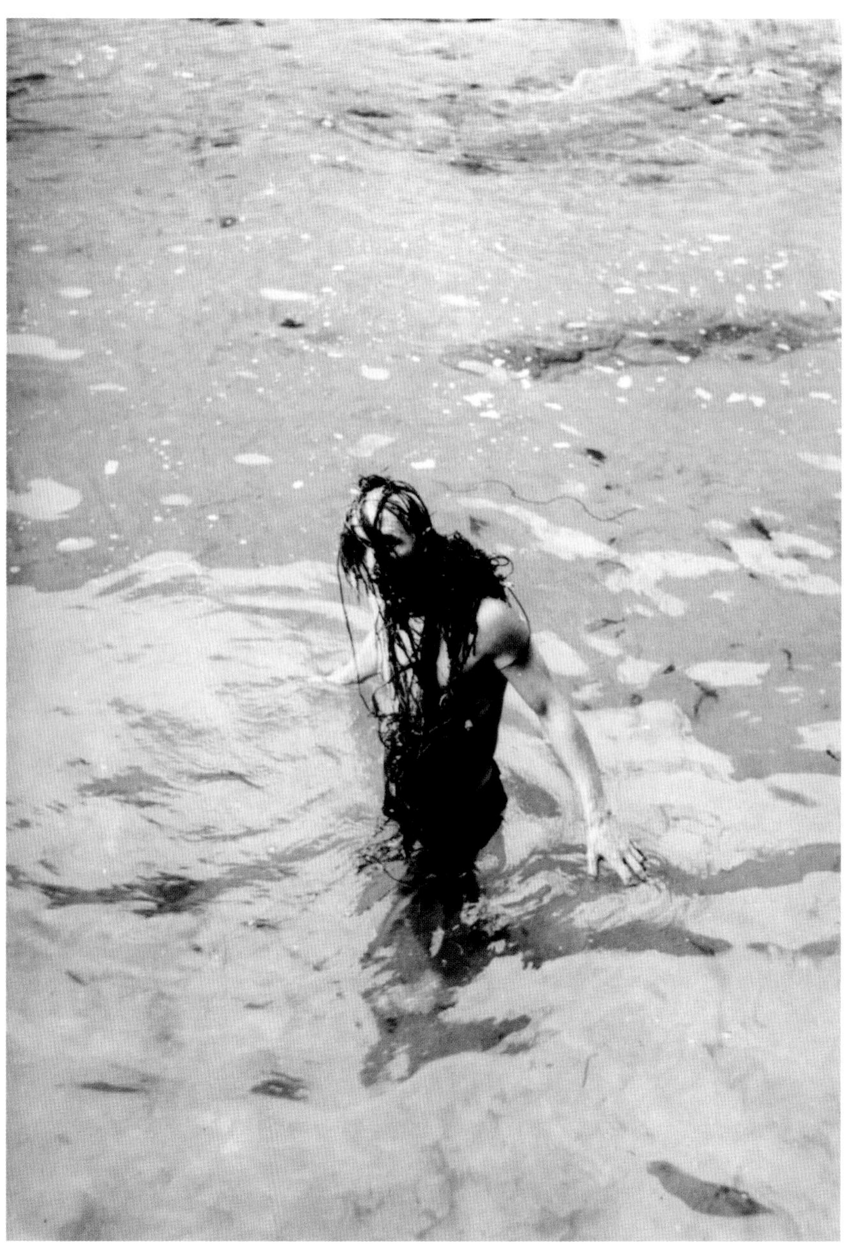

Max Ernst and seaweed, Lambe Creek, Cornwall, England 1937

Roland found no time to paint, but he drew. A portrait of Nusch reclining with her eyes closed dates from this holiday.[23] He also made a series of drawings of a small boat beached in the shallows; a surf of fine blonde hair tumbles out of the hull like a massive breaker completely swamping it. He developed the drawing into a painting titled *Cheveux et Barque* the following year and took up the theme again in 1948 as *Une Chevelure*

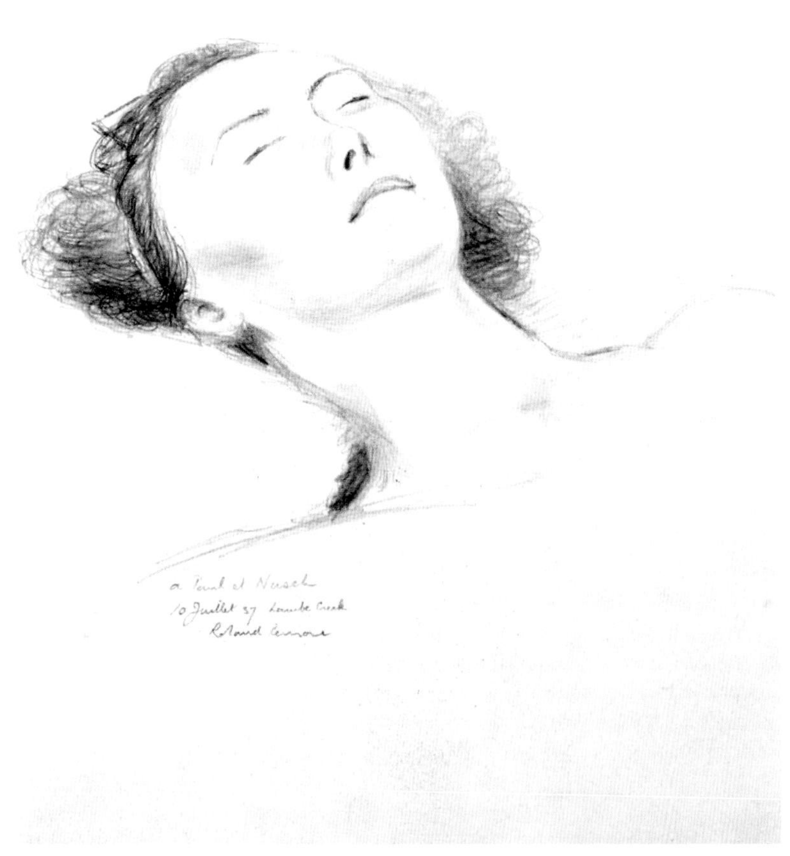

Portrait of Nusch Eluard, pencil on paper, Lambe Creek, Cornwall, England 1937

Blonde Dans Une Barque, reproduced in *Voir* with a poem by Eluard. Paul Eluard was excited by the image and references to it and to Lee appear in his poem *The Last Letter to Roland Penrose* from which the following lines are extracted;

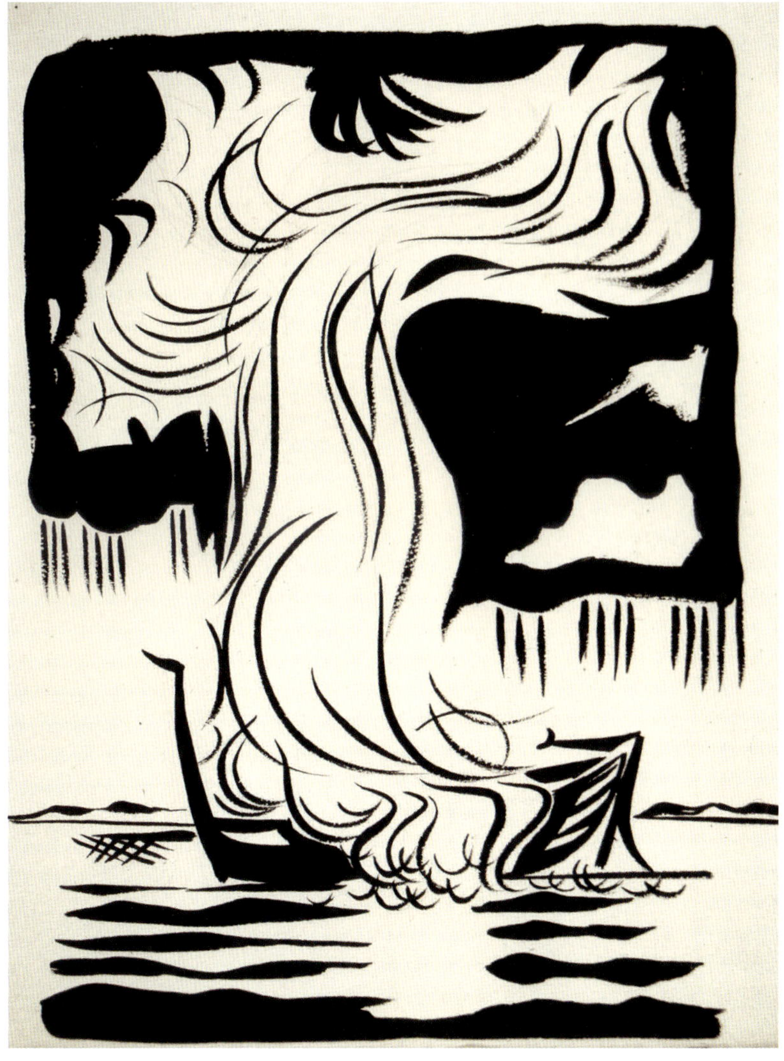

Une Chevelure Blonde dans une Barque, 1948, work on paper

The softness of the seafaring climate
Of blonde hair in a boat
And the ground that rises up
That trembles at the water's edge
Showing me a woman from abroad
[...]
The reflection of a body naked and hard calms the flood tide
The blonde season is favourable to my caresses
Your blonde hair opens to me the boat of your body.

Paul Eluard 1936–48
Translated from the French by Roland Penrose

The poem confirms that the wild waves of hair bursting from the boat relate to Lee and her uncontrollable, naturally wavy locks. The connotations of the boat and a woman's pudenda were recognised by Eluard and by Roland who used the symbol in his wonderfully playful and enigmatic object *Le Paradis des Alouettes.* A tiny wooden boat, closely inspected by a pair of dark glasses, features outsized hairs growing on the blade of one of the oars, which is positioned lengthways in the hull, like a clitoris.

We see Lee's wavy hair again in another drawing titled *Nourishment From Heaven*. Her head reclines corpse-like on a flat landscape. A woman's hand appears to delicately insert a coin into Lee's mouth. The coin bears connotations of death from the ancient practice of placing a coin in the mouth of a corpse for the deceased's soul to pay Charon the ferryman to convey it to the afterlife. But Roland's love of ambiguity gives us other possible readings. If the coin was being taken out of Lee's mouth like a sleight-of-hand conjuring trick, we would have abundance appearing by magic. Roland leaves us to decide.

The party broke up at the end of July and, before leaving for Paris, Eluard suggested they should all meet again at Mougins. They shipped

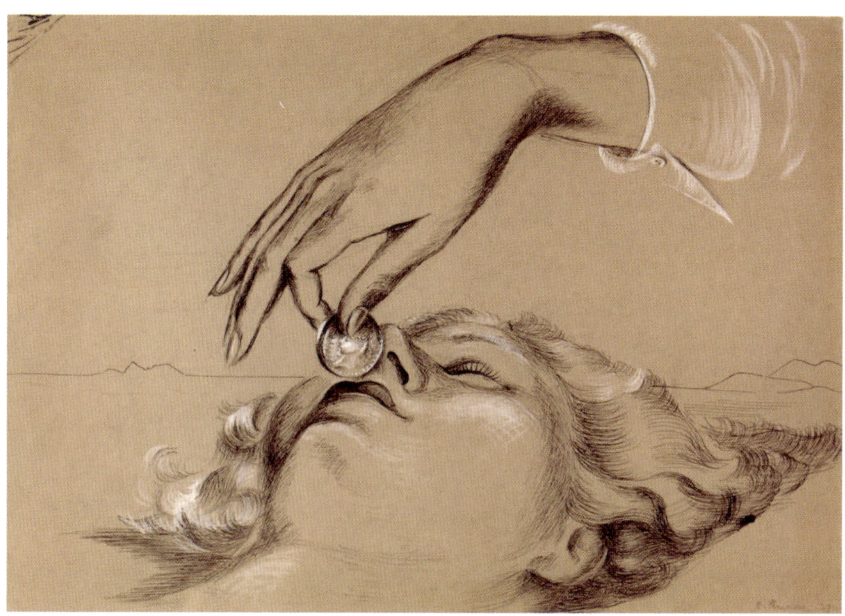

Nourishment from Heaven, 1938, ink, graphite and watercolour on paper

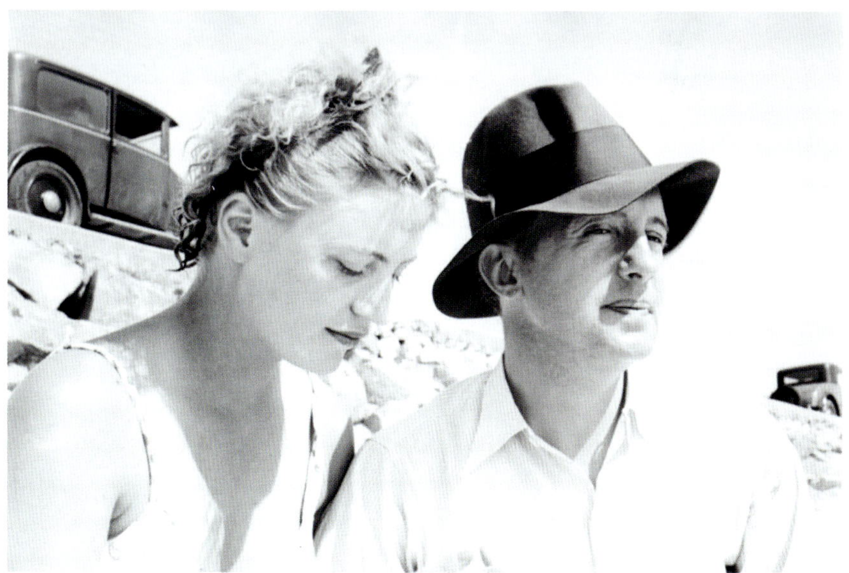

Lee Miller and Paul Eluard on the beach, Côte d'Azur, France 1937

Roland's Ford convertible on the ferry to Belgium and met Mesens in Brussels. Lee shared Roland's affection for Mesens and respected his understanding of Surrealism and his own considerable ability as a poet and collagist. It was probably his fondness for groping women that earned him the nickname of Tripotin, which also carried the implication of shady activities as an art dealer. Mesens was evidently proud of his sobriquet and on occasions used it as his signature. He was delighted with Roland and Lee's visit and introduced them to the Belgian Surrealist painters René Magritte and Paul Delvaux and the collector van Hecke, all to remain friends for many years.

When they arrived in Mougins on 19 August Picasso and Dora Maar, the Eluards, Man Ray and Ady were already there. A few days later Roland and Lee motored to the outskirts of Cannes to pick up Eileen Agar and Joseph Bard. The party was complete.

Picasso was attracted to Lee's large firm breasts and robust physique, but he was also charmed by her wit and ebullience.

He was enchanted by the way she drove them all down to the beach topless in an open car and generally behaved with her own brand of stylish outrageousness, like the night when she danced trouser-less in the car headlights.

Relationships within this group were very free and easy, with the exchange of partners being openly accepted. Eluard, who had had his own liaison with Eileen Agar, had at times encouraged Nusch to sleep with Picasso. It was an act of homage – to offer the man he admired most the gift of the woman he loved most. It is my guess that Roland, who told me he had taken an interest in Ady, paid homage in a similar way. It is easy to imagine that Lee, with her great affection for Picasso and her remarkable sexual emancipation would have enthusiastically made the most of the occasion. Forty years later Roland told me that in all the years he and Lee had been together, they had never been unfaithful to each other. I was astonished, knowing something of their many liaisons, but he went on to explain that he and Lee had agreed at the beginning they were free to sleep with whomever they chose but their love for each other was to remain forever sacred.

For part of every day, usually in the afternoons and evenings, Picasso worked. He had taken the biggest room in the hotel with a balcony and he surrounded himself with a huge amount of *objets trouvés* collected from the beach that awaited their chance to become part of a work. Canvases were piled against the walls and every available space was crammed with evidence of his tireless capacity to work and invent.

In this atmosphere of easy sexual liberation, he chose the theme of *L'Arlesienne.* Women from Arles were renowned for their beauty and their particularly flattering local costume, but *L'Arlesienne* had a secondary significance. A popular short story of the time told of an Arlesienne of legendary beauty who drove the young peasant boy who loved her to madness and suicide with her deceit and thus epitomised the dangers of love and eroticism.[24]

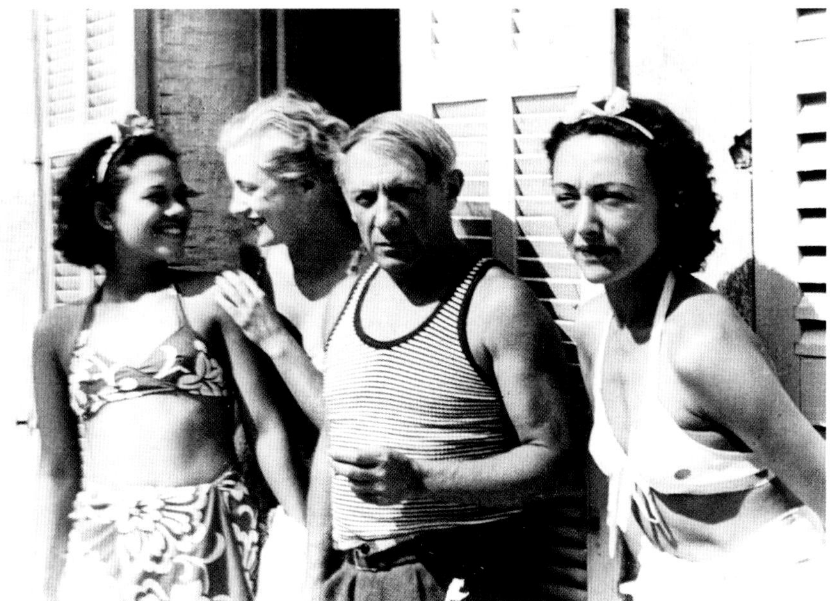

Ady Fidelin, Lee Miller, Picasso and Nusch Eluard, Mougins, France 1937

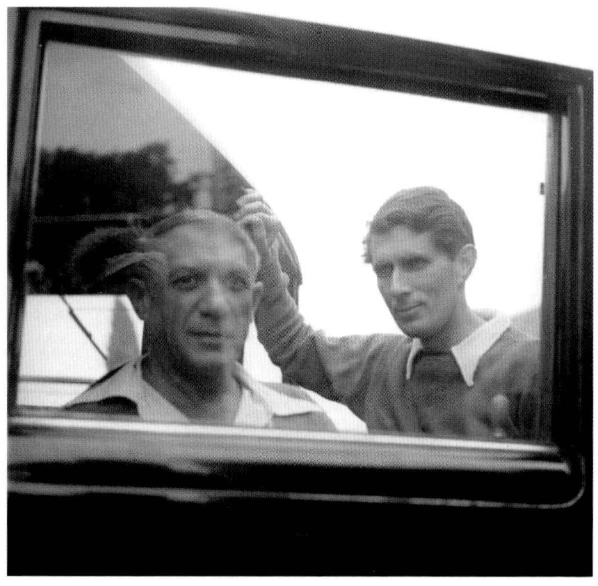

Picasso and Roland Penrose, Mougins France 1937 by Lee Miller

One of Picasso's first *L'Arlesienne* portraits is unexpectedly identifiable as Paul Eluard shown breast-feeding a small tabby cat. The next day Picasso announced he had painted a portrait of Lee and in the days that followed his portraits of Lee mounted up until there were six in all. The theme of the flamboyant shoulders on the costume and the hat that sometimes gives way to Lee's hair ribbon runs throughout and her much-admired breasts are prominent. The key features that make the likeness unmistakably Lee are the profile of the head, the green hair and the lips with the gap-toothed smile. Her face is shown devoid of modelling often in a bright yellow, perhaps in recognition of the sunny warmth of her character, against backgrounds that vary from garish pinks to yellow. With a few notable exclusions such as his portrait of Gertrude Stein, the subjects of Picasso's best female portraits tend to be the women he slept with and Lee was no exception.

Picasso's joy was nearly cut short as a few days later Roland was driving him in his Ford on the mountain roads when an oncoming car hurtled round a bend on the wrong side of the road. They crashed head on and Picasso was thrown around inside the car, bruising his chest. Picasso's injuries were not severe but to torment Roland he made much of them. It is ironic to think how close Roland came to being known as the man who killed Picasso, a turn of fate he would have found impossible to endure.

Taken during this time one of Lee's best-known photographs is of the Eluards, Roland, Man Ray and Ady seated on the ground around a low table under the shade of pines. Unconsciously imitating Manet's *Déjeuner sur l'Herbe* the men are clothed but Ady and Nusch are topless. Paul Eluard is kissing Nusch tenderly. Ady and Man Ray look happy. Next to them, Roland has the look of complete ecstasy on his face. This

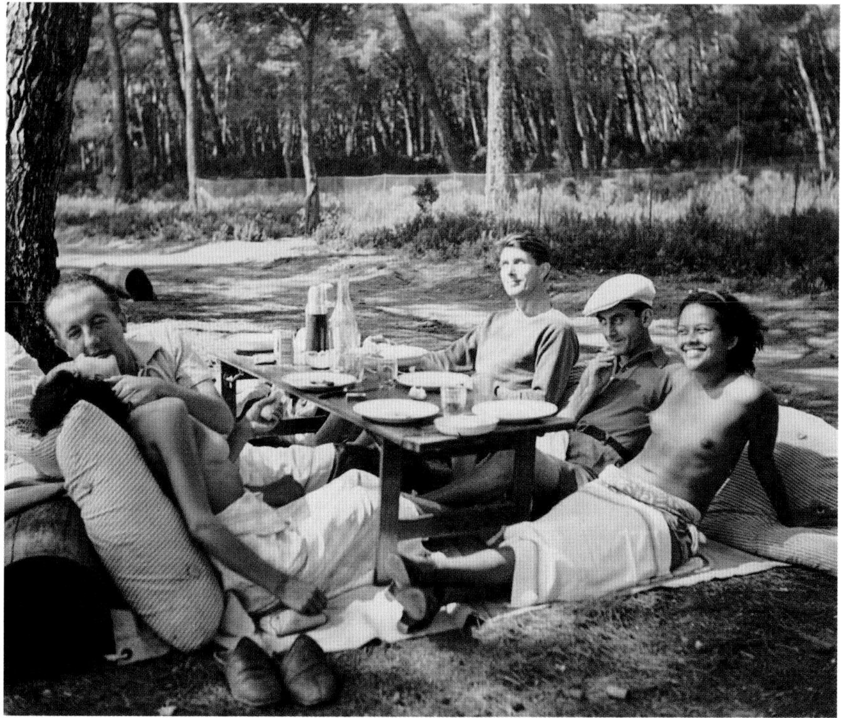

Picnic, Ile Sainte Marguerite, Cannes, France 1937 by Lee Miller

is the appearance of a liberated Englishman freed from the burdens of his puritan past.

This heady mix of sex, freedom, friends and all the other good things to be found on the Côte d'Azur sixty years ago triggered the most important development in Roland's art. One rainy day with Lee in bed with a cold, he crouched on the tiled floor of his hotel room and began using coloured postcards as elements in collages. He chose images of local scenes with bold patterns, picked for their form rather than their detail. Among the first was *Soleil de Mougins*.

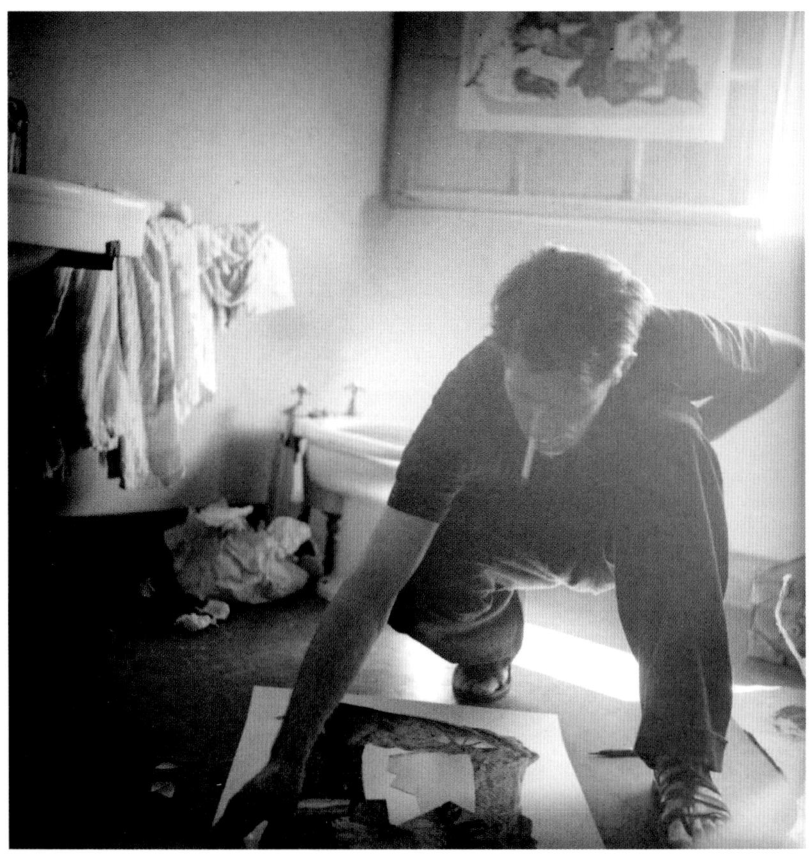

Roland Penrose, Mougins, France 1937 by Lee Miller

In his new style, Roland used large sheets of paper and prepared the background with gouache textures or cut-out papers of different colours. The cards usually form fan-shaped or linear rhythmical patterns in a method that owed a little to the Cubist technique of breaking down the surface of an object and reconstructing it as a series of planes.

One of the best-known works is a celebration of Lee called *The Real Woman*. Lee's nude torso fills the right hand side. For this, he first made a frottage on a surface with a pronounced wood grain. He cut from it the silhouette of the torso and then modelled the contours of her body by lightly erasing the areas that should be dark. This produced an effect like a photographic negative where dark is exchanged for light and perhaps was a reference to Lee's career as a photographer. By contrast a hot vivid sunset aligned vertically forms her vagina. The torso is the core of the real woman who had just arrived in Roland's life – robust and charged

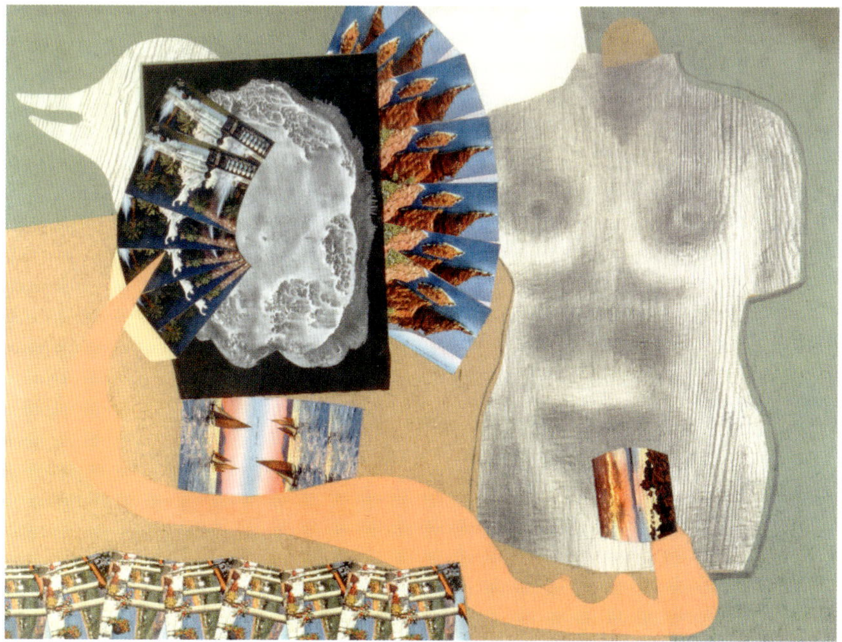

The Real Woman, 1937, Collage Collection: National Trust, Willow Road.

with sexuality. The left side of the picture is given to what is perhaps Lee's alter ego, a large bird with fantastic plumage. Her tail feathers are formed by a spread of seven cards of the rocky headland of Les Roches du Trayas on the nearby Corniche d'Or. Scenes of municipal Cannes are repeated to form the breast feathers (Lee always was a town bird) and her body is a lacy effect of white gouache on a rectangle of black card. Another cut-out piece of frottage creates the bird's head, beak open and ready to make some colourful American wisecrack.

After Roland's postcard collages had been exhibited in the 1938 Paris *Exposition Internationale du Surréalisme* at the Galerie Beaux-Arts René Magritte and Paul Nougé wrote;

> It may well be that the strangeness of the light-effects in England, which never cease to permeate the painting and photography of this country, offers sufficient explanation of why Penrose's attention should have particularly been focussed on the problem of colour. Roland Penrose, however, has thought of formulating the problem in entirely new terms; up till now, he says, colour has been used for no other purpose than the creation of the image of the objects. But what if we tried to use the image of the objects to create colours? Roland Penrose has succeeded in this experiment.[25]

Many more works were to follow and, as the idea developed, all kinds of items rapidly found their way into the composition – tickets, book illustrations, newspapers, tin lids, string and even a fragment of a painting by Roland's aunt in his collage *Magnetic Moths*.[26] The scene of a stone bridge over a river is turned upside down and becomes the moth's body and tail. A double row of Eiffel Towers make the thorax and two views of Parisian nocturnal illuminations give it a pair of bulbous eyes registering distress at the sight of a huge alluring candle formed by images of urban sophistication. From here on, many of his paintings also contained the exciting addition of unexpected fragments of almost

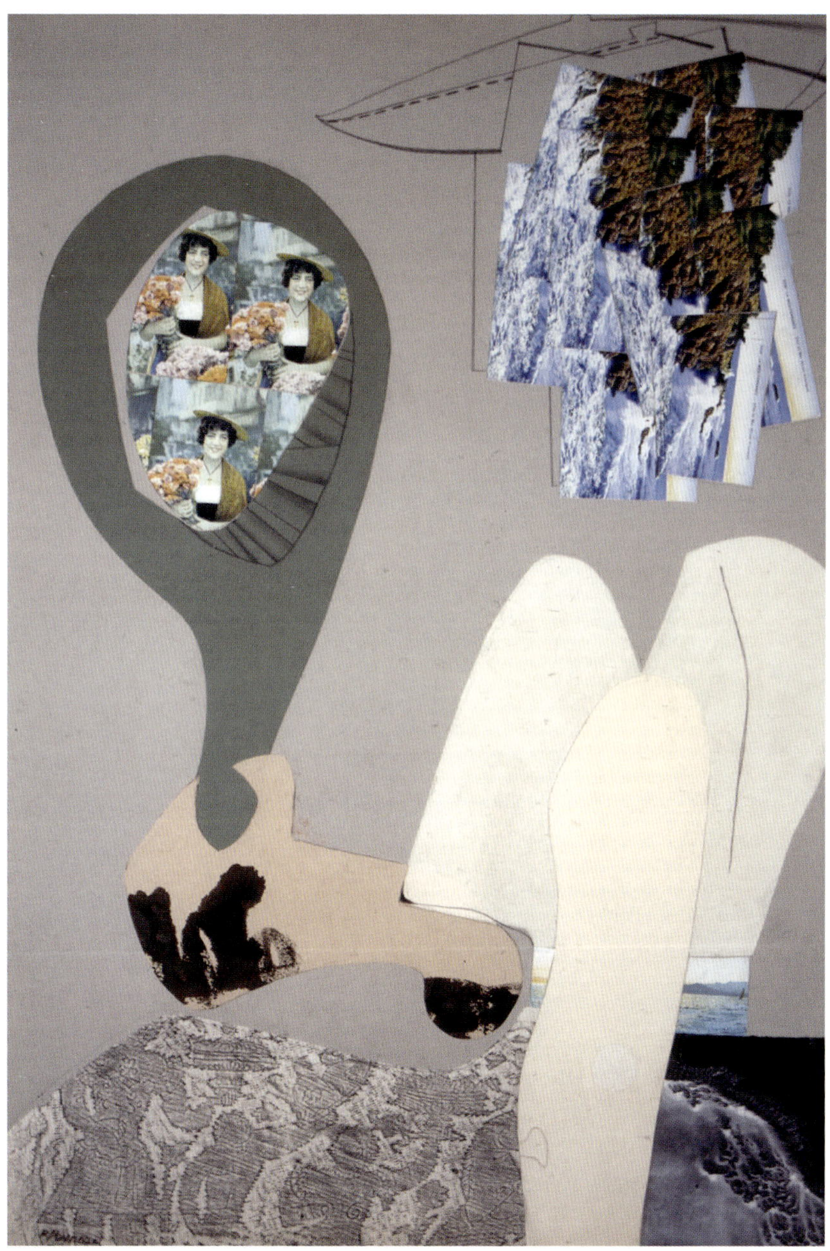

La Mediterraneé, 1937, collage. Collection: National Galleries Scotland

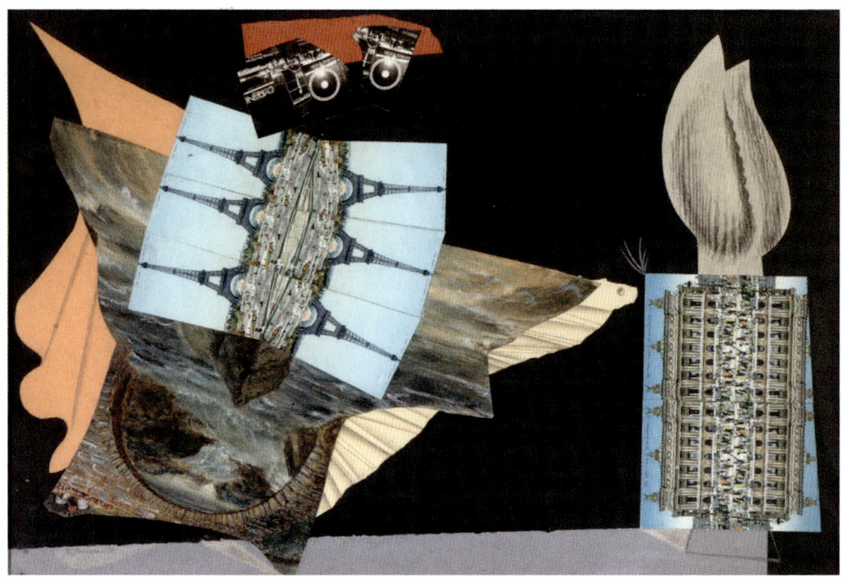

Magnetic Moths, 1938, collage Collection: Tate Modern

anything, press-ganged into the service of his work and transformed in the process.

It was a sad parting when Picasso and Dora Maar crammed themselves, the paintings and most of the *objets trouvés* into the Hispano Suiza and left for Paris. Lee sensed she had stretched Aziz's indulgence to the limit, so they made a short tour of the Côte d'Azur and then drove back to Paris. With heavy hearts they parted a few days later at the Gare de Lyon. They both clung to the comfort of the many plans they had made for future adventures as Lee returned to Cairo via Marseille from where she posted a note scribbled on a page torn from her notebook;

It's cold in the train – I'm alone with the noise
– and my tears, unlike your chains
– bind me –
it was true – it is true
– I'm leaving – I love you
and I'll return.[27]

Back in London after a brief stay in Paris Roland replied;

> London Wednesday evening.
> My love, I'm back here where I started from – stacks of fatuous unanswered letters, pictures, objects and an intolerable silence, a blank, everything tries to look as though nothing had happened and to hide the fact that all has changed, that a marvellous presence has been here and has gone. … I can never say how much I love you, it is beyond all powers of expression. You have given me something new, something so potent that it is either life or death. Darling I want you. Darling come back.[28]

6 1937-39 The Road Is Wider Than Long

'The important thing about being a Surrealist is to never discover one's self and to try anything once, except incest and folk dancing.'

Conroy Maddox, with reference to Sir Thomas Beecham.
Address at the opening of the Eileen Agar Retrospective Exhibition, Scottish National Gallery of Modern Art, Edinburgh, 1 December 1999.

On his way through Paris in October 1937 Roland had called at Picasso's studio in Rue des Grands Augustins on the Rive Gauche opposite L'Île de la Cité. Before leaving Mougins, Roland had persuaded Picasso to sell him one of his portraits of Lee. For once Picasso turned down the chance to torment Roland, who for £50 bought the pick of them all and returned with it to England. There he delighted in Lee's surrogate presence in his house until he reluctantly shipped it to Cairo.

Roland was tortured by Lee's absence. He was aware he had by chance stumbled through a door into a new life of full-blooded sensuality, the complete antithesis of his experience with Valentine. He wrote in a letter to her that reveals the honesty of their relationship;

> Actually darling most people would think that I had forgotten you already, your bed has not been empty for the last four nights but Thea[1] who occupies it is so different that I almost feel ashamed to make love with her. She is very sweet and is perhaps the only person who could console me of this bitterness. She puts up with my gloom

> with great patience though I talk of you whenever I can and tell her of the lump that I can't move at the bottom of my heart.[2]

Roland in his younger days could not be described as 'good looking' but all through his life women found him extremely attractive. He had a way of listening attentively that made a woman feel she was the only person in the world he found important. It was not contrived; most women genuinely fascinated him. His old-world style manners were impeccable, borne with a kindness and sensitivity to others that made them feel at ease. Within his charm there was the irresistible cachet of mystery that so irritated Valentine – the inaccessible part of him some women saw as a fortress to be sieged. He was never alone for long.

A week later Lee replied to his letter;

> It's very nice that Thea is with you – I liked her very much – which is a great deal, … I hope you are as tender with her as you know how to be – because if she likes me and is replacing me, especially so soon, it's as if she were me – and I could feel it.[3]

Roland, Eileen Agar and other English Surrealists frequented the Caledonian Market in North London, a marvellous source of bric à brac and *objets trouvés*. It was there that for three shillings and sixpence he bought a model of a girl's head and shoulders with what he described as;

> … very naughty eyes. She is an old hairdresser's model and will make a very pretty object when I have cut her head off and repainted her cheeks.[4]

His creation was to be titled *The Dew Machine*.

Roland had a wig made of long blonde straight hair, added false eyelashes, and completed her transformation by painting the eyes, lips and skin tones. The head, elegant but banal, hovers upside-down above

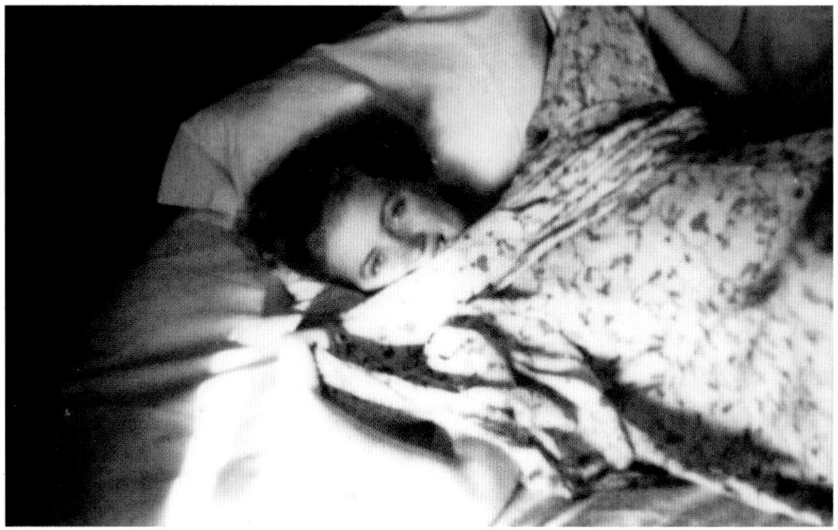

Lee Miller in bed, Bruges, Belgium 1937

a base board and funnels from chemical apparatus filled with coloured beads, tacks, shells and seeds are inserted into the neck. The part of the hair that caresses the base board is dyed bright blue. A further wineglass-shaped apparatus completes the object, strengthening the conjunction between the forces of arcane magic and science. It is easy to imagine the object scaled up to a gigantic size, the funnels loaded with mysterious substances feeding the hair that softly trails across the countryside wherever dew is needed.

A reprise of *The Dew Machine* greets us from within Roland's painting *Seeing Is Believing*, also titled *L'Île Invisible.* Here the head reaches down from the sky where day and night are simultaneous, and the tresses caress a small island densely covered by houses and a port with the masts of sailing boats. A strand of hair tumbles from a street like surf, recalling the simulacrum of hair as surf found in *Une Chevelure Blonde Dans Une Barque,* begun in Cornwall and developed at the same time as *L'Île Invisible.*

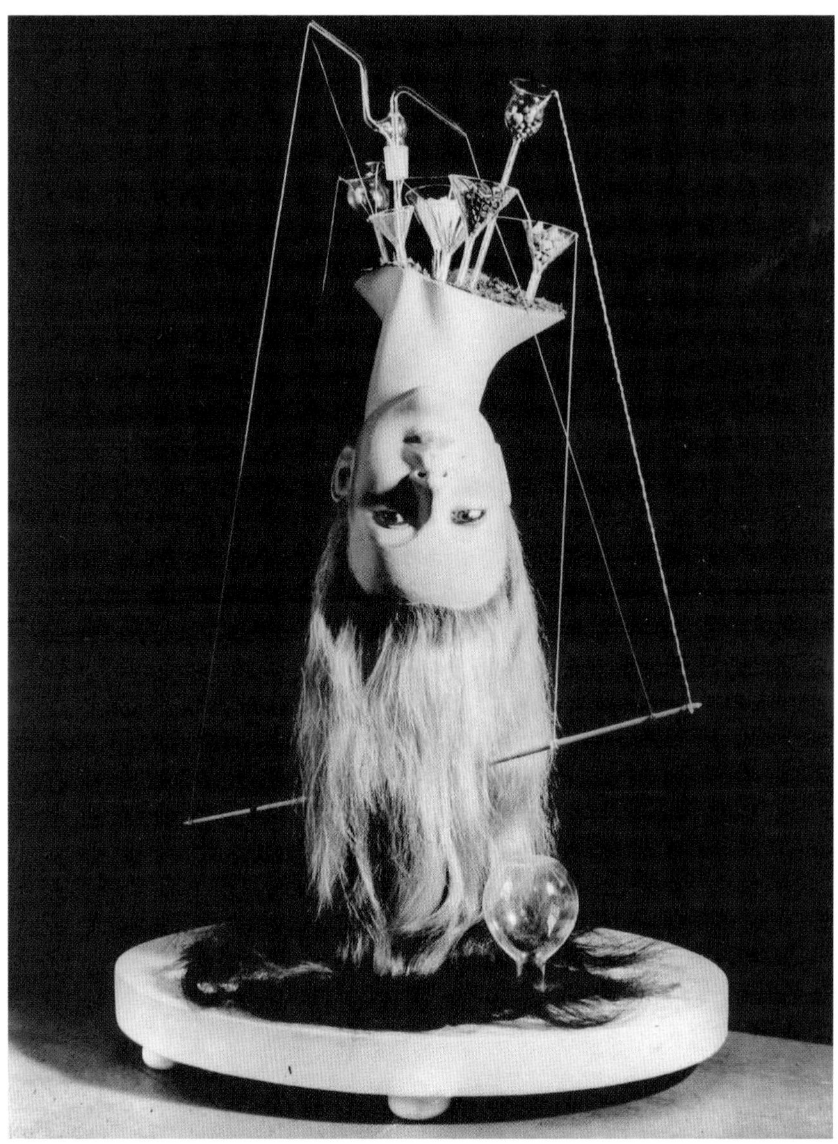

The Dew Machine, 1937 and *Untitled Object*, 1937

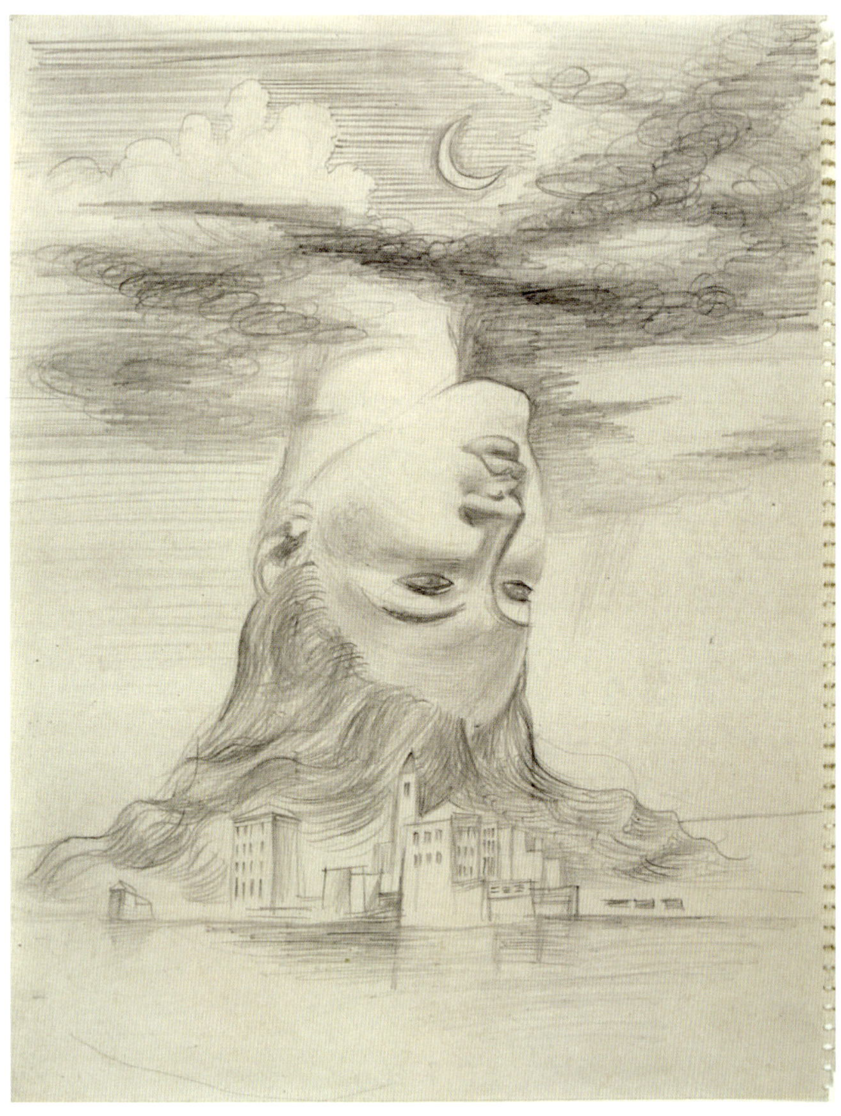

Study for *Seeing is Believing*, 1937, Pencil on Paper

In *Seeing is Believing* also known as *L'Île Invisible* the woman's hair becomes a conduit for magic connecting terrestrial dwellers to the mysteries of the arcane forces of the heavens. Good and bad weather, night and day are conducted down to the island village. The head is not Lee's, she is in the room with us observing the scene. Her hand is present on our side of the picture plane casting light instead of shadow. Perhaps she brings us enlightenment.

In the early spring of 1937 René Gaffé, a Belgian perfume merchant, bibliophile and art collector had been told by his doctor that he had only a few months to live. With his Belgian love of order he began methodically tidying up his affairs and decided to dispose of his large collection of Surrealist and Cubist paintings through a sale at the Zwemmer Gallery in London. An exhibition of forty paintings by Picasso, Miro and de Chirico was held and very few sold. Mesens, who in his capacity as a dealer was already associated with the London Gallery, immediately proposed Roland should buy the collection as a whole, and pursued him to Cornwall to close the deal.

On the 4 July Roland confirmed the purchase for the sum of £6,750. A comparison with the £50 he paid for the Picasso portrait of Lee made the average price of the paintings at £169 seems expensive, but in truth it probably reflects a prix des amis between Roland and Picasso. In late October, after Roland's return from Mougins the collection, less six pictures already sold, was delivered to his home.[5]

Among the works were twelve Picasso paintings, some of them great Cubist works such as *Girl with a Mandolin, Portrait of Uhde* and *Nature Morte au Bec de Gaz,* Miro's, *Tête du Paysan Catalan and Maternité,* both from the early 1920s and twelve early de Chiricos including *L'Ange Juif* of 1916. Thirteen of the less important paintings were sold on by Mesens, allowing Roland to recoup some of his outlay.

Strangely, Roland never regarded himself as a collector, in that his purchases of work did not follow a pre-determined theme, and nor did he ever buy a painting speculatively. He bought works of art solely because he loved them, and up to the purchase of the Gaffé collection, nearly all his acquisitions had been direct from the artists themselves with the additional motive of helping his friends through hard times.

Roland was not naturally acquisitive. His grandfather Alexander's passion for curios repelled him – he could not grasp the point of surrounding oneself with trophies from all over the world. For Roland and the Surrealists, objects and paintings had to reveal a marvellous world beyond the banal. He was more delighted with an odd-shaped bone or a piece of driftwood found on the seashore than the most amazing treasure from Alexander's glass-fronted cases. Alec was scornful and reproached him for squandering his money on what he regarded as the worthless daubings of madmen. Others in the family cautiously distanced themselves from Roland, believing he had clearly taken leave of his senses.

Roland did nothing to allay their fears. On a visit to Moore's studio at Kingston near Canterbury, Roland found and was instantly captivated by a large sculpture in Hopton stone, *Mother and Child.* The gentle foetus-like profile of the head with its vestigial features inspires a need to protect, and the figure's tender embrace envelops her child with a truly maternal strength. Roland was so taken by the mystic beauty of the piece that he bought her, and Moore duly arrived at 21 Downshire Hill with the sculpture. Roland recalled;

> He came and set her up in the front garden in Downshire Hill where I lived, saying 'If ever you get tired of this, change it, I will give you another one instead', which I thought was wonderful. It made me love him as much as the sculpture.[6]

The closeness of the friendship and collaboration between Roland and Mesens at this time had a lasting effect on art in Britain. It seemed at first sight an unlikely match. Mesens was inclined to be pompous, argumentative and dogmatic, but no one could deny his love and deep understanding of modern art and that is what linked him to Roland. Mesens encouraged Roland's work, in particular the postcard collages, and demanded more to show in Brussels and at the London Gallery. In particular he wanted objects for the forthcoming *Surrealist Objects and Poems* exhibition.

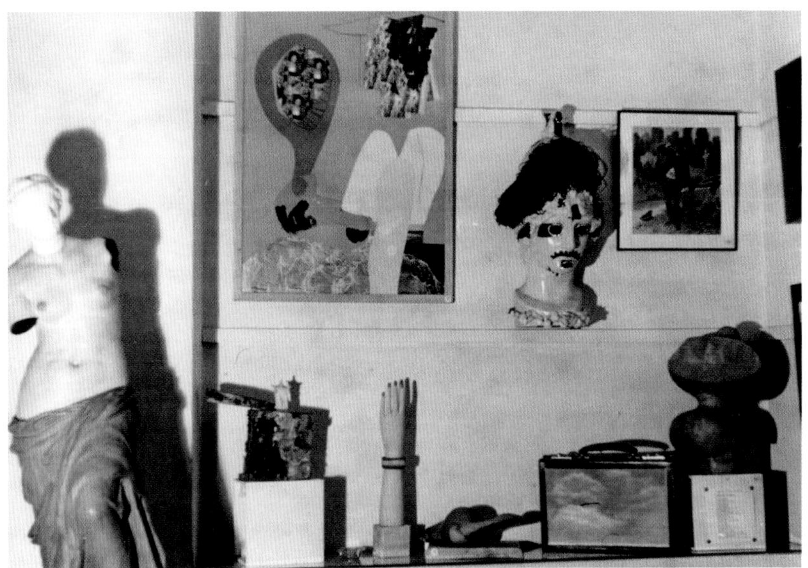

Objects and Poems Exhibition, The London Gallery, London, England 1937

Roland set to work with a will writing to Lee;

Yesterday I went to the Caledonian market and came back in triumph with a phrenologist's head – like the ones at Brighton – six pairs of dolls' eyes looking like false teeth and an elephant's tail. I have constructed several strange objects, the piece of wreck from the beach at Juan-les-Pins looks fine with a plumb line for a nose and nails for eyes, and the fish spinners from Toulon have come in very useful hung in a row inside a garden hoe which I picked up in my brother's garden.[7]

Roland titled the driftwood piece *The Survivor*, and the curiously beckoning figure of the garden hoe, *Condensation of Games*. Sadly both were later lost or destroyed. This was also the period in which the unremitting grey skies of England prompted his witty *Guaranteed Fine Weather Suitcase* with its bright summer painted skyscape framed on the side like a window displaying the contents. In his letter to Lee he remarked;

> I have just completed another 'Valise beau temps' for the object show – rather better painted than the last as I am beginning to discover the right process. Tripotin thinks I shall have to set up a factory producing blue skies 'en série'. I have rashly promised another for Irena Moore who wants to walk about London with one.[8]

Lee had drifted back into the easy life of Cairo, but tales of Surrealist adventures made it increasingly unsatisfactory and she chafed with

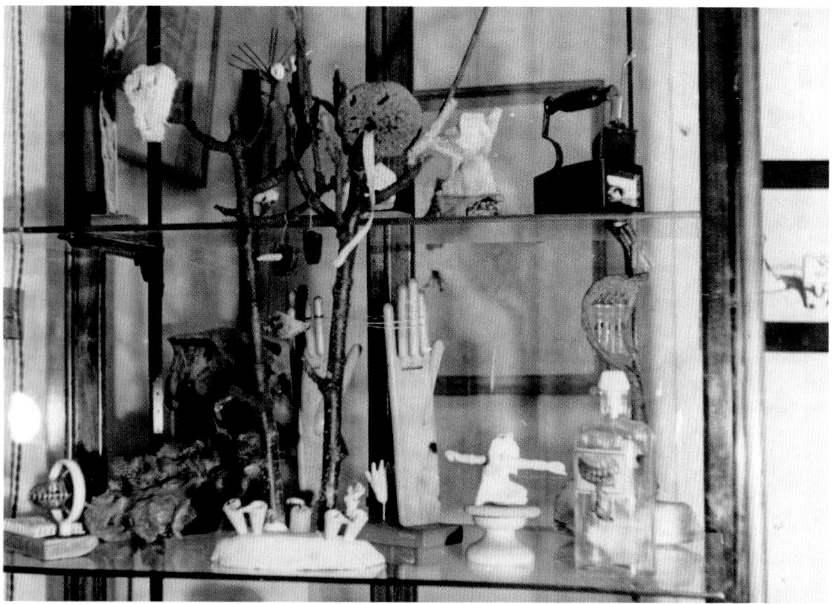

Objects and Poems Exhibition 4, The London Gallery, London, England 1937

frustration at being excluded from Roland and his circle. As the opening of the *Surrealist Objects and Poems* show drew closer, Lee wrote to Roland;

> I'd like to have an object in the Surrealist show if possible. [...] If you would like to, you could make it for me as it is very simple. It is a very beautiful wax hand, like in a manicurist's window standing up from the wrist, vertically, and on it I'd like a bracelet made of false teeth mounted in particularly false pink-coloured gums.[9]

When Roland tried to track down the hand he met with difficulty;

> I must tell you about your object – to begin with there are no wax hands of the right type in London. ... So I bought a wood one which has a really good shape and I painted it with the greatest care inspired by your hands which I can still see with some accuracy ... The second hunt was for the teeth – finally ... I found two old men, in white coats sitting in an attic making the most rosy pearly false jaws I've ever seen.[10]

At midnight on 24 November a large crowd gathered at the London Gallery for the opening of the *Surrealist Objects and Poems* exhibition. The word had got around that something scandalous and exciting was afoot. The press by now appreciated that Surrealism gave them good copy, and there had been some encouraging advance notices. Read's solemn appearance gave him gravity incongruous with the outrageousness of both the objects and his opening remarks which he intoned with the mannered modulation of a BBC newsreader;

> If you were listening carefully, you will have heard the thirteenth stroke of midnight. This is the post-ultimate stroke, which transports us to the world of steel swans and tender glaciers, to the fortunate handcuffs of manacled policemen, pouring fire through feather

> funnels into the vortex of our desires. … Approach, for we have names to sell – angels of anarchy and machines for making clouds, the caged bunyip and the virgin washerwoman. … Do not weep for these objects – they are happy in their nests of wild stones. The dew machine sprinkles sphinx's eyes on the gorse roots and the time tables. … But ladies and gentlemen, the jacket is off the peg and Nature takes the chair.[11]

Mesens had helped Roland arrange the show, and they were both delighted with the success of the opening. It was so crowded that for about an hour the place was completely blocked with people so tightly packed they could not move. Upstairs generous quantities of Black Velvet were served. Dylan Thomas had a spectacular fight with an unknown drunk who insulted him, smashing a picture in the process. The unexpected arrival of Ernst and Leonora Carrington crowned Roland's evening. They had come from Paris and intended to stay secretly in London to conduct peace negotiations with Leonora's parents.

Of the 138 objects, 88 were from British artists, although two thirds were 'temporary members' of the Surrealist group.[12] Maddox and the Melville brothers were conspicuously absent, possibly because they had upset Roland and Mesens with their protests at the 1936 *International Surrealist Exhibition*. Roland contributed a collage and four objects, *The Dew Machine, Guaranteed Fine Weather Suitcase, Condensation of Games* and *The Survivor*. Under Roland's collage titled *La Méditerranné* Lee's object titled *Le Baiser* was prominently displayed, holding its own in the company of Eileen Agar's *Angel of Anarchy,* Julian Trevelyan's *Machine for Making Clouds* and Geoffrey Graham's *Virgin Washerwoman* referred to by Read in his speech.

The assembled community of objects almost appeared to take on a life of its own. But it was the flirtatious gaze of *The Dew Machine* that earned her the position as their spokesperson and her portrait appeared in several national papers.

There are few words, written or remembered, that tell us of Roland's underlying thought processes. He placed great importance on the Surrealist value of the spontaneous connection with thoughts and emotions buried in the subconscious beyond the reach of intellect. There is no conscious explanation but the meaning lies in the poetic, the marvellous – a revelation which is experienced on a non-rational level, which we are invited to reject or accept on our own terms. When pressed to offer a meaning of a work, he would say *'Whatever it means to you is the meaning'*. This was an unsatisfactory response for those who wanted clear interpretations, but one that generously enrols the viewer as a participant.

Roland spent a very boozy Christmas at Lambe Creek with Beacus and his wife Joy. Roland's half-Spanish girlfriend Juanita accompanied him and on their return, she installed herself in Downshire Hill. At a distance, Lee afforded Roland protection against the commitments he did not want. He wrote to her about Juanita;

> She's much happier and keeps telling me she's glad I'm in love with somebody else, so we get on in a loose temporary way.[13]

On 14 January 1938 Roland was back in Paris among old friends such as Wolfgang Paalen, Georges Hugnet, Oscar Dominguez, Paul Eluard and Ernst. On 17 January he went with Eluard to visit Picasso in Rue des Grands-Augustins. As they entered the studio they were both stopped in their tracks by a small canvas placed on an easel as though work was still in progress. Roland wrote;

> I have more than once been shaken by the emotional strength of a painting seen for the first time in an artist's studio, but this contained an unprecedented blend of realism and poetic magic.... It came as a postscript to the great mural [Guernica] and contained again a cry of agony caused by the fascist aggression on humanity.

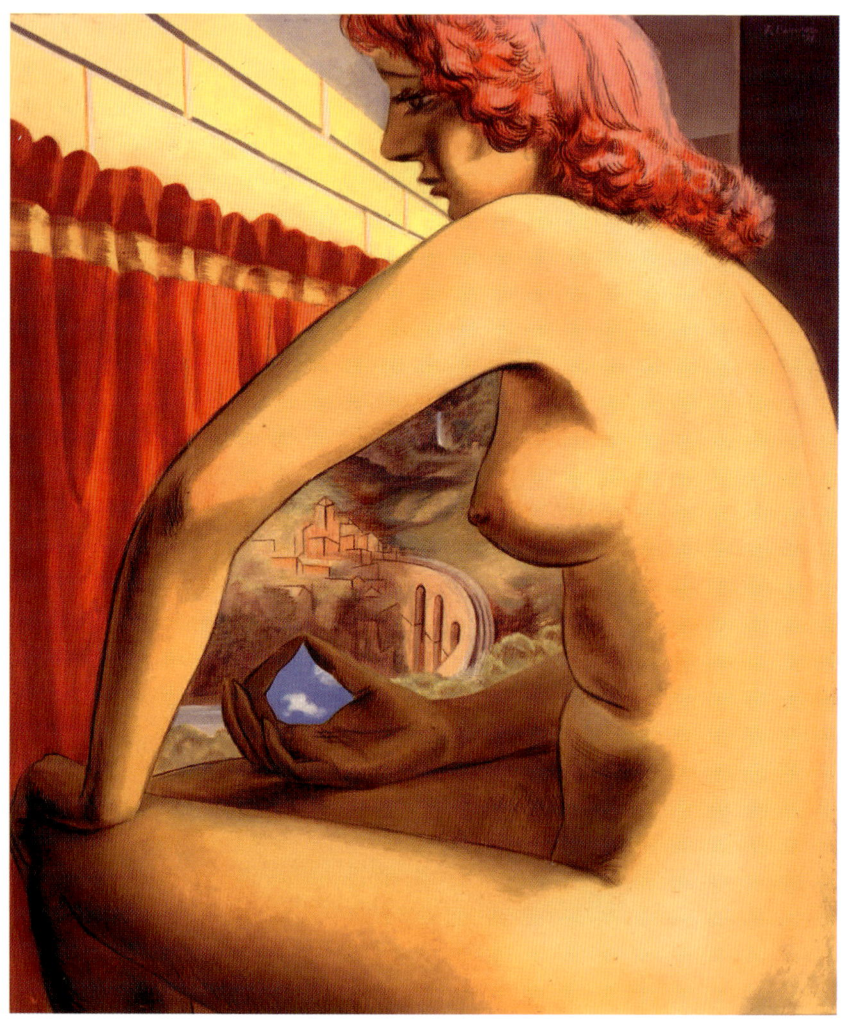

The Human Frame or *Nude in Window*, *c.*1937, oil on canvas, Private Collection, England

> The sombre monochrome of Guernica had given place to brilliant contrasts of red, blue, green and yellow in a highly disconcerting way. It was as though this girl, seen in profile, but with both the dark passionate eyes of Dora Maar, dressed as for a fête, had found herself suddenly faced by heartrending disaster. For a while the impact of this small brilliant canvas left us speechless, but after a few enthusiastic exclamations I heard myself say to Picasso,
>
> 'Oh! May I buy that from you'?
>
> and heard in a daze his answer;
>
> 'And why not?'
>
> There followed the exchange of a cheque for almost nothing for one of the masterpieces of this century.[14]

He had bought the *Weeping Woman* [*La Femme qui Pleure*] of 1937 painted after *Guernica*, now in the collection of Tate Modern. Roland left the studio walking on air, with *Weeping Woman* under his arm. The paint was scarcely dry on the canvas that became one of the best-known paintings of Picasso's entire oeuvre. Roland told me years later his bank manager was utterly dismayed. The purchase had pushed his account sharply into overdraft, and more dismay was to follow as Roland bought an etching in the same series, and two etchings of *The Dream and Lie of Franco.* Picasso's outrage towards fascism in Spain found ready accord in Roland but not with his bank manager.

The main purpose of Roland's visit to Paris was to attend the opening of the *'Exposition Internationale du Surréalisme'* at the Galerie Beaux-Arts, organised by Breton and Eluard during a temporary break in their feuding, with the collaboration of Marcel Duchamp. Roland lent six de Chiricos from his collection, including *L'Inquiétude du Poète* and *L'Ange Juif,* Ernst's *Déjeuner sur l'Herbe,* and *Joie de Vivre,* Eileen Agar's *Quadriga* and Picasso's portrait of Lee listed as *Portrait de Mme Eloui Bey.* His own work was well represented with five works from 1937, two collages *Real Woman, and Venus of Montecarlo,* the object *Condensation of*

Games, *La Promenade*, and *L'Île Invisible* which now belonged to Ernst.

At home, The London Gallery was facing an uncertain future. It had been founded in 1936 by Lady Noel (known as Peter) Norton, the wife of Sir Clifford Norton, a diplomat. Peter Norton and her partner Marguerite Strettel had run the gallery for over a year, during which time they had mounted one-man shows for Munch, Moholy-Nagy, Léger and Naum Gabo among others. Now, following Sir Clifford's posting to Poland, Peter Norton had to withdraw the generous financial support with which she had kept the gallery afloat, and closure looked inevitable.

The London Gallery was by now well known to Roland, who immediately saw a possibility. Recognising the small size and fragmented nature of the British Surrealist movement, he wanted to create a centre that would become a nucleus to attract young artists. He saw the need for a library and a bookshop to provide access to the steady stream of Surrealist literature and poetry arriving from other countries, and also for an exhibition space. He wanted to show the work of young artists, both British and international, alongside the paintings of well-established modern artists such as Picasso, Magritte, Ernst, Man Ray and Miró.

After prolonged and difficult negotiations, Roland, with Anton Zwemmer, the Dutch proprietor of Zwemmer's Bookshop and Gallery as his partner bought the London Gallery at 28 Cork Street. Roland appointed Mesens as the manager, and the gallery re-opened on 1 April. It was a bold stroke, and one that was to cost Roland dearly, but by providing gallery space and a point of focus for the movement, and by publishing the *London Bulletin* under the imprint of the gallery he and Mesens made a key contribution to Surrealism in Britain.

Roland raised about three-quarters of the capital, and to do so he sold the farms he had inherited in Suffolk and Norfolk, but there was an additional emotional cost. Lee had written an impulsive letter begging him to meet her in Athens where she had gone at a moment's notice to join her friends the British diplomat Henry Hopkinson and his wife Alice. Overwhelmed with the preparations for purchasing the gallery,

Roland could not get away, and a hint of coolness began to creep into the correspondence, with Lee's letters becoming more widely spaced.

As galleries go, the venture must have seemed like a reasonably good risk. The success of the *Surrealist Objects and Poems* exhibition and the reverberations from the *Exposition Internationale du Surréalisme* in Paris had created the most receptive atmosphere yet to be found. The timing was good, and the London Gallery was in the right street. Next door at 30 Cork Street, Peggy Guggenheim, the free-spirited renegade of New York society, had opened her Guggenheim Jeune gallery in January with a show of Jean Cocteau's work. The gallery windows adjoined one and other, and Peggy and Mesens kept in step ensuring their shows were co-ordinated. She also found her way into Roland's bed on a number of occasions, but they both agreed that their shared passion for the arts was more notable.

Another Cork Street friend was Freddy Mayor, who had re-opened his Mayor Gallery a few doors away five years earlier. Freddie Mayor was well known for loving all the pleasures of a *bon viveur*, and The Mayor Gallery always closed on the days of important horse races. It must have been the gambler's streak that had prompted him to champion such rank outsiders as Paul Nash, Fernand Léger and Juan Gris in the mid-1920s, but he studied the form and by the late 1930s had built a fine stable of the best names.

Nearly all aspects of running The London Gallery were delegated to Mesens. Roland by now understood Mesens well and, trusting him implicitly, gladly gave him a free hand. Right from the beginning all invitations and catalogues all conspicuously proclaimed;

The London Gallery
E.L.T. MESENS PRESENTS ...

No mention of Roland or Zwemmer is made, and this is clearly how both men wanted it. Zwemmer, as a minority shareholder was more

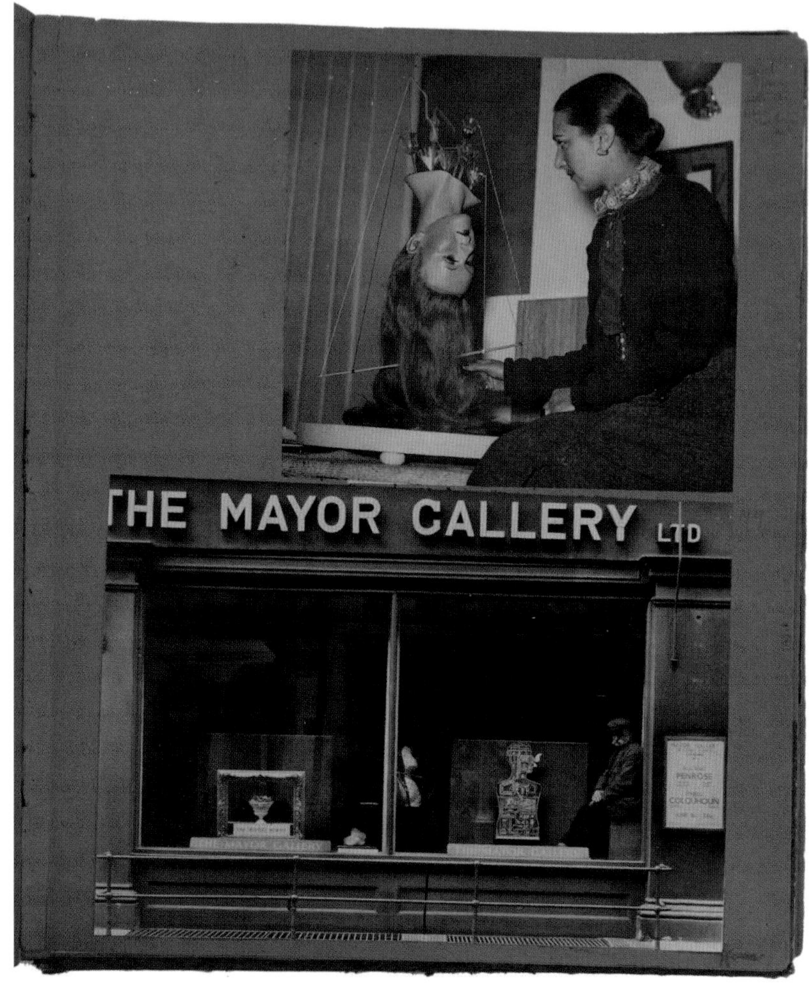

Wartime scrapbook – The Mayor Gallery. Collection: Scottish National Gallery of Modern Art Edinburgh

concerned with his own gallery, and Roland liked to keep in the background. Although entirely competent with financial matters, he simply hated the mechanics of running a business. He loved and excelled at the creative process of selecting the right artists and mounting their shows but in time his refusal to assert more control over the Gallery contributed to its demise.

In the years of the depression Mesens had been a shrewd buyer of Magritte's work. He had his own collection of about 150 paintings and these formed the basis of the London Gallery's first exhibition. The show was opened at midnight on 1 April 1938 by Julian Trevelyan dressed as an explorer in a dinner jacket, a topee, red gloves, and huge spectacles with mirrors instead of lenses. Magritte himself came over for the opening, and later wrote to Roland thanking him warmly for his generous contribution to the success of his exhibition.[15] The reviews in the press were gratifyingly acerbic with the art critic of the *Scotsman* declaring that it was; 'quite wonderfully disgusting ... almost persuaded to be a Nazi. Goebbels, at any rate will not tolerate such stuff'.[16]

In the next two years, the London Gallery succeeded admirably in promoting British Surrealism and reinforcing the links with the continent. Under Mesens's inspired management, eighteen exhibitions were organised by or with the participation of the gallery. His plan was to exhibit Surrealism on the first floor, and on the second work of a less challenging nature. It was hoped the latter would sell better and help support the space allocated to the surrealists, particularly ones that could not normally hope to be exhibited and were highly unlikely to sell. There was also a social dimension of great importance. The gallery operated a lending library that became a magnet for artists, poets and writers, making a significant contribution to the development of Surrealist activities in Britain.

The political arguments, alliances and biases within the British Surrealist movement make up a complex history. Most were Communists, Marxists or sympathisers of one shade or another, but the main conflict centred on the attitude surrealists should take towards the Communist parties controlled by Moscow. There was, however, agreement about the need to oppose Fascism in Spain.

One of the British group's most impressive displays of united strength was their participation in the Trade Unions march in Hyde Park on May Day 1938 (where the Surrealist contingent demonstrated their opposition to the British government's policy of non-intervention in Spain, which in effect aided Franco. Roland, James Cant, Geoffrey Graham and Julian Trevelyan dressed themselves in top hats and tail coats, with placards hung round their necks declaring *CHAMBERLAIN*

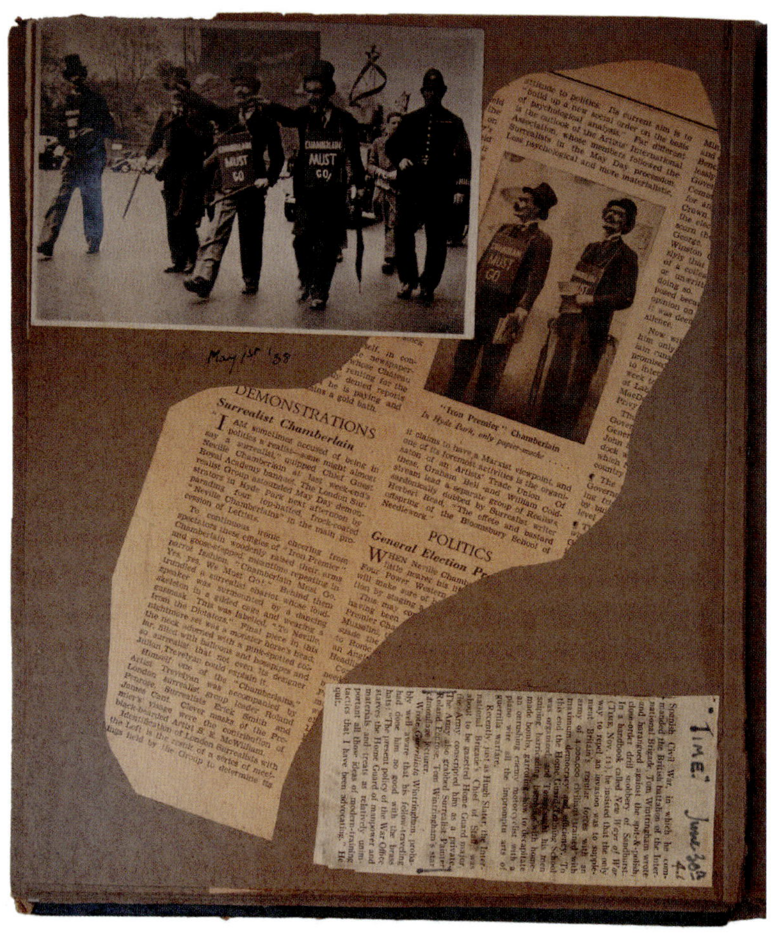

Wartime scrapbook – Trade Unions march in Hyde Park on May Day 1938. Collection: Scottish National Gallery of Modern Art Edinburgh

MUST GO! Masks of Chamberlain made by F. E. McWilliam completed their transformation into the object of their protest. About 100 surrealists and their supporters marched, determined to prove as much as anything that Surrealism as an art movement was also their way of life.

Lee had not been forgotten amid all this excitement. The correspondence recovered its warmth, and by June plans for a rendezvous in Athens were laid. On 26 June 1938 Roland passed through Paris and lunched with the Eluards. Out of the blue, Paul Eluard proposed that Roland should buy the greater part of his collection that he had gathered over the years mainly as gifts from the artists or in exchange for his writings on them. Paul Eluard had been hungry long enough, and wanted to make better provision for himself and Nusch, whose health had become delicate. Paul Eluard insisted there should be no argument about the prices, and whatever the outcome they would always remain friends. The list of over one hundred paintings and objects he offered Roland included some of the greatest modern works of this century. Notably there were forty Ernst's which reflected the close friendship between Eluard and Ernst since the early 1920s. They included *The Elephant of Celebes*, *Oedipus Rex* and *La Révolution dans la Nuit*. The six de Chiricos included *The Uncertainty of the Poet* and among the four Magrittes was *Threatening Weather*. Picasso's works included a delightful portrait of Nusch and a copy of *Grand Air*, the poem of Eluard's that he had illustrated. Miro's *Horse* was among the eight works by him, and there were pictures by Klee, Chagall, Tanguy, Arp, Paalen, Picabia, Giacometti, Dali, Hayter, Victor Brauner, Dominguez, Bellmer and Toyen. There were three excellent Man Rays, including *Le Logis d'Artiste* which, unknown to Roland at the time, contained the image of Lee's head and neck with her throat slashed – painted after one of her many quarrels with Man Ray. There was also a fine selection of ethnological objects from the Pacific Islands, Africa and British Columbia.

For all this Paul Eluard asked £1,500 and stifled Roland's protests at the ridiculously low price by insisting on his condition of no arguments. The next day Eluard documented the sale with a letter, and Roland boarded the night train for Marseille. The purchase was clearly at a *prix d'ami*, and later in the 1960s when the value of these works skyrocketed Roland began to feel uncomfortable, as if he had robbed his old friend. With this purchase and the Gaffe collection, Roland now had the finest collection of Surrealist and Cubist art in the country.

Roland took a freighter from Marseille to Athens, where Lee had arrived a few days earlier. Lee had shipped her new grey Packard convertible to Greece, but their first journey was by sea to Mykonos. The art of the ancient Cycladic civilisations had interested Roland for a long time, and he owned examples of the mysterious goddess figures from the third millennium BC. The hilltops were populated with deities that were more modern – white painted windmills whose sails, when animated by the breeze, groaned and sighed like weary Cyclops.

Delos was their next call, travelling on the deck of a local boat amid its cargo of nuts, cheeses, grain and honey. The remains of the vast marble phallus saluting the sky in the Sanctuary of Dionysus fascinated them both. Roland was carrying a new compact 35-millimetre camera, and he made good use of it in a very 'front on' documentary style.

Back in London months later Roland's photos would become the basis for his Surrealist odyssey titled *The Road Is Wider Than Long.*[17] In this work of poetry he uses his photographs in a non-chronological order with his text, which although surreal in its dreamlike style often refers to real incidents. The poem follows the manner in which sequential events are randomly recalled to memory in a non-linear order. The real itinerary is replaced by a narrative that zig zags across place and time.

A photograph of the amphitheatre of Epidaurus, which they reached a few days later after returning to Athens by way of Syros, is connected to the lines;

the stage of a Greek theatre echoing
the smile that drops from her lips.

At once he reminds us of the incredible acoustics of the steeply raked amphitheatre, and transforms Lee's bewitching smile into an audible, physical entity.

Their next visit was to Delphi, and his reference invokes the ancient oracle, which is thought to be caused by an emission of volcanic gas that gave oracular powers to those who inhaled it;

Vapours escape from the rocks
writing tomorrow's news in the sky
...
At night we found a deserted city
water ran under the streets
the houses dry and full of herbs
formed the labyrinth of a dead shell
...
At Dephi the mountain
Translated her voice.

It may have been at Delphi that Roland acquired a Mycenaean votive in the form of a small blue striped terracotta female statuette. She became a cherished companion piece for his Cycladic figures.

A day's journey took them to the northern limit of the plains of Thessaly where the monasteries of Metéora perch on top of the sheer rock pinnacles forming the abrupt beginning of the mountains. The legend tells that an eagle carried St Athanasios aloft on its back to found the first of the twenty-four monasteries and hermitages early in the fourteenth century. Roland and Lee's ascent was more prosaic but no less dangerous, and they set out from Kastráki on mules with a local guide and a basket of food and wine. Whilst some monasteries could be reached by climbing,

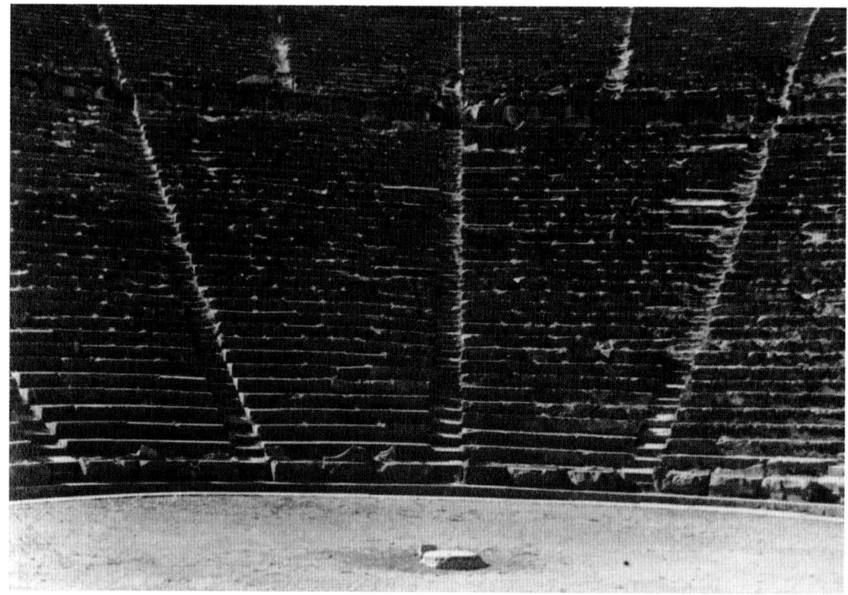

Amphitheatre, Epidaurus, Greece, 1938, used in *The Road is Wider Than Long*

most were so inaccessible that the only way in was to sit in a basket and be hoisted up two hundred feet by the monks at the top.

The name Metéora literally means 'between earth and heaven' and it seems this and the fact that the cliffs were once a seashore was not lost on Roland;

> Each rock that floats above is
> crowned by a monastery and
> the monks can lift a man
> from water as deep as the eye of a goat

On the north coast of the Aegean they visited the ancient port of Kavála, where the accretion of different cultures over the centuries has left overlapping remains of Byzantine, early European, Roman, Venetian and Turkish civilisations. For some unaccountable reason

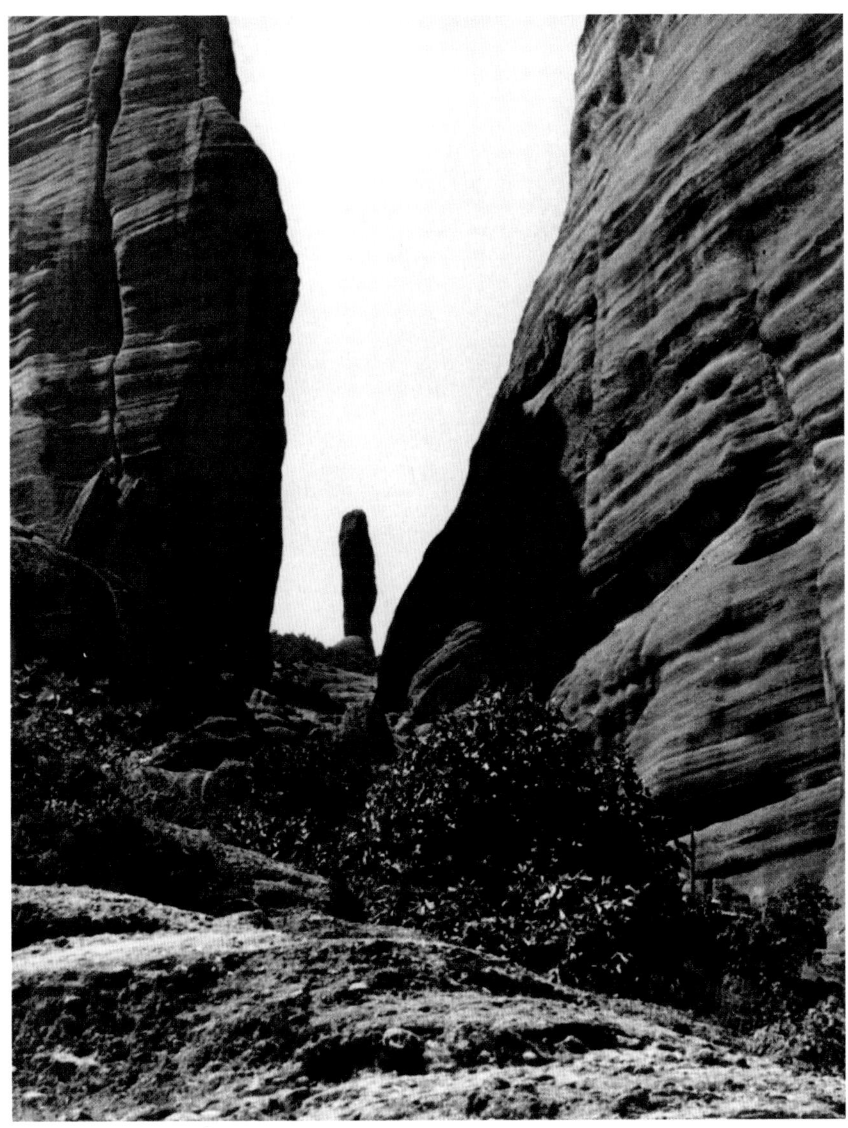

Rock Pillar, Meteora, Greece, 1938

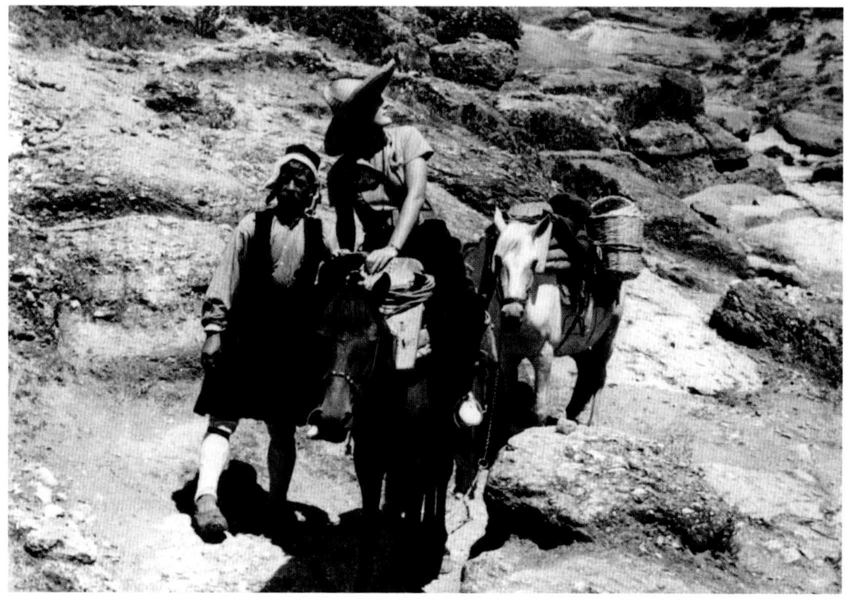

Lee Miller on a mule, Meteora, Greece, 1938

the equestrian statue of Mehmet Ali, Pasha of Egypt, was shrouded in canvas, tightly bound by ropes. Roland photographed it and as well as finding his way into *The Road Is Wider Than Long,* Mehemet Ali and his high-stepping steed also appeared in a painting, *Enemy The Sun.* The statue appears beside the sea, back-lit by a fan of sunlight blazing up from behind clouds. The sun also illuminates a bare tree, floating in space with birds flying around it. In the foreground a weeping ash tree – a variety much loved by Roland – is cloaked in foliage; but here it refers to another series of photographs of Lee's hair, combed forward over her face. This time instead of foaming breakers, her hair has become leaves, but the resonance with the sea is not forgotten. As the branches extend downwards, they brush ripples of water that lap the tree like an incoming tide. This symbolism became partly transformed into reality when a weeping ash was among the first trees Roland planted at Farley Farm fifteen years later.

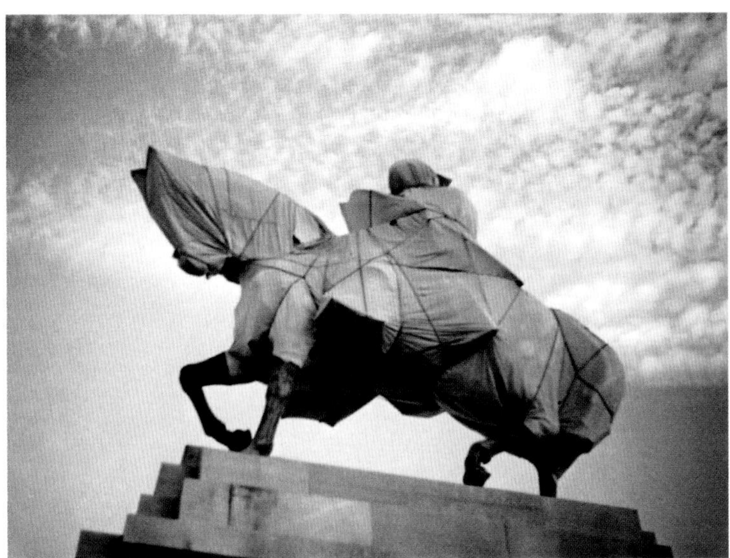

Statue of Mehmet Ali, Kavala, Greece, 1938

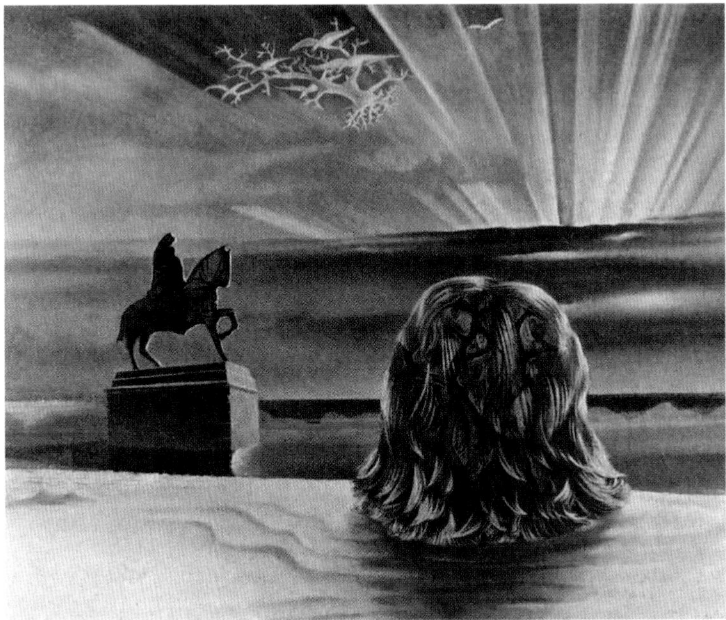

Enemy the Sun, 1938, oil on canvas, Private collection

The motif of wrapped or draped sculpture appears on other occasions in the work of both Roland and Lee, and resonates with the work of other Surrealists including Man Ray with his wrapped sewing machine, *The Enigma of Isadore Ducasse*. Roland painted a large undated canvas that although untitled I feel sure is a portrait of his mariner brother Beacus. A powerful figure of a man stands at a ship's wheel. The nude body of a beautiful woman lies at his feet as if expended, her foot snagged in the rigging. His face is shrouded in canvas, tightly lashed by a cord, perhaps a metaphor for Beacus's inscrutability. Inside his chest the weights from a grandfather clock are visible. Perhaps they represent the oppressive influence of grandfather Peckover who would have deeply disapproved of his grandson's velvet smoking jacket and his wild ways, funded by the inheritance he left to Beacus who literally could not tick without the weight of his grandfather.

Roland and Lee left Kavála by ferry for the island of Thasos, and strolled among the groves of ancient gnarled olive trees, whose shade harboured neat lines of beehives. The deeply furrowed stems of the olives gave an impression of battle-scarred muscles, with many crevices containing preying mantises and cicadas that sang constantly to accompany the dance of the brightly coloured swallow-tailed butterflies. Beside the sea, secluded niches among the marble cliffs gave them the opportunities for days together that would have gratified Dionysus, the god of wine and mystic ecstasy.

They headed the Packard north from Kavála, across Bulgaria and onwards to Bucharest in Romania. Here they sought out Harry Brauner, the brother of Roland's friend the surrealist painter Victor Brauner, who lived in Paris. Harry was an eminent musicologist at the University of Bucharest, and had dedicated himself to the study of folk music. Harry was delighted to see them and he quickly put together an itinerary for various folk dance and music events in the villages in and around the Carpathian Mountains.

At Runcu a fair was in progress and hundreds had come into the

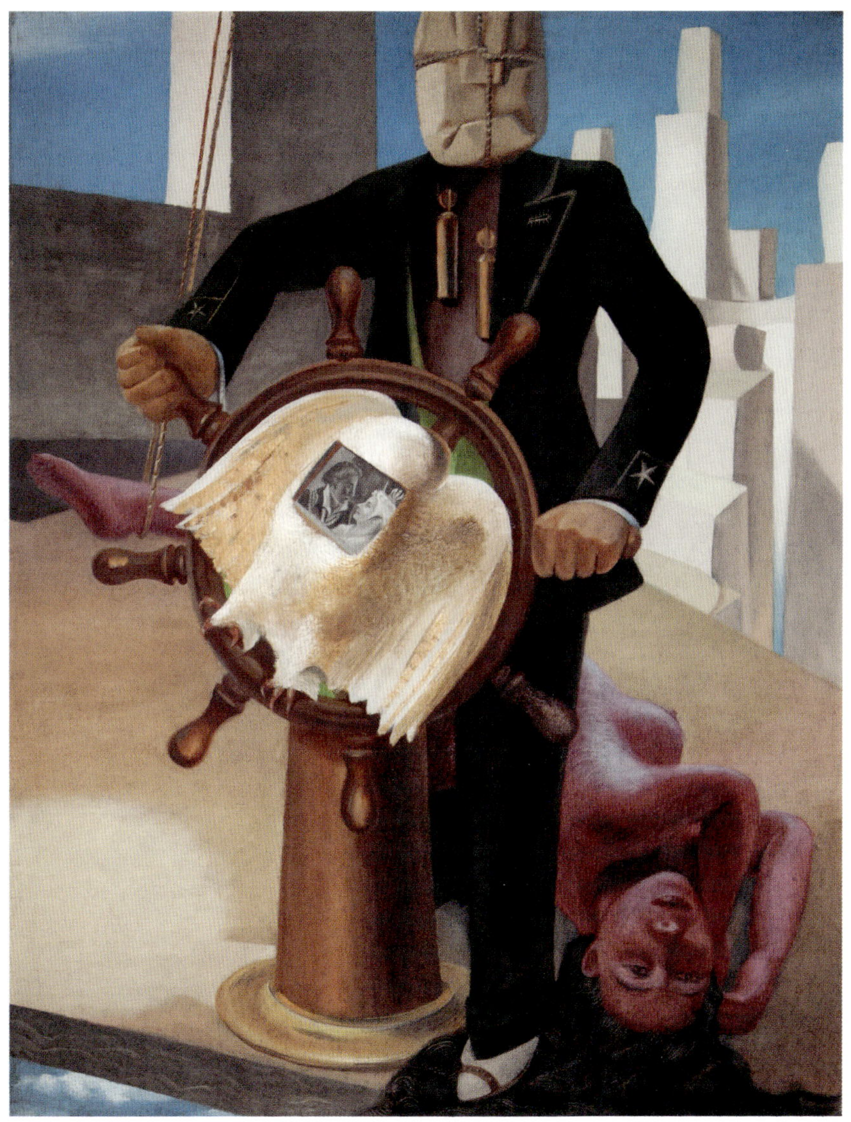

Beacus Penrose at the Wheel, c. 1937, oil on canvas

village in gaily painted horse-drawn carts. Under Harry's aegis Roland and Lee were welcomed by the priests and the notables, and moved freely among the peasants. Lee bought a complete peasant woman's costume. The idea was to disguise her so she could take pictures more readily, but it was a total failure as her hair showed through the thin muslin headscarf proclaiming her as the only blonde for miles. The open friendliness of the women rendered any disguise quite unnecessary and they showed her how to spin with a distaff.

The nomadic gypsies of the region struggled for their survival. The women's faces have great beauty and strength. Their gaze is direct, looking straight into Roland's camera, their babies on their hips, children clustered around them. They wear their ragged clothes with a natural dignity. They talked openly to Lee through Hari, their ease transcending their differences. These people who willingly suffered the hardship of their existence for the sake of their freedom earned the admiration of Roland and Lee. *The Road Is Wider Than Long* Roland wrote;

In the river a gypsy washes
the inflated bellies of her children
bellies full of wood pulp
yelling and government regulations
NOMADS may not move their tents
The Markets are closed to them
The Prefect has no time to waste.

It was hard to find any gypsies when Lee returned eight years later at the end of the war as so many had been murdered in Nazi death camps.

Their road took them out to the Bulgarian coast of the Black Sea at Balchik and then swung back to Bucharest. There, with Harry and other friends they celebrated their last evenings together in an open-air nightclub near the North Station, listening to the songs of Maritza, the renowned gypsy musician. Roland ends *The Road Is Wider Than Long*

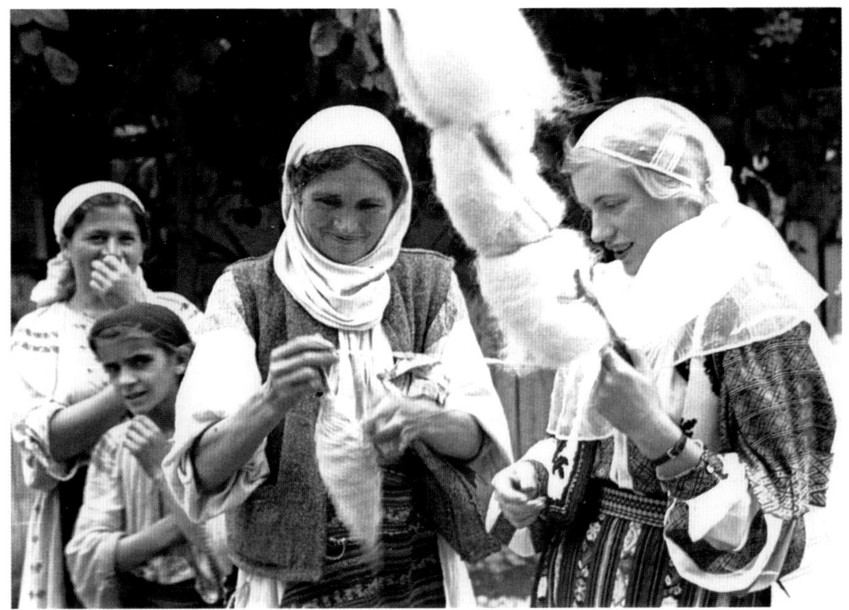

Unknown Romanians and Lee Miller, Transylvania, Romania, 1938

with these lines that wistfully evoke his wish for permanence. There were some things that not even a Surrealist wanted to change;

> Maritza is strong
> the porter puts his sou
> into the belly of her guitar
> her understanding is his security.
>
> The cockpit the bull ring the open air
> Cinema the dance hall the committee
> room and the black exchange
> are at work
> turning their bloodshot melodies while Maritza
> tunes the two chords of her guitar.

Roland and Lee kissed a passionate farewell on the platform of Bucharest station. He was heading back to Paris to complete the arrangements for an ambitious English tour of Picasso's painting *Guernica*. Lee was heading off for another two weeks of travelling with Harry and his friend Lena to a festival in Bucovine, and then back to Egypt from the Black Sea port of Constanta via Athens. At their parting, Lee had pointed out a pretty French girl on the train whom she felt should console Roland. As the train rolled through the night, the girl who had been much aroused by the sight of the amorous farewell turned Roland's journey to Munich into an erotic encounter.

The sight of Munich station on the morning of 9 September brought all romantic thoughts to a crash stop. Vast red and black banners bearing the swastika celebrated Chamberlain's first appeasement visit to Hitler, forming a brutal reminder of the threat of war that everyone faced.

On reaching Paris Roland waited there for a few days. He wanted to finalise the arrangements with Eluard for the shipping of his newly acquired collection, and before he returned to London he needed to see Picasso. After the showing of *Guernica* in the Spanish Pavilion at the Paris *Exposition Universelle* in August 1937 Roland arranged with Picasso that it should tour England to raise money for The National Joint Committee for Spanish Relief. Now it was time to finalise the arrangements that had been progressed by Mesens while Roland was travelling in the Balkans.

Mesens had formed an exhibition committee chaired by the Member of Parliament, Wilfred Roberts, with Read as vice-chairman, and a varied spread of patrons and donor that included E.M. Forster, Virginia Woolf, Edward James and Harry Pollitt, the chairman of the Communist Party. Roland was the honorary treasurer, and Mrs Sybil Stephenson, the secretary of the London Gallery, and soon to be Mrs Mesens, was the honorary secretary.

The private view of the great canvas and 67 of its preparatory and related drawings and paintings such as Roland's *Weeping Woman* opened on 3 October at the New Burlington Galleries in London's West End.

The reviews were poor and the show had an attendance of only about 3,000 over three weeks. Public interest picked up as the exhibition toured to Leeds, Manchester and Oxford. When it returned to London's Whitechapel Gallery in the East End in December it found a warm welcome, particularly among working-class people. Clement Attlee, the Leader of the Opposition, opened the Whitechapel exhibition with Roland among the officials on the platform, and about 12,000 visitors attended. It marked a rising of public indignation at the consequences of Britain's policy of non-intervention in Spain, but it was too little and too late to make a significant political impact.

The political solidarity among the British Surrealists back in May was short lived, as alignment shifted among the various factions. In October Breton tried to assert his preferences on the group as a whole. He had met the exiled Trotsky and the artist Diego Rivera in Mexico, and on his return to Paris he had formed FIARI *[Fédération Internationale de l'Art Révolutionnaire Indépendant]*. It was intended to free artists and writers from Moscow based Stalinist control, and widened the rift between him and Eluard who remained pro Stalin. Breton circulated his FIARI manifesto among the British Surrealists who met to consider their position. With Read an anarchist, Banting a Stalinist, and others like Gascoyne strongly opposed to the way Moscow-led communists had suppressed the POUM in Spain, there could never be any hope of agreement.

Since his work on the cause of the Spanish Republic, Roland had been on good terms with Harry Politt and the other organisers of the Communist Party of Great Britain. He did not become a member, but probably due to his links with Paris he became the political spokesman for the British Surrealists. He found himself in an impossible position. On a personal level, he refused to allow any political disagreement to come between him and Eluard, and on top of that, he could not assure Breton of the support of the British group as it was looser and tolerated a wider range of views. Many also held that the brand of Communism or socialism a person adhered to mattered less than the fact that it inherently opposed Fascism.

Roland's refusal to turn on Eluard signalled the flaw in his relationship with Mesens, whose dogmatic views allowed no compromise. How much this rift detracted from the effectiveness of the London Gallery can only be guessed, but certainly, if Roland and Mesens had been able to keep in step even greater things might have happened. It was a measure of Roland's commitment to the higher purpose of Surrealism that he continued to share his house with Mesens and wholeheartedly support him, in spite of their often acerbic differences.

The increasing Nazi persecution had prompted an exodus of artists, poets and writers from Germany. Roland and others formed the Artists' Refugee Committee in November 1938, with representatives of the New English Art Club, the London Group, Artists International Association and other bodies. The purpose of ARC was to raise funds for refugees and to find them host families and employment, without which they could not get a visa. Roland himself represented the Surrealists.[18] Stephen Bone was the first chairman and Roland's friend and neighbour in Downshire Hill, Diana Uhlman, was the secretary. She was married to Fred Uhlman, the Jewish lawyer turned painter, who had fled from Germany in 1936.

There was much excitement about Hitler's shows of so called 'degenerate art' *[entartete Kunst]* in Munich and other German cities in 1937, which was intended to discredit works by Ernst and other modernists held in high esteem by British artists. It was decided to mount a counter exhibition in London titled *20th-Century German Art.* Mesens, Read and Roland were among the organisers, and the show went on at the New Burlington Galleries. It was a financial disaster and made a huge loss, to some extent countered by two successful exhibitions at the London Gallery.[19] Overall ARC was a success, raising about £4,000 and helping between 20 and 30 people, mainly artists, to escape to Britain. Immigration rules required the refugees to be guaranteed employment and Committee members took in many. Roland himself employed Margarete (Greta) Klopfleisch (née Grossner) as his cook.[20] She had escaped via Finland and Sweden arriving in London on 9 March 1939. It is unlikely he needed any full-time staff, but it served to legitimise her visa. The arrangement did not last long as when war was declared she and her husband had to endure two years of separation in internment camps.[21]

Roland spent Christmas with Beacus and Joy in Cornwall, and then hurried back to London. Harry Brauner had arrived with a troupe of Calusari dancers from Romania that had proved a great success at a folk-dance festival in London. A couple of days later Roland was at Victoria station saying goodbye to Harry and the Calusari troupe when he met an old friend Beryl de Zoëte, an authority on folk dance. She mentioned she was just off to Egypt on a field trip, and Roland who, until Romania, had not held the slightest interest in folk-lore, immediately volunteered himself as her photographer.

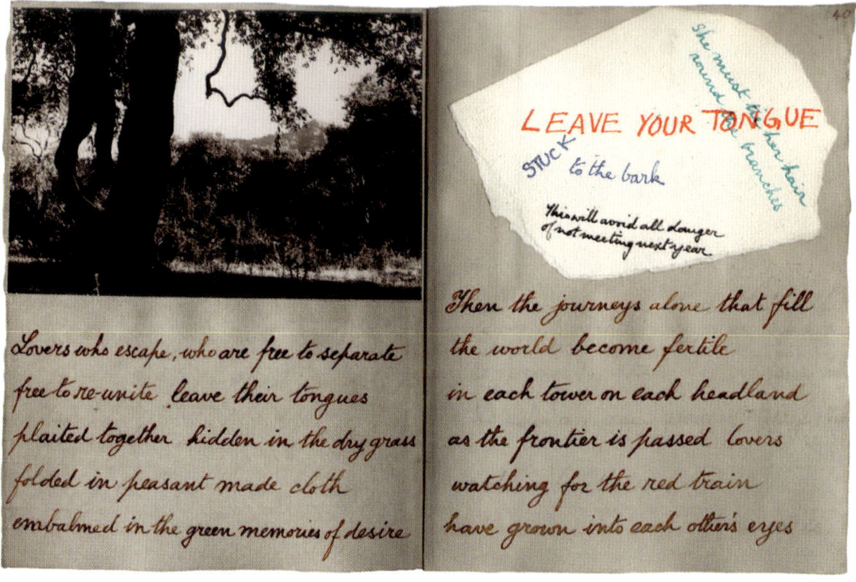

The Road is Wider Than Long, 1938

He arrived in Cairo on 30 January 1939, and found a note from Lee. She had misunderstood the dates of his arrival and had gone off on a lengthy desert trip, but mentioned that on the way back she would be calling on her friend Gerti Wissa. The Wissas were a Coptic family who owned a cotton farm at Beni Kora, near Asyut, two hundred miles south on the Nile. Roland caught a train, and then walked the final distance carrying his suitcase in the full heat of the afternoon sun. Nothing was going to delay him from reuniting with Lee, and as luck would have it he managed to catch her there. The expedition returned to Cairo without Lee, who remained at Beni Kora with Roland.

In Roland's case were two precious gifts he hoped would fascinate Lee. The first was the manuscript for *The Road Is Wider Than Long*, laboriously calligraphed with his photographs and a small collage pasted to the pages. The second was a pair of real handcuffs made from gold, signed *Cartier.* Lee was ecstatic about her gifts. She wore both the handcuffs on the same wrist as a chic bracelet by day, always ready to gratify Roland's desire by snapping one on the other wrist. Some months later she tried a Houdini trick while very drunk, and broke the link. Thereafter they became two individual bracelets until they met their ironic fate of being stolen by burglars after the war.

In Cairo, Roland was astonished to find he had met Aziz previously. Aziz and Nimet had entertained him and Valentine when they were in Cairo with the Dobrées in 1927. The occasion had slipped his memory until he recognised Aziz's house, the Villa Al Beit near the island of Gezira. It is a measure of Aziz's big-heartedness that he welcomed Roland a second time.

Aziz and Lee had realised their life together was not working, but he declared he was not going to set Lee free until there was someone in her life capable of looking after her. Although he accepted Roland might be this person, both he and Roland respected Lee's insistence that she was not going to be pushed into any move. In giving his tacit blessing on her being with Roland, he was allowing Lee time to define her own path. To avoid embarrassing Aziz, Roland kept up the pretence of being Beryl de Zoëte's photographer, and continued to use this cover during an expedition to the oasis of Siwa, nearly five hundred miles to the west on the border of Libya. They went in the Packard and another car, accompanied by Lee's sister-in-law Mafy Miller, and George Hoyningen-Huene, the photographer.

After Alexandria the road follows the Mediterranean to Marsa Matrûh, and then swings south-west inland across the Libyan Plateau on rough tracks. Lee described a previous journey like this;

> There is no road, just desert tracks, rock, sand and space … no water, no rest, jolting, jouncing, cursing – followed by a hot wind going the same twenty kilometres an hour as we could make, sweating, parched, aching back and swollen feet.[22]

Alexander the Great reached Siwa on foot with his army, and was rewarded by the oracle of the temple Amman confirming him as a son of Zeus, but this was small comfort to Lee and Roland's party.

Close to the oasis, wind-eroded rock formations became the subject for Lee's now famous *Cock Rock* photograph, published in the London Bulletin June 1940, coyly titled *The Native.* Roland also photographed the rocks, but it was the village of Siwa that really captured his imagination. Restrictions of land ownership had forced the Siwans to build upwards, and the mud buildings rose above the date-palms like giant ant-hills, five or more storeys high. Some of Roland's watercolours from this period refer to this bizarre settlement where the buildings seemed to have an organic life of their own like the humanoid shapes of the rocks beside the road.

Back in Cairo Roland and Lee made some more leisurely trips along the Nile to the ruins of Memphis and Saqqâra and then out to the Red Sea. They loved the adventure of travelling together, and made a good team – Roland cautious and well prepared like a good boy scout, Lee impetuous and disorganised but always very resourceful, especially in a crisis.

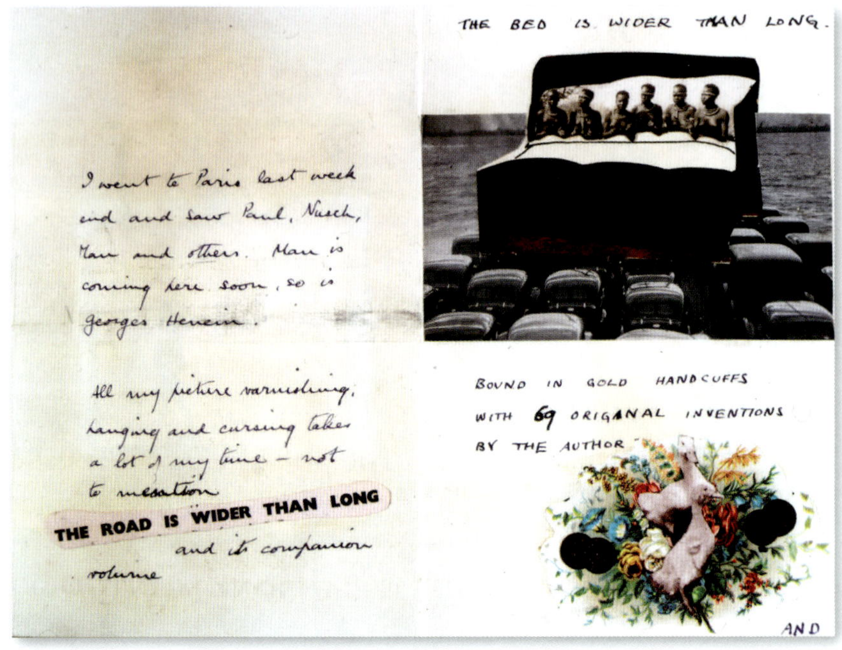

I went to Paris last week end and saw Paul, Nusch, Man and others. Man is coming here soon, so is Georges Henein.

All my picture varnishing, hanging and cursing takes a lot of my time – not to mention THE ROAD IS WIDER THAN LONG and its companion volume

THE BED IS WIDER THAN LONG.

BOUND IN GOLD HANDCUFFS WITH 69 ORIGANAL INVENTIONS BY THE AUTHOR

AND

Letter to Lee Miller, Collage and Handwritten, 1939

Roland pleaded with Lee to return with him and live in England. The political situation was worsening daily, and in the war that now seemed inevitable it was certain that Egypt would be fought over as a British territory. But Lee was not sure. She did not love Aziz, but was loyal to him and wanted to avoid hurting him. She loved Roland, but was uncertain if she was ready for another long-term relationship. It was a sad parting at Alexandria as Roland boarded the *Marco Polo*, bound for Venice.

In Paris he launched himself into a frenzy of activity, lunching with Man Ray and Paul Eluard, and later visiting Man Ray's show of paintings and drawings where Roland bought the beautiful silver-point *Eyes and Hands*. Breton's exhibition of Mexican folk art was on at the same time, and he met Frieda Kahlo who had an exhibition of her paintings in the same gallery, where he also met Leonore Fini. He lunched with Picasso and Dora Maar, dined with Ylla, the Hungarian woman photographer famous for her animal portraits, and visited a brothel with Paul Eluard.

Back at Downshire Hill he found Moore's *Mother and Child* was the subject of press attack initiated by his neighbours. He fell ill, and his doctor Karl Goldman confined him to bed in a nursing home for two weeks. Frolics with Lee in the wilds of Greece or Egypt must have seemed remote.

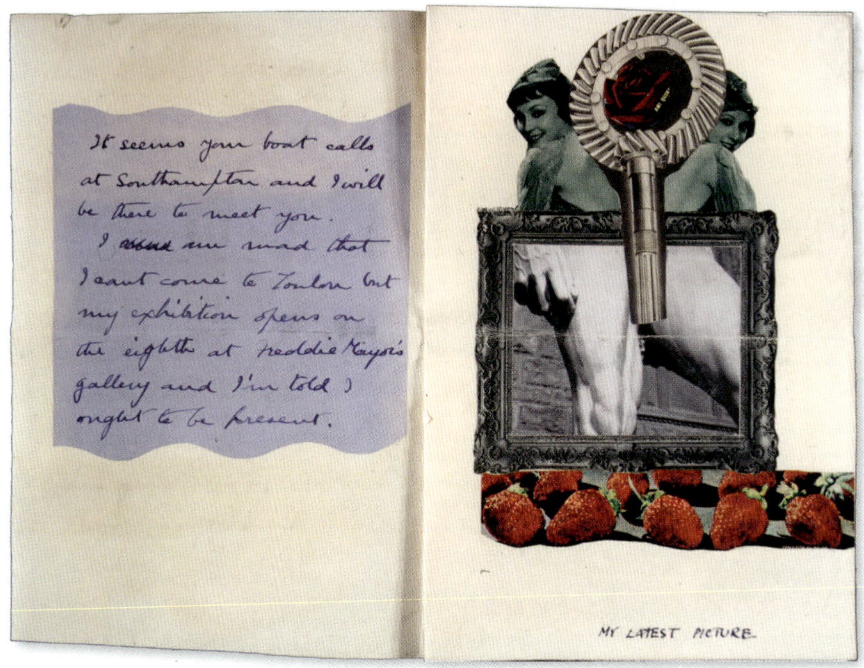
It seems your boat calls at Southampton and I will be there to meet you.
I am mad that I can't come to Toulon but my exhibition opens on the eighth at Freddie Mayor's gallery and I'm told I ought to be present.

MY LATEST PICTURE

Letter Collage to Lee Miller, 1939, Collage and Handwritten

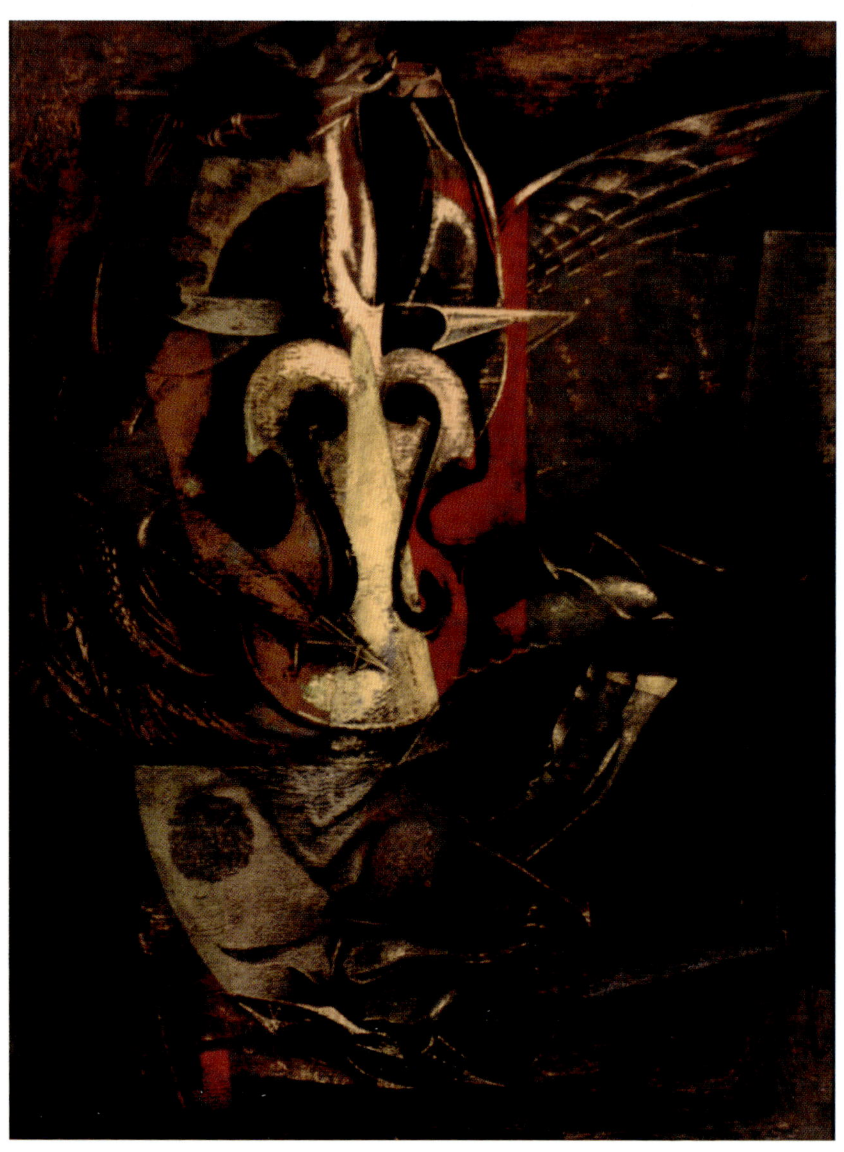

Black Music, 1940, oil on board

7 1939-46
Black Music

'Don't reject the flames just because the cold coals are easier to handle! … It is better to be a conscious servant of fire than the king of the ashes.'

Valentine Penrose. Letter to Roland from India, 5 October 1935.[1]

Aziz had recognised that nothing he could do would ever make Lee happy and her best chance of a fulfilled life lay with Roland. He gave her his blessing, a generous portfolio of shares as insurance and a steamer ticket for England. Their elegant parting after five years together was in keeping with his unfailingly gentle and kind nature. Roland met Lee when the liner Otranto docked at Southampton on 14 June 1939 and whisked her back in triumph to Downshire Hill, where Man Ray was staying as Roland's guest. Five days later, Roland's divorce from Valentine became absolute, but while marriage to Lee was safely out of the question – she was still married to Aziz – Roland and Lee were a couple straightaway.

Roland took Lee to the London Gallery with great pride to introduce her to the *Weeping Woman* in the 'Picasso in some English Collections' exhibition. They went on to the Mayor Gallery for the combined show of Roland and Ithell Colquhoun's recent work that had opened on 8 June. I am sure Roland would have worn the agonised expression customary in moments when he was deeply proud of something but far too modest to enjoy recognition. Lee was delighted with her portrayal in *Night and Day* and *Good Shooting*, but the press were less enamoured.

The *Evening News* printed a photograph of Roland's painting *Seeing Is Believing* beside an acerbic review by J. B. Manson, a former director of the Tate Gallery titled *This Modern Art Misses So Much.* After a lengthy eulogy on landscape painting and the beauty of nature, he went on to urge readers to visit the *Milestones in French Painting* exhibition to see selected works from Corot to Cézanne.

Stung by Manson's article, Roland countered the critique with a letter to the paper saying that he had too little in common with the ex-director of the Tate to challenge his views on the beauty of nature. Instead he suggested that the public should make their own minds up by seeing works by painters who admire the merits of the French masters, citing Julian Trevelyan's show at the Guggenheim Jeune, Picasso's at the London Gallery and his and Colquhoun's shows at the Mayor Gallery.

Night and Day, Good Shooting and *Octavia* were new works, all inspired by Lee. *Night and Day,* which Roland painted casually as design for a fancy dress costume for Lee remains as his most perceptive portrayal. Her body is divided into the elements of earth, air and fire. Her legs are earth, appropriate as Lee was well grounded. Her body is air, perhaps a comment on her ability to dissociate from her feelings and her face has become the sun in keeping with the strength and radiance of her intellect and personality. Water is absent, to the point where the earth forming Lee's legs is parched and cracked. Water usually symbolises emotion and Roland, who like Lee tended to be embarrassed by demonstrations of feelings has thoughtfully provided some funnels to safely conduct away any water that might appear.

Good Shooting was titled *Bien Visé* in French, literally *Well Aimed* but as slang translates as *Well Screwed.* Lee's nude body stands against a brick wall already pockmarked by the bullets of the firing squad. She waits calmly defiant, without needing the strong chain provided to secure her. Her upraised arms enclose the space where her head should be, which is replaced by a peaceful scene of the Norfolk Broads, with a sailing boat and pollarded willow trees. As in *Night and Day*, the elements of earth,

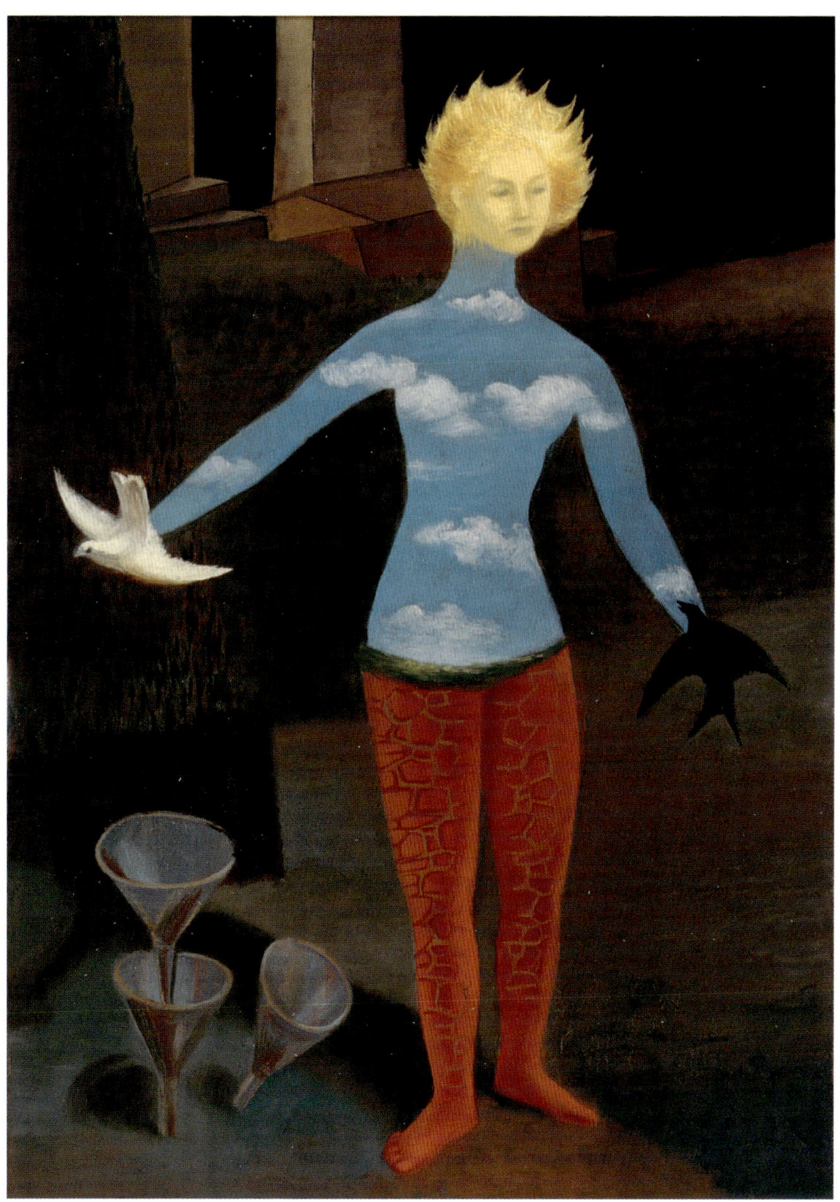

Night and Day, 1937, oil on canvas. Private collection

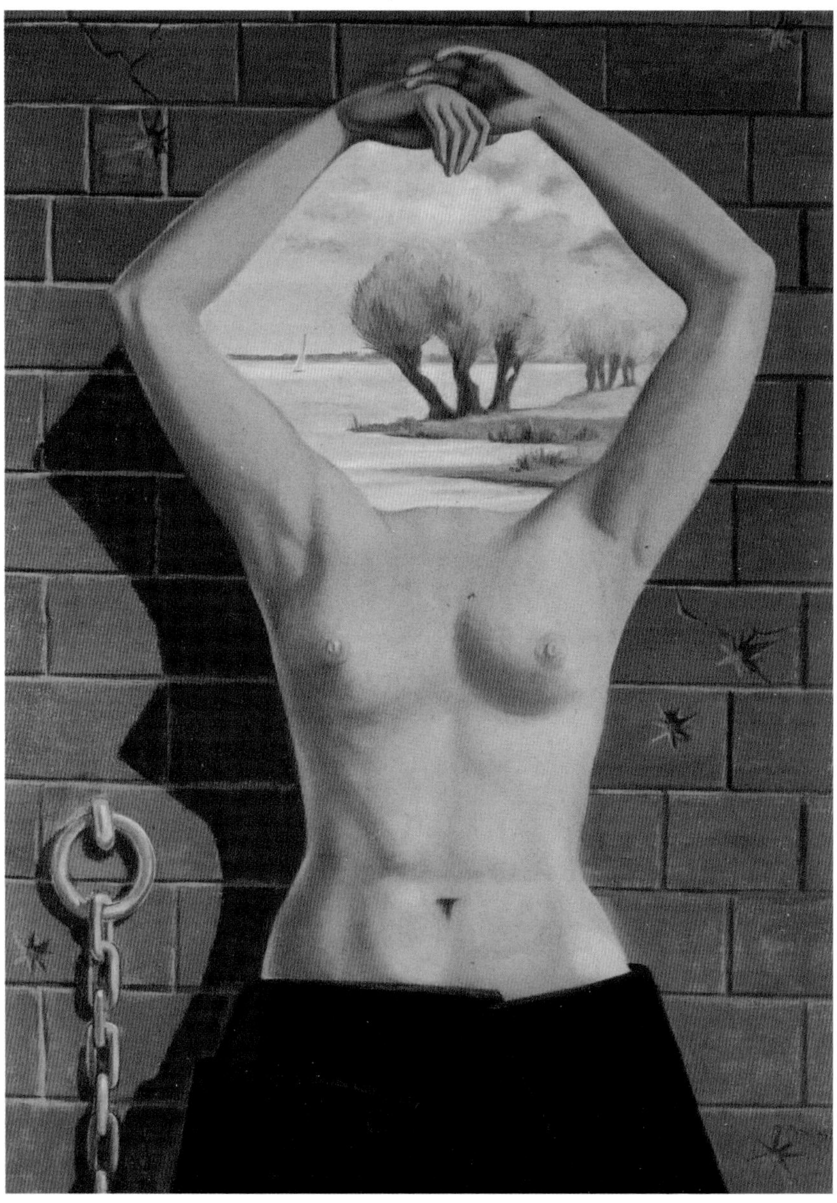

Good Shooting (*Bien Visé*), 1939, oil on canvas. Collection: Southampton City Art Gallery

air, water and fire, alluded to by the bullets, are present. In contrast to *Night and Day*, Lee's body is flesh, although her pubic area is protected by what seems like steel armour. This time water is present, tranquil, sustaining and contained by Lee's arms it replaces her head. Perhaps this is symbolic. She had willingly given Roland her body, but with this metaphor he acknowledges he would never have control over her emotions or her thoughts.

Octavia presents us with a more puzzling if not threatening enigma. Roland, Man Ray and Ernst, with his *Femme Sans Tête*, both explored the theme of the headless woman. The obvious interpretation of this is that without a head a woman cannot answer back, have a mind of her own or be independent. Roland's headless women take the form of *The Last Voyage of Captain Cook, The Real Woman, The Revolving Statue* and *Good Shooting*. The latter three bear reference to Lee Miller and it seems Roland may have taken the headless theme to signify his re-connection to the visceral Roland made with Lee. She was the antithesis of Valentine's ethereal qualities.

In these headless works Roland explores his fascinations with the mystery and contradictions of the women he loved. After he discovered women he did not seek to repeat the homosexual experiences of his youth, although he remained completely accepting of it in others. Valentine was bisexual, as were some of his later lovers and Lee, although stridently heterosexual, had some strongly masculine traits. For Roland the person was more important than their sexual predisposition.

Octavia has a head, but the long arms become legs and the stance of the hands reinforce this ambiguity. The head becomes a male genital, chained to the ground by essentially female bonds.[2] In that the head has become the sex, the two sources of a man's driving force are interchanged. Roland constantly fought with this juxtaposition in his struggle to resolve whether to allow himself to be ruled by his intellect or his hormones. The eight spikes in *Octavia* could represent the dangers inherent in penetrating the organic dimensions inside a woman. This

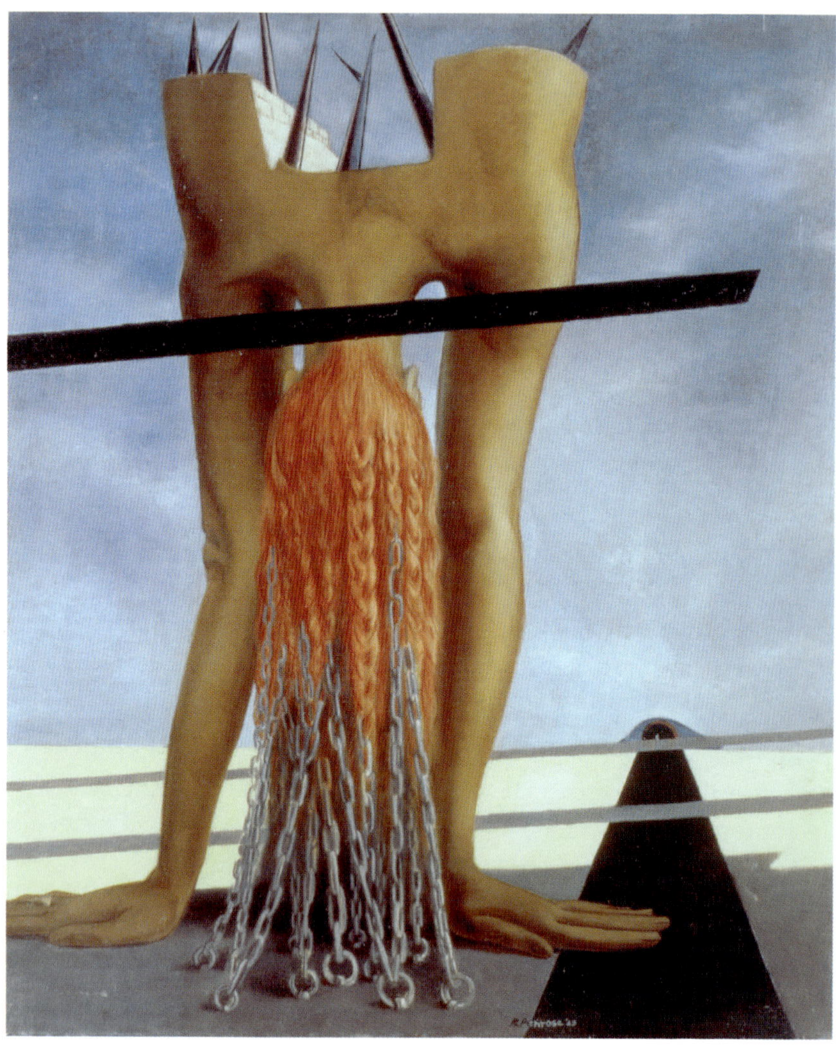

Octavia (Aurelia), 1939, oil on canvas. Collection: Ferens Art Gallery

can be defined as the fear of castration, in that women can engender a fear of emasculation or more simply the fear of the unknown – like the 'virgin territory' of a woman's body.

The hair becomes chain fastened to rings triggering associations of bondage. Perhaps it also relates to Roland's extensive knowledge of the Bible and refers to the legend of Samson and Delilah where hair is a symbol of male strength – in this case a captive strength that anchors his genitals to the ground. The mysterious assembly of icons for power, sex, bondage, mutability and danger combine in one of Roland's most disturbing and enigmatic images.

The twenty-seven exhibits of Roland's exhibition show his work at its apogee and alongside *Winged Domino* which was not included, many are the images for which he is best known today. *The Last Voyage of Captain Cook*, the painting titled *Portrait* that was soon to scandalise the Royal Academy and two collages, *Le Grand Jour* and *Magnetic Moths* are now part of the Tate Gallery collection, a turn of events which would have astonished J. B. Manson. The New Orleans Museum of Art bought *The Veteran*, *Octavia* resides at the Ferens Art Gallery in Hull, *The Conquest of the Air* at Southampton Art Gallery and *My Windows* is part of the Scottish National Gallery of Modern Art collection in Edinburgh. History shows us that J. B. Manson got it wrong, but then Roland, Lee and Freddy Mayor would have been horrified if the establishment Manson represented had praised the exhibition.

Freddy Mayor had invited Roland to decorate the whole window of the gallery, which Roland recalled with affection in an interview for BBC TV;

> In the late 1930s I had this exhibition in Freddy Mayor's gallery in Cork Street with Ithell Colquhoun and there were various Surrealist objects in it. I was particularly interested in having this frame on the left, which framed an actual vase of fruit and flowers, which I called the painter's problem, but it was the real thing. Next

> to it there was just a loaf of bread and then there was this study, this scheme of the inside of a man making it look like a factory and next to that we found a very nice old boy, a charming old man who was a sandwich man and we got him just to sit there as the real thing again. And he sat there all afternoon with a bottle of beer hidden underneath him and he went to sleep most of the time. But we did get blamed, this was something – cruelty to men, sitting them up in a window and showing them off like that. He didn't think so at all – he was delighted.[3]

A woman had spotted the tramp snoozing in the window and lodged a complaint. The Police came round to 'have a word' with Freddy and that was the end of the man's stay in the window, much to his annoyance.

'Best job I ever had – paid to sup ale!' he muttered as he stumped off.[4]

Roland's painting of the man whose insides resembled a factory may have been inspired by the exhibition at the London Gallery the previous July, *'The Impact of Machines'*. Mesens had enlisted the help of Arthur Elton and Humphrey Jennings in assembling the show. In an article titled 'The Iron Horse' in the June *London Bulletin*, Jennings stated; *'Machines are animals created by man and every machine has a latent human content'*.[5] Roland reversed the concept and painted a human with machine content. Roland loved nature but was squeamish about the deeper realities of biology. I remember him going green at the sight of a difficult calving, so the idea of his insides being a reliable and repairable machine must have been appealing.

Next door at Guggenheim Jeune, Peggy was pursuing a more ambitious project to create a British Art Centre inspired by Alfred Barr's achievements at the Museum of Modern Art in New York. Roland wrote;

> Peggy Guggenheim has been all honey to me and what she wants in return is that I should be one of the three big bugs on her selection committee. She is starting a Museum of Modern Art in London.

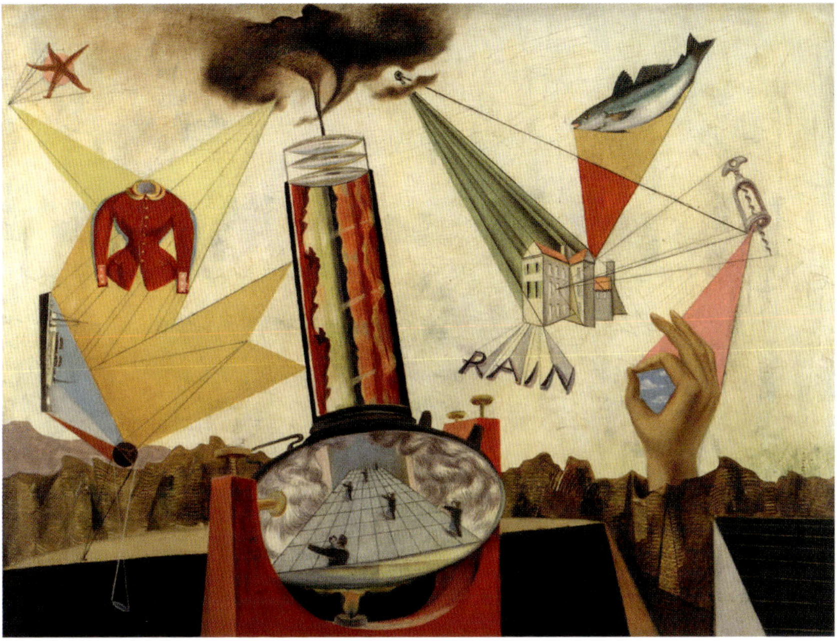

Le Grand Jour, 1938, Oil on Canvas, collage. Collection: Tate Modern

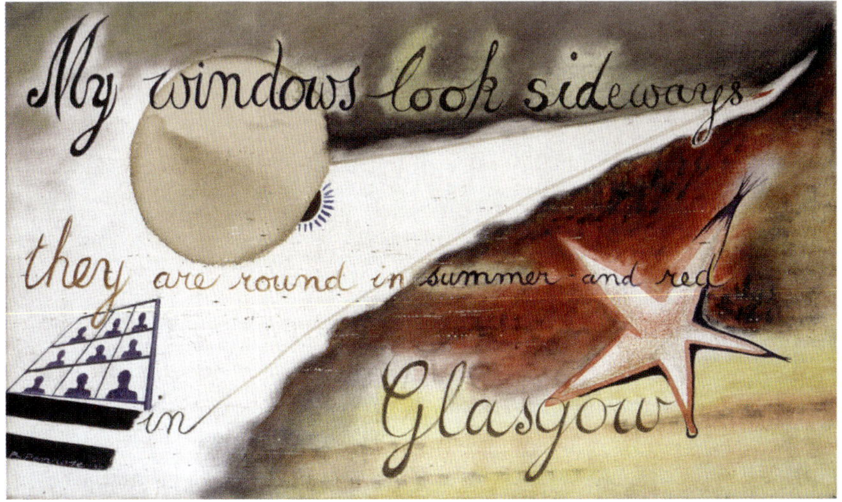

My Window Looks Sideways, 1937, Oil on Canvas. Collection: Scottish National Gallery of Modern Art

> Read is to be director and it is to be a grand effort to establish a 'home' for art in this barbarous country. All very ambitious and rather lacking in funds – (I am not going in on that side).[6]

Roland's instincts were right, but not because the project was ill-founded. Both Peggy and Read committed themselves fully but Mesens, judging Peggy to be motivated by mainly commercial interests that could rival his own, did what he could to discourage Roland.

Roland trod a middle path for reasons of his own. He knew from his experience with the London Gallery that the timing was wrong for such a grandiose scheme. As it happened, the impending threat of war prompted Peggy to halt the plan, close Guggenheim Jeune and leave for Paris. The idea itself did not die, but remained dormant until awoken by Roland and Read nearly ten years later as the Institute of Contemporary Art.

When Roland and Mesens started the London Gallery, instead of having a series of exhibition catalogues they published *The London Bulletin,* a periodical intended for a wide circulation. The first issue, in April 1938, contained articles by Read and Jennings about the Magritte exhibition. The scope broadened with poems by Eluard and Paul Nougé and short pieces on Degenerate Art, Surrealism and Fashion, Joan Miró and the discussion between realists and Surrealists.

Surrealism inspired the mix of painting, prose, photography, drawing and some insulting comments about the shortcomings of the Tate Gallery and Sir Kenneth Clark. Mesens' skill with typography and layout gave a stylish presentation to contributions he chose wisely. It was a groundbreaking magazine that became widely known and today exists as an eloquent chronicle of British Surrealism.

Picasso in English Collections was the London Gallery's most widely acclaimed show, so successful that the closing date had to be extended by two weeks. Eighteen of the fifty-one works were from Roland's collection, including some major Cubist works such as *La Jeune Fille à la Mandoline*

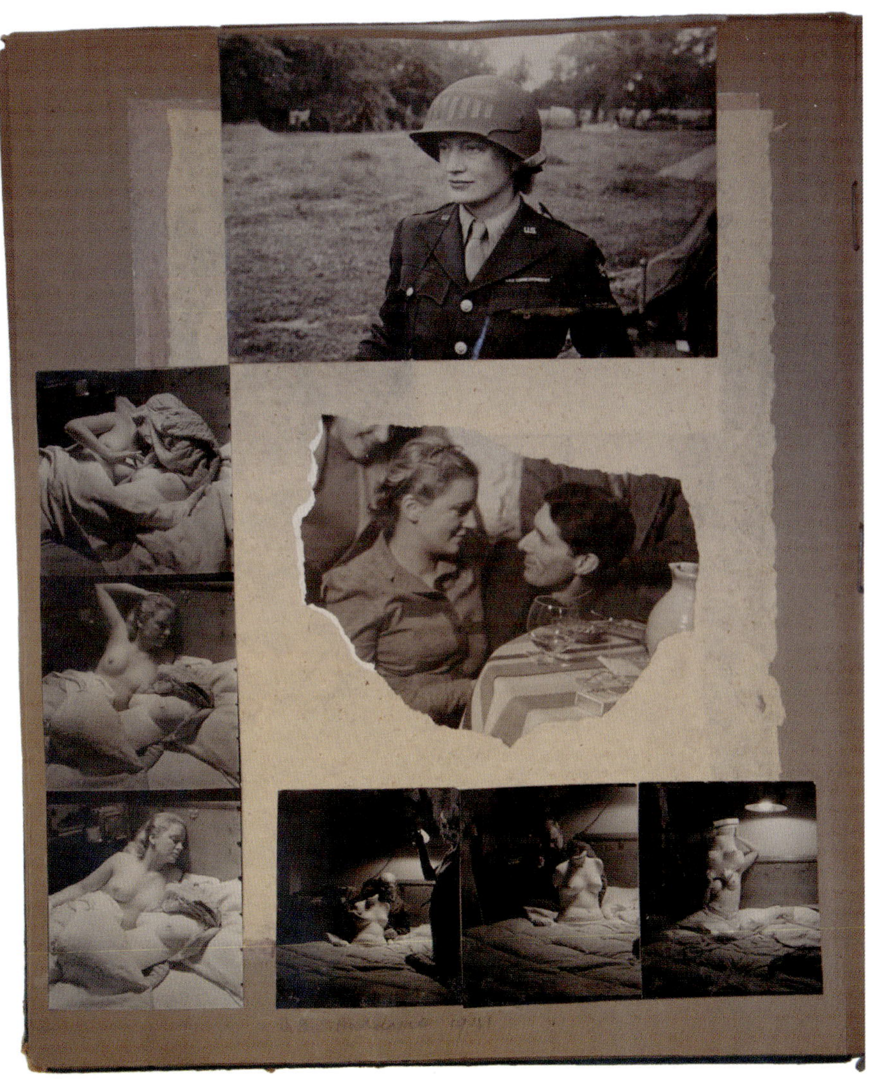

Wartime scrapbook. Collection: Scottish National Gallery of Modern Art Edinburgh

and *Portrait of Uhde*, the exquisitely drawn *Fin d'un Monstre* and the intimately tender *Portrait of Nusch Eluard*. The forceful eloquence of the *Weeping Woman* was noted by reviewers.

But it was the gallery's swan song. Mesens had been grumbling for some time that 'the street too is quiet' and they had to accept that the success of the Picasso show was against the trend. At the end of July 1939, Roland and Mesens announced the closure of the London Gallery. Two months later Freddy Mayor shut the Mayor Gallery.

Roland and Lee were determined to visit their friends in France before the evil of war was unleashed. They headed for Antibes in the hope of finding Picasso, Dora and the Eluards, but first visited Ernst and Leonora at their house in Saint-Martin d'Ardèche, thirty miles north of Avignon. Léonor Fini was staying there when Roland and Lee arrived and they made a brave attempt at merriment. Ernst had decorated the house with giants, ghosts, dancing birdmen and other fantastic creatures made from cement and stone, creating his own monsters for protection against the monsters to come. Lee photographed the beings of Ernst's creation. She photographed Ernst tenderly embracing Leonora, so young, vulnerable and beautiful, with tinkling bells sewn round the hem of her jacket. She photographed Léonor Fini looking as mysterious as ever. Maybe she thought that by capturing the images of the people she loved inside her camera she could keep them from harm. They all knew it was the twilight of innocence.

Within weeks, Ernst would be led away to an internment camp for enemy aliens. To Leonora's relief he would be rescued through the influence of Roland and others only to be re-imprisoned after the fall of France. They had the idea of getting to London, but it proved impossible and eventually Ernst took up with Peggy Guggenheim who had him flown to America. Leonora fled to Spain, where she suffered incarceration in a lunatic asylum before a marriage of convenience to Renato Leduc, a Mexican poet and diplomat gave her an escape to Mexico in 1941. Man Ray left Ady in Paris and fled to America and Léonor Fini survived the war in Monte Carlo and Rome.

In Antibes Roland and Lee found Picasso working on his giant canvas *Night Fishing at Antibes.* Picasso bravely insisted that the whole war had been invented to stop him working, but refused to oblige and carried on despite the ominous military build-up in the port. The animated talk around the café tables had been replaced by earnest discussions of where to escape to and how obtain visas and money. The days were punctuated by strained silences as everyone tried to hear the latest news on the radio until the announcement of Hitler's invasion of Poland swept away all the last vestiges of the old life forever.

The first air-raid siren wailed above Waterloo Station as they arrived back in London. War had been declared and the city was seething with activity. Lee presented herself to *Vogue* studios, but to begin with was politely brushed off. Her professional career had lapsed for six years and she was considered *passé*. Soon the military call-up began to thin *Vogue* staff and as her long association with Condé Nast was remembered, new opportunities opened to her. What started as a few minor assignments led to a constant stream of work, as *Vogue* bravely continued to put an aspect of normality into a mad world.

Following the fall of Barcelona in January, Roland became an active supporter of the National Joint Committee for Spanish Relief, which sought to rescue Republicans from concentration camps in Spain. Picasso supported the movement and supplied drawings for use as publicity and at Miró's request Roland stood as guarantor for the artist's two friends, the painter Antonio Garcia Lamolla and Enrique Crous Vidal, a writer and the director of a revue called *Art* in Lèrida.[7] It seems that Vidal at least was successfully liberated.

Roland faced the crisis of the war with a sense of impotent gloom. Undoubtedly the memory of the carnage of World War I was still in his mind and he felt appallingly frustrated that no political solution had been found to the crisis. I recalled the agony he felt years later during the Yom Kippur War and even more acutely at the time of the Falklands War. Losses from either side plunged him into the depths of despair.

When the news of some dreadful slaughter came, he was deeply affected.

'Why?' he would ask, his face crumpling, *'why do we have to still do it like this. We have all these people in the UN – if only they talked more they could put a stop to it – there is no need for this. If our politicians were serving us at all they would prevent wars, not make them'*.

Cut off from Paris and with life in London slowing to a halt, Roland felt a growing isolation and loss of freedom. Many of his friends had dispersed into military jobs. His brother Alec was considered too old to enlist but was forced to evacuate his beloved Bradenham Hall, which was requisitioned by the Army. In April Lionel had accepted the post of Director of Psychiatric Research in Ontario, Canada.

Before he left, Roland had managed to establish a new rapport with his hyper-intelligent brother;

> I showed him my photos of Siwa and the desert at which he said – 'Come and look at my slides of nerve sections and brains' – So I spent a whole afternoon squinting down a microscope at the most beautiful formations which looked like rippling sand, wind blown rocks, the Red Sea coast, it all being bits of imbeciles.[8]

The common ground of aesthetic values bridged the gap between Surrealism and the far shores of genetic science. The link was to endure and give Roland interesting insights into the Surrealistic qualities of mental illness.

Beacus did not aspire to pacifism and he joined the Royal Navy. Roland wanted to make some kind of non-combatant contribution and searched around for a venture by like-minded people. Fortunately Bill Hayter, who had seen camouflage in the Spanish Civil War had founded The Industrial Camouflage Research Unit with Helen Philips, Julian Trevelyan, John Buckland Wright and Denis Clarke Hall and Roland joined them. They rented space in Ernö Goldfinger's office at 7 Bedford Square and set to work to get contracts from firms who were worried about the vulnerability of their factories from air attack.

In the late autumn of 1939 the Royal Academy invited contributions to an exhibition titled *United Artists* and Roland sent in two pictures;

> One was a collage – no objection was raised to that, but the other picture was a sort of abstract form over which I had written the description of an imaginary person, which they did not like. I got a letter from the Royal Academy saying 'Would I please remove this picture and send another picture, if possible without writing'. So at Lee's suggestion what I did was to go down town and to get a card in deaf and dumb sign language from which I chose a four-letter word S-H-I-T and painted a row of hands saying this and I titled it *From The Housetops*. They accepted that at once, in fact they hung it exactly opposite an enormous portrait of His Majesty the King. I didn't ask them to do that but they did. People got the idea – in fact I think it all happened through one of the cleaners at the Royal Academy being deaf and dumb and looking at this picture he started hooting with laughter and gave away what it said. At this, Tom Driberg, who then wrote the 'Hickey' column in the *Daily Express*, went to see Lutyens, the President of the Royal Academy. He said;
>
> 'I hear there is a picture with a dirty word in your exhibition – what are you going to do about it?'
>
> Lutyens said; 'Oh, let's keep it – it may bring in a few more people'.[9]

The replacement *From The Housetops* was lost during the war, but Roland had made a monotype at the same time which he gave to one of his closest friends, the artist and film maker John Banting. After the war, Banting was so upset to hear of the loss that he insisted on returning the work to Roland, his friendship for Roland overriding his Marxist opposition to the upper classes.

In the spring of the 1940 Grace Pailthorpe and Ruben Mednikoff

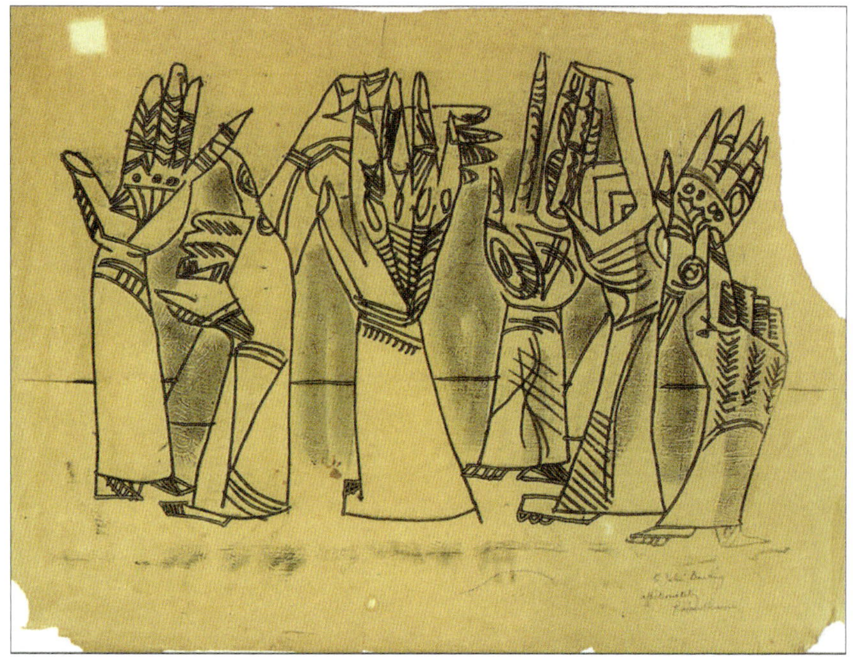

From the Housetops, 1939, Mono print on paper

called a meeting of the Surrealists at the Barcelona restaurant and with the best of intentions made an attempt at reviving the group on a non-political basis. They proposed a group show at the British Art Centre for June, but Mesens, sensing a challenge to both his position as leader and the movement's political goals launched a counter-attack. He demanded adherence to the support of the proletarian revolution. There was to be no membership of any other group and no exhibiting or publishing outside approved Surrealist channels. Surrealist writers should not work for or contribute to non-Surrealist publications. His edicts fell on ears deafened by the inherent British resistance to group activities. Some members left, others including Pailthorpe, Mednikoff and Ithell Colquhoun were later expelled, but few took much notice of Mesens.

There was flicker of revitalisation and although hopes for a show at the British Art Centre vanished when Peggy Guggenheim left for Paris, on Roland's initiative the exhibition *Surrealism Today* took place at the Zwemmer Gallery in June. John Banting and Maddox designed the window display which mainly featured an armchair that Eileen Agar had converted into a seated black woman. Roland painted the window with the banner title SURREALISM spanning the glass and at Maddox's suggestion added 'art' repeated in a circle so that the word read 'tart…'. It only lasted a day as Zwemmer objected.[10]

One of the exhibits was a list of painters who were not allowed into the gallery. The impossibility of shipping new works from Europe meant Delvaux's latest work was represented by photographs, but the overall effect of the eighty-two exhibits was a *tour de force* for the Surrealist Group in England. Roland exhibited five of his most recent paintings and Lee four of her Egyptian photographs. Eileen Agar, Banting, Hayter, Paul Nash, John Tunnard, Matta Echaurren, Conroy Maddox, Edith Rimmington, Henry Moore and Tanguy were among the other artists.[11]

Roland began his contribution to the war effort by joining the Air Raid Protection corps, the ARP. The initial amusement he felt at wandering around in a tin hat with his friend Jean Arp's name on it soon evaporated in the tedium of walking the streets at night and yelling at people who let a chink of light shine through their blackout curtains. Then things began to get more serious, with training for dealing with incendiary bombs and the other ghastly devices that began to rain from the sky.

When the full fury of the Blitz was unleashed in the autumn of 1940, the main target areas were the docks and the East End of London. Roland and the other North London ARP men could only watch in horror as the sky to the south-east turned orange in the glow of massive fires. Searchlights criss-crossed the sky probing for the insect-like bombers, their beams followed by the firework bursts of flak shells and streams of tracer. In the hellish din, spent ammunition and off-target bombs would come their way, but it was nothing compared to the dreadful destruction they were compelled to witness nightly to the south.

Roland's formerly well-ordered house filled up rapidly with friends bombed out of their own homes in central London and every available space was taken with people sleeping all over the floor. Freddy and Pam Mayor were among the most welcome guests who stayed several months. Kathleen McColgan, a journalist on the *Evening Standard*, moved in and with Mesens and Sybil living upstairs it was a tight fit. Other arrivals included two stray tabby cats Lee had befriended, named Jeep and Taxi and a goose named George given to Lee as a birthday present. George cultivated a taste for gin and tonic but sadly a conflict arose between his artistic decalcomania on the carpet and those who slept on the floor, so he was packed off to a farm.

Out of the blue, Roland was surprised to receive a phone call from Valentine who he had thought was safely in India. She had been trying to get back to her parents in Gascony, but after the fall of France the British ship taking her to Marseille would not put into an occupied port and brought her on to London. She had avoided approaching Roland, not wanting to intrude on the new life he had made with Lee, but turned to him when she was bombed out of her hotel. He arranged a rendezvous at the Three Horseshoes, a pub frequented by the Surrealists where he was sure she would find people she knew, such as Mesens and the French writer and broadcaster Jacques Brunius. He was delayed and when he arrived an hour late he was astonished to find her quietly chatting to Lee;

> On seeing me Valentine leapt to her feet, saying how glad she was that I had turned up at last as she had heard that Lee Miller, who of course she did not want to meet, might be arriving any minute. 'But', I exclaimed, 'that's Lee you were talking to', in answer to which came Valentine's spontaneous exclamation; 'Oh! but she's wonderful!'[12]

Lee generously insisted that there was room in the house for her. She stayed for nearly a year and enlisted in the Free French Army as a *soldat*

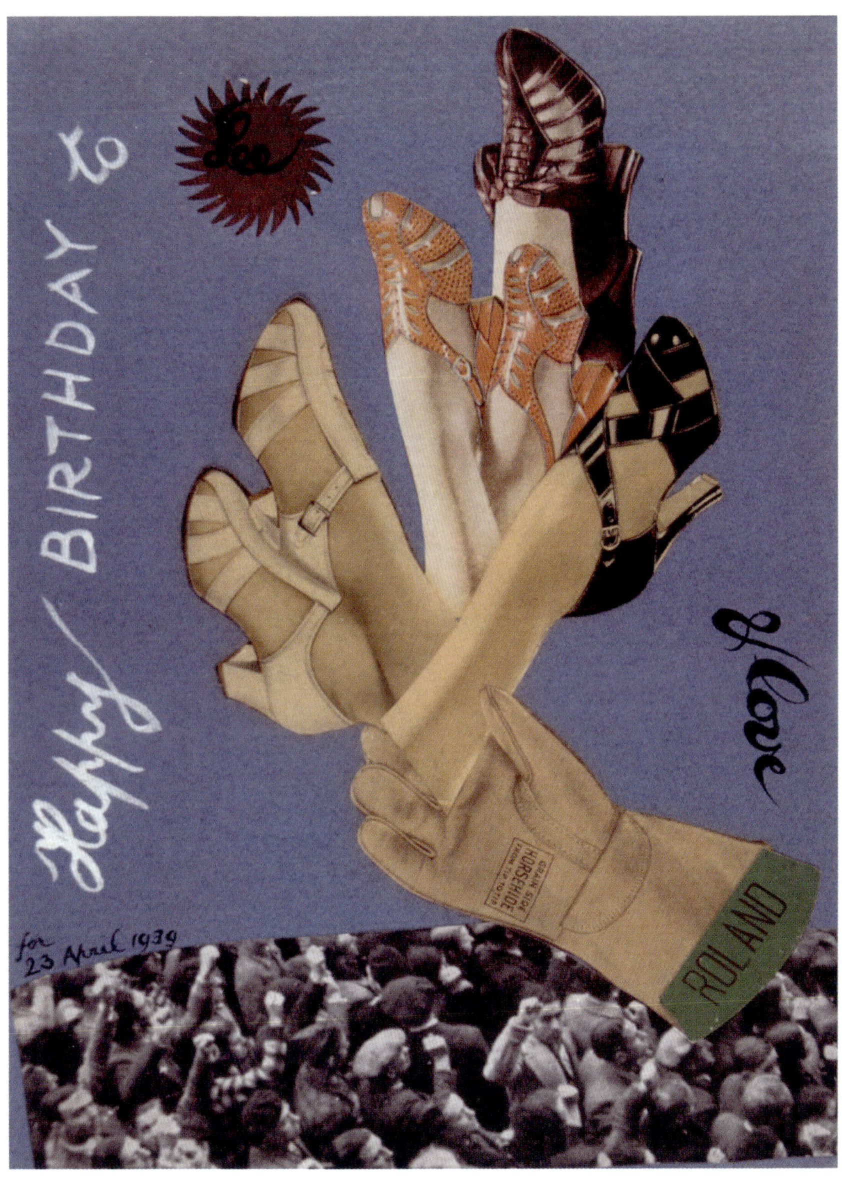

Birthday card to Lee Miller, Collage on card, 1939

de troisième classe serving, by some mad quirk of fate, as a driver for senior officers, creating great peril on the streets of London and later Algiers. She was posted there to her brother Gilbert's unit for a while, before returning to London for the remainder of the war. The liberation of France did not come soon enough for her father who died in 1945, a few days before Valentine managed to get through to him in Condom.

Vogue's offices and studios were wrecked several times and Lee took to the streets, shooting fashion in all kinds of unlikely locations such as the basement of the Natural History Museum crammed with stuffed animals, or paper and rag recycling depots. She was instinctively more interested in the surrealistic scenes around her and began assembling a series of photographs of the strange conjunctions of lyrical poetry and violence she found every day. Many of these pictures were published in a slim volume called *Grim Glory, Pictures of Britain under Fire,* edited by *Vogue* staffer Ernestine Carter with a preface by the American broadcaster Ed Murrow. It was designed to give an up-beat *Britain-can-take-it* image to the American public and the humour of Lee's pictures was essential.

Lee was not the only Surrealist photographing amid the rubble. Roland recalled encountering Humphrey Jennings with his film crew amid the debris. His memorable documentary *Fires Were Started* so precisely portrayed the surrealistic aspects of the war including dream-like sequences of people moving about normally in completely unreal circumstances.

'Get away from here! Can't you see it's dangerous!' bellowed Humphrey Jennings seeing Roland, oblivious of the shattered remains of a building likely to collapse and bury him at any moment.

When the London Gallery closed Roland and Mesens carefully placed their stock of art works, office furniture and files in store at Taylor's Depository in Pimlico. There were eighty-three paintings and objects including nineteen Magrittes, thirty-one Ernsts, six Delvauxs and a selection by Agar, Brauner, Braque, Chirico, Dominguez,

Giacometti, Man Ray and others, two-thirds of them belonging to Roland. In December the warehouse was hit by German bombs and burned to the ground. Not a trace remained of the paintings. The insurance company was not liable for war damage but Mesens claimed their entitlement to government compensation of ten percent on the value of £807.[13]

Roland's involvement with The Industrial Camouflage Research Unit gave a start to his army career as a civilian lecturer in camouflage at the Home Guard School at Osterley Park, a position that still allowed him enough time to paint. The Blitz brought an abrupt new style change into his work with music as the theme. I asked him what lay behind the series, *Night Music, Black Music, Night Orchestra, Nightfall* and *The Dance,* all from 1940. He was characteristically reticent, but ventured;

> It was the noise of the bombardment at night. It was so overwhelming I felt it was the relentless work of demons, so to make them less terrifying I tried to see them as a group of musicians. They seemed less threatening that way. The art of primitive man always seemed to me to have been doing just that, converting hideous intangible fears into art that might still frighten us, but we can see it and touch it so it becomes a little more controllable.

It was not until I found in Roland's studio a copy of a small volume titled *The Home Guard Manual of Camouflage* by Roland Penrose – Lecturer to the War Office School for Instructors to the Home Guard, that I had any real respect for his war career. Other kids had dads who had flown fighters, driven tanks or landed from rubber boats with blackened faces and done deeds of great heroism. My dad had been in camouflage, for me a non-event until I found *the* book. Then his war history suddenly became real, not heroic, but useful and clever, in ways that my pals and I put to good use for years when playing our war games in the woods.

In his manual, Roland used many examples of camouflage in nature.

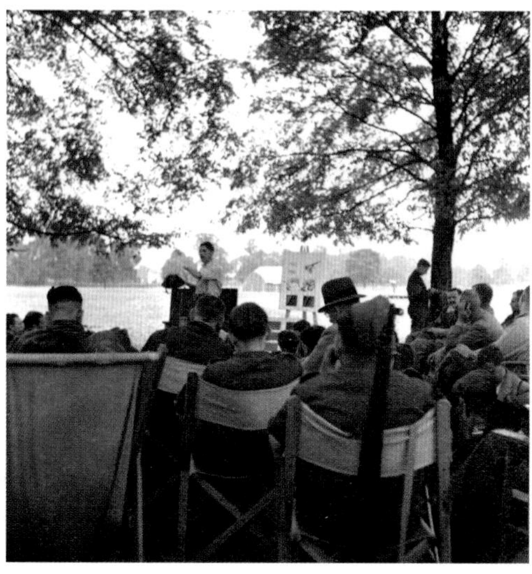

LEFT: Roland Penrose lecturing on Camouflage, England, *c.*1943, by Lee Miller

BELOW: Camouflage Car (detail), England 1941

His inherent love of wild things gave him a sound understanding of natural concealment that harked back to the woods of Oxhey Grange. In Chapter III – *Nature as a Guide*, he wrote;

> For instance, the night-jar nests on the ground in a wood, choosing a background of dry leaves and sticks with which its own colour harmonises so exactly that it is very difficult to see. Another is the yellow-underwing moth which lies flat on the bark of a tree, so that it eliminates its own shadow and becomes almost invisible.[14]

The book contains instructions on making almost anything disappear as well as various designs of sniper suit that confer total invisibility on the wearer; at least that is what we believed when as kids we made them from old sacks stolen from the barn.

Roland once told me that in the summer of 1943, as an enlisted man in the 19th Battalion of the Home Guard Middlesex Regiment, was lecturing to a large group of Home Guard officers when an army staff car drew up. The occupant appeared to be eavesdropping on Roland's

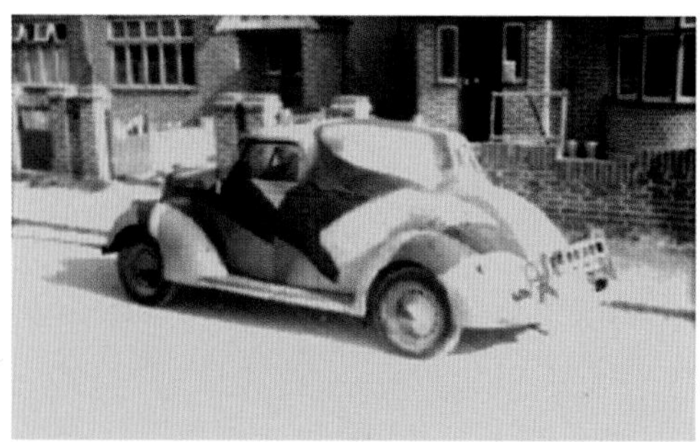

lecture and at the end he was summoned by an immaculately dressed aide. He found himself face to face with General Montgomery and was informed that as of now he had a commission in the regular army.[15] Before Roland knew what was happening, he found himself Captain Penrose in charge of Eastern Command Camouflage School, which had its headquarters in the elegant eighteenth-century Assembly Rooms in Norwich. Roland's major was his old friend the painter John Lake and a surrealistic blend of characters formed the camouflage corps; Oliver Messel the designer, Jasper Maskelyn the conjuror and the couturier Victor Steibel.

In Hampstead Lee was not alone. In the autumn of 1941, David E. Scherman, an eminent American *Time-Life* photo-journalist had arrived in England. He had just produced a distinguished report on the demise of the Zam Zam, an unarmed passenger ship taking him to Africa that had been sunk by a German raider disguised as a merchantman. Scherman's photographs in *Life* magazine later led to the identification of the raider which was sunk in turn by a British warship. Soon after his arrival in England he met Lee and Roland and recalled;

> Twenty-five years old and a brash and bumptious squirt, I had the eternal good fortune to be invited by Roland to visit – and later move into – his house in Hampstead. Its walls were completely covered with what I thought were absolutely first-rate copies of the works of Picasso, Braque, Miro, Tanguy, Chirico, Brancusi, Giacometti, Tunnard, Ernst, René Magritte and a dozen by Roland Penrose himself. Only they were not copies, Lee explained to me patiently. They were originals and what's more they were merely the few that Roland wanted to keep near him – the main body of his work was hidden away safely out of the blitz in Devon. The house was mind-boggling and so were Roland and Lee's regular soirées, the guest list of which reads like a Who's Who of modern art, journalism, British politics, music and even espionage, though we did not know about

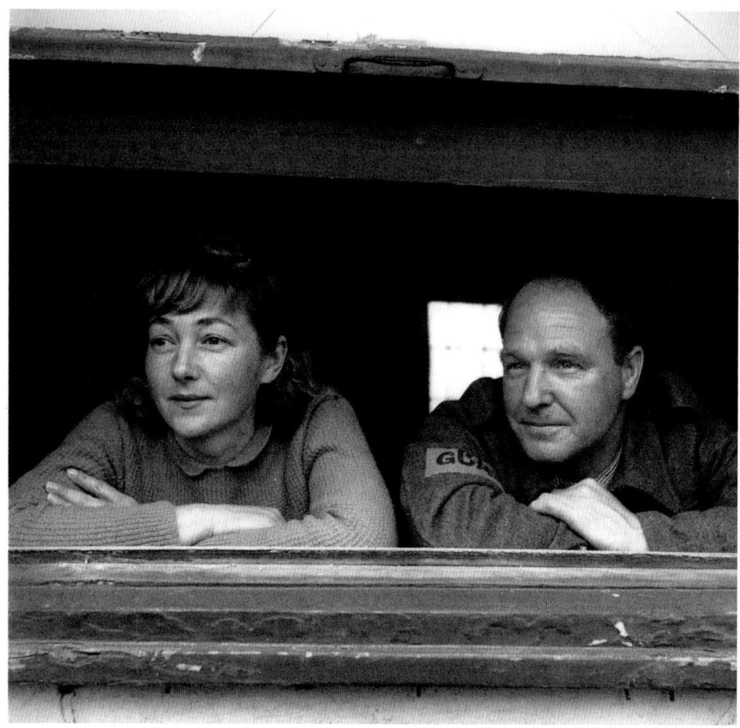

Irina and Henry Moore, Oxford, England 1942, by Lee Miller

> the latter until years later. Communists, Liberals and Tories drank and jostled one another in an amicable mélange that will never be seen again, anywhere. Among them were Michael Foot, then a young Labour stalwart, Alfred J. Ayer, … and Spanish War veteran named Tom Wintringham. … Another visitor was Tom's friend, a small, quiet, violent man with a bandit's moustache, a professional guerrilla named Yank Levy, who would teach us how to disarm and strangle would-be assailants.[16]

It was Scherman who suggested that Lee should apply for accreditation as a war correspondent with the US Army for *Vogue*.[17] They worked closely together for the next two and a half years, sharing assignments and facilities all over England and Scotland. Together they produced features on Moore and the ATS searchlight battery near Hendon where they came under fire from a German aircraft. Scherman also helped Lee with her coverage of the Women's Royal Naval Service, known as the WRENS, which later became a picture book called *Wrens in Camera.*[18]

A French friend claims that the shortest distance of the affections between two men is the love of the same woman and that was the case with Roland and Davie as he was known. It is hard to know how else such a close friendship would have formed between this small, fast-

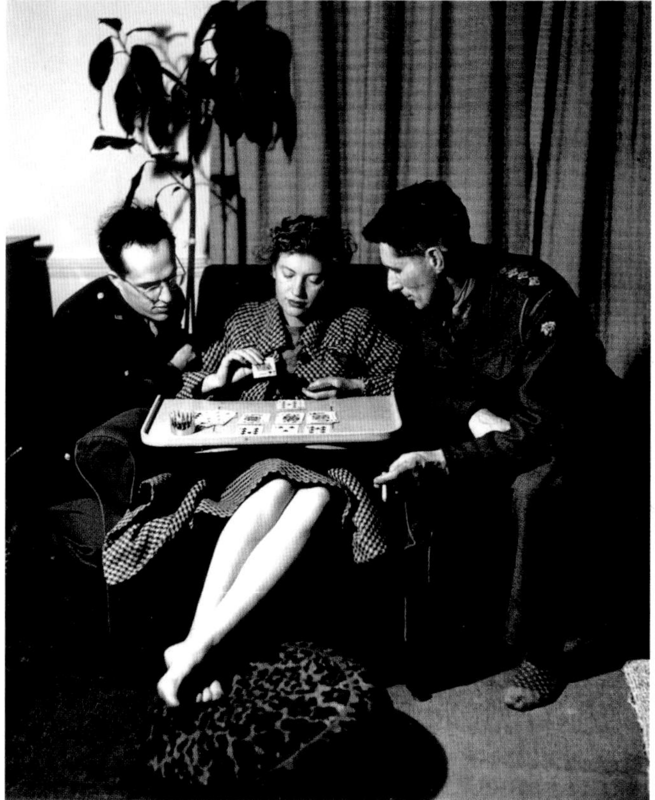

David E. Scherman, Lee Miller, Roland Penrose, Downshire Hill, London, England 1943, by David E. Scherman

moving, wisecracking, Jewish New Yorker and the reserved Englishman he always addressed as 'Rollers'. The household at Downshire Hill became a *ménage à trois,* a situation that brought Roland some comfort, as he did not like the idea of Lee facing the bombs alone. He wrote from his posting in Derbyshire;

> Darling, I'm so glad Davie's home again, hang on to him as long as you can ... give my love to Davie.[19]

When I asked Roland if he felt jealous about sharing Lee in this way, he was emphatic.

'No, not at all, I was very fond of Davie and admired him greatly. I was glad he could keep Lee company and look after her while I was away,' he said. Then he thought for a while and added with a wry smile, *'Well, I did find it a little upsetting to come home on leave and find Davie Scherman's pyjamas under my pillow'.*

The allied landings at Anzio in January 1944 signalled the escalation of the Italian campaign and by March Roland had arrived in Italy to report on developments in camouflage potentially useful for the invasion of Europe. He witnessed the allied bombardment of Monte Casino and whilst he was in Naples Vesuvius erupted, its display of menacing fiery clouds a reminder of the far greater power of nature. He found Beacus on board his flak ship in Naples, where the squadron under his command had put in for repairs after the heavy fighting at Anzio.

Roland always acknowledged what he regarded as far greater bravery in others, including Beacus whose seamanship and dogged toughness had earned him promotion to the rank of commander but he rarely talked about his feelings for his role as a non-combatant. He sometimes said *'I knew I would never be much good at killing people, so I did what I could do best'.* Little evidence remains to suggest there was a conflict between his Quaker pacifist principles and the societal pressure to comply. Being aged thirty nine at the outbreak of the war made explanations of his non-combatant role less necessary but it cannot have been easy for him when his brother and others close to him were fighting men. It was not an issue of courage; sometimes it takes more resolve to resist the norm, but the greatest test of his inner strength was just beginning as Lee's career took off.

The long awaited D-Day invasion of 6 June arrived and soon after Lee went to France on assignment. Roland wrote;

> I've realised again that it's worse to stay behind when it's a question of goodbye – into the bargain my jealousy of anyone going to France and my misery at being separated from you make me a poor individual to live with just now.[20]

For her first story, Lee was flown into the huge 44th US Army Evacuation Hospital at Bricqueville, inland from Omaha Beach. Her brief was to cover the hospital, but Lee soon worked her way forward to the front-line casualty clearing station where the medics tended the wounded under makeshift conditions within range of the enemy's guns. On her return the pictures and words she filed established her dominance of *Vogue* features for the next eighteen months.

Her next assignment was to cover the Civil Affairs Team in the port of St Malo, which was reported as having been taken by the US Army. The German commander Colonel von Aulock had not heard this news and doggedly held the fortress Citadel d'Aleth against the heroically brave but futile infantry assaults by the US 83rd Division. Lee found she had a scoop; a medieval-style siege all of her own. She quickly made friends with the commander, Major Speedie, who allowed her access into observation posts to witness the action. Lee entered into the camaraderie of the fighting men and became their interpreter. The men of the 83rd were to be her buddies right across Europe. During the fighting she was briefly reunited with Scherman who had landed from a US warship.

She was with Major Speedie when he took von Aulock's surrender and then was arrested by the Military Police for violating the terms of her accreditation by entering a combat zone. On her release she headed for Paris, arriving on 27 August, two days after the surrender of the German garrison. As soon as she could Lee went straight to Picasso's studio. Hugging her, he exclaimed;

> 'It's incredible, the first allied soldier I should see is a woman and she is you!'
>
> Picasso and I fell into each others' arms and between laughter and tears and having my bottom pinched and my hair mussed we exchanged news about friends and their work, incoherently and looked at new pictures which were dated on all the Battle of Paris days. [...] I found Paul Eluard; he was talking on the telephone in the back room of a *librairie*. He didn't notice who had come into the gloomy little den and waved for silence. Then he noticed my uniform and froze a little. He hadn't been on sitting terms with a 'soldier' for a very long time. ... There was almost nothing to say to each other – stupid things about how I had traced him – idiotic remarks on the weather. ... We went back to the address where the concierge had denied ever having heard of the Eluards – or any other occupants of the flat.[21]

The flat belonged to Yvonne and Christian Zervos,[22] and there, in front of the un-stretched canvas of Picasso's *Night Fishing at Antibes*, Lee photographed Paul and Nusch. There was not much left of Nusch except her luminous smile. Paul Eluard's role as the poet of the Resistance had put them both high on the Gestapo wanted list. The starvation and strain of the years they spent on the run from one hiding place to another had wasted her to a skeletal thinness. This beautiful woman, beloved of so many, was to die the following year because of the privations she had suffered. Eluard was distraught, saying to Roland; *'Je dormis dans un lit moitié creusait par mort'* [I sleep in a bed half gouged-out by death].

Roland was determined to reach Paris. He managed to get some leave and on 28 September, with uncharacteristic shamelessness, he bluffed his way onto a supply plane to Le Bourget and headed for the allied press headquarters in the Hôtel Scribe. There, Lee and Scherman were sharing connecting rooms 412 and 413. Lee's room looked more like a supply dump, crammed with equipment, looted weapons and other barterable items. The American journalist Catherine Coyne remembered being invited to the room for a drink with Lee and Scherman when Lee received a telegram announcing Roland's imminent arrival;

> Suddenly she took off all her clothes, right there and said, 'I'm going to have a good clean bath for this'! and Davie [Scherman] took me by the arm and said, 'Come on, let's you and I go get our drink'.[23]

Roland's return to Paris was bittersweet. He was exhilarated at being back among the familiar sights and smells and everywhere he went his British uniform earned him masses of kisses from unknown Parisiennes. Beautiful girls whirled past on bicycles and the redolence of baguettes, Gauloise and drains produced its familiar evocation. He wrote;

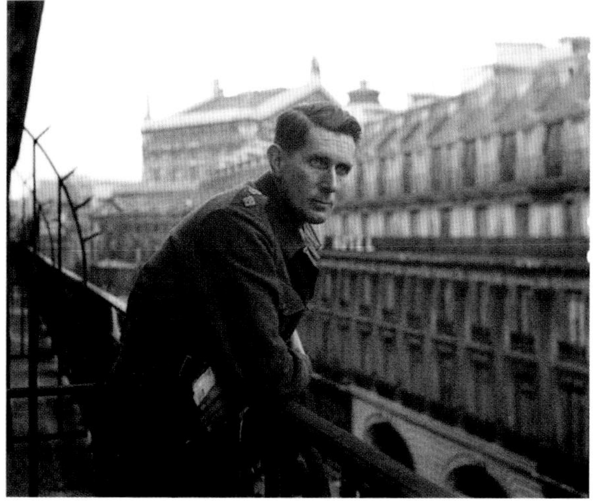

Roland Penrose, Hotel Scribe, Paris, France 1944, by Lee Miller

> My first evening in the old high-windowed studio of Picasso, surrounded by a mass of new paintings and sculpture, a dozen of my old friends were there. I had never wept tears of joy until then. Questions followed. What had I been doing? What had they? Four years of agony of different brands had to be crammed into a few minutes. They were all in tremendously high spirits, their enthusiasm hid at first glance the signs of strain they had been through. Much worse, more sustained than I had ever imagined. … As early as the first winter of the occupation, a full-scale campaign began against scientists, artists, lawyers, doctors, even students regardless of age or creed. … Not a single friend that I met was without personal stories of sickening barbarity. My surprise was that any should have survived.[24]

Picasso, Dora Maar, the Eluards, René Char, George Hugnet, Tristan Tzara, Oscar Domínguez, Louis Aragon, Elsa Triolet and Jean Cocteau had survived, but amid joyful reunions there were ghosts. The poets Max Jacob and Robert Desnos had been murdered. So had Jacques Decour, a professor at the Lycée Rollin who had founded the clandestine journal *Les Lettres Françaises* that had published Eluard's poems during the Occupation. Lou Straus-Ernst, Ernst's first wife and the mother of his son Jimmy had been shipped out of Drancy by freight car to her murder in Auschwitz. *Vogue* editor Michel de Brunhoff's son had been killed fighting with the Resistance a month before.

Eluard gave Roland a large collection of clandestine publications, which he stuffed into his bag and bluffed his way back to London hidden under a pile of mailbags. Roland was expecting a reprimand from his C.O., but instead John Lake gave him additional leave. The material Eluard had provided became source material for a small book he wrote titled *In the Service of the People*.[25] It is an articulate and forcefully written account of the French Resistance movement, compiled using underground newspapers and letters from victims of the Gestapo. In it Roland wrote;

> These letters, written in the anguish of waiting for death, were some of the earliest and most potent forms of resistance literature. They spoke with such eloquence of the courage among young and old alike.[26]

Using prose by Jean-Paul Sartre and poetry by Eluard and Aragon, Roland paid tribute to the sacrifices made by intellectuals such as Jacques Decour. He and his printer were murdered before the first edition came out, but the journal survived and lived on openly after the Liberation.

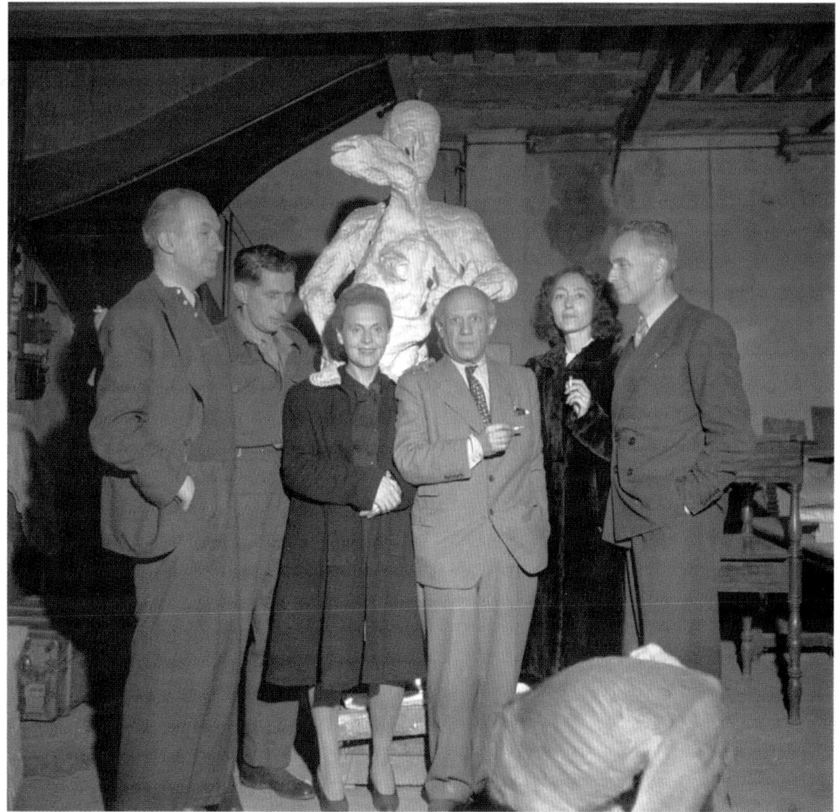

Paul Eluard, Roland Penrose, Elsa Triolet, Picasso, Nusch Eluard and Louis Aragon, Picasso's studio, Paris, France 1944, by Lee Miller

The egalitarian revolutionary essence of the Resistance appealed deeply to Roland; '*A true democracy in which all were equal in danger and held equal responsibility*'.[27] The book's simple cover design shows the Cross of Lorraine patriotically printed in *tricouleur*; a choice that was to have repercussions later.

On 22 February 1945 the tensions within the British Surrealist group reached flashpoint. The main issue echoed the row provoked by the Surrealist painter Tony del Renzio, that challenged the leadership and direction of the group. Mesens and Jacques Brunius countered that there were too many neophytes of doubtful conviction, stating that the most they shared was a refusal to accept ready-made ideas.[28] He in part blamed himself and Mesens for not publishing a manifesto of the fundamental points of Surrealism, which illustrates the paradox. How can people whose basic tenet is the rejection of ready-made ideas accept a manifesto in the first place? Perhaps this is an over simplification but it does demonstrate the contradiction inherent in Brunius' and Mesens' ideals.

This row was more destructive than most. Incensed by Mesens' animosity, Brunius walked out of the meeting and the next day wrote Mesens a twelve page densely typed letter. He made a critical assessment of the group's history and devoted a paragraph to each member. His remarks about Roland are particularly revealing. He starts by attacking Roland's publication *In The Service of The People*;

> It seemed to me inevitably pointless to suffer the pain of a discussion caused by the publication of his tricoloured book under the sign of the Cross of Lorraine. It simply remains for you to rule whether he can continue to be used as a sleeping partner. I know how much this question is serious and distressing for you and I share your anxiety. If you consider, which I believe would be useful, that you must maintain a contract with Penrose that will enable you to publish something good, to open the gallery, I agree in advance.[29]

The Cross of Lorraine was the symbol of the Free French and Brunius scathingly referred to it as *l'emblème du morpion de Lorraine,* the 'crab louse of Lorraine'. Ironically, although Roland got the blame, I suspect Mesens designed the cover,[30] but apart from blatantly revealing their regard for Roland as the source of funds these remarks by Brunius indicate just how contorted the reasoning had become. The left saw De Gaulle, the leader of the Free French as a Fascist and hated him and the 'Stalinist' Eluard equally. In their characteristically righteous and self-contradictory way, Brunius and Mesens reviled Eluard, Aragon and Roland by association for supporting the Communist Party. Brunius and Mesens' cynical repudiation of Roland's homage to the sacrifices of the Resistance fighters and the war time work of Eluard and Aragon does not come well from two men who sat out the war in the comparative safety of England.

Brunius and Mesens were presiding over the death rattle of the British Surrealist group. The war had turned the Surrealist world of imagined unreality into reality. People had lived, died, suffered and loved in a real unreality and now the imagined dreams of Surrealism looked insubstantial. The movement had passed but it had served its purpose in the unfettering of artistic talent and public acceptance that continues today in advertising, pop videos, fashion, design and every other dimension where the spirit of Surrealism has escaped from art to cross-fertilise thinking world-wide. There were many spasms, aftershocks and meetings of like-minded people, but after 1945 the Surrealist movement was dead in Britain, although Surrealism will continue to inspire and delight forever. The genie will remain out of the bottle.

Lee heard of the German surrender in Rosenheim, where she sat in a schoolhouse typing her despatch. She had arrived at Dachau concentration camp on 30 April, the morning after its liberation. Touring the camp, consumed by an icy rage, she had photographed with unflinching professionalism. Many of Lee's closest friends were Jewish, or political dissidents and that alone had been sufficient cause to become one of the emaciated corpses piled in heaps like cordwood, or a living skeleton in striped garb. As Lee photographed, she was constantly checking the faces of the living and the dead to see if any of her friends were among them. She saw and recorded prisoners who died as she stood there. She photographed the battered faces of the captured guards and of the dead SS soldiers, some of whom had been beaten to death by the prisoners.

At the edge of the camp, they found a train. It had left Buchenwald a month earlier with 2,310 prisoners on board. On arrival in Dachau, the SS commanders were preoccupied with the fighting nearby so they

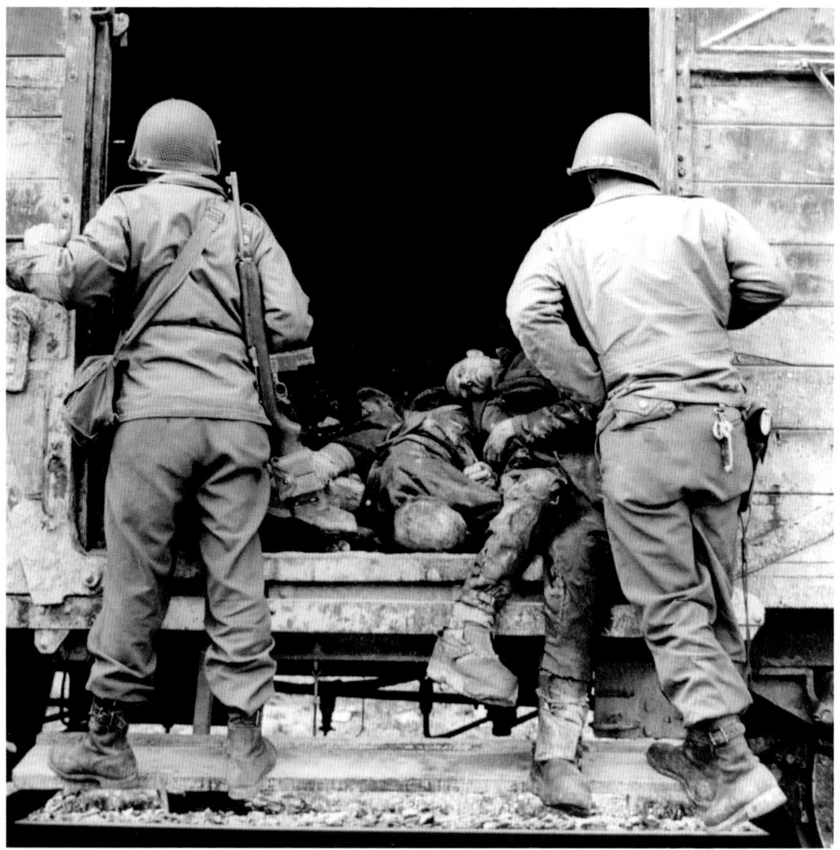

US soldiers examine a rail truck loaded with dead prisoners, Dachau, Germany 1945, by Lee Miller

posted guards with orders to shoot any escapees. The guards were not kept busy. By that time the prisoners were mostly dead and the GIs found only one survivor. Dr Jacques Hindermeyer, a French medical expert who was an eyewitness, told me Lee took a photograph that he himself could not take because he was too overcome with revulsion when the GIs opened the door of a rail car and the rotting corpses flopped out.

That night Lee and Scherman found a billet in Hitler's apartment in Munich. They typed their dispatches, looted the place and drove east to Berchtesgaden, at that moment the front line of the US Army. They persuaded two GIs with a weapons Jeep to take them four kilometres into enemy territory to Obersalzburg where they arrived as Hitler's house was going up in flames. Ignoring the danger of presenting their silhouettes to snipers, Lee and Scherman photographed what Scherman later described as *'the funeral pyre of the Third Reich'*.

It was the last time they worked together. Scherman went west to Paris, London and eventually New York and Lee was soon to follow the GIs into Denmark and then Austria. Scherman must have been the best friend she ever had. He loved her and understood her better than anyone, but he could not live with her. Later he told me that being part of her creative process was like feeding his brain through a meat grinder, but he remained steadfastly loyal to her for the rest of his days. He also became one of the most important people in my life in his role as something of an alternative father after Roland died.

Months later in London Scherman had second thoughts and put an idea to *Vogue* for a joint project with Lee. Roland could see this was likely to lead to Lee's permanent disappearance from his life and with the collusion of *Vogue* studio boss Sylvia Redding persuaded Scherman to kill the idea.

I don't know where Roland was on Victory in Europe Day, 8 May 1945 and perhaps he did not remember. He told me he got terribly drunk and climbed up a lamp post with a flag; but looking at the news photos from that famous day it seemed that his behaviour was quite normal. It is possible that Eluard was staying with him. He had come over from Paris as a guest of the British Council ten days earlier and would have relished the fun.

Lee came home in July for a month. Roland was in Norwich much of the time, but Scherman was still there. Outwardly, things seemed normal; however Lee and Roland found that severe tensions had arisen between them. I think Lee's combat experience made Roland feel somewhat inadequate and jealous. His Surrealist muse had leapt from her pedestal and against the odds had made an outstanding career as a combat photo-journalist. For Lee's part, she was at a fork in the road. She had been highly acclaimed for her work, which gave her a real purpose in life. Roland wanted her at home as his partner and she felt torn by the choice between the man she loved and a career she felt she could not quit. The injustice of murdered people, dying children and homeless refugees burned within her and she wanted to use the power of her journalism to put things right. Like thousands of other couples, they found living with peace was a greater challenge for their relationship than surviving the war had been. There was a full-scale row with screaming and door-slamming and Lee left for Paris.

Roland, who still had six months to serve in the Army, immediately added to his distractions by burying himself in the plans for re-opening the London Gallery. He regularly wrote to Lee, beseeching her to return, or even just to write. But not the faintest echo came in answer to his pleas.

8 1946-50
Forks in the Road

'My work is a life's dream.'

Scottie Wilson. Title of his exhibition at the London Gallery, 18 February 1948

Lee left Paris alone, heading for Vienna in Scherman's big olive drab Chevrolet emblazoned with the US Army star. Her photograph of the opera star Irmgard Seefried singing an aria from *Madame Butterfly* in the remains of the burned out Vienna Opera House gives us an image of the triumph of art and culture over the surrounding horrors. Behind the scenes in the Wilhelmina Children's Hospital Lee found few triumphs. It was the true story behind the film *The Third Man.* The black-marketeers had stolen all the drugs and people were dying for lack of medication. Lee wrote;

> For an hour I watched a baby die. He was the dark dusty blue of these waltz-filled Vienna nights, the same colour as the striped garb of the Dachau skeletons, the same imaginary blue as Strauss' Danube. I'd thought all babies looked alike, but that was healthy babies; there are many faces for the dying. This wasn't a two months baby, he was a skinny gladiator.[1]

Lee began to recognise that the war had failed to cleanse all the demons from Europe. Her depression and disillusionment encircled her and made it impossible for her to write to Roland as this unfinished and unposted letter shows;

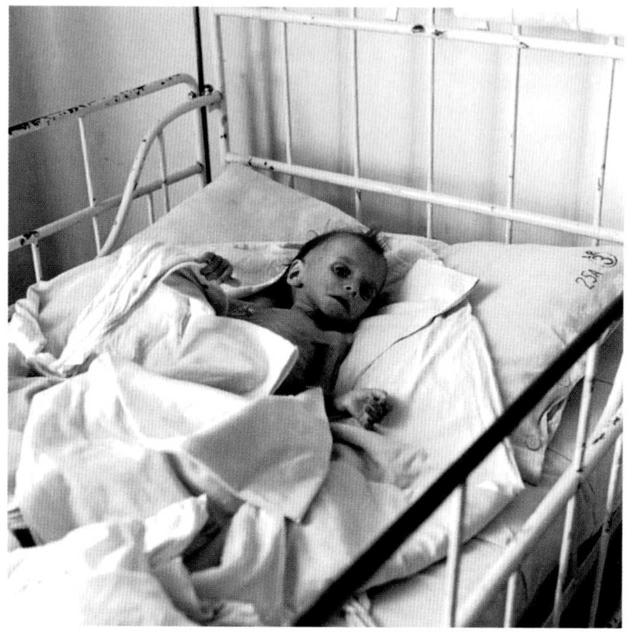

'Nearly all these children will die in next few years if not now.'
Wilhelminenspital, Vienna, Austria 1945, by Lee Miller

> Darling Roland, I haven't forgotten you. ... Every evening when I could take the time and certainly have the interest to write you I think that tomorrow I'll know the ultimate answer or that my depression will have lifted or my exaltation ebbed or whatever so that I'll be able to write a more balanced report ... containing some sort of decision ... staying or coming home licked.[2]

Despite Lee's silence, Roland persisted, regularly writing letters that were never answered. Audrey Withers and other *Vogue* staff helped him keep track of Lee through her despatches and service messages. Inevitably, Roland was not alone for long. Emma,[3] the niece of a famous German art historian entered his life. She was soft and gentle, with blue eyes set in a pleasant open face capped with fair hair. They took long walks together on Hampstead Heath. At the most, she would drink a small sherry; she was kind and steadfast and she loved Roland selflessly. Before long, she had moved into Downshire Hill and further into Roland's heart than either of them expected. Roland was torn between his two loves and in January 1946 wrote Lee an ultimatum;

> Darling
> For so long I have tried to understand your silence. A silence which not only touches me deeply but, so I'm told affects your dealings with your office, your parents and Aziz. … Darling Lee, I ask you for an immediate reply – cable me as soon as you get this – what are you doing, when are you coming home? My reasons for asking are vital. You asked me before leaving if I had some girl I loved as well as you – now I have.
> Lee – my darling – answer
> Roland.[4]

When the letter caught up with Lee in Budapest, she ignored it. She and *Time-Life* photographer John Phillips had just witnessed the execution by firing squad of László Bardossy, the former Fascist Prime Minister of Hungary. Lee and Phillips were billeted together in a convent, but Lee got them both thrown out, mainly due to her propensity for hard drinking and filling up the place with refugees. Lee drove the Chevrolet to some remote villages with her assistant, a young photographer Robert Halmi. The Russians, who had occupied the country, pounced on her and locked her up. Halmi forged her a pass that got her out after a week, during which time she had charmed her captors and consumed all their vodka.

In the meantime, Scherman had heard about Emma. Realising Lee's position with Roland was threatened, he cabled her via John Phillips. The message was brief; GO HOME YOUR POSITION WITH ROLAND IS THREATENED. Lee's reply to Scherman was one word; OK.

Roland had been 'stood down' from active service for some weeks before his de-mobilisation from the army on 31 January. After the obligatory shattering binges, he celebrated further by taking a trip to Paris. There he reconnected with Picasso, Eluard and other friends such as Parisot, Hugnet, Fin Vilató and Alain Gheerbrant, the anthropologist. It was he who Roland was with on 16 February when, out of the blue, Lee arrived. She had crashed and abandoned Scherman's Chevrolet some weeks earlier and had begged rides across half of Europe. She looked like a character from a horror movie, suffering from a debilitating disease that made her face haggard and chalk white and her gums bleed continuously. Extremes of physical, mental, emotional and spiritual exhaustion had driven her into a crashed heap. Roland tenderly scooped her up and they returned to Downshire Hill. Emma, ever-loving of Roland and mindful of the longstanding relationship between the two, moved out. Re-establishing their relationship proved difficult after so much in both of them had changed. Superficially Lee's health recovered quickly. The effect of traumatic events she had witnessed was for the moment delayed like a time bomb.

To distract themselves from painful issues, Lee forced herself back into mainstream fashion work for *Vogue* and Roland kept up his frantic pace with the London Gallery. The re-opening at 23 Brook Street was an act of faith that bordered on the reckless. Behind Roland's back, Mesens vituperated openly about the 'Stalinists' Penrose and Eluard in a way that must have reached his ears. In the face of Mesens's disloyalty, it is almost unbelievable that Roland should have wanted to press ahead; but he did. He was so fervent in his passions he was blinded to the perfidies of others.

Previously, in January 1946, Mesens himself had reawakened another sleeping genie. Mesens and Read invited Roland to a meeting to discuss the creation of a Modern Arts Centre from which a Museum of Modern Art in London could eventually be planned. Others attending were Peter Watson, a wealthy and well-connected man rumoured to be

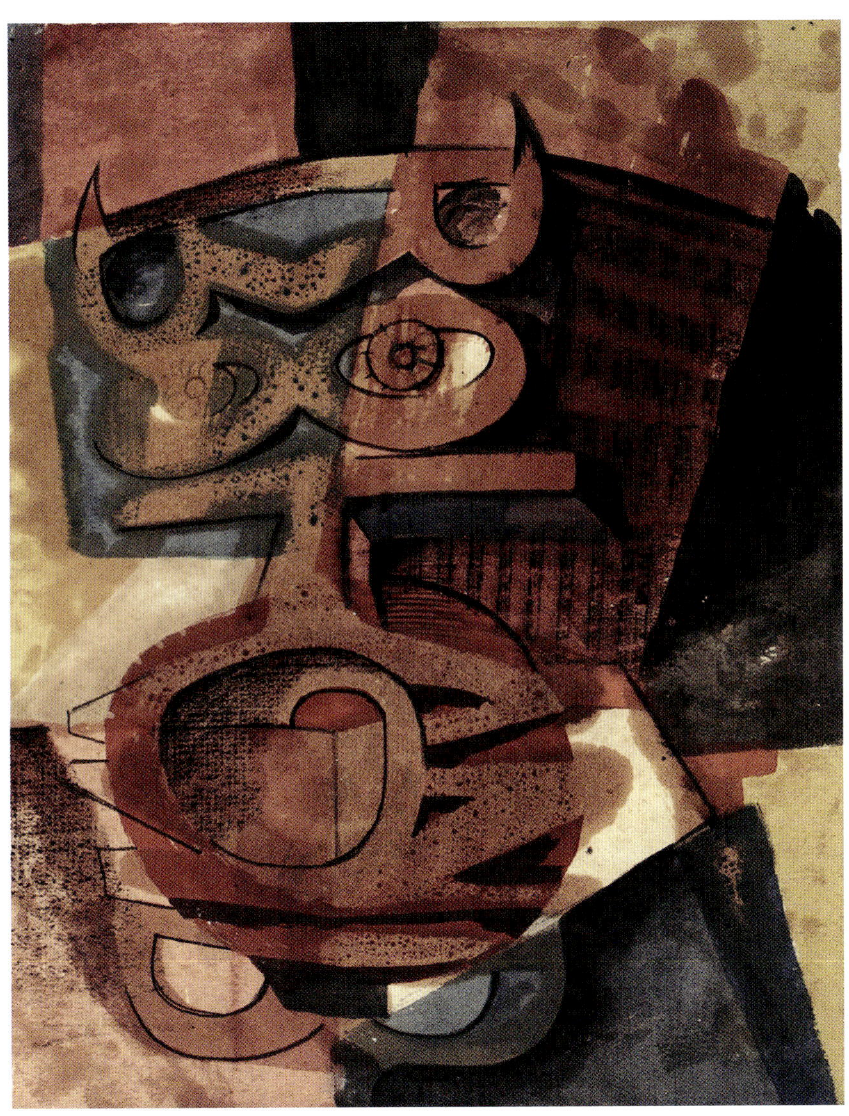

Self Portrait, 1947, Gouache and pencil on paper

the illegitimate son of Edward VII, E.C. (Peter) Gregory, the Director of the publishers Lund Humphries and George Hoellering, the manager of the Academy Cinema in Oxford Street which showed arthouse films.

The art historian Douglas Cooper attended the next meeting where Read formulated this statement of their objectives;

> Such an institution as we have in mind should be international in scope, should cover all the arts with a view to promoting their inter-relationship and should be open to experimental manifestations which are outside the scope of commercial enterprise and not yet given official or public recognition.[5]

They were well aware that Alfred Barr's success with the Museum of Modern Art in New York was largely due to his ability to persuade rich patrons to donate or loan works to the museum, giving it a superb permanent collection. Although some potential patrons were rankled by the refusal of the British public art galleries to buy modern works, it was obvious that no real support existed in England and the cost of housing such a permanent collection would be crippling. More importantly it would bring a static influence where versatility and quick response were needed. The committee's left-wing views also gave them concern that rich British patrons might have too much power to interfere and they wanted above all to keep their organisation independent.

Roland suggested that a manifesto should be drawn up and circulated among potential backers to raise funds. In the short term, the committee met the expenses from their own pockets, supplemented by donations from Roland, Watson and Gregory. Five sub committees were envisaged to cover the fields of Painting and Sculpture, Architecture, Music, Film and Literature.

Subsequent meetings refined the ideas and James Richards the architect, Frederick Ashton the choreographer, the actress Peggy Ashcroft, Brunius, Geoffrey Grigson and Robert Melville joined the committee, but trouble soon appeared. Cooper had his own agenda for using the Modern Arts Centre as a weapon in his vendetta against the Tate and Mesens launched vicious attacks on Read and Roland, expressing his annoyance at *'... gentlemen of leisure on the Committee'*, as opposed to *'businessmen like himself and Hoellering'*.[6] This was ironic, considering that Mesens's ability to run the London Gallery was already being badly compromised by his dissolute behaviour and could never have existed without Roland's financial support.

Vogue invited Lee to New York for a celebration of her achievements as a photojournalist and Roland accompanied her on one of the new scheduled air services, arriving on 19 May 1946. Lee was much fêted by Condé Nast, the *Vogue* publishers, with glamorous events including a dinner. The art dealer Julien Levy lent them his apartment which was filled with Surrealist works such as examples of Joseph Cornell's boxes, early work by Dalí and the wartime work of Ernst, Tanguy and Man Ray which was new to Roland.

By chance Paalen was in New York and made a happy reunion with Roland, but to Lee's concern, Emma was also there. It was the first inkling that Lee had of Roland's inability to detach himself from a beautiful woman. Over the next two or three years Lee became resigned to her rival's intermittent appearances in Roland's life. *'I accepted your life with Emma'*, she wrote later, *'as gracefully as possible, to prove that I loved you and the fact that your love for me was diluted and weakened was unimportant as long as you were happy'*.[7]

Lee's parents were to know nothing of this and they welcomed Roland with their characteristic generosity. Theodore loved the excitement of all new discoveries, but modern painting was an extreme challenge for him. It was the obvious affection between Roland and Lee that caused him and Florence to accept Roland with enthusiasm and forgive him his art.

Another flight took them to Phoenix, Arizona and they drove to a remote spot in the desert near Oak Creek Canyon, Sedona.

Here Ernst had come to live, building a small wooden house for

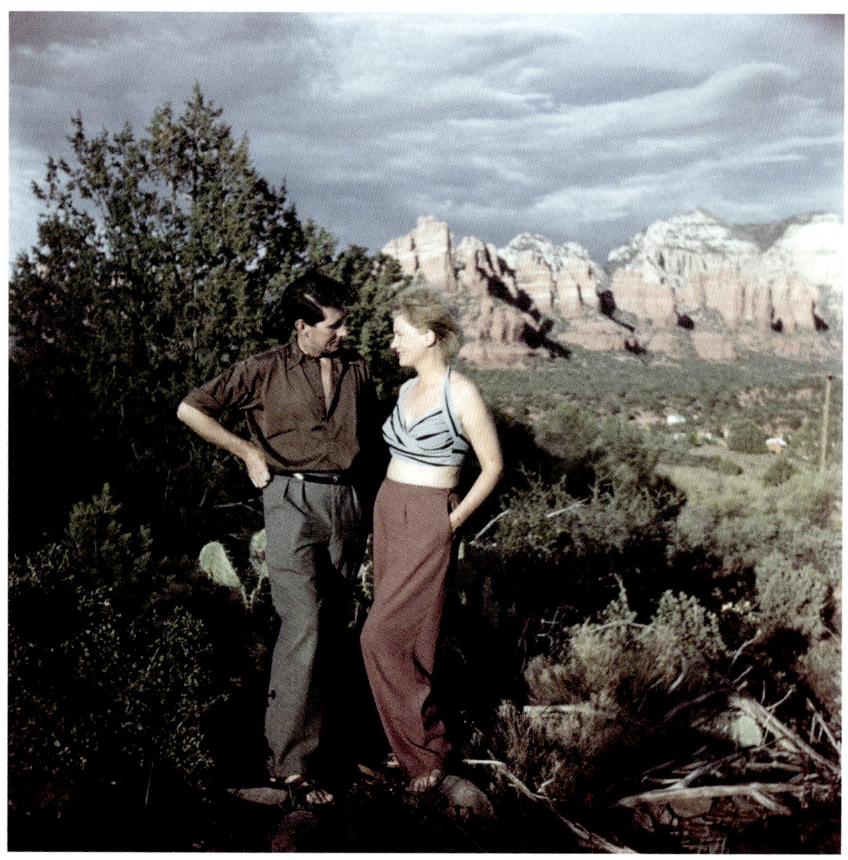

Roland Penrose and Lee Miller, Sedona, Arizona, USA, 1946

himself and his new love, the painter Dorothea Tanning. Roland felt he had stepped into a landscape created by his friend. The harsh surfaces of the sheer-faced canyons glowed in the raking evening light, resembling Ernst's paintings from Paris before the war.

Ernst was fascinated by the cultures of the native Americans. Evidence was all around him of the great antiquity of their civilisations, but more importantly, he had managed to make friends with the Hopi Indians on the reservation eighty miles to the north-east. They drove

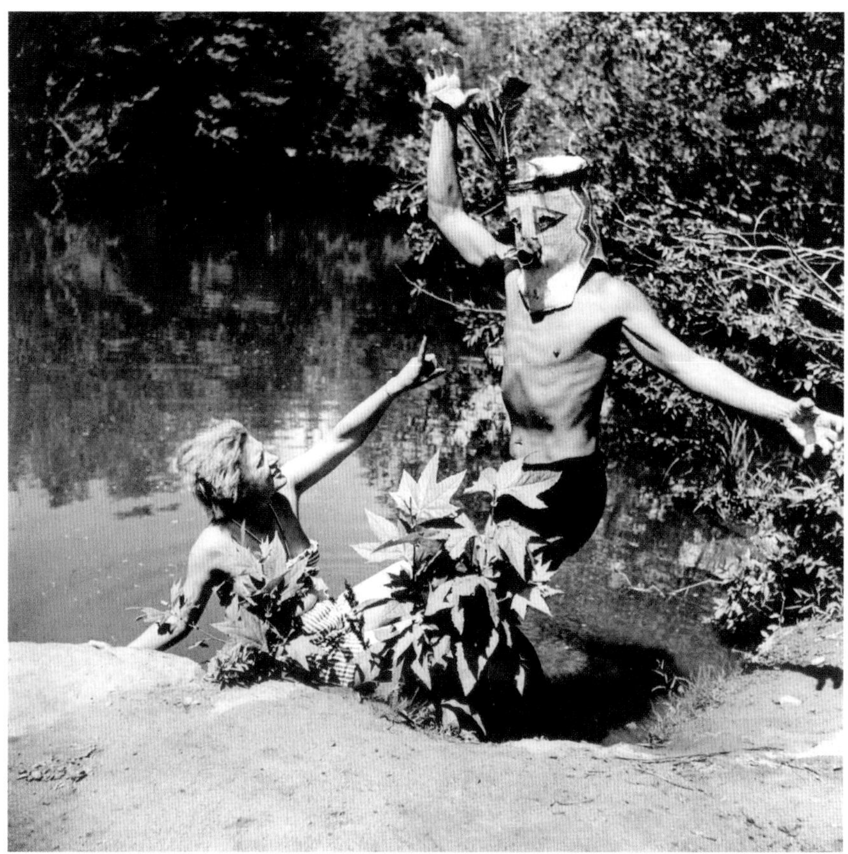

Lee Miller and Max Ernst, Oak Creek Canyon, Sedona, Arizona, USA, 1946

there to watch a rain dance where the dancers performed holding live rattlesnakes. The dance worked, a down-pour ensued and they were only saved from becoming hopelessly bogged in the mud because Ernst knew what was coming and insisted on leaving early.

Nearly thirty years later I had the great good fortune to witness a similar event in the village on Second Mesa. A double file of dancers stamped and swayed to the rhythm of a drum. Their Katchina masks and costumes bore bold geometric designs and strong patches of colour, adorned with feathers, pine branches and leaves. Chanting swelled out to us from inside of their masks, penetrating to the marrow of my spine, bringing fear inextricably combined with exhilaration. All the little hairs on the back of my neck stood up; I was light-headed and cold despite the sun. The invocation soared to the sky and then one at a time the dancers disappeared into the earth, into their kiva, their sacred place. We stayed until dusk and then drove off into the desert and slept under the stars. It seemed that merely by witnessing, I had undergone an initiation. I could feel life in the stones of the desert.

Roland was always fascinated by the connection between art and magic. He had been deeply moved by the Hopi dancers and it reinforced his belief that the truest forms of art and magic come from similar places deep inside the human spirit.

Ernst and Dorothea had endured a tough time following Ernst's acrimonious split from Peggy Guggenheim in New York and they had come to Arizona to build a new life. Ernst's sales had practically dried up. He would set off on long journeys in his car towing a trailer loaded with paintings wrapped in blankets and return without one sold. He decided to paint small works that could be easily transported in a suitcase. Roland bought an exquisite example, *Microbe Vu a L'Œil Nu,* that despite its miniature scale (55 by 70 millimetres) perfectly conveyed the vastness of the canyons.

In Los Angeles, they stayed with Lee's brother Erik and his wife Mafy. Roland had met them previously in Cairo, where Erik had been working for Aziz as an air-conditioning engineer. They visited Man Ray who had taken a studio in a courtyard off Vine Street, where he was living with Juliet Browner, a woman of gazelle like delicacy who had been a dancer with Martha Graham.

In Roland's absence, Read had returned from New York and with the information gained from his own meetings with Alfred Barr had developed the ideas further. He rejected the use of 'Museum' in the title as too far removed from the experimental side; and after much discussion

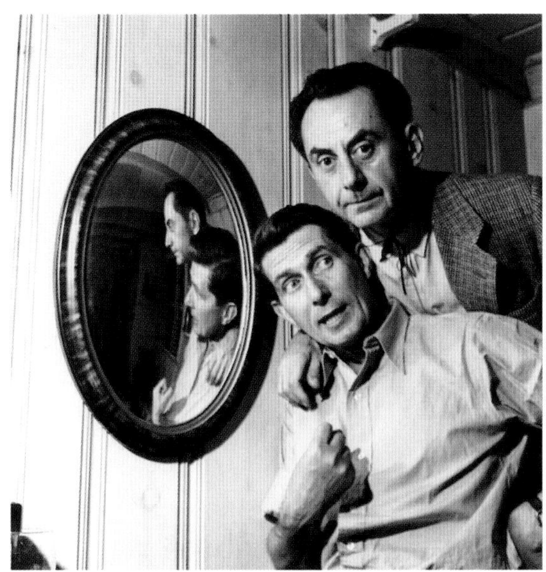

Roland Penrose and Man Ray, Vine Street, Los Angeles, California, USA, 1946, by Lee Miller

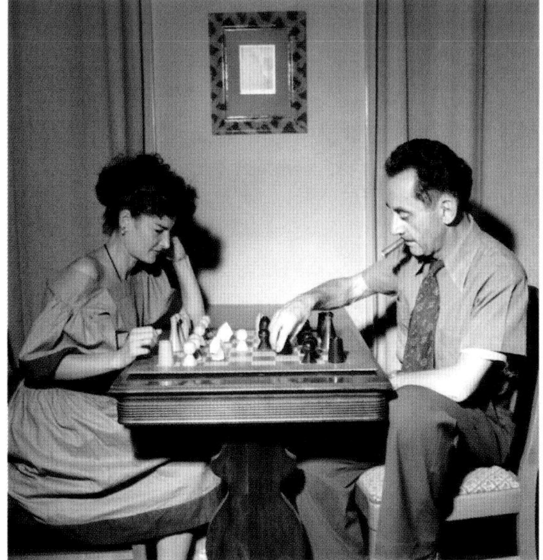

Juliet (Browner) and Man Ray, Los Angeles, USA, 1946, by Lee Miller

the new name of the Institute of Contemporary Art was adopted, to become known as the ICA.

Roland returned to find battle-lines drawn up in the committee. Mesens, Brunius and Cooper had aligned themselves against the other members, but when Cooper resigned Mesens and Brunius toned down their objections. I have often heard it said that Cooper was the only enemy that Roland had and it was also commented that with an enemy like Cooper he needed no others.

On 5 November the bookshop of the London Gallery reopened with the show of Wilfredo Lam's drawings and then a month later a large collective exhibition marked the opening of the ground floor. Surrealism was strongly represented in the show with works by Miró, Delvaux, Magritte, Masson, Paalen and others, mainly taken from Roland and Mesens' stock that had survived the war. In keeping with the principle of the gallery, the show included lesser-known artists such as Craxton, Lake, Morton and Scottie Wilson, who Mesens simultaneously showed at the Barcelona Restaurant in Beak Street.

To support herself and Mesens, Sybil had gone to work and risen to become chief buyer at Dickens and Jones and this vacated the post of secretary in the Gallery. The young George Melly eventually took the position, recently de-mobbed from the British Navy and soon to become the renowned jazz musician and indefatigable champion of Surrealism. Melly and Roland did not hit it off. Roland was appalled by Melly's egregious behaviour, frequent drunkenness and the recurring absences caused by his other life as a jazz singer but later Melly earned Roland's respect when he threw Douglas Cooper bodily out of the London Gallery.

In France the official version of Surrealism still rumbled on. Breton had returned from the United States and was trying to rally the faithful with a new manifesto and exhibition. The June 1947 *Exposition Internationale du Surréalisme* in the Galerie Maeght, Paris, had a deluxe version of the catalogue with a foam-rubber breast on the cover, surrounded by a black velvet collar titled *Prier de Toucher*[8] by Marcel Duchamp. Roland had a copy in his library and I can remember from experience that the breast's realism was such that its detached form chilled even rampant teenage ardour but might have suited a necrophiliac. This isolated fragment of a woman became a metaphor of the movement; a small part of a once beautiful entirety, with its adornments failing to hide its artificiality. Despite Breton's pleas for works, the British group was represented by only eight living artists including Maddox, Banting and Scottie Wilson. Roland showed two paintings, *Jacobite Jacobin* and *Moon Tiger Night.*

In March Mesens mounted *The Cubist Spirit in Its Time* with a wide range of artists including Wyndham Lewis, Marcoussis, Masson, Severini and others beside classic works by Braque and Picasso from Roland's collection. The show, which intelligently explored the links between Surrealism and Cubism, drew the scorn of Cooper, who by now considered himself the pope of Cubism and excluded all but Picasso, Braque, Gris and Léger from his canon.

After Christmas Lee left for Saint Moritz on an assignment with her friend and colleague Peggy Riley, then *Vogue*'s European features editor, who later became the well-known art critic and presenter Rosamund Russell. Lee wrote to Roland;

> Darling, This is a hell of a romantic way to tell you that I'll shortly be knitting little clothes for a little man – but it seems to be true. […] So far no resentment or anguish or mind changing panic – only a mild astonishment that I'm so happy about it. Let me know how you feel about being a parent – sure you want it? and why? There is only one thing,– MY WORK ROOM IS NOT GOING TO BE A NURSERY. How about your studio? HA HA. […] Love Lee.[9]

The threat of using his studio as a nursery jolted Roland and when a larger house across the street, number 36, came up for sale, he arranged to trade it for 21 Downshire Hill. It was a bitter winter and, once the move

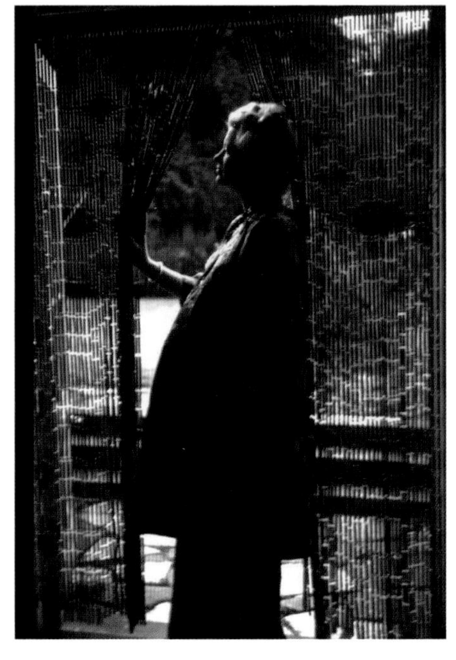
RIGHT: Lee Miller pregnant in doorway, England 1947

was complete on 28 February 1947, they were miserably cold in their new home devoid of carpets, curtains and fuel due to post-war shortages. They smashed up furniture for the fire, burned the bed legs and the bases of the sculptures. Lee was on the verge of consigning some of the ethnographic works to the flames when a neighbour loaned them some coal.

Lee's pregnancy was fraught. She became ill with pleurisy that developed into pneumonia and then a viral infection like mumps. Nurses attended by day and night and her doctor, Carl Goldman stood over her and said; *'You are going to have that baby if I have to stand here for the next three months with my knee in your crotch'*. Lee complied. People have often told me that Lee became pregnant to ensnare Roland, but that does not square with my parent's account. They told me that medical opinion had informed Lee it was impossible for her to become pregnant. Later I discovered she had been infected with gonorrhoea resulting from rape as a seven year old. This with later miscarriages and abortions were thought to have finally rendered her infertile. My arrival was contrary to all medical opinion and a great surprise.

Although repelled by the messier aspects of biology, Roland had always been fascinated by Jeep's pregnancy and had done an enchanting decalcomania of the cat, drawing the kittens in her womb. Now Lee's pregnancy produced a sense of wonder in Roland that prompted a

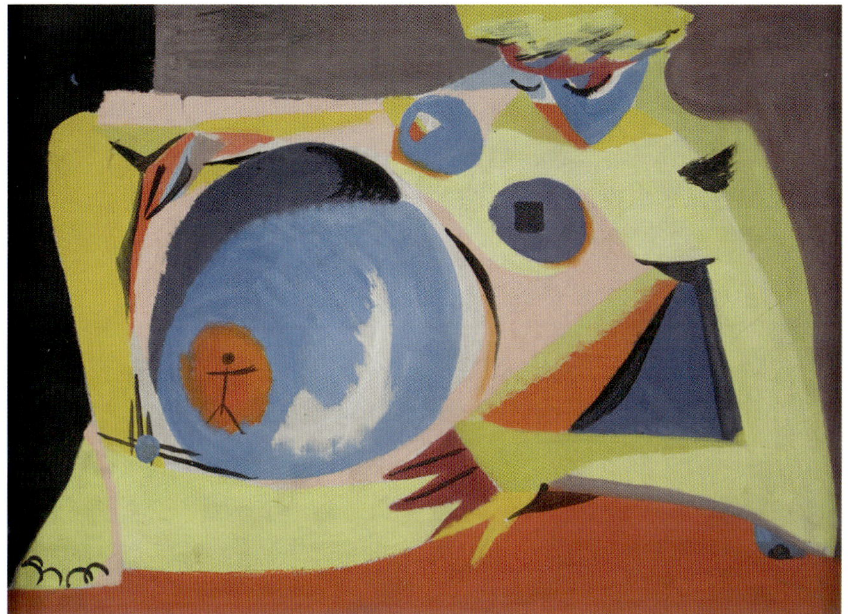

Nude, 1947, Oil on Board. The Penrose Collection

new series of photographs, paintings, drawings and an engraving. The paintings signalled another radical style change. Many works became dominated by primary colours, some with yellows that took on a strident acidic edge.

Lee appears as a deity, presiding over the feminine mystery of creation. The rounded swelling of her belly, both threatening and inviting, contains symbols that vary through the different versions from a Greek temple to the aqueous blue of oceans on the surface of our planet in *Faites vos Jeux*. In this work, amidst a mass of crumpled bed sheets Lee is seen knitting – a rare event that would have been a last resort to stave off boredom. The woollen yarn connects to an illustration of a four-wheeled carriage, a typically Roland pun on the 'carriage' of pregnancy. The title, translatable as *Place your Bets* perhaps refers to the hazards inherent in the process. The climax of his celebration of Lee's

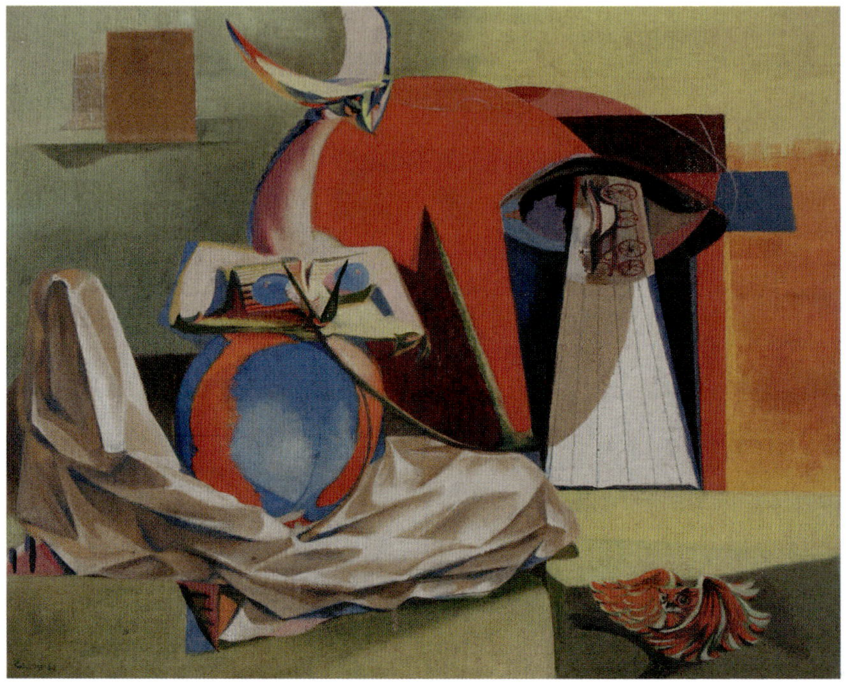

Faites vos Jeux, 1947, oil on canvas with collage

pregnancy is a large painting titled *First View*, here I appear as a small inquisitive green lizard, poised to grapple life with enthusiasm. He was right about me, except for my colour, but maybe I lost that together with the tail he gave me.

Roland's household continued true to form, run by Annie Clements, his Scottish housekeeper who remained utterly unfazed. In the spring Valentine came to stay for a long period and Aziz arrived. Lee was confined to bed, but Roland set up a card table in the bedroom and in the evenings they all dined together, with Aziz telling marvellous stories such as adventures from *The Arabian Nights.* Aziz had come to give Lee her divorce, which he did under Muslim law by saying, '*I divorce thee*', repeated three times.

Roland and Lee's wedding at Hampstead Registry Office was

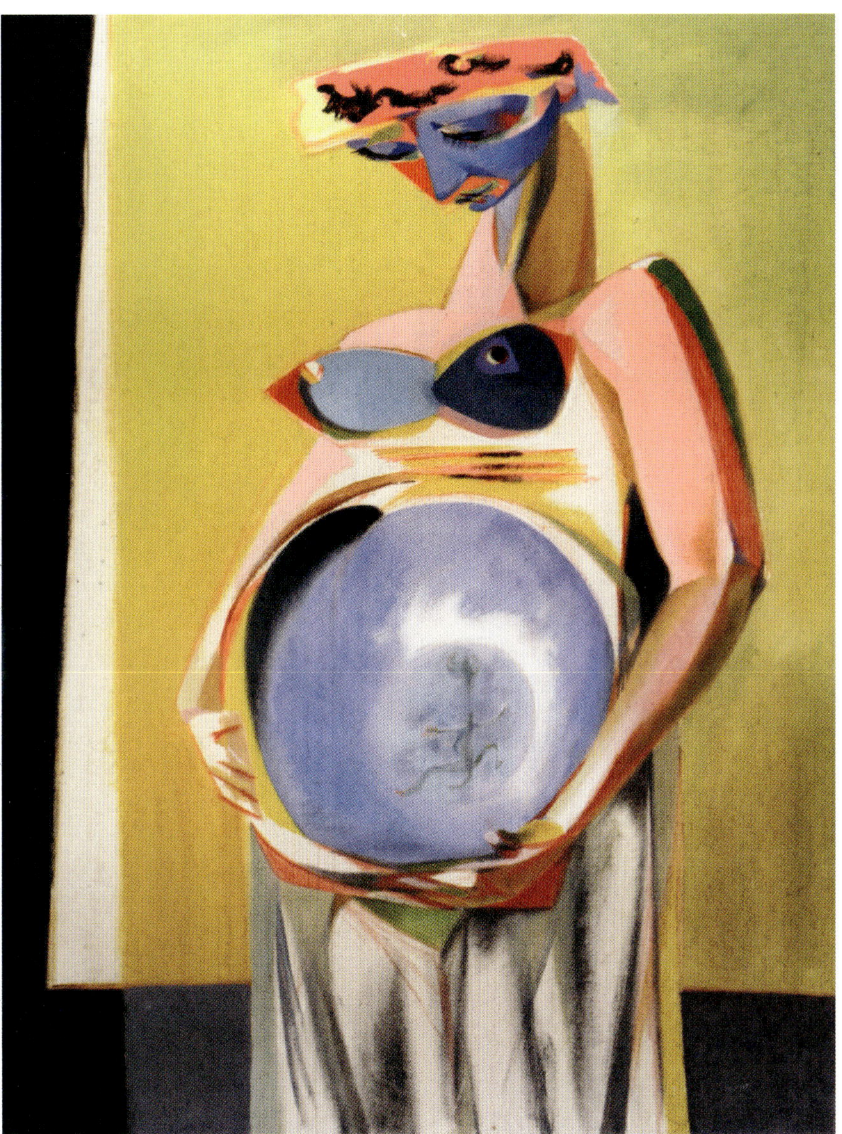

First View, 1947. Oil on Canvas

attended by Valentine and Aziz, two close friends, Timmie O'Brien, managing editor at *Vogue* and her Australian husband Terry, John Lake and Sylvia Redding as their witnesses. Outside a street photographer rushed up to take a picture of the newly-wed couple and at the sight of Lee's bulging midriff, apologetically backed off, sure that they would not want their 'indiscretion' recorded.

It was straight back to bed for Lee, but Roland made her a special letter he called *The First Letter to Mrs Penrose.* He made a decalcomania with gouache and using a wet brush calligraphed *Mrs Lee Penrose* and the address, later picking out the letters in red. He added in crayon a red stamp and a postmark with the date, 4 May 1947. He glued the work to an envelope in which he placed three playing cards from the word game *KAN-U-GO.* They were the letters I-O-U and went with the ace of diamonds, a heart shape cut from silver paper and a corner torn from a piece of blue cardboard bearing the words '*and love Roland*'.

For the second time in their lives two Surrealists, who had repudiated family values and civil contracts as bourgeois, had married. Roland would later try and dissuade me from marrying the woman I loved, saying;

> Lee and I only did it when we knew you were on the way. There is no need for it unless you want to provide a secure home for a child.

I never could understand how marriage automatically created security as he implied and although on that occasion I did not marry, it was for other reasons.

Lee, who had comforted battlefield casualties and faced the living dead of Dachau, had a pathological fear of maternity. The idea of breast-feeding was abhorrent and she was relieved when Dr Goldman decreed that she would have a Caesarean delivery. Secretly, Lee was sure she would not survive and in the early morning of 9 September she wrote a message for Roland;

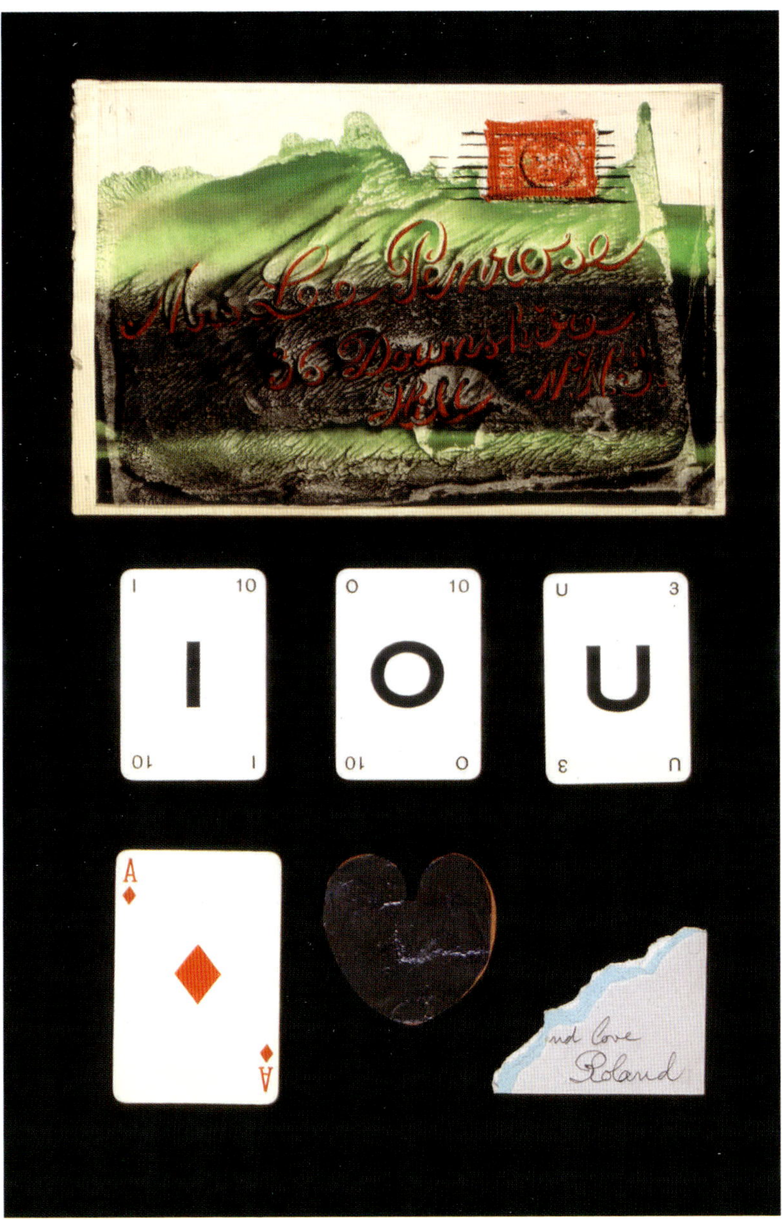

First letter to Mrs Penrose, 1947, Collage

> I keep saying to everyone – 'I didn't waste a minute, all my life – I had a wonderful time' but I know, myself, now – that if I had it all over again I'd be even more free with my ideas – with my body and my affection. Above all, I'd try to find some way of breaking though the silence, which imposes itself on me in matters of sentiment. I'd have let you, Roland, know how much and how passionately and how tenderly I love you. Next week, if I am still here I will probably be as off-hand again as in the past … .[10]

Roland waited at home and recorded in his diary *a morning of great beauty*.[11] Eluard was staying with him and when the call from the London Clinic came announcing my arrival, he took an exquisite Man Ray photograph of Nusch and wrote on it;

> Pour notre amie Lee
> et son petit garçon nouveau neé
> que Nusch aurait tant aimé,
> elle t'aimait vraiment,
> Lee chérie
>
> Paul Eluard
> 9 septembre 1947[12]

A few days later Eluard visited Lee and me. On his return he drew on plywood the figures of two birds, one tall and elegant, the other a stubbly chick with an air of intense demand on its face. He signed it;

> La beauté de Lee aujourd'hui
> Anthony
> C'est du soleil sur ton lit
> Paul Eluard
> 15 septembre 1947[13]

'... *he is so ugly, snout like a pig, hands like a bruiser and the toughest looks ever known* ...' Roland wrote to Lee's parents.[14] It seems he was a little slow in bonding with me. In keeping with his own upbringing, Roland was a remote parent, entirely unskilled around babies, but in time he became thrilled to have a son. He told me I was named Antony because he loved temptation and bestowed it on me as my cradle blessing. It might have had something to do with the show the London gallery was running, *The Temptation of St Anthony*, a competition set up by the MGM Studios Inc. to provide a painting that would serve a dramatic purpose in a movie. Among the contestants exhibited in the show were Carrington, Dalí, Delvaux, Ernst and Tanning. Ernst won, a fact Roland attributed to his susceptibility to temptation and his consequent understanding of it.

Being born a baby was inevitable and risky, as Lee was an avowed child-hater but my smartest move was being born a boy. Lee had written to her parents saying that she wanted a son she could teach him to use bad language becomingly and she could play with trains and have a workshop to tinker in.[15] I eventually gratified those three desires, but in the beginning things went wrong fast.

Roland had no way of understanding that Lee was suffering from acute post-traumatic stress syndrome. She never spoke of her war experiences, but Scherman and others who knew her at the time told me her witnessing the liberation of Buchenwald and Dachau affected her profoundly and irreversibly. In 1947 little was understood about her condition. Today there are many approaches, but Lee and the thousands like her had only the coping strategy of the *stiff upper lip*. If that failed there was always the whiskey bottle to anesthetise the unbearable turmoil of suppressed anguish.

Fortunately for me, Nanny Woodward was engaged to dote on me. Although protective and on occasions tender and affectionate, Lee found motherhood a repugnant process. Lee's reserve towards expressing affection and 'sentiment' is something that can probably be attributed to her early childhood traumas, which led her to live her life in a series of watertight compartments. People from one compartment were seldom allowed into another and some areas were off limits to all.

Roland may have intuitively recognised this compartmentalisation in his painting *Unsleeping Beauty*. The sleeping female figure lies on a rectangle of blue as if she is floating over water. Her body is composed of elements clearly not connected to each other. Breasts, abdomen, pelvis and legs lie in the right order, but separated. The background shows a landscape of mesas that corresponds to the view from Ernst's studio in Sedona, a sliver of a new moon glimmering over the hills as dusk settles. A lone figure from a companion painting titled *The Duchess* stands behind the sleeper. Her head is one large eye, perhaps a reference to Man Ray's famous *Indestructible Object*, or alternatively it may play with the way Lee's camera gave her the monocular vision of a Cyclops.

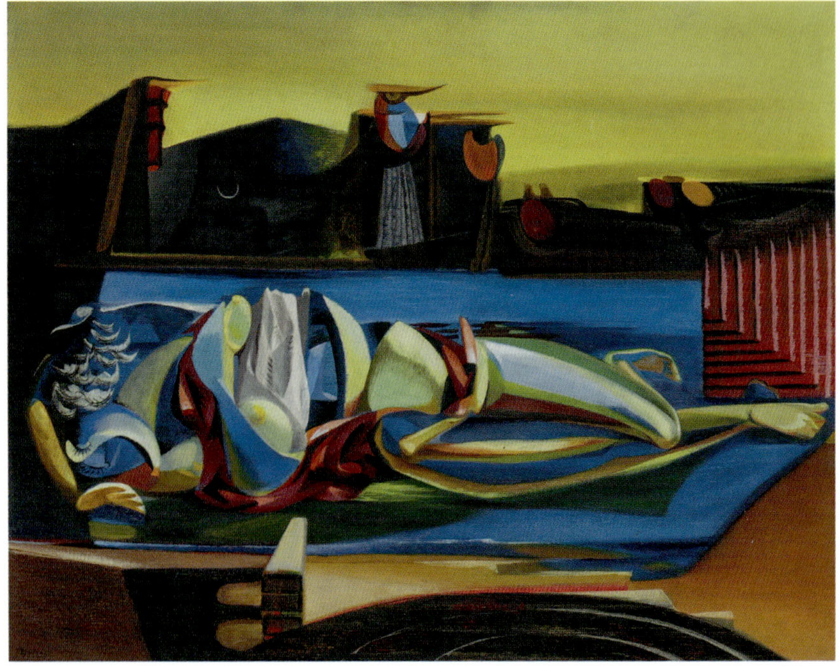

Unsleeping Beauty, 1946, oil on canvas. Private Collection

The ICA's first exhibition opened on 10 February 1948. Called *40 Years of Modern Art*, 1907–1947. A Selection from British Collections it was run on a wing and a prayer at the Academy Hall, Oxford Street. The hall was the basement of the Academy Cinema and managed by George Hoellering who had generously guaranteed the hire of the space against loss. Outside in an open space provided by a German bomb, a Surrealist nude sculpture titled *Kneeling Woman* Roland had bought from F. E. McWilliam (known as Mac), presided on a tall plinth. It was Mac's first commission and a marvellous advertisement for the show, as her photograph appeared in the press and so many people stopped to look that the police tried to charge the ICA with obstructing the thoroughfare.

Private collections were the source of the loans as the national museums had made virtually no acquisitions of modern art. Roland, Read, Mesens, Mayor, Watson and a handful of others provided most of the 127 paintings and sculptures including five Picassos, three Braques, three Matisses and works by Dalí, de Chirico and Magritte. In response to criticisms from the committee about deviating from the aim of fostering new talent, a group of young artists was added that included Lucien Freud, John Craxton and Eduardo Paolozzi.

Today it is unthinkable that an 'amateur' exhibition in an ordinary hired hall could attract loans of key paintings, but then the comparatively low value of the works and the pioneering generosity of the lenders made it happen. Many had a sense of evangelism and were glad to make loans even under very risky circumstances. Lucien Freud told of how during the war Roland lent him Picasso's *Weeping Woman* for a private exhibition in his friend Hugh Willoughby's flat in Brighton. Freud left Hampstead with the unwrapped painting under his arm and on the train sat it on the seat opposite him. He recalled how the sunlight splashed on the colours and revealed their brilliance.[16] Today, on the rare occasions that she is allowed out of the Tate Gallery, she travels inside a sealed crate in an air-conditioned truck with special suspension and maximum security.

Over 20,000 people visited *40 Years of Modern Art*, marking it as an outstanding success. But although it raised the profile of the ICA, it failed to swell the membership and altercations behind the scenes had reached ugly levels. A faction headed by Geoffrey Grigson accused the ICA of being deflected from its original purpose at the head of the avant-garde and launched a vicious attack on Roland who had earlier called for his resignation on the grounds of non-attendance;

> What is one to think of Mr Penrose's snobbish jesuitry? … I propose thinking that the resignation of Mr. Roland Penrose be also called for, on the grounds that his position as a minor painter, buttressed by wealth and indeed by taste and his sincere energy in furthering the ICA, does not outweigh his zealous pursuit of compromise which is making the ICA ridiculous to those very artists it should help.[17]

Ultimately Roland's detractors had to concede that without Roland's effort there would have been no show and the ICA's financial survival depended on him and Watson. Management changes took place and the new committee found a permanent office in rooms at Edward Clark and Elizabeth Lutyens' home in 6 Fitzroy Street. Ewan Phillips was appointed as the first director. He had been trained at the Courtauld Institute as an art historian and had been known to Read since before the war. He was soon to be joined by Julie Lawson, a Javanese woman of great intelligence and beauty, who was fluent in five languages.

Concerts, film, poetry readings by T.S. Eliot, Cecil Day Lewis, Dylan Thomas and others and sell-out lectures on architecture organised in conjunction with the MARS group, all held in hired spaces, had filled the programme for the year. A few days before Christmas the ICA opened a show that became a landmark, *40,000 Years of Modern Art – A Comparison of Primitive and Modern,* again at the Academy Cinema.

In support of the ICA and in recognition of his gratitude to Roland who had loaned paintings to the Museum of Modern Art during the war,

Barr loaned Picasso's *Les Demoiselles d'Avignon*, asking only that Roland should meet the cost of the insurance. Cunard sponsored the show by shipping the large painting on the Queen Elizabeth, arriving only six days before the opening. Delays occurred in clearing customs and when the painting reached London, it was the day before the opening. It was then that Roland had one of the worst moments of his career. The painting was far too big to go through the door. Taking it off its stretcher was out of the question. They were stuck with it in the truck outside until someone realised that the same bomb that had provided the exhibition space for McWilliam's sculpture afforded their solution. A section of the gallery wall faced the bomb site and Hoellering agreed to allow a hole to be broken through to admit the painting. The exhibition attracted around forty thousand visitors and its impact on the press and young artists was gratifying. The sculptor William Turnbull, who was twenty-seven at the time, recalled.

> The exhibition 40,000 Years … meant a breakdown of certain hierarchical attitudes to art. I remember a discussion at the ICA in the 1950s about ethnographic art where there was someone who absolutely refused to accept the idea that it could be art. To him it was just a manifestation of a culture. So the outlook of the ICA towards European and international art was important and it was a view characteristic of Roland Penrose as well. It seemed an alternative to the British Romanticism going on after the war. … It was also the first place I'd come across in London outside a pub where you could meet friends in a casual way, it was as close as you could get to café life in Paris.[18]

The ICA was now on the map and set to become admired and sometimes envied internationally for its independent and radical stance. Its success sounded the death knell of the London Gallery. In May 1949 the London Gallery held a show of Roland's recent works, featuring *Faites vos Jeux* and *First View* among forty-two other paintings and drawings. A series of works tracing movement included *The Flight of Flies*, a magnified diary of insects that trailed threads as they buzzed around cavities in a log before disappearing into the blue. In *Getting Up And Going Out* the threads give us the track of a person who gets up, goes downstairs, walks down the street, meeting a friend who has emerged from the house opposite. The houses, which are shown in section, become two heads in conversation reflecting the friend's greetings.

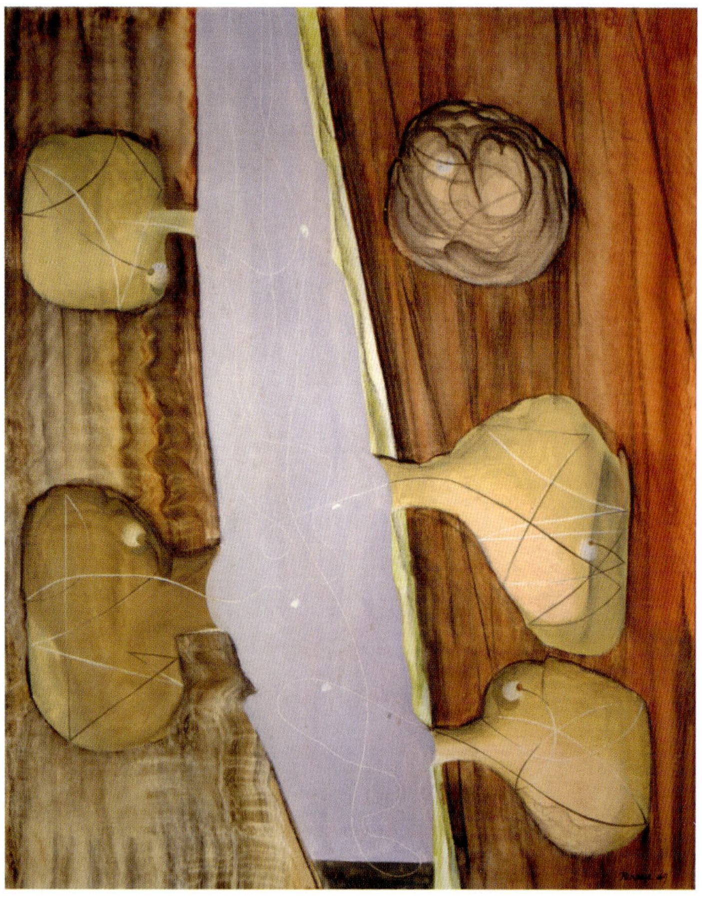

The Flight of Flies, 1949, Oil on Canvas

The painting titled *Don't You Hate Having Two Heads*, is almost certainly a self-portrait. Roland's body has become encased in steel armour like a medieval knight, perhaps to keep out the slings and arrows of people like Mesens and Cooper. A window allows us to see inside his abdomen where the tightly coiled black knots of bowel show the effects of extreme anxiety, deeply held inside the impenetrable metal casing. Between his thighs, he awarded himself an impressively long and sharp steel penis, with steel balls to match. He clearly still placed a high value on his virility.

Protruding from the top of the breastplate, two ovoid heads are engaged in a tense dialogue. For me this represents his internal conflict between his desire to continue promoting the work of others and organising the ICA and the desire to be an artist in his own right. Some of the preparatory sketches show a third head in place, possibly a premonition of his career as a writer. The exhibition at the London Gallery was to be his last one-man show for thirty years.

The London Gallery itself had less than a year to run. The subsequent programme of exhibitions concentrated on young artists such as Lam, Craxton, the first one-man show for Desmond Morris and a new discovery, Austin Cooper. The bold high profile exhibitions were absent. Roland's focus had been on the ICA and the gallery had suffered from the tensions between him and Mesens. Heavy losses over two years forced the directors to close. Watson, Zwemmer, Mesens and Roland gathered one foggy day to auction among themselves the remaining stock owned by the gallery. George Melly wrote;

> My task was to remove the works one by one from the stacks and show them to the reluctant punters. Edouard [Mesens] (in part out of pride?) bought most, Roland very little (understandable in that his walls were already crammed with masterpieces), Zwemmer a few things to show goodwill, while Pat Pat (Watson) bid for nothing … The amount realised was laughable … .[19]

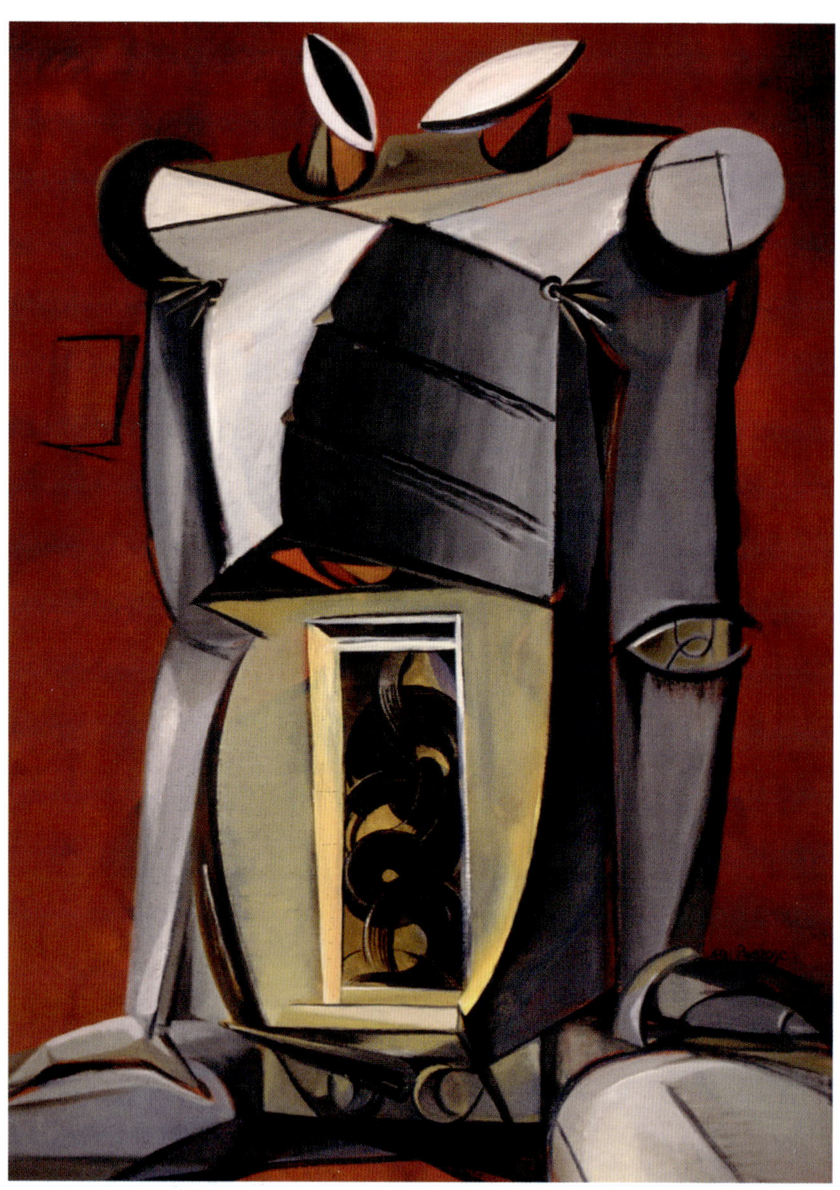

Don't you hate having two heads, 1949, oil on canvas

9 1951-59
Surrealism in Muddles Green

'He remained silent for a while, his face a mask of chagrin. 'It's sad, mon cher Luis,' he added, 'but it is no longer possible to scandalize anybody!'

André Breton speaking to Luis Buñuel, Paris 1955.[1]

The air of permanence about Farley Farm led me to believe it had been part of my parents' lives since the beginning of time but in fact I was eighteen months old when we moved there. Since the war, stirred by childhood memories of his uncle's farm at Herstmonceux, Roland had been looking for a small farm in the south-east. He wanted a country property to escape to and re-affirm his contact with nature and he had an instinct that a quiet peace in the country might help Lee in overcoming the result of her wartime traumas. He did not care for the showcase houses of the landed gentry. It needed a life and a purpose of its own to make it real, a place with genuine roots.

It was a friend of Lee's at *Vogue*, Harry Yoxall, who alerted them to the auction of Farley Farm at Muddles Green in the parish of Chiddingly. The map showed it to be in the Weald, in similar country to Herstmonceux, fifty miles from London and close to the port of Newhaven which was a key link to Paris.

When they visited on a cold February day, the place was fog-bound. They found a large farmhouse with a stark but kindly air. The oldest part, which is now the kitchen and dining room, dates from around 1735, progressively rebuilt over the years with puzzling complexity. A

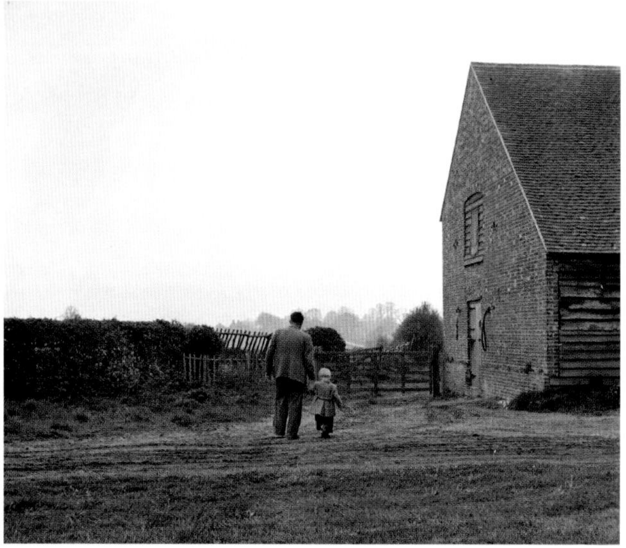

Roland Penrose and Antony Penrose outside Farleys Barn, East Sussex, England 1949, by Lee Miller

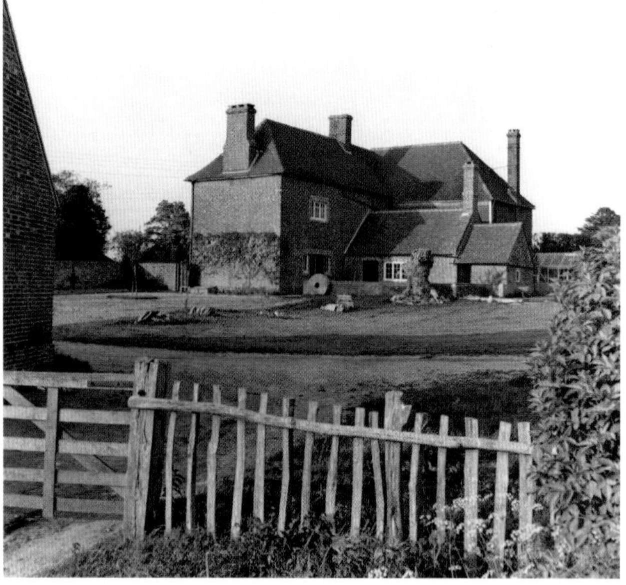

Farleys House, Muddles Green, East Sussex, England 1951, by Lee Miller

Georgian front overlooks the garden and a later Palladian-style facade overlooks the road, giving a false sense of formality to the rambling house behind. The rooms and passages are spacious and as the windows are small, there was plenty of wall space for hanging pictures.

With great excitement, Roland and Lee went to the auction at the George Hotel in Hailsham on 16 February 1949. The price of farmland in the post-war years was at an all-time low and Roland was delighted to get two hundred acres, the house, cottages and farm buildings for twenty-nine cows knocked down to him for £22,500. They hurriedly motored the four miles to Muddles Green to admire their purchase. As they stood in front of the house in bright sunshine, they were embraced by the rolling green panorama of the South Downs spanning the whole horizon from east to west. The Long Man lay flat on his hillside, where he remained discretely in the shadows.

Roland could hardly believe his luck. Here was all the romance of Le Pouy, but without the isolation he had found so stultifying. He could have the buzz of London and Paris and the earthy harmonies of rural Sussex. Lee, however, was a city person at heart. *'Fuck living in the country'*, she would complain. In her view it was *'too goddamn cold and uncomfortable'*, with plumbing that, when it worked at all, delivered a trickle of well-water stained by its iron-oxide content the colour of thin tomato soup.

Roland, who was impervious to most discomforts including extreme heat and cold, made letting in more light his first priority. On the south elevation he had dormer windows installed in the attics, enlarged the windows of his bedroom and put French doors from the sitting room through to the brick courtyard. He had a porch built to shelter the back door from the westerly winds but he stopped there. It took Lee years of agitation to get the kitchen modernised and it was more than a decade before central heating arrived.

To fund the purchase of the farm Roland sold 36 Downshire Hill and leased 11ᴬ Hornton Street, a small flat in a row of Edwardian houses in Kensington. After Hampstead the flat was cramped, but most of the collection and furniture was installed at Farleys. We commuted by car at weekends to begin with and I am told I hated the cold and the gales that swirled in the dark corridors making the doors bang. When the move was complete, I stayed all week at Farleys with my nanny and an adoring maternal golden Labrador named Heather.

It was the following summer that Roland put his mark on the house. John and Cynthia Thompson[2] recalled how they visited to find a mural that filled the inglenook fireplace had transformed the dark north-facing dining room. In the centre above the fire a bright sun figure sails over the Downs, radiating warmth and light across the farmland. To the left, planets drift in their circular orbits and on the door of a cupboard to the right a full moon lights a shimmering path in the blackest night, her light revealing her own provocative breasts. In the alcoves each side two voluptuous female cornucopia figures display the fruits that result from the fortuitous conjunction of the sun, moon and planets. Roland had installed the household deity to protect us all.

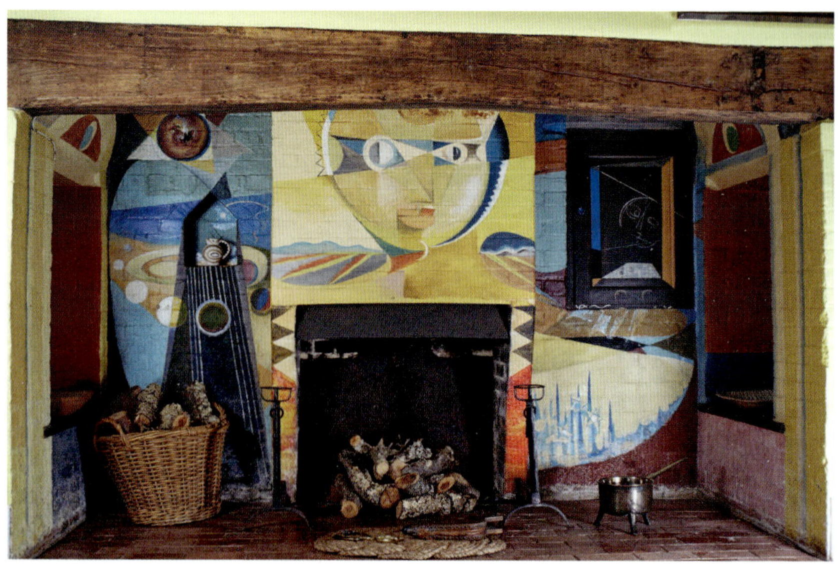

Dining Room Fireplace Mural, Farleys House, Muddles Green, England

From the beginning, Roland had understood that he needed a manager to run the farm. He told me;

> Strutt & Parker [local land agents] produced a whole range of bright young men in flat caps and green wellingtons and I did not like any of them – they were all too glib. Then we found this bear of a man, a real son of the soil, who I knew right away was the right person. We walked round one Saturday and I asked him; 'Could you make this pay?'[3] He said; 'It's a poor old farm, much neglected. It's going to be very difficult as it is in a terrible state.'

He had found Peter Braden who ran the farm for the next thirty-seven years, building it up to a well-run modern enterprise. As time passed and Roland suffered frequent betrayals, he came to value Braden's loyalty and steadfast honesty even more highly.

In April 1950 the ICA had moved into its first permanent home, a gallery on the first floor of 17 Dover Street, Piccadilly. T. S. Eliot opened the first exhibition, *James Joyce, His Life and Work* and Osbert Sitwell the second, titled *Symbolic Realism in American Painting*. Both shows were well received and marked the start of a decade of programming that changed the British art scene but before this could get underway the gallery closed for refurbishment.

The architect Jane Drew designed the large room that formed the exhibition space for maximum versatility in a relentlessly modern style – chromed steel tubing, dark hardwood cabinets and bright pastel colours on the walls. The furniture and fabrics were designed by Eduardo Paolozzi, Terence Conran, Neil Morris and Ernest Race.[4] There was a bar, a room for smaller shows and some excruciatingly cramped office space. Despite the ultra-modern design, the place had an informal atmosphere, where improvisation and sheer determination nearly always won the day.

Later in the year, Roland and the ICA assisted Phillip James with his Arts Council exhibition *Picasso in Provence* at the New Burlington Galleries. The show coincided with the Peace Congress in Sheffield organised by the Communist Party and Picasso arrived in England on 11 November for the event. Since the start of the war in Korea, the first hard frosts of the Cold War had been felt. Roland wrote;

> I hurried to Victoria Station to meet him. The night-ferry was unaccountably late and to my surprise, when I finally caught sight of the small figure of Picasso dressed in a grey suit and a black beret and carrying his suitcase, he was alone. As soon as we met he explained that his friends, almost without exception, had been turned back from Dover as dangerous revolutionaries, 'and I', he said with anxiety, 'what can I have done that they should allow me through?'[5]

Picasso had sent Marcel, his chauffeur ahead with the car and to escape the attention of the press, Picasso, Roland and Lee and two of Picasso's friends sped off to Farley Farm. It was a bright autumn day, with the leaves turning. The farm enchanted Picasso, who admired the bull and the red and white Ayrshire cows with their elegant horns and the Wessex Saddleback sows and their litters. He had a natural affinity and understanding of animals and of children and was very good at cuddles in the way of so many Mediterranean people. The outer fringes of my memory still hold the coarse feel of his tweed jacket and the tang of strongly scented soap and Gauloise cigarettes. Lee wrote for *Vogue*;

> Our son Tony was three years old. He was in ecstasy. Picasso and he became great friends, telling secrets in some secret language, finding treasures of spider webs and seedpods, roughhousing and looking at pictures. In Tony's early vocabulary the words picture and Picasso were synonymous. … Later he realised that Picasso was a man who, like Daddy, made pictures. Thus all pictures were made

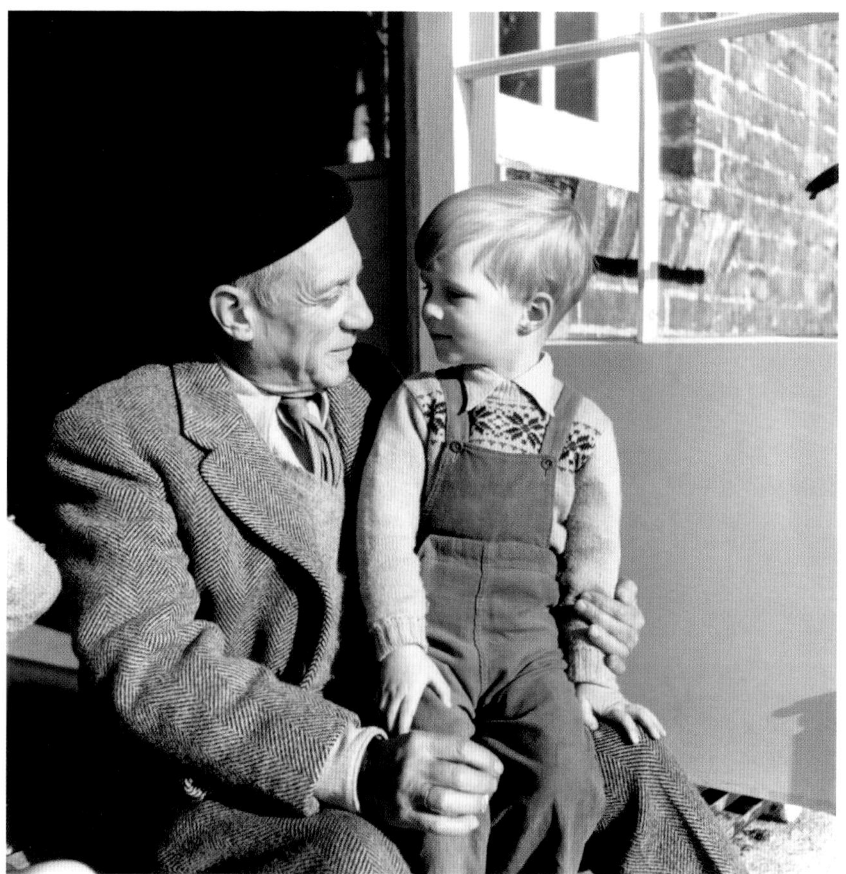

Picasso and Antony Penrose, Farleys House, Muddles Green, England 1950, by Lee Miller

by Picasso, Daddy and himself. His expertise is wildly incorrect, but perfectly consistent. 'Pictures' include Matta, Craxton, Ernst, Klee, Calder, Braque, Tanguy etc. … Naturalistic or whimsy illustration, however and of course photographs are NOT 'pictures'. Picasso and he agreed on this instantly and illustrated books, particularly *Farmer's Weekly*, became tools to clarify misunderstandings in their mysterious mutual language.[6]

Perhaps meeting our big Ayrshire bull gave Picasso the idea of initiating our game of 'bull fights'. It was long before I understood how obnoxious and cruel bullfighting really is so for me it was a wonderful role to be the bull. Picasso was the toreador flicking his jacket like a cape. With my pointed fingers as my horns I charged across the room at him. He nimbly skipped out of the way at the last second and after a few attempts I gave up. Then I thought of another strategy. When he was not looking, I crept up and I bit him, hard. Picasso immediately bit me back and in the astonished calm that followed before I began to yell, Lee heard him remark; *'Just think, that's the first Englishman I ever bit!'*[7]

Picasso left for the Congress the next day. Government pressure forced its closure after its first day and on the 14 November he returned to London, where he refused to attend the private view of *Picasso in Provence* as a protest against the government. Still hounded by the press, he retreated to 11[A] Hornton Street where Roland recalled;

> He looked out of the window and astonished me by saying 'Pitt Street!' which was the name of the street in front of him. I said 'Yes, Pitt Street?' He said, 'That reminds me of Lady Hester Stanhope' [William Pitt's niece who wrote about her travels with the Bedouin]. Little did I think that Picasso knew much about British history, but on the contrary, he had heard all about Lady Hester Stanhope and when he left Barcelona for the first time in 1899, he said it was not to go to Paris, it was to go to London, where he wanted to go particularly because there were wonderful emancipated women like Lady Hester Stanhope and the beggars went round in top hats. And he said 'Well, I got on the train and I got to Paris and I got stuck there.'[8]

The conference was being reconvened in Warsaw and Picasso needed to return to Paris so they all set off towards Newhaven via Farleys. On the way, Roland took Picasso around the sights of Brighton, hunting for what he regarded as typically English souvenirs. Picasso chose postcards of the Brighton Pavilion, a peaked school cap for himself and his son Claude, a jar of Bournvita, a plastic mug with a sleepy man wearing a night-cap embossed on the side and a packet of Kwells seasickness tablets.

At Farleys Picasso had quickly defined the things he liked. Lee listed them as;

> Open log fires, a whiskey and soda night-cap, hot water bottles, cooked breakfasts and tea. He could scarcely know that besides modern pictures, an English farmhouse doesn't have rows of French sabots inside the back door, garlands of garlic and furniture which lived its first hundred years in Gascony. But the tinned plum pudding on my menu, holly wreathed and flaming was indeed English, VERY English and superb.[9]

That evening Roland got out some brushes and coloured Indian inks. Seated before the fire Picasso covered two pages of the ICA visitors' book with a drawing of grasshopper bulls perched on twigs against a background of yellow suns with pink rays. Then he moved on to a copy of *Góngora, vingt Poèmes* he had illustrated with twenty etchings and filled the flyleaf with an exuberant picture of a satyr mounted on a horse and dedicated it to Roland.[10]

The next day Picasso and Marcel returned to France and life resumed its more normal rhythm, except that for me something happened the following February that changed the course of my life. My current nanny was indisposed and a twenty-three-year-old woman of Irish descent arrived to take care of me. She had black hair and sparkling blue eyes set in a kind, intelligent face that carried the wistful humour of her Irish ancestry. She came for two weeks and stayed for fifty seven years. Patsy Murray found an immediate rapport with Roland and Lee. Her own upbringing had prepared her well for life at Farleys.

Patsy had been brought up in a kind of commune in Doddington, Kent, run by Dr. Josiah Oldfield, an eccentric physician. He was an ardent educationalist and insisted Patsy went to school, although the spindly girl had to walk two miles in all weathers to catch the bus. At the age of sixteen she began training as a children's nurse, went on to become matron of a private school and then looked after three children for a family who were in Malaya.

Patsy was the one permanent fixture in my ever-changing world and Farleys became a real, solid home. Roland had engaged Fred Baker and Fred's father-in-law known as Old Whitey as gardeners and soon Paula,

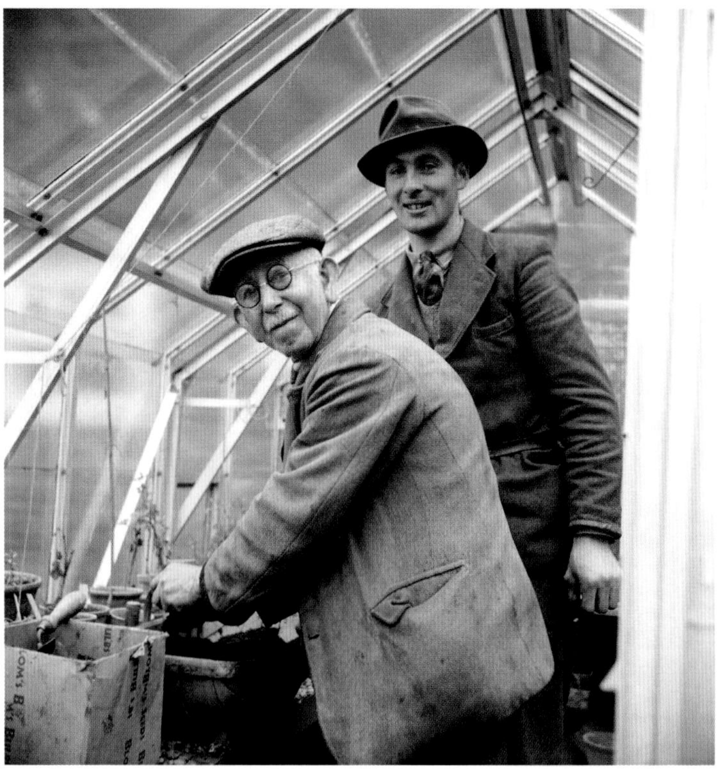

Grandpa White and Fred Baker, Farleys Garden, East Sussex, England 1953, by Lee Miller

Patsy's mother, arrived as housekeeper. The Victorian style household that Roland had tried to escape from had replicated itself, but Lee's down to earth friendliness made sure the expected divisions of class did not apply. Roland was often heard to say in later years, *'If it were not for Patsy, I would never have been able to keep Farley Farm'*. Lee agreed; she wanted no part of the housework, but loved entertaining at weekends when guests from many parts of the world would arrive, creating an almost non-stop arts conference.

Socialising locally was always a problem. One of the first visitors was a retired colonel who informed Roland that the local branch of the Conservative Party were accustomed to using Farleys as the venue for their garden party. He gave Roland the benefit of his long experience: the cars would park over there, the guests would be received here, the speeches would come before the refreshments and so on. In the first lull, Roland said quietly; *'But Colonel, I always vote Labour'*. There was a pause and the Colonel's face turned an interesting shade of puce. *'Then you won't find many friends around here'*, he growled and stormed off. *'I think I'll manage'*, said Roland to the retreating figure.

As their contribution to the Festival of Britain the ICA mounted the exhibition *Growth and Form*. The show was inspired by Scott D'Arcy Wentworth and organised by Richard Hamilton, a young student championed by Roland. Hamilton wanted to demonstrate in detail the natural phenomena of growth, ranging from atomic particles to crystals and living organisms. He saturated the environment of the gallery with photographs and projected images, some in extreme magnification to demonstrate the ingenuity and astonishing beauty of his subject. *Growth and Form* challenged the accepted wisdom that beauty was a cultural issue that could be decided according to the formulae of taste and judged as 'good' or 'bad'.[11] The show was a key part of the debate that is still running today, linked to a trail of movements ranging from Pop Art through Grunge and ever onward.

Growth and Form lost money and was an example of the difficulty

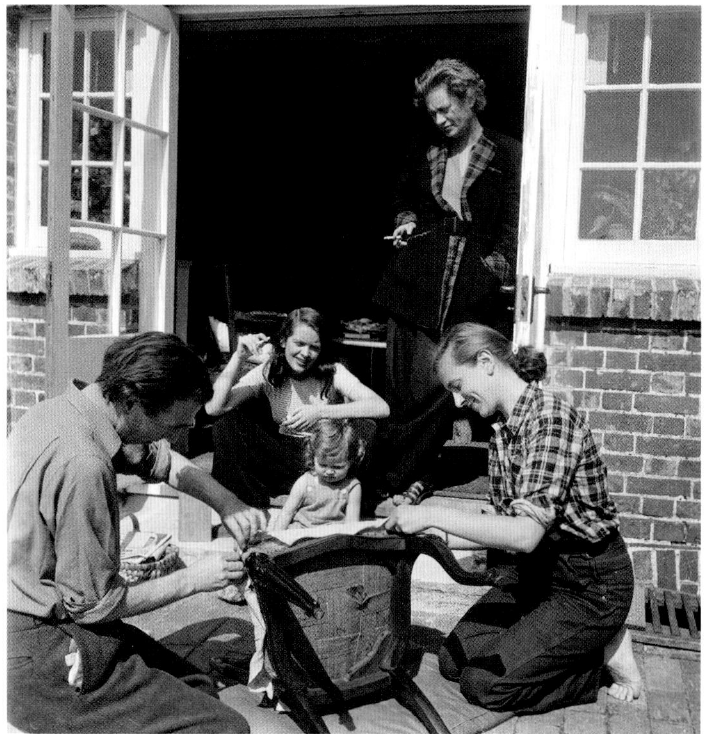

Outside sitting room, Lee Miller, Richard and Terry Hamilton with others, Farleys House, Muddles Green, Sussex, England 1951

facing the ICA. Some on the committee, Read included, insisted their function should be the promotion of young artists. Roland and Peter Gregory, who dipped heavily into their own pockets to keep the place going, recognised that they needed to mount a strong proportion of shows by known artists to bring in the revenue and raise the ICA's profile, benefitting the emerging artists. Some funding had been provided by the Arts Council whose undisclosed strategy was to use public money to support exhibitions that would have invited severe criticism if they had been organised by the Arts Council itself.

In that summer of 1951 Roland, accompanied by Lee and myself, was in Paris doing what he loved best, organising a show of Picasso's work. Scheduled for October at the ICA, it was titled *Picasso. Drawings and Watercolours since 1893.* After making the selection we all journeyed south to Saint-Tropez for the wedding of Paul and Dominique Eluard. The ceremony was incomprehensible to me as Paul Eluard and his warm, smiling Dominique stood in a room that smelt of damp paper, being harangued by a grumpy nervous man. Françoise Gilot was there, young, beautiful and very kind. Afterwards in the restaurant she gave me wonderful chocolate patisseries as an incentive to keep quiet. Picasso made a drawing of the scene with us all sitting round the table.

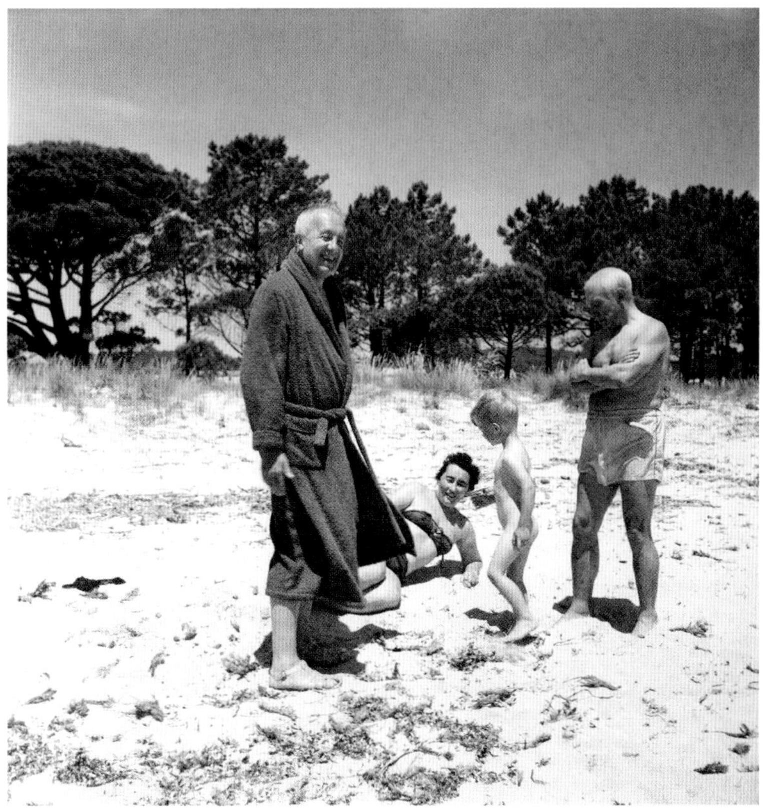

Paul Eluard, Dominique [nee Odette Lemort] Eluard, Antony Penrose and Picasso, St.Tropez, France 1951, by Lee Miller

Picasso's wedding present to Paul and Dominique was a tall vase decorated with dancing figures that he made in his Vallauris studio. Dominique was strong and kind and loving. Paul Eluard adored her. We were all happy for them. Who was to know that in just over a year Dominique would be a widow?

Eluard's death on 28 November 1952 came soon after the untimely demise of Roland's brother Alec on 23 August 1950.[12] Roland told me; '*Losing Alec was the first time I was really touched by death*'. I marvelled he had reached his fifties before being hit by bereavement. He had fallen out with his brother more than once, usually due to Alec's dismissive attitude to Roland's apparently frivolous lifestyle and the art he loved but there was a very deep bond between them. Alec had represented the old values of their parents and Roland unexpectedly missed him for that as well as his role of confidant. Now nothing remained of the old ways. Roland made a contribution in his memory to the restoration of the Guildhall in Kings Lynn, a magnificent seventeenth-century building that Alec had saved from demolition and converted into a performing arts centre.

Picasso. Drawings and Watercolours since 1893 at the ICA coincided with the artist's seventieth birthday.[13] Peter Gregory's firm Lund Humphries produced a fine catalogue with the grasshopper bull design from the ICA visitor's book as the cover and many full-colour plates within. Roland's catalogue essay presents Picasso and his work in an affectionate and penetrating way, with the romanticism of an amateur rather than the cold erudition of a scholar.

At the ICA, Dorothy Morland had replaced Ewan Phillips as director. For more than ten years, she managed the ICA during what many regard as the most productive and exciting period of its existence. Lawrence Alloway was to become Director of Exhibitions and an American, Anthony Kloman, was appointed Director of Publicity, a title that thinly disguised his real purpose of fund-raising.

One of Kloman's most successful ideas was the holding of the ICA

Picture Fairs. Artists of all calibre, from Picasso, Ernst and Miró to total unknowns were persuaded, mainly by Roland, to donate a work to the ICA. The collection was exhibited briefly and people invited to buy tickets that cost £25 each for the draw. Roland augmented the prizes with works from his own collection and frequently gave tickets as presents to those who could not afford them. I remember in the late 1950s the actress Eleanor Bron was the celebrity who pulled the numbers from a large pot. Roland had generously bought me a ticket and I became the proud owner of a large painting by Richard Coote-Smith, a minor artist. Roland was relieved – it would have been bad form if I had walked off with the little gem of a Miró (which was won by Cynthia Thompson) or the Picasso drawing.

Kloman was conscious of the impoverished nature of most of the 1,500 people who made up the ICA membership. He tried to entice donors from the upper echelons of society and worked on driving the ICA upmarket with prestigious openings reported in the glossy magazines for companies like Shell who sponsored *The Old and New in South-East Asia*.

Among the shows his American connections helped bring to the ICA was *Saul Steinberg's Drawings* coinciding with the publication in Europe of Steinberg's new book *The Art of Living*. *Life* magazine sponsored the show, a nice connection for Roland and Lee as Steinberg was a close friend of Davie Scherman. American art, which had been ignored in Europe, was suddenly in the ascendant and other shows included *Opposing Forces,* which showcased the work of Jackson Pollock.

Kloman secured £16,000 of sponsorship towards an international competition to be run by the ICA for a large-scale sculpture titled *Monument to the Unknown Political Prisoner*. The winner was Reg Butler. His maquette and other selected entries were exhibited at the Tate Gallery. The House of Commons and Winston Churchill condemned the work and worse, no one could agree where the monument should be sited. A hill overlooking the Russian sector in Berlin was favoured by many, but in the escalating tension culminating in the erection of the

Berlin Wall it was deemed too provocative and the project was allowed to die quietly. For many years, Roland was completely unaware of a suspicion known all along to Alfred Barr that the money, which had ostensibly been donated by John Hay Whitney, originated from a sinister source. In her recent book, Anne Massey writes;

> It could be claimed that the Unknown Political Prisoner competition was a CIA exercise in promoting liberal, individualist politics and the avant-garde.[14]

The internal culture of the ICA was being pulled in three directions. America provided cash, but threatened to replace the rich European diversity with what some saw as a monoculture of US Modernism. Read and Roland were becoming increasingly retrospective in their thinking and still wanted to promote Surrealism and modern masters from the continent. Others demanded greater support for young British artists. More importantly, as the ICA expanded, Roland and the members of the management and committee were, with the exception of Gregory and Hoellering, mainly artists and not businessmen. They were ill equipped for navigating in the dangerous waters of finance and political pressures and mistakes were inevitable. The miracle was that the place functioned as well as it did, a fact that owed much to the personal commitment of those involved.

In his day, Alloway and in particular Morland were the ones who held the interest of the young artists at heart, forming first an ad hoc *Young Group*, followed by the *Independent Group*. This initially consisted of Hamilton and his ex-Slade friends Eduardo Paolozzi and Nigel Henderson. They insisted on responding to the excitement of American culture on many levels. The new shapes of cars, trends in the design of advertisements, technical drawings and the intricacies of new scientific discoveries provided them with the raw material for their work, particularly collages, at which Hamilton, Henderson and Paolozzi excelled.

But for Roland a schism was appearing. He had strongly supported Hamilton and championed Paolozzi, but those who knew him could see that these developments were not to his taste. He was seen bravely trying to cope with books on cybernetics and to interest himself in science fiction, all part of the *Independent Group's* scene. This was brave, but futile, as nothing would replace his love of Surrealism and the eclecticism of shows such as *The Wonder and Horror of the Human Head* of March 1953.

The show was a marvellous anthology of the treatment of the human head in art. Palaeolithic sculptures, tribal masks and the famous Mexican rock crystal skull from the British Museum contrasted with Picasso's Cubist *Portrait of Uhde* and other works by Hieronymus Bosch, Paul Klee, Brancusi and Goya. In the catalogue,[15] Roland's essay shows perceptive research and imaginative connections, with references ranging from the cultures of the Haida to the Celtic. Lee had helped him extensively with the research and he acknowledged her in the dedication;

> To my wife, without whose help this essay could not have been written.

By now not even Lee's friend and *Vogue* editor Timmie O'Brien could get Lee to focus on her work and her drinking bouts and procrastination left everyone in shreds. Roland told me he wrote to Withers secretly, begging her to stop giving Lee assignments, as the suffering it caused Lee and those around her had become unbearable. Lee realised what had happened and sank further into depression, a bad place for her to be as something much worse was just about to occur.

One day in the summer of 1953 Diane Deriaz walked into the ICA and introduced herself as having been a friend of Paul Eluard. She was a circus performer, an artist of the flying trapeze, who following a fall had come to England looking for some bears to buy for a new act where the danger of being eaten would replace that of plunging to earth. Tall, with the figure of an athlete and a spring in her stride, she carried an aura of excitement, glamour and rebellion. Roland was instantly smitten.

Lee openly stated that after my birth she lost interest in sex, but encouraged Roland to have as many lovers as he wanted. She had felt secure in this, knowing the promises they had made would mean he would never allow another to supplant her in his affections and to begin with she welcomed Diane, encouraging her to sleep with Roland.

The decisive moment came at Christmas 1953. Farleys was crammed to bursting with Ernst and Dorothea Tanning, Valentine, Timmie and Terry O'Brien, Dominique Eluard and her daughter Caroline, Patsy and her mother Paula, Diane and me. It was fraught. On Christmas Eve at dinner there was a scene and Diane fainted. Roland panicked;

'*Oh Patsy, please do something!*' he begged.

'*There is nothing wrong with her*', declared Valentine angrily, '*Look, her face is still pink!*'

Diane soon revived, but Lee took to her bed and refused to come downstairs. With thirteen people to feed, Patsy and Paula were run ragged by Boxing Day, when a taxi drew up in the drive.

'*That's it, if one more person comes into this house*', said Paula, '*I am leaving!*'

She did not leave. The new arrival was James Dugan, deep-sea diver and photographer, whose charm did much to smooth things along.

Lee's drinking had reached the serious level at which it would more or less remain for the next fifteen years. She drank because she felt unloved and she was unloved because she drank. Extreme mood swings would sweep over her without warning, transforming her in minutes from a benign, witty person into someone that would lacerate everyone within reach and then attack herself. Friends such as Valentine, the O'Briens and the French food writer Ninette Lyon loved her enough to weather the storms, but many were alienated by her egregious behaviour. I opted out as best I could, avoiding Lee whenever possible and we consequently grew apart.

Roland begged Diane to marry him. His plan was for Lee to take me to live in America and he would live in Paris with Diane. To Roland's astonishment, Diane refused point blank. Years later she told me it was because she did not want to break up my parents and destroy my life and while I believe this to have been a compelling reason, I felt her own determination to remain independent carried similar weight. Whatever her reasons for so doing, for my own sake I will always be glad Diane refused to marry Roland. How would I have survived on my own with Lee, without Patsy and the sustaining environment of Farley Farm is a chilling thought. We stayed together as a family, although at times life for Lee was unbearably tough. Roland had made no secret of his desire to abandon her for Diane and she left for a long visit to America, uncertain if she would return.

After several months with her father in Poughkeepsie and friends in New York, Lee did come back, accompanied by crates of kitchen gadgets she had bought. I was glad to see her and so was Roland. They found they loved and needed each other, although they still found it hard to get on together. Their relationship settled into a fragile balance that alternated between affection and uncomprehending strife. Lee accepted that Diane was part of Roland's life, but he was more discreet now and he did not try bringing her to Farleys again. Fortunately, a project that would give Lee and Roland a common interest arose.

From the faltering way he read out loud and the mistakes in his manuscripts, I suspect Roland was acutely dyslexic. Certainly, reading and writing were always a struggle for him. With this disadvantage and his inexperience of writing major works, he was understandably baffled as to why the renowned publisher Victor Gollancz should approach him to write the first full length biography of Picasso in English. It turned out that when Gollancz was looking for an author, Alain Gherbrandt, who had become a writer and explorer, had recommended Roland.

Before accepting, Roland, who was concerned about Picasso's reaction, went to visit him in Perpignan where he and his new love, Jacqueline Roque, were staying at the house of Comte Jacques de Lazerme and his wife Paule. Françoise Gilot had ended her relationship with Picasso a year earlier, but she was there on this occasion to collect their children, Claude and Paloma, who had been staying with their father.

Soon after Roland arrived, they all set off to Collioure, a small fishing port with a beach they all enjoyed frequenting. It was close to the Spanish frontier and Picasso loved to tantalise himself with the proximity to his own country that he had exiled himself from in protest against Franco. From now Roland would keep detailed notes of all his visits to Picasso, a practice he continued until Picasso's death. He wrote of this occasion;

> Claude and Paloma looked wonderfully brown and healthy on the beach. We played with them and bathed. As we were leaving the beach, I told Picasso that I wanted to write a book about him. His reaction was more encouraging than I had dared to hope. He seized me with both hands and his black eyes looked deep into me as he said; 'C'est vrai? C'est bien!' I told him that I had had an offer from a publisher and that I had considered all the obstacles – my own inability, heavy competition, vastness of subject etc. He said – hit by some doubt – 'But is this an idea you have just had now or have you already written something'. I told him the idea had always been there and that I had written prefaces and lectures but that it now took on new and greater proportions. I told him I would have to come to France to write it and see as much as I could of him without getting in his way. In general, I think he likes the idea and certainly has nothing against it. He said; 'Even if there are other books each person has his own views, sees the question differently and that's what makes a book worthwhile'.[16]

It was four years before *Picasso, His Life and Work* was published. Two or three times a year Roland would visit Picasso in Paris or in his new house, Villa La Californie in Cannes. Roland's long-standing friendship made him a ready target for the various capricious torments Picasso

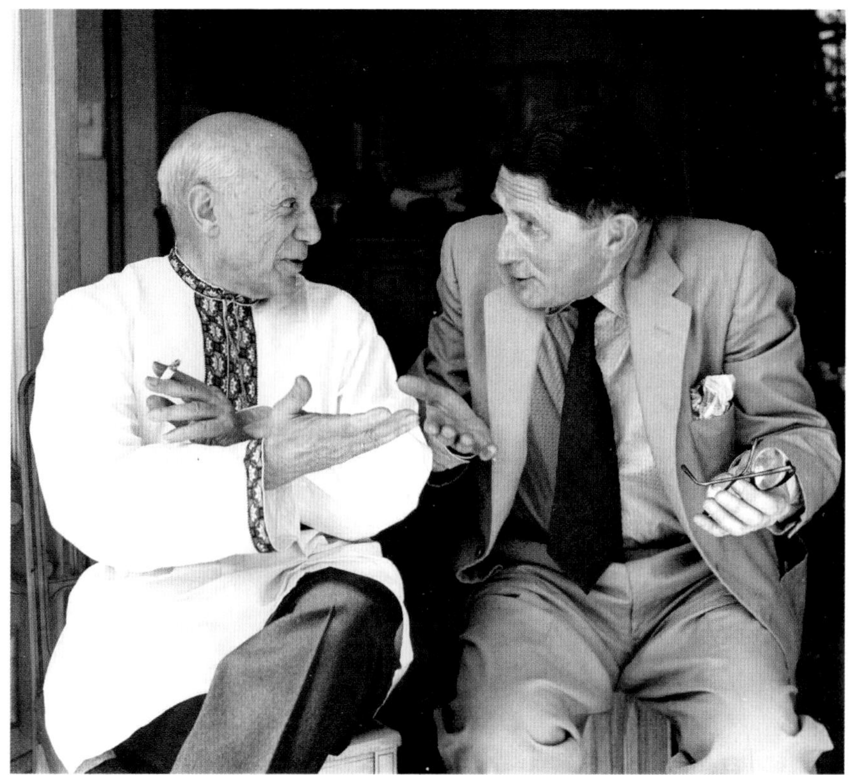

Picasso and Roland Penrose speaking French, Villa la Californie, Cannes, France 1956, by Lee Miller

randomly inflicted on those who loved him. Picasso sensed the rivalry between Roland and Cooper and at times baited them with each other. One of his most sardonic tricks was to give Roland a copy of the poster he made for the 1951 Nice Carnival, dedicated *Pour Roland Penrose*. It shows a broad, grinning face topped by a series of yellow points that could be a crown. Roland was delighted with it and it still hangs beside his chair in Farleys kitchen. He must have been wholly unaware that the figure with its fair hair *en brosse* and asymmetrical eyes set in a podgy face, has every appearance of his arch rival, as John Richardson points out in his autobiography.[17]

The distractions of Picasso's court made it hard for Roland to form the questions he needed to pose for his research. He once told me that during a lull, Jacqueline had prompted him; *'Now we are alone, you can ask all the questions you want'*. Roland shrivelled with nerves. *'I am afraid I might ask you the wrong questions'*, he blurted. *'Yes'*, said Picasso emphatically, *'and if you ask me the wrong questions, you can be sure I will give you the wrong answers'*. In his notebook Roland recorded;

> Answers cannot be expected easily. Some questions can imply a falsehood and therefore, can only merit a lie or a paradox as an answer. There are no definite answers. Is that blue? No it is red. There is no such thing as blue by itself. It is a balance between intuition and intelligence. Science tries to force us into precise answers, black or white, but the theory of relativity should admit that there are no precise answers where art is concerned – only appreciation and paradox. Without appreciation no explanation is possible. Picasso

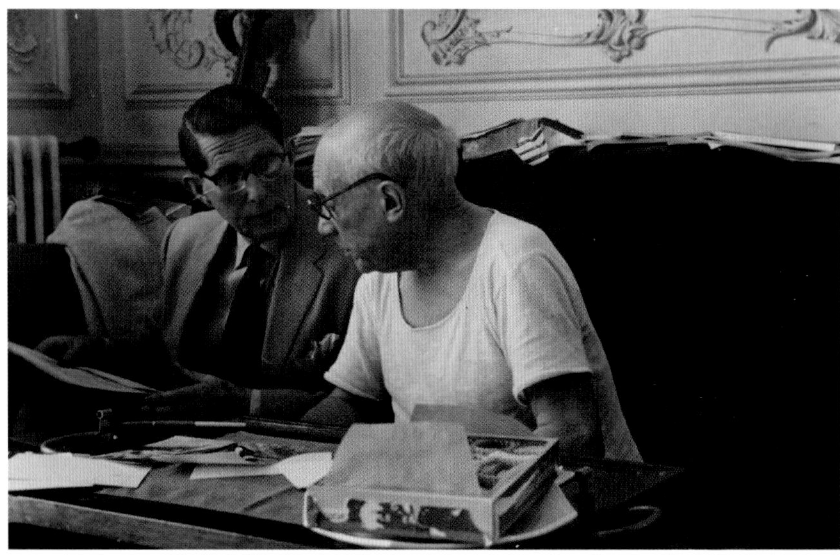

Roland Penrose and Picasso, Villa la Californie, Cannes, France *c.*1955, by Lee Miller

said; 'What I say should not always be believed, the questions you tempt me to answer are lies because there is no answer'.[18]

Roland and Lee made research trips to Malaga, Madrid, Barcelona and many other places where Picasso had lived and worked. Lee photographed as a visual record and many of her pictures were used in the ICA exhibition that Roland organised for Picasso's seventy-fifth birthday in 1956. Titled *Picasso Himself*, it was a biographical selection of over two hundred photographs and works Roland had borrowed from Picasso including portraits of Picasso by Cocteau and Derain as well as some recent works and a portrait of Jacqueline. Alfred Barr wrote the foreword for the catalogue that was published as *Portrait of Picasso*.[19] Joanna Drew of the Arts Council organised the show's tour of England and then Paris, ending with the Museum of Modern Art in New York. Using his current research material, Roland wrote *Portrait of Picasso* concisely and fast. The result is informative and flows with an ease. Roland, a visulate person found it easier to communicate through images and this work formed the story board for his main feature, the biography.

Picasso, His Life and Work, first published in 1958, was translated into seven languages and some editions are still in print after more than sixty years. It was not until the French translation appeared that Roland had Picasso's reaction. *'I read your book'*, he said to Roland, *'It's good, in fact so good that often it seemed to me that we were sitting at the same table and writing it together'*.[20] He could not have paid Roland a more perfect compliment. Later when the Spanish edition appeared thirty pages covering communism, the painting of *Guernica* and the Spanish Civil War had been cut by the censor, but although they were both angry at seeing history distorted Picasso understood the cuts had not been Roland's decision.

For three years from 1956, Roland and Lee spent half of the year in Paris. He was Fine Arts Officer for the British Council promoting the work of British artists in Paris, the city which was still seen as the hub of the art world. Old friends, Ernst and Tanning, Man Ray and Juliette, Giacometti, Miró, Braque, Matta, Dominguez and many others abounded. There seemed to be no limit to Roland's energy and he produced a constant flow of catalogue essays and lectures. The British Council sent him to Lisbon to lecture, Brazil to help select for the São Paulo Bienal, then on to Mexico, for more lectures and home via the United States. It was a dazzling whirl, but closest to his heart remained the championing of young artists and in particular two young sculptors, Kenneth Armitage and Lynn Chadwick, the rank outsider who won the 1956 Venice Biennale. Armitage recalled;

> Roland had a lovely flat in the Île de la Cité. … Roland gave me a party in his flat at the time of my exhibition in Paris. Roland was ideal as the British representative in Paris because he knew everyone! He asked Giacometti, Man Ray and Miró to my party. […] The thing about Roland was that one felt safe with him. You know the vulgarity of a lot of the art world? Well, Roland was never going to exploit me or use me. He stands out as one of the best people I've met ... I feel privileged to have known him.[21]

10 1960-70
Sir Realist

'To punish me for my contempt for authority,
Fate made me an authority myself.'
Albert Einstein

Roland was unusually quiet as we climbed Windover Hill above the Long Man. Not even my chum Johnny and I kicking sheep turds at each other interrupted his thoughts. At the top, we sat on the Neolithic barrow in the warm sunshine. The liquid song of the meadowlarks poured down over us from such a height that the birds were too small to see. In the distance, we could see the spire of Chiddingly Church and guess where Farleys lay hidden among the trees. Cowslips grew on the springy turf and below us the Long Man spread his arms wide to welcome the spring sunlight. But none of this seemed to be important and Johnny and I were awed into a respectful silence.

On the way back down, Roland said;

'*When I have a big question in your mind and I can't decide what to do, I find taking a walk helps me find the answer*'.

'*What was the question?*' I asked, hoping it might be something important like buying a new tractor.

'I have been asked to organise an exhibition about Picasso. It is a big and difficult task and I am not sure if I am capable, but I have decided to do it'.

Since starting on his book researches, Roland had taken advantage of his frequent visits to Picasso to press for things on behalf of the Director of the Arts Council. He had been unable to get the Pushkin Museum collection of Picassos transferred to London after their exhibition in Paris, but he resolutely continued to lobby Picasso and his dealer, Daniel-Henry Kahnweiler, for a major show in London. When it became evident that Roland had won Picasso's commitment for an Arts Council show at the Tate Gallery in 1960, a curator was needed.

Apart from Roland, the only other possible choice was Douglas Cooper. Museum directors knew that they would want to borrow works from both Roland's and Cooper's collections in the next few years and favoured them more or less equally. Cooper was the stronger of the two

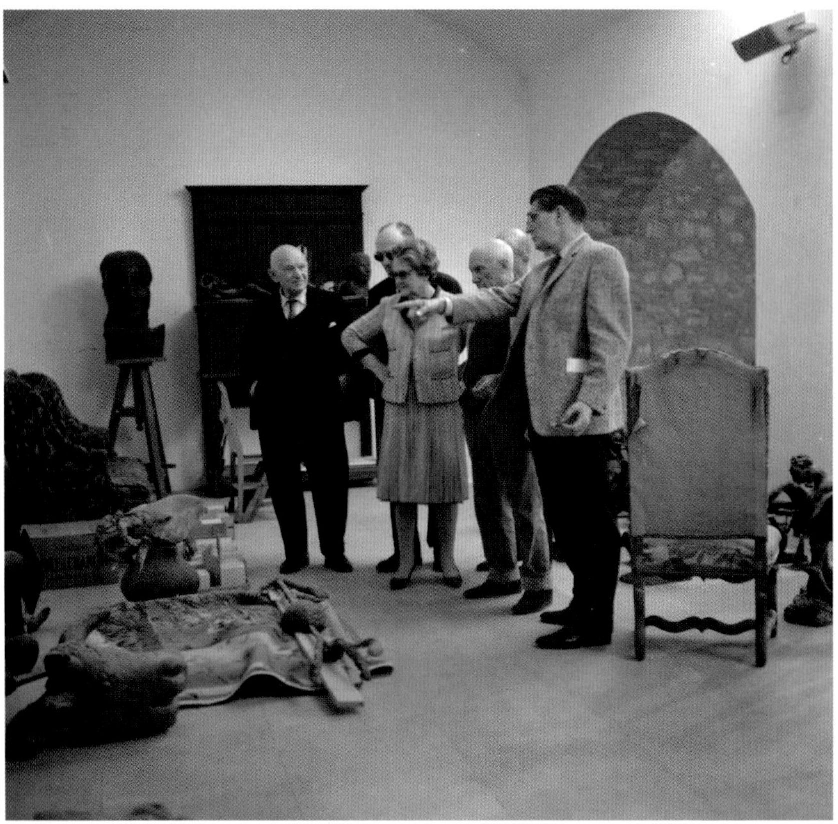

Daniel-Henri Kahnweiler, Maurice Jardot, Zette Leiris, Pablo Picasso, Michel Leiris and Roland Penrose, Notre Dame de Vie, Mougins, France 1966, by Lee Miller

academically, but he had upset many potential lenders. Roland's tact and integrity had earned him such a good reputation that many people would lend simply because it was he who asked.

By a large majority the Art Panel of the Arts Council confirmed Roland as their choice of curator.[1] Roland had already been asked informally and had accepted after his walk over the Long Man. Cooper's spite knew no bounds but Roland, as always seeking conciliation, visited him offering to share the job.[2] Fortunately Cooper turned it down, as the outcome of such a joint venture could only have been disastrous. As it was, Cooper did everything he could to sabotage Roland and the exhibition, spreading malicious gossip and refusing all Roland's pleas to loan his remarkable Cubist works. I remember Roland's anger and frustration when at the opening Cooper stated in the press that he was surprised he had not been asked to lend.

The exhibition organiser at the Arts Council was Joanna Drew and she took care of loans, correspondence, catalogue production and shipping. Roland was in his element, flying around Europe and America coaxing loans from collectors and museums. His knowledge of Picasso's work enabled him to assemble key works representing each period and if a work was denied, then he would track down another to fill the gap. Letters and telegrams flew back and forth to the Arts Council headquarters in St James's Square as Roland pleaded, flattered and on occasion invoked the influence of the Arts Council Chairman Sir Kenneth Clark with particularly stubborn lenders.

Cooper, in his efforts to sour things for Roland, had overplayed his hand with Picasso, who, angered at Cooper's presumptions, retaliated by backing Roland beyond his dreams. From Cannes, Roland wrote to Gabriel White at the Arts Council;

> I have asked him for all the paintings I have on my list and he is willing to lend some 32 paintings dating from 1895 to 1955. In addition to this he will select some 10–12 paintings from 1956

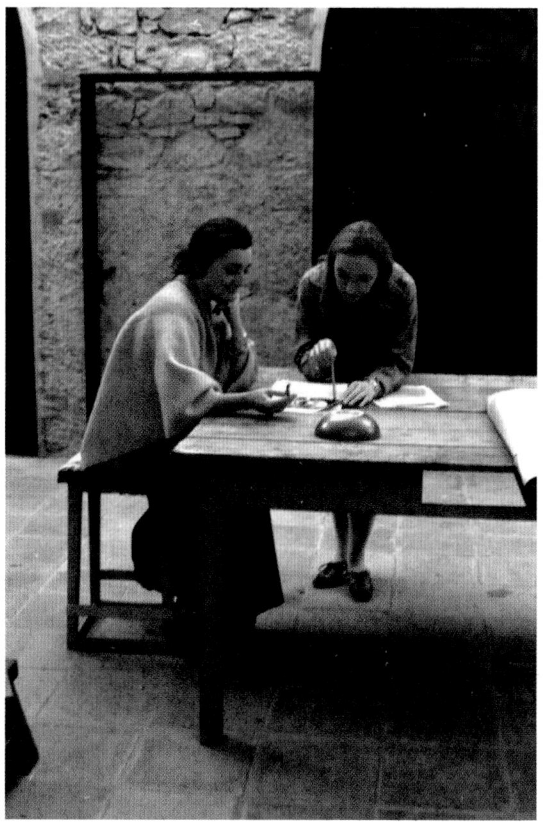

Jacqueline Roque and Joanna Drew, Mougins, France 1970, by Lee Miller

onwards. ... They are all items of importance for our show which now promises to be the most complete exhibition up to the present time as far as painting is concerned. ... He has again told me he does not want to lend any sculpture. ... On the other hand he is willing to lend the entire series of Las Meninas which has only been seen once at the Galerie Louise Leiris last summer. The condition is that the whole series amounting to some 50 to 60 paintings be shown together. ... I am very anxious we should try to get this, as

> the Meninas are an item of great importance and will make the show unparalleled.[3]

The show had already grown beyond the space allocated. Further negotiations were needed with Sir John Rothenstein, the Director of the Tate, to use the South Duveen Sculpture Gallery to accommodate the *Las Meninas* series and the North Duveen Sculpture Gallery for the vast drop curtain from the Ballet Russes production *Parade*. The two hundred and seventy loans came from over eighty named lenders and more than thirty private collections. Even with Drew coping with the blizzard of paperwork, Roland was run ragged by the catalogue essay and notes. He and his secretary Joyce Reeves took over the dining room at Farleys with masses of small photos clipped to cards. As loans were unexpectedly granted or withdrawn, the whole catalogue had to be reshuffled. There was no word from the Soviet Union about their loan and at the last minute Roland even approached Ilya Ehrenburg, the famous Russian writer and friend of Picasso's who was visiting England.

The catalogue reflected the format of the show, which Roland divided into distinct periods. The sections begin with an informative essay and a chronology of the events and places prominent in Picasso's life and each painting has its own succinct note with a small black and white illustration at the end. Even for a major show like this, the lavish colour printing we take for granted today was many years away. Given that resource the catalogue would have been a masterwork in itself.

The ICA organised the gala Picasso Party for the opening night of 5 July 1960 and Lee, after trying every avoidance dodge she could think of, wrote the preface for the booklet. A pink-and-white-striped marquee was erected on the lawn of the Tate and a scaffolding stairway was constructed to connect with the main entrance. Patsy, Julie Lawson and half a dozen others were roped in to fill the place with flowers and the caterer struggled to produce a mountain of paella.

HRH THE DUKE OF EDINBURGH HAS GRACIOUSLY

CONSENTED TO ATTEND, announced the booklet. There was some concern about seating him near Lee. The sight of her Surrealist husband and other members of the avant-garde being deferential to royalty might have made her unable to resist the temptation to shock HRH with outrageous behaviour. But she held firm and in fact, they were observed enjoying each other's company. Roland conducted the Duke on a tour of the show, where the early work was more to the royal taste.

Five hundred thousand people visited the exhibition and some who were then part of the Arts Council look back on it as the best show they ever mounted. Ticket sales generated such a profit that the Arts Council was able to allocate £30,000 (about £300,000 today), to a special projects fund for future exhibitions.[4]

The partying with lenders and visiting VIPs went on for days. About two weeks into the show the eleven pictures from the Soviet Union arrived without warning, causing total consternation and an overnight re-hang. There was great excitement one evening when Roland was asked to take the Queen around the exhibition. He was very nervous.

'I can't understand why she should be interested, there are no pictures of corgi dogs', he said to Lee.

'Don't worry, she will love Pegasus and her foal in Parade', replied Lee, *'maybe you should go straight to that'*.

The desolation of the Blue Period work, *The Blind Man's Meal*, visibly moved Her Majesty, but Roland was still on tenterhooks. The strident leap of *Les Demoiselles d'Avignon* heralded the Cubist period that he had been advised to skip by Anthony Blunt, Keeper of the Queen's Pictures, who was part of the entourage. But the Queen cut no corners, examining all the paintings attentively until they came to the beautiful wooden Cubist construction *Still Life*. A knife, cheese, salami and a glass complete with a slice of lemon stand on the fringed edge of a table. The Queen declared;

'Oh! How delightful. I would so much have liked to make something like it myself'.[5]

She had no way of knowing it was part of Roland's collection. He was enthralled. The Surrealist anarchist had on the spot become a royalist. Picasso understood. He had often told Roland about the extraordinarily erotic dreams he had about the Queen and Princess Margaret;

'*If they knew what I had done in my dreams with your royal ladies, they would take me to the Tower of London and chop off my head*'! he said with pride.

Some of Roland's friends were much less charitable. Mesens was predictably caustic and almost certainly retaliated by discouraging Magritte from letting Roland show his work at the ICA. George Melly, who was particularly incensed by the Duke of Edinburgh's presence at the opening, wrote Roland a blistering letter;

> Honestly, I find the whole concept an insult to a great painter. What are you after? A title? A ticket to the Royal Enclosure? I wish to put it on record now that I shall lend no picture to any exhibition in the future under the aegis of yourself or the ICA.

Before signing off as *Yours disgustedly*, Melly concluded with a quotation from a similar lambasting given to Read by Jean Dubuffet, the artist famous for Art Brut, a friend of Roland, who was later to have a show at the ICA;

> What he [Dubuffet] says is entirely relevant to your own shabby and opportunistic little marriage of art and the establishment. I am absolutely opposed to the whole concept of merit in relation to art. The true mission of art is subversive; its true nature is such that it would be quite legitimate to forbid it and persecute it.[6]

Roland's critics got plenty more ammunition when he accepted his knighthood on 1 January 1966. Even Ninette Lyon's teasing had a cutting edge to it;

'How can you call yourself a Surrealist now you are Sir Penrose?', she demanded.

'It's alright, I am now a Sir-realist', replied Roland.

Ninette laughed and forgave, but others were less easily mollified and at times Roland had people haranguing him at his lectures and seminars.[7]

His appointment as a Trustee of the Tate Gallery in 1959 had been less controversial, as he was seen as a rebel working inside the establishment. Besides, the Tate's post-war exhibitions policy had eventually embraced modern art. Roland regarded their former director J.B. Manson's scathing condemnation of his 1937 show at the Mayor Gallery as a thing of the past.

The Arts Council followed the Picasso show with a major Ernst retrospective at the Tate the following year, for which Roland was responsible. The exhibition was similarly prestigious, but it was a less Herculean task to assemble because, of the 205 works, 141 had previously been shown at the Museum of Modern Art in New York and the Art Institute of Chicago. Roland and Lee visited Ernst and Dorothea in France where in 1955 they had bought a house in Huismes, forty kilometers south-west of Tours. With the help of Ernst and Dorothea, he selected the works from the American show. Bill Lieberman, the Curator of Drawings at MOMA and his staff gave marvellous co-operation and the lenders, who were mostly private, were persuaded to extend their loans for another three months to allow that part of the show to come to the Tate. The balance of the loans was made up by European collectors who were mostly friends of Roland, although Melly, true to his word, refused even Ernst's plea to lend his *Portrait of Marie-Berthe*.

Ernst and Dorothea came for the opening, another celebrity bash for the ICA, with a more modest party to follow up so that artists and the less well-heeled could meet Ernst. The show attracted some satisfactory vitriol in the press but John Russell in *The Sunday Times* declared;

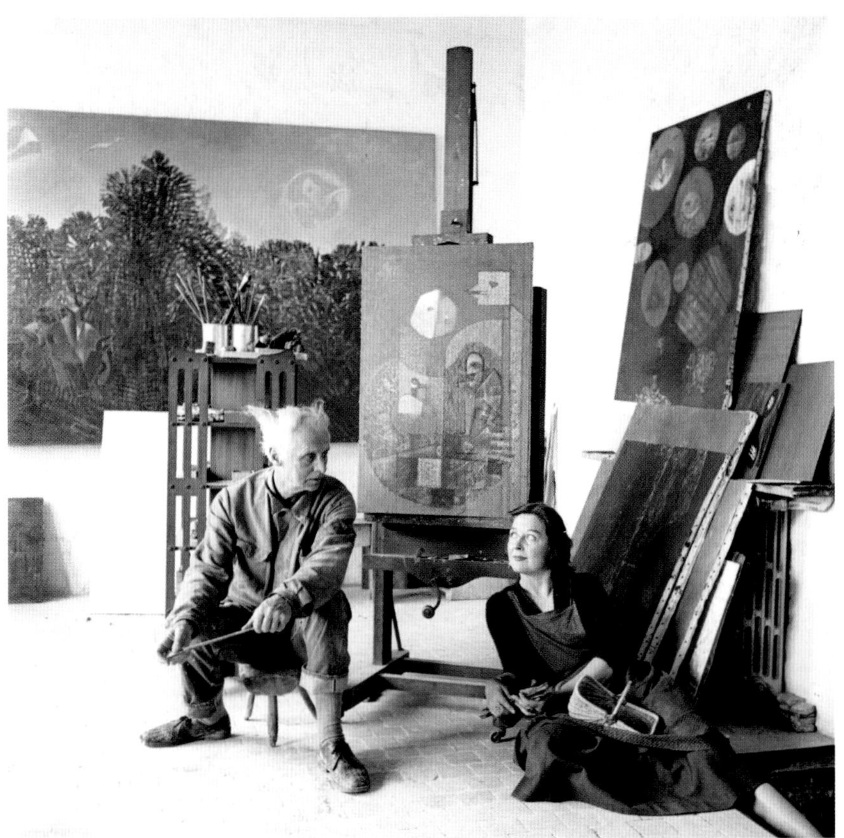

Max Ernst and Dorothea Tanning, Huismes, France 1955, by Lee Miller

> Something in the art of Ernst has always dismayed our local donkeys and they are likely (to be badly affected) for having seen the compendious homage to Mr. Ernst which has been arranged by Mr. Roland Penrose under the auspices of the Arts Council … . [8]

Stephen Spender, Robert Melville, Denys Sutton and David Sylvester wrote perceptive and glowing reviews. *The Times* echoed; '*One of the most arresting exhibitions ever to have been mounted at the Tate*'.[9]

The next year Roland and Lee went to the Venice Biennale and took me with them. There was a party at Peggy Guggenheim's palazzo on the Grand Canal that housed her famous collection. Although there was no evidence of it on this occasion, there had been a frost between Peggy and Roland. In her memoirs, referring to him as 'Donald Wrenclose' she commented he *'was a bad painter himself'*.[10] She had also catalogued in detail his exotic methods of tying her up by the wrists. He grumbled;

'I only used an ordinary pair of police handcuffs – I can't think where she got her ideas about ivory bracelets'.

But the comment about his painting really stung and he told her. She removed it from subsequent editions, gave him back his real name, but retained the reference to the ivory bracelets.

By the time I was sixteen, I had been at Bryanston School for a couple of years, arriving there after a spell in a London crammer. At the end of the Easter holidays, I passed through London to see Lee and Roland before catching the school train. Roland summoned me into the sitting room and shut the door. My schooling was never successful and I expected another exhortation to work harder, but I was wrong. He stood beside Picasso's *Weeping Woman* and told me how he had bought the painting from Picasso. Then he spoke about how he periodically sold works from the collection to 'replenish the family coffers' and I thought I saw his strategy; it was going to be a guilt trip about how much my school fees were costing, but I was wrong again.

'This painting is the most important one I own and I am going to give it to you partly to make sure that I never sell it. Also one day it will be worth quite something and you can sell it if you want. In the meantime, I have to live another seven years to make this gift free of tax'.

He went on to explain that the painting was constantly in demand as a loan and I would now have to be the one who decided which shows she went to. Of course he would help me if I wanted – and would I mind if he went on enjoying the painting in the flat?

I did not know what to say. The painting had always haunted me. When very young, I had asked why the lady was crying. Lee had explained that she had lived in a Spanish town called Guernica and a bomb dropped by an aeroplane had killed her little boy. The randomness of the deed horrified me and not knowing a thing about the atrocity that inspired the painting, I found myself apprehensively watching passing aircraft in case I should be the next little boy to be blown apart. Now I was starting my apprenticeship as a lender with one of the most important works in a private collection. For years I was able to chart the travels of the *Weeping Woman* by the private view invitations and catalogues that arrived in a bewildering variety of languages.

There was a hidden side to all this. Roland had made similar arrangements for Lee and it was not only his advancing years that made him concerned about providing for our future. He was again thinking of leaving Lee. At the time I could not blame him, as I had become embattled with her in relentless hostilities. She and I escalated our quarrels into an art form as her alcohol misuse and depression bit hard, exacerbated by her chosen method of giving up smoking sixty a day by stopping in the middle of a cigarette for a bet.

In the depth of her despair she would lash out and tell me in detail that I was thick and useless and a waste of money. *'You are boring!'* she would growl, her glassy eyes trying to lock on to mine. All drunks are boring and Lee was more boring than most. At dinner she would shout at Roland in front of the guests;

'God, not that story again, Christ, what a fucking bore you are' and then go droning on with some incoherent saga of her own. I avoided her whenever possible.

But Roland did not leave Lee. I will never understand what motives of loyalty, love or simply convenience bound them together. With the exception of Diane, whom Lee openly loathed and banned from proximity, she welcomed most of the girlfriends in Roland's life. Some, whom Lee perceived as spongers, were eventually sent packing, but those she approved of she treated as guests.

Roland's best antidote for the pressures of his household was to disappear overseas on a lecture tour or to visit Picasso. At the close of the Picasso show, Sir Colin Anderson, the Chairman of the Tate Trustees, asked Roland to see if he could try and persuade Picasso to sell the gallery one of the stars of the exhibition, the *Three Dancers*. The Tate could only offer about half the painting's value. It would have to be a *prix d'ami* and Roland was aware that Picasso had rebuffed several other museums who had made high offers.

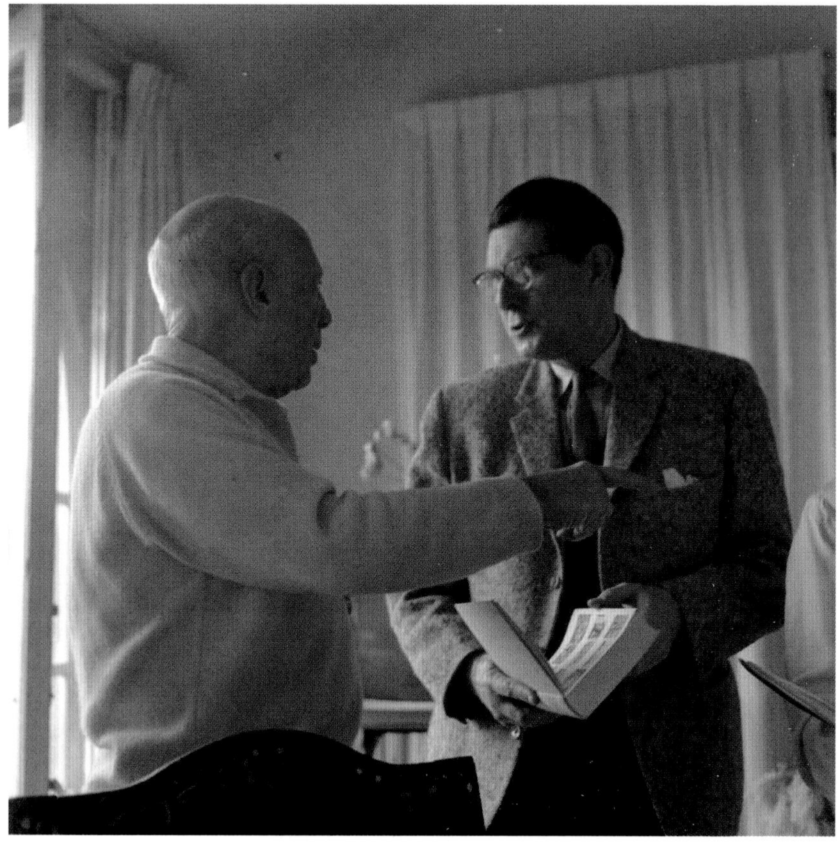

Picasso and Roland Penrose with the first French edition of *Picasso – His Life and Work*, Notre Dame de Vie, Mougins, France 1961, by Lee Miller

Roland was also in the process of organising the Arts Council Miró retrospective at the Tate. With the opening only nine weeks away, he was desperate to secure the loan he had previously negotiated for two Miró portraits Picasso owned, one of them being the key *Self-Portrait.* Roland noted;

> I then chose a moment when he was out of the room to ask Jacqueline about the loan of the two early Mirós for the London Exhibition. He came in just then and asked suspiciously what I wanted. 'It's the two Mirós that you kindly said you will lend for London', I told him. 'You mean the Mirós that I am not lending to London', he retorted angrily.
>
> 'You are not going to lend them! That's a disaster for us all.'
>
> 'Well that's how it is, I have had enough of people asking me for things, always making demands. I bought them. They are mine and I'm keeping them here'.
>
> 'Yes, I know people are always asking for things and it never stops and now it's me who is giving you the most shit in that sense.' I continued to exaggerate and just as suddenly as his anger had risen it disappeared and in a voice of resignation he said; 'OK, I will lend them if you want'. [...]
>
> An hour or two passed very pleasantly and we offered to leave; 'We could go and have dinner in Nice, if you like'. General delight at this suggestion – some time before Jacqueline had been talking to Lee in the house; 'I bet', she said, 'he will suggest that we go out to dinner – he will want to make amends for his peevishness about the Mirós'.[11]

Picasso finally agreed to sell *Three Dancers* to the Tate on 30 November 1964. It was the first painting he had ever sold directly to a museum. During the long negotiations Roland had endured every torment Picasso could devise, simply to see his old friend's masterpiece hang permanently in the Britain's foremost modern collection. It gave him great satisfaction to have Picasso's work thus validated by the institution that formerly represented everything he despised about art in Britain.

The Arts Council *Picasso Sculpture* exhibition was another marathon drama as Picasso, at the last minute, announced that the show was off. He was persuaded to change his mind and the show, including ceramics and drawings, opened at the Tate on 9 June 1967 to the kind of reviews that by now seemed habitual. The Tate exhibition was subsequently shown at The Museum of Modern Art in New York. Roland expanded his Tate catalogue essay for their superb book of the exhibition.

The 1964 Tate retrospective of Miró ran from 27 August to 11 October and the concurrent show at the ICA, *Miró, Thirty Years of his Graphic Art,* also drew excellent reviews. The tragic death of Miró's son-in-law prevented him from coming over for the openings, but he arrived in September with his wife Pilar. Miró was delighted when Desmond Morris, a great admirer of his work, proposed a visit to London Zoo. With his inherent sense of poetry, when asked what he wanted to see, he replied; '*Serpents, small birds and creatures of the night*'.

In the reptile house Morris gently draped a huge python around Miró's shoulders, where it lay motionless. Miró, with a beaming smile and no trace of fear, studied every detail of the animal's markings, its hard bright eyes and incessantly flickering tongue. In the bird house, Miró and a giant hornbill fell in love with each other. The bird, with its huge beak and erect crest looked as though it would have been as comfortable in one of Miró's paintings as it was perched on his wrist while he fed grapes into its vast beak.

Roland's friendship with Morris went back to 1950, when The London Gallery showed Miró, Morris and Cyril Hamersma. Then in 1957 ICA held an exhibition of paintings by a protégé of Morris's, Congo the chimpanzee. Morris ran the Granada Television programme called *Zoo Time*, where Congo was one of the regular stars. By chance, Morris noticed Congo could use a pencil to make patterns and built

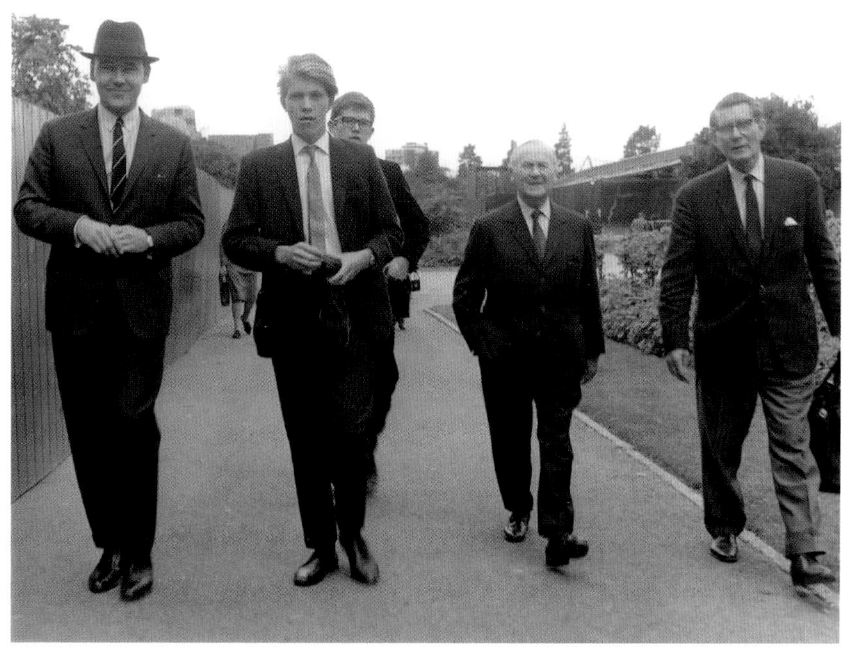

Desmond Morris, Antony Penrose, Ian Barker, Joan Miro and Roland Penrose, London Zoo, London, England 1964, by Lee Miller

on this. Soon Congo was turning out a steady stream of paintings and Morris started looking for a gallery for his first one chimp show. Roland and Read visited Morris and finding the work entirely genuine, scheduled an exhibition for Congo on 17 September.

The American artist Bill Copley, a dedicated supporter of the ICA, flew in especially to try and dissuade Roland from mounting the show Copley was sure would be the end of his credibility as a curator. Roland was undeterred. The opening was an outstanding success. Many came to the private view to scoff, but it was immediately realised that the work held something unique. The more scholarly looked for clues to the origin of painting in primitive man, while the Surrealists regarded it as one more celebration of the effects of chance and spontaneity. Satisfaction was derived from the scornful comment filling the letters columns of London's papers, but among Congo's adroit defenders was David Sylvester, the art critic of *The New Statesman.* As befitted a leading artist, Congo had his biography published. Congo's painting days were soon over, as after he matured he abandoned art for an interest in sex. Morris used some of Congo's earnings to buy him a chimpanzee wife and he retired happily.

After Françoise Gilot parted from Picasso, she remained friends with Roland and Lee and several of her drawings and paintings used to hang on the walls of Farleys where she visited a couple of times. I had remembered her as being kind to me as a child and my parents always talked affectionately about her. That was until she wrote her book *Life With Picasso*,[12] and became a demon in their eyes. Roland took down her paintings and spoke of her with angry bitterness. Today, it is hard to understand the furore caused by Gilot's book, which gives a valuable insight into both the genius and the human failings behind Picasso's deified persona. In 1964, when the book was first published in America, it was as if a deadly contagion had appeared among Picasso's friends and admirers, intellectuals and members of the French Communist Party. They made an unattractive spectacle as they denounced the book and its author, personally and in the media. When the book was published in Britain, Roland confronted Gilot on BBC Radio.[13] Gilot, as an old friend, a beautiful woman and a person whose art and intellect Roland admired, was the last person he could be expected to turn against, but she had hurt and enraged Picasso and that, for Roland, was a crime in the face of god.

Roland's need for refuge had changed Farleys from being the easy-rolling artist's colony into something more sedate. The hectic pace he maintained with his lecture tours, exhibitions and the ICA left him in need of time to recuperate and to write an endless number of catalogue essays and monographs such as his biography of Miró. The numbers of visitors to the house had declined slightly and as if in compensation, the

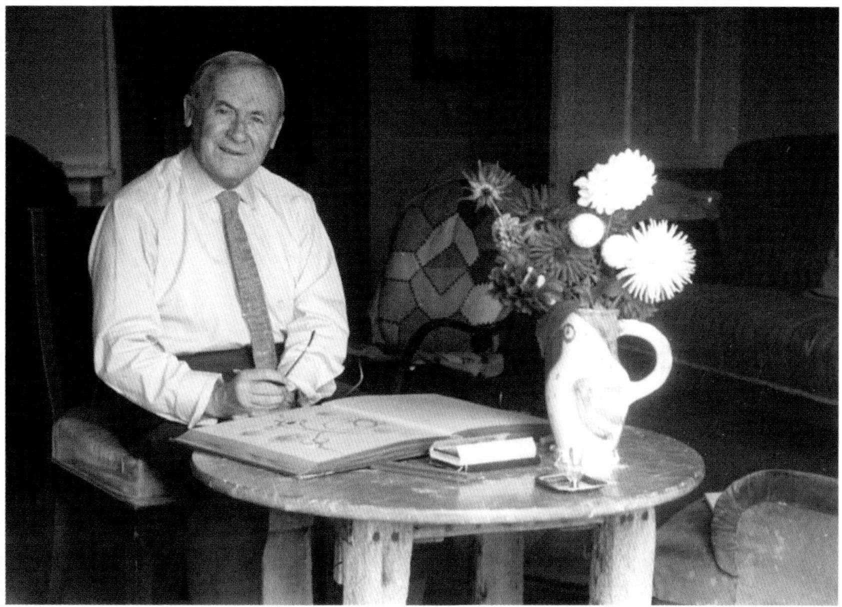

Joan Miro signing the visitor's book at Farleys House, Muddles Green, East Sussex, England 1964, by Antony Penrose

garden filled with sculptures. F. E. McWilliam's *Kneeling Woman* who had halted the London traffic in1948 was given a serene spot in a bower of apple trees. Germaine Richier's little naked *Bird Man* stood on the flat roof of the porch. In the orchard Michael Werner's vast disjointed *Fallen Giant* would soon lie prone beside the beehives, awaiting the harvest moon when he would assemble himself and feast on the apples from the tree tops – as I used to tell my children when they were little.

Moore's *Mother and Child* had adjusted happily to her new position on the lawn. Roland became interested in the theory of ley lines, the invisible channels of energy that link ancient sites. He was delighted to find he had sited *Mother and Child* on the line that linked the Long Man of Wilmington to Chiddingly Church, built on a site of far greater antiquity. He also noticed that standing beside the sculpture on Midsummer's Day,

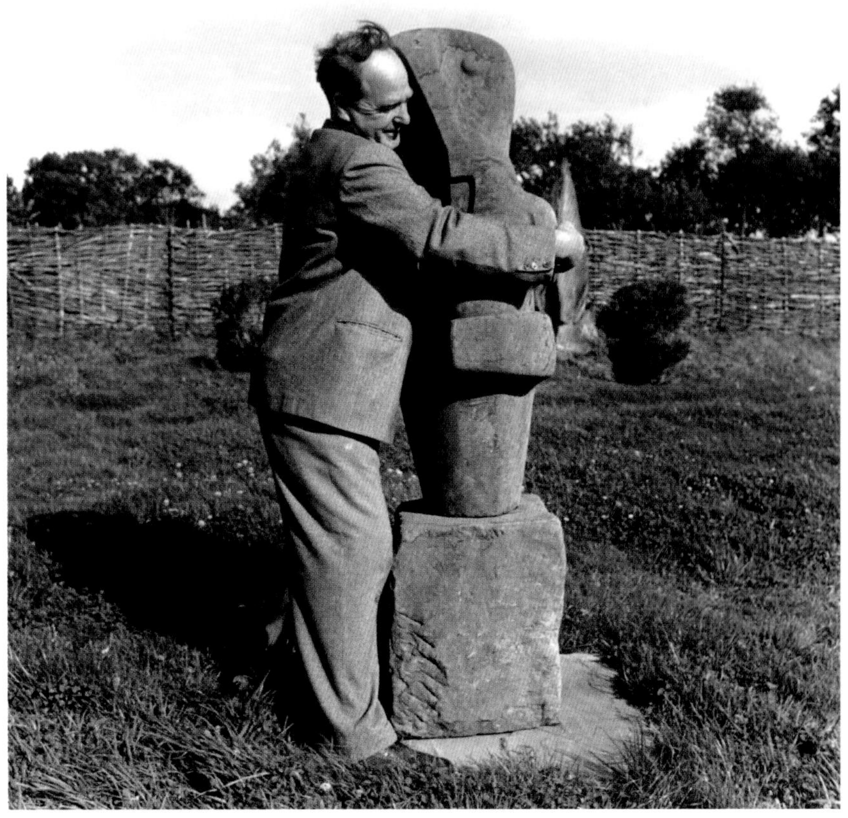

Henry Moore with his sculpture 'Mother and Child', Farleys House, East Sussex, England 1953, by Lee Miller

the sun was directly over the Long Man at midday and at midnight on Midwinter's Night, the great celestial giant of Orion hung in the same space. He loved this conjunction between the heavens, the farm and the sculpture and it became the source for some of his works.

By the gate Kenneth Armitage's bronze *Girl Without a Face* stood flirtatiously on a breast-like mound, contemplating Bill Turnbull's weathervane that surmounted the dovecot, home to a flock of tumbler pigeons that Roland loved for their acrobatic displays. On the other side of the drive he had constructed a fish-shaped fishpond on the same lines as the one he made at Le Pouy.

Another magnificent bronze female figure overlooked a pond on the kitchen side of the house. She was Bill Turnbull's *War Goddess* Roland had bought after Turnbull's show at the ICA. A fountain had the central place in the pond – the life-sized figure of a woman I had made from copper to Roland's design. He made a cardboard maquette and I

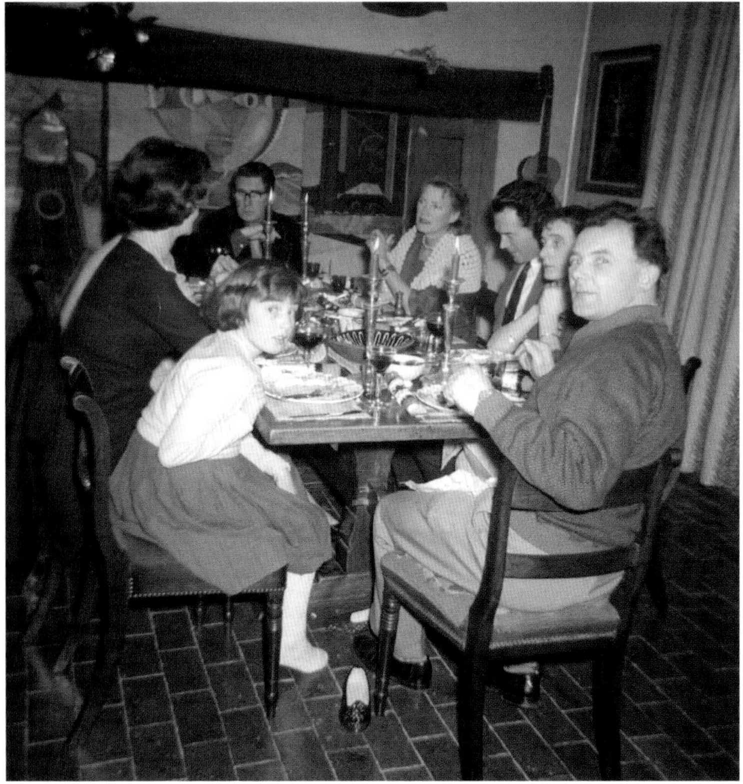

Christmas at Farleys House, clockwise – Georgina Murray, unknown woman, Bettina McNulty, Roland Penrose, Lee Miller, Henry McNulty, Patsy Murray and Stan Peters, Sussex, England 1961, by Antony Penrose

hammered out some of the components, putting others out to a firm of sheet-metal workers who enjoyed the figure's modest nudity. This work had special significance, as it marked a rapprochement between Roland and me after some bad events.

In the early 1960s Patsy's daughter Georgina came to live at Farleys. At a stroke, Patsy no longer belonged to me and to make matters worse, while I was away at school, it seemed that Roland and Lee had formed an increasingly close attachment to Georgina. School was the obvious place to get a reaction. For the first few years at Bryanston I worked hard and did well. Then I found a similarly disaffected pal and gradually things began to go wrong. We were quite creative in our mischief, but inevitably, we went too far. A series of nightmarish events followed. My pal ran away. Unknown to everyone he was a diabetic. In a state of mind altered by several days without food, he tied himself onto the railway line. He lived, but he lost both legs below the knee. His greatest hero had been Douglas Bader, the similarly disabled Spitfire pilot.

My friend's sacrifice of his legs gave me back Roland, Lee and Patsy. They were kind, forgiving and unexpectedly understanding. Back at Farleys I realised Patsy had enough love for both Georgina and me if I was prepared to receive it and Roland and Lee showed they were not going to give up on me. While my reconciliation with Lee was still another decade away, I found a deeper understanding and affection with Roland. I left Bryanston and before I went off to my first job as a machinist in a factory in Dorset, Roland and I built the fountain together. Copper has pleasantly durable, malleable and forgiving qualities that seemed symbolic and as we worked on the sculpture we began to get to know each other.

Roland continued to enjoy excellent health and looked younger than ever. In happy defiance of his upbringing, he attributed this to his liberal consumption of good wine and indifferent whiskey and the constant kippering of his lungs with cigars. But not even Picasso could escape growing old, although that was not evident in the vitality of work that

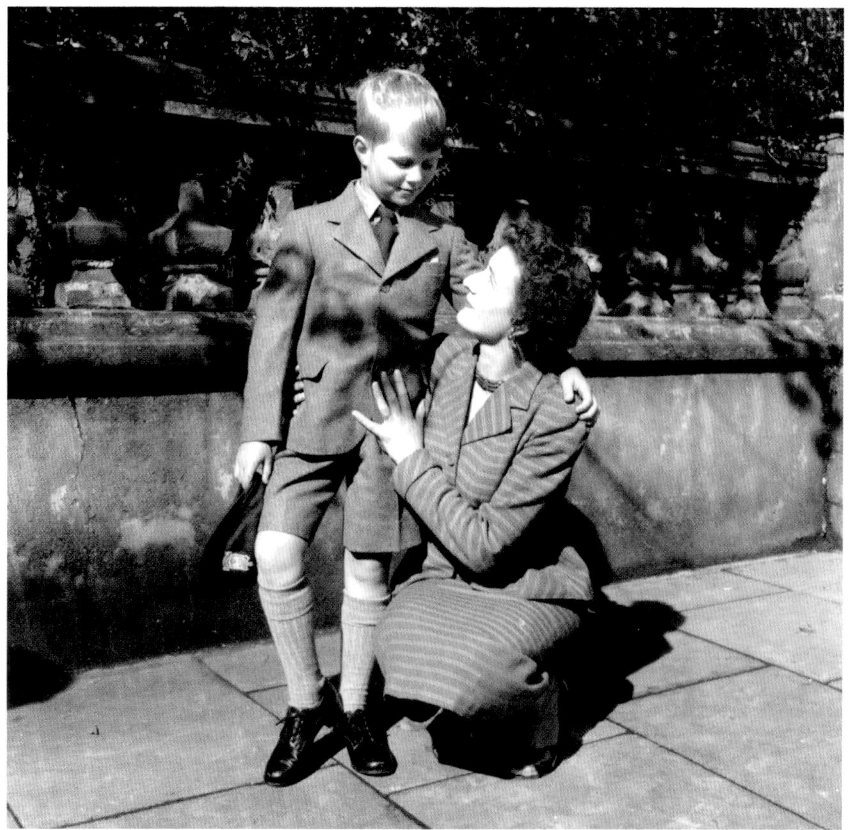

Antony Penrose and Patsy Murray, London, England 1957, by Lee Miller

still flooded from him. His eighty-fifth birthday in 1966 had been widely celebrated and provided an opportunity for Roland to express the ICA's gratitude to him in their Bulletin.[14] Picasso's support had been most notably the drawing in their visitor's book and the three drawings of Shakespeare and a painting he gave to the ICA to be auctioned for fundraising.

Fundraising had never been more of a priority. The lease was up on the old premises in Dover Street and a move was afoot to Carlton House Terrace, an august Nash mansion on The Mall. Most people agreed that the ICA needed to redefine its direction, as Dover Street was showing signs of losing its asperity and becoming a chummy, elitist club. The arts had become an accepted arena for political and social protest but the main action was now overtly in the street. CND [Campaign for Nuclear Disarmament] rallies had changed the face of public protest, achieving the largest mass arrest in British history. The CND demonstrations metamorphosed into protests against the war in Vietnam, in the time of Flower Power, The Beatles, Carnaby Street, minimalist and conceptual art and a haze of marihuana smoke.

Roland was enthusiastic about doing things on a grander scale, wanting the ICA to be a centre frequented by local artists that would have enough punch to feature internationally. He was concerned about Britain sinking back into its pre-war parochial isolation and saw the need to maintain the stimulation of work from overseas. Arnold Goodman, the Chairman of the Arts Council, recognised this and steered him towards taking the lease on Carlton House Terrace, together with four other societies for design, landscape architecture and advertising who were thought to share compatible aims.

It was the beginning of a long struggle to raise the £500,000 (about £5 million today) needed for the alterations to the building, rent and the extra staff required. It put Roland in the position he hated most – begging from his friends for gifts of paintings and sculptures or hosting expensive dinners for fundraising. Sotheby's gave their services free for two auctions on 23 June 1966 and 12 December 1967. To set the ball rolling Lee gave her cherished Braque Cubist painting *La Mandore* to the first auction. Arp, Bacon, Caro, Ernst, Hayter, Hepworth, Lam, Man Ray, Matta, Miró, Moore, Nicholson and Picasso were among the sixty-seven artists who generously gave first rate examples of their own work, with a further fifty-four donations coming from collectors and dealers. The Queen had her own private view, escorted by Roland. The auction was a great success, with the Tate buying *La Mandore*. Roland could not keep his hands still and bought Lynn Chadwick's *Dancers II*. The auction raised £119,600. The point of no return in the move to Carlton House Terrace was now passed.

Roland had anonymously presented Picasso's *Le Crayon qui Parle* to the first auction and intended to make a very generous gesture to the second auction eighteen months later. Joanna Drew recalled;

> I remember collecting Picasso's Nu sur la Plage from Hornton Street for Roland, as he wanted it to be in the auction. I was just leaving with it when Lee arrived. She asked me what I was doing so I told her. She said 'If that goes, I go!' I just put it down and fled! Roland was persuaded to change his mind and donate another work. It was the first Picasso that Roland had acquired.[15]

The opening party in April 1968 was the first time I set foot in the building and I had come straight from the farm in Norfolk where I had gone to work. If I had landed on another planet it would have been less of a jolt; the cavernous gallery was pulsing with the brain-pulping sound of an African rock band. The walls reflected ever-changing amorphous psychedelic colour patches projected from a series of ingenious lanterns. Various 'happenings' were staged around the gallery, some erotic, others just bewildering. It was hot, dark and jammed tight with merrymakers in the trendiest of costumes who danced, drank and enjoyed the sight of each other as much as the 'happenings'. Indeed it was a great event, but it was so un-Roland with its noise, garishness and raw licentiousness.

The new Director, Mike Kustow, had an understandable problem changing the culture of the old ICA that was based on gifted and dedicated amateurs who for twenty years had delivered world class programming on a shoestring. They had been accountable mainly to themselves and took risks that could now not be considered.

The first exhibition was a show proposed by Julie Lawson, titled *The Obsessive Image – Man 1960–1968.* Organised by Robert Melville and Mario Amaya, with work by Picasso, David Hockney and Claes Oldenberg, it was deliberately designed as an antidote to minimal and conceptual art and was seen by some as playing safe. *Cybernetic Serendipity* and *Play Orbit*, both organised by Jasia Reichart were adventurous and in the mode of the time, as were the shows *American Contemporary Prints – ONE* and *Fluorescent Chrysanthemum*, the work of two Japanese sculptors.

In the first six months, the programming had run £40,000 over budget, which was mainly attributed to poor financial control. Roland lacked the gritty authority to stop the slide and the Arts Council ordered severe cuts. The hubris of April had led to nemesis in December. Read was spared this last crisis, as in November he lost his battle with the cancer he had bravely fought for so long. Roland was deeply saddened. Read had been his travelling companion for more than forty years.

The ICA's next challenge to authority was not ingeniously subversive; it was just a crass stunt with a predictable outcome. Kustow hired Rosalie, an American performance artist, to produce a happening. The cinema was filled with cylinders of foam rubber, among which Rosalie frolicked naked to the blast of over-amplified music, lit by a movie film. Some members of the audience stripped off and joined in and the police took a big interest, not least because drug abuse was now rife in the ICA.

A few days later Roland and Kustow were summoned to attend a breakfast meeting with Arnold Goodman, the chairman of the Arts Council. Goodman made it plain that such programming betrayed those who had worked hard to secure the funding and influence to establish the ICA in its new home. While no boundaries were stated, an understanding was expected about the severity and the quality of the insults to the establishment, which clearly could not be expected to support embarrassments of the nature of Rosalie's happening.[16]

The ICA's autonomy was irreparably damaged. Further disasters followed and Kustow was suspended in October 1969. Goodman obliged Roland to take Read's role as President and he appointed Harry Kissim as the new Chairman. Roland wrote;

> Our new much needed helmsman, who soon after received a peerage, was according to Arnold Goodman 'a tycoon not yet

> submerged in good deeds,' but I soon began to have fears about his ability as a navigator in uncharted seas. The paintings chosen to decorate both his office and his home showed no signs of interest in contemporary art. Faultlessly lighted and framed in gold they were all conventional Dutch scenes … [that] reminded me of the taste of the myopic dons I had known at Cambridge.[17]

The following Easter we were all at Farleys when Roland received a devastating phone call from Elsa Fletcher, who looked after the Hornton Street flat. Thieves had ransacked the place and stolen a large number of the most important paintings. Roland, Lee and I arrived in London a few hours later to find Elsa in tears, broken glass strewn over the floors and a pile of empty frames. From them we identified that among the twenty six paintings stolen were four Picassos, the *Weeping Woman,* the Cubist *Nature Morte au Bec de Gaz, Head of a Woman* and *Negro Dancer.* De Chirico's *Uncertainty of the Poet* 1913, Ernst's *La Joie de Vivre*, Miró's *Head of a Catalan Peasant* and works by Braque, Man Ray, Magritte and others, including ironically a reproduction of Picasso's *Jeune Fille à la Mandoline,* made up the roll-call of paintings denied to Roland and the world in general. We were bereaved. Roland wrote to Picasso;

> Lee and I are both desolate and heart-broken, […] . The only consolation is that they have left the little Object that came from Paul and the little watercolour La Danse and a few drawings that still remind us of your presence and its enormous influence.[18]

The police acted swiftly and Detective Chief Superintendent Frederick Lambert was put in charge of the case. A conservative estimate valued the paintings at £300,000, but Roland had insured them mainly for fire, with only minimal cover for theft.

'Why should anyone bother to steal them?' he said, *'They could never re-sell them because they are too well known'.*

He reckoned without the trend of stealing for ransom. Samuel Jaffe, the film producer had his collection stolen a few months earlier and it was rumoured that his insurance company had paid a ransom to recover the works. It was not long before an unidentified caller began trying to contact Roland.

A few nights later Roland appeared on the BBC-TV programme *24-Hours.*[19] Without warning, the interviewer asked him if he would be prepared to pay a ransom. He reacted as though stung; '*I will have no dealings whatsoever with these people*', he retorted. Afterwards he said to Lambert that he felt sure the thieves would now destroy the paintings. Lambert reassured him, saying that Roland's commitment to standing firm actually strengthened their chances of catching the thieves.

Messages of sympathy and support poured in from Roland's friends and there was no shortage of crackpot advice, including a seriously advanced theory that the Kremlin was behind the theft. John Russell sent a message saying that the paintings belonged to the world and not just to Roland and he should not be so upright and Quakerish and pay the ransom demand. Roland furiously countered that if other owners had not done deals his pictures would still be on his walls.

In the months that followed Lambert's informers established the thieves' identity, but not where the paintings were hidden. A sting was set up to catch the whole gang red handed. On the day, Roland waited anxiously for news. None came and then he was astonished to see in the *Evening Standard* news of the discovery of an art haul.

Plain-clothes police had followed the thieves as they visited several places in south London, but had not been led to the paintings. Unknown to their observers, the gang had gone to the place where the paintings were hidden in a disused shop in Ealing, only to find it was impossible to recover their loot as builders had just started work.

Two workmen, Eddie Mitchell and Aubrey Worman, discovered the paintings, which narrowly escaped being tossed on the bonfire. Mitchell took one, the *Weeping Woman,* to a nearby art shop, to see if was 'worth a bob'. The owner identified it and phoned the police and before long the workmen and the disused shop became the focus for great excitement.

Roland went to Chelsea Police Station where, on seeing his paintings stacked around the walls, he wept openly. The paintings spent the night locked in the cells for security and then were whisked to the Tate where Stefan Slabczynski, the famous restorer, took them into intensive care. The most seriously damaged was Picasso's *Negro Dancer*, from which the thieves had cut the signature with the intention of sending it to Roland as a ransom note.

A skilful repair made the damage unrecognisable and Roland took the painting to Picasso to be signed once more. Picasso did not miss a chance to torment Roland.

'Every brush stroke is my signature: why should I sign it again?' he said.

Then he tried to sign it in Indian ink, knowing it would not take on oil. Finally, he protested that the packing would smudge the wet paint. Roland pointed out a cavity had been made in the crate to accommodate the signature and having run out of ideas for mischief, Picasso signed the canvas.

The informer narrowly escaped with his life. The ringleader avoided justice, but members of the gang were jailed. Some paintings, such as the *Weeping Woman*, remained at the Tate for safekeeping. Thereafter we lived among burglar alarms and security systems. Worse, a slight suspicion now greeted new requests to view the paintings. The casual accessibility that Roland gave others to both the collection and his life was ended.

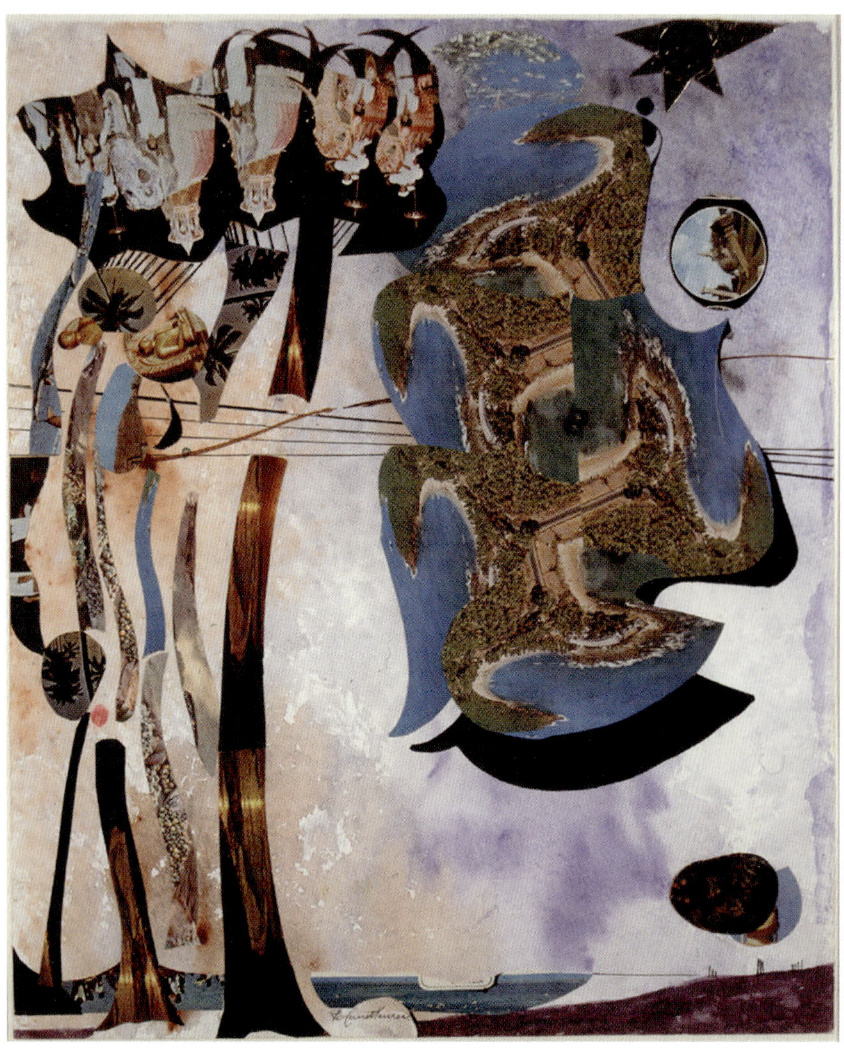

How do you like Sri Lanka Sir? 1981, collage

11 1970-84 Illusion and Reality

'Surrealism is no more dead than a dead flower containing seeds.'

George Melly, *The Savage God*. Lecture at Lewes Live Literature Festival, 27 June 1999.

In 1966 Roland sold the Cubist Picasso *Portrait of Uhde* and used the proceeds to buy Burgh Hill Farm adjoining Farleys. He happily told Picasso;

'The farm as a whole is now big enough that you would need a day to walk round the outside of it'.

'Have you tried that yet'? asked Picasso.

'No', said Roland.

'Well you had better be sure of some fine weather', replied Picasso.

Roland was relieved by his friend's reaction, as he felt that he was confessing the sin of selling a member of the family.

When I passed my final exams at the Royal Agricultural College in Cirencester Roland was worried. He could picture me coming back to the farm bursting with new ideas and upsetting everything.

'Before you settle down', he advised, *'why don't you do some travelling'?*

I needed no second bidding and teamed up with Peter Braden's elder son Robert, later known as Bozourg and my cousin Dominic, the son of Annie and Beacus. In the farm workshop we fitted out a Land Rover and crammed it with spares and equipment. Roland painted her name *Que Sera* ... on the front. We named our adventure *Muddles Overland Trek* after Muddles Green and our destination was Australia.

Roland tracked our journey across Europe, Asia, by sea to Malaya, overland to Singapore, then another voyage to Western Australia. We were broke and found jobs on wheat and sheep farms. Roland's letters were full of encouragement, but the tone changed sharply when I announced after six months that we had earned enough money to press on and my girlfriend Suzanna was joining us to go round the top end of Australia and through to New Zealand. I could not understand their misgivings, as in their brief meeting with Suzanna before I left England they had greeted her warmly. True, Bozourg and Dominic were apprehensive about having an elegant ballet teacher on board, but Suzanna soon won their hearts and they hers.

After touring New Zealand Dominic returned to England. Bozourg and I worked in a factory assembling bulldozers. Suzanna ran the Rembrandt Hotel, the cheapest flophouse in Auckland, filling a position made vacant by the murder of the previous incumbent. The New Zealand economy was booming and we worked all hours to raise cash, as our objective was to return to England via the Americas.

Roland was working on the *Illusion in Nature and Art* exhibition at the ICA,[1] a project he had nurtured for some years. He assembled a group of scientists centred on Richard Gregory whose work on perception had long fascinated Roland. Gregory and Sir Ernst Gombrich edited the book of the same title accompanying the show.[2]

In his essay titled *In Praise of Illusion*, Roland wrote;

> My praise of illusion is given not only because of its ability to create amusements, but also because it can sustain a power which is of inestimable value in our search for knowledge, our lasting enjoyment of life and our search for the fragile key to reality.[3]

A conjuror gave a performance and the ten-pound notes he produced from thin air proved as illusory as the ICA budget. Sadly the success of the *Illusion* … show was not typical of events at the ICA. Earlier in the year Roland had contributed £5,000 to ensure the show would be mounted. The new director, Ted Little, had rapidly moved into conflict with Roland who now found himself openly insulted and obstructed. Despite the success of the *Illusion* ... show, he encountered bitter opposition to the exhibitions he planned for Man Ray and Ernst. He persisted in going ahead, but at the same time put more effort into his own work.

1970 had seen the publication by Thames & Hudson of Roland's biography of Miró. Roland gives us a picture of the artist that is as compelling as his work; the reclusive peasant-like figure who loved poetry, who Ernst nearly hanged in drunken jest,[4] and who was wracked by the torments of the Spanish Civil War; a man who showed his most extreme savagery in some of his paintings of women, yet treated his wife and daughter with heartfelt tenderness. He understood the fine balance of cruelty and delicacy that is ever present in nature, as it is in the innermost parts of man and rendered this truth visible on canvas.

Roland found writing so hard I often wondered what strange puritan work ethic drove him. Perhaps he sought absolution through this extreme form of penance. He wrote in long hand, laboriously, burdened by what must surely have been dyslexia, his many changes making the page look like a collage. The flowing text of his book *Man Ray* refutes the agony of Roland's creative process.[5] This scholarly and affectionate work tells us a great deal about the oeuvre, but Roland is too discrete about the artist himself.

Of all Roland's Surrealist friends, it was Man Ray I liked the most with his dry wisecracks and his Brooklyn accent. He and Juliet often welcomed me to his Paris studio at 2 bis rue Ferou. Once, as a brash teenager, I had the temerity to ask him his real name. He flipped from being a benign, melancholy owl to an ogre. '*I am here to give inspiration, not information*', he growled. Man Ray invented himself and he was the most effective of his own creations. He had transformed himself from Emmanuel Radnitsky, the son of a Russian Jewish immigrant tailor, into

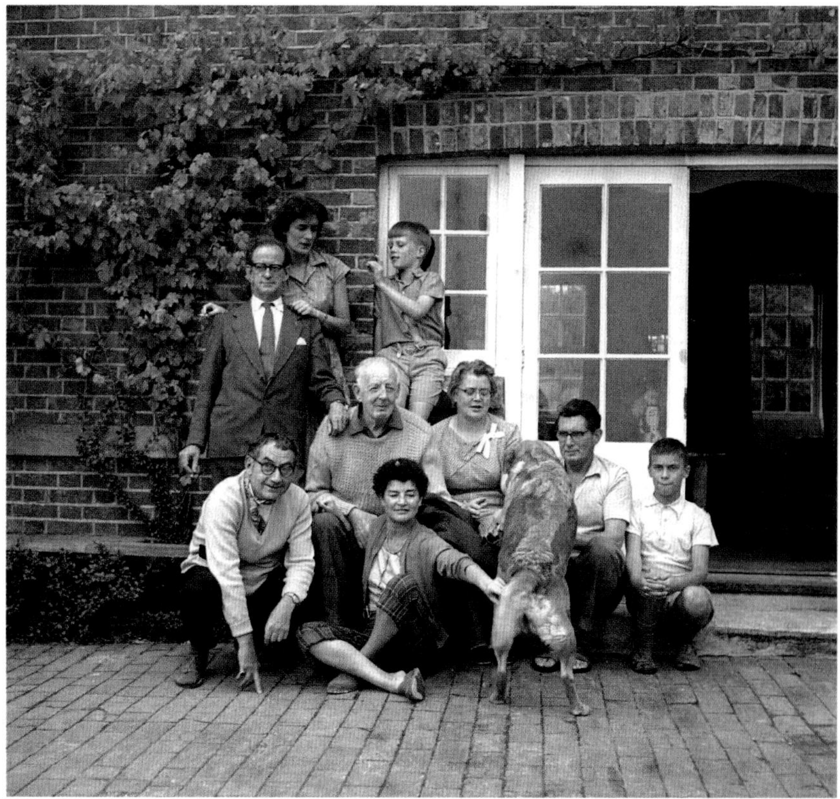

Man Ray, Juliet Browner, Heather the dog, Peter Gregory, Joyce Reeves, Roland Penrose and John Funnell, Maxwell Fry, Patsy Murray and Antony Penrose, Farleys House, East Sussex, England 1957, by Lee Miller

an enigma, free from history, limitations and dependants.[6] He recorded his persona in his autobiography *Self Portrait*,[7] and Roland, out of respect for his friend, refused to reveal more, thereby perpetuating Man Ray's legend.

In our little flat in Auckland we heard the news of Picasso's death and I could feel echoes of Roland's extreme grief in my own heart. The passing of time gave him the perspective to write;

The shock and implacable finality of the news on the morning of

> Sunday 8 April 1973 that he had died at first seemed incredible – another of those diabolical jokes he delighted in inflicting on his friends to test their perception of the uncertainty of our human condition. Slowly I realised that the only consolation that remained was the knowledge that beyond death, his work would live and his influence would endure.[8]

In the controversy surrounding Picasso's estate, Roland sensed he was offered a poisoned chalice when he was invited by Dominique Bozo to join Jean Leymarie and Pierre Daix on the committee to select the works for the *dation* of Picasso's works to the French nation in settlement of tax.

Day after day they filtered through the thousands of works going back to 1895 when Picasso was fourteen, up to the end of his life. Roland told me that at times he felt as though he was burgling his old friend's house. The process of selection took two years and in the autumn of 1979 the collection of nearly seven hundred paintings and sculptures was exhibited at the Grand Palais and *le tout Paris* turned out.

A large part of the show travelled to Minneapolis and then to MOMA in New York, where it joined other loans and great works of the museum's collection such as *Les Demoiselles d'Avignon, Guernica* (still on loan to them) and *Jeune Fille à la Mandoline,* formerly of Roland's collection. It was the largest and most complete show of Picasso's work ever assembled and drew crowds for four-and-a-half months. The following year Roland and Joanna Drew were able to secure for London a magnificent selection of the works that would form part of the Musée Picasso in Paris. John Golding collaborated with Roland on the catalogue for the exhibition, which was called *Picasso's Picassos.*[9] It was the last great show of Roland's career as an exhibition organiser and as the gallery was crowded to capacity with extensive media celebrations, it proved a very suitable note to end on.

Roland was still in demand as a lecturer, but his presentations were an ordeal for him and at times for the audience. He insisted on reading and stumbled over his lines in a monotone. He used unimaginatively chosen slides and frequently bungled the cues. He did not have enough confidence in his recall to memorise the script and remained stuck to the ground. But on the rare occasions when he spoke without notes, his words had wings and his love for the subject came straight from his heart.

The year of Picasso's death found my friends and I preparing to leave New Zealand. Bozourg and our new friend Peter Comrie accompanied *Que Sera …* on the MV Tropic to Matarani in southern Peru. Suzanna and I stayed on in Auckland with Lowell and Tony Cotton, two friends who had recently married. The Cottons' happiness prompted romantic thoughts in Suzanna and me. Roland had severely discouraged us from marrying, so on the afternoon of our departure without a word to either of our families we were wed in Auckland registry office. Tony and Lowell were our witnesses and covered us in confetti as we boarded our flight for Tahiti. After two blissful, romantic days we flew to Lima and then reached the southern port of Matarani in time to see the MV Tropic sail in with Bozourg, Peter and *Que Sera …* on deck. We were conveniently still a month away from our first mail pick-up in Lima.

I opened Patsy's letter first, receiving her warmest congratulations. She told me Roland did not take the news well. He felt that I had betrayed him and spurned his good advice. Lee wrote with great warmth and instantly enveloped Suzanna as a friend and Valentine affectionately confirmed that our horoscopes were auspicious. Suzanna's parents were so excited they forgot to be cross.

For seven months we travelled up through Latin America and took a ship round the impassable isthmus of Darien, finding our way to Mexico City where we stayed with Leonora Carrington. She directed us to the Sonora market where every possible accoutrement for witchcraft was sold. Seeking a reconciliation present for Roland I bought an *ojo de venado,* a charm made from a seed resembling a deer's eye and also a strange dried flatfish. Leonora approved of the *ojo de venado,* but the fish threw her and her friends into disarray. It contained powerful forces that could be used for bad magic, they said. I proposed chucking it away, but no, even if I burned the fish I would still own the magic and it could settle on anyone who angered me. The thought of Roland sprouting fins or Suzanna shrivelling up after a row was too much, but what should I do? One of Leonora's friends wrote out a mathematical mantra in red ink, to be tied round its neck. The magic force would spend the rest of its life trying to solve the riddle and would thereby be rendered safe. Roland loved it and it hung in his study for many years.

In Los Angeles, we stayed with Lee's brother Erik and his wife Mafy and went on to tour the USA and Canada for seven months. We shipped from Quebec to Southampton a few days before Christmas – three years, three months and seventy thousand land miles after leaving England.

Roland and Lee were not among those who welcomed us. They had gone to New York for the opening of the show *Man Ray. Inventor, Painter, Poet* he and Mario Amaya had curated at the New York Cultural Centre. The signature emblem was a giant version of Man Ray's *Indestructible Object,* his metronome with the image of Lee's eye slowly arcing to and fro on its pendulum. They were staying until mid-January for the opening of the show *Max Ernst, A Retrospective* at the Guggenheim Museum.

Roland and Lee had suggested that we meet for Christmas in Florida, but we were tired, broke and after three Christmases on the road wanted to be home.

'We will give you a second Welcome Home in January', they had offered.

It was all so logical and all so bitterly disappointing that my return as the prodigal son complete with my adored wife should lack the approval I most wanted. Suzanna and I moved into our beautiful early Victorian house on a hilltop close to Farleys and grappled with a settled life.

When Roland and Lee did come home, we met like strange dogs sniffing at each other. Questions such as; 'Do I have a place on the farm/ in your life/ in this family?' were impossible to approach given Roland's aversion to confrontation and I settled uncertainly into an ill-defined role on the farm.

By this time, Lee had won control of her drinking and had become celebrated in *Vogue* and *House & Garden* as a gourmet cook. It takes great courage for a young bride to invite a gourmet cook mother-in-law to her home, but that is what Suzanna did. She constantly made Lee and Roland welcome in our home and gradually Lee and I made friends. It was not a mother–son relationship, but more like a grudging affection between two battle scarred warriors who suddenly find they would have been fighting on the same side if only they had known differently.

I discovered Roland and Lee had at last found an accord, although the nature of it was still baffling. Roland had a new girlfriend, Daniella, a young Israeli film editor. Daniella's lovely, open face with dark eyes was topped by a mass of dark curls. She appreciated art, she loved Roland and treated Lee with respect. Lee became fond of Daniella and recognising her integrity and the happiness she gave Roland, she encouraged them to enjoy each other.

The New York show *Man Ray. Inventor, Painter, Poet* transferred to the ICA from 11 April to 1 June 1975 and Man Ray and Juliet came over from Paris for the opening. Man Ray was in a wheelchair, desperately frail, but greatly enjoying the attention from the large numbers of young people his shows always seem to attract. Watching him and Lee together, it was plain to see the strong bond of love that still existed between them.

The cash crisis at the ICA had worsened and mounting the Man Ray show was only possible because Roland made substantial donations. In their efforts to stay afloat, the ICA had sold nearly all the works of art donated by artists, including the much-treasured Visitors' Book. Dating back to the earliest days of the ICA, the book contained the Picasso grasshopper bulls drawing. Dedications by Sutherland, Masson, Chagall, Moore, Kokoschka, Keyt, Steinberg, Ernst, Tanning, Dubuffet and others adorned pages in what amounted to a roll call of the leading figures of international modern art.

In 1973, Alistair McAlpine, a property developer and later Deputy Chairman of the Conservative Party, who was then an ICA Council member, loaned the ICA £15,000, taking the Visitors' Book as surety. Two years later, needing the money himself and as the ICA were not in a position to pay off the loan, he consigned the Visitors' Book to auction at Sotheby's. The way the Sotheby's catalogue was worded made it look as if the ICA was behind the sale and this was likely to cause offence to the artists who had contributed their works. Roland was appalled. The agreement had been that if McAlpine ever sold the Book, it should go to the Tate.[10]

At the auction, the Visitors' Book was knocked down for £28,000 to gallery owner Leslie Waddington.[11] Roland had arranged for it to be 'bought in' by Sotheby's and paid them £10,000 with a further £1,179 direct to McAlpine as a half share in the auction expenses.[12] The Visitors' Book was presented to the British Museum on behalf of two anonymous donors. Roland was clearly one donor, but the identity of the other and their contribution was never conclusively disclosed.

In his autobiography, McAlpine records his version of events;

> I offered the Visitors' Book for sale at Sotheby's. Roland Penrose was furious. Why, I can never really understand, for he had sold the book to me for far more than it was worth. Why should I not sell it on to someone else and try, at least, to recover part of my money? I had never made any promises to Penrose and at the time I bought the book, he needed money at the ICA to put on a show to enhance his reputation.[13]

McAlpine shows an unusual perception of events. The Sotheby's auction price of £28,000 after only two years would generally be taken as an indication that when he bought the Visitors' Book for £15,000 he paid way *under* its value.

Ted Little objected strongly to the next show Roland proposed, scheduled for 15 January to 29 February 1976, which was *Max Ernst. Prints, Collages and Drawings 1919–1972.* The main exhibition space had become more focussed on trendy shows and Little complained that '*another major retrospective show would damage the balance and overall direction of his "arts centre" programming*'.[14]

Encouraged by Little, the staff began a war of attrition against Roland and Julie Lawson. On one occasion Roland arrived in his office to find Little's henchmen removing his desk. *'You won't be needing this'*, they told him, *'you're finished here'*. Sabotage became rife and just before the opening of the Ernst show the gallery and foyer were vandalised with purple paint daubed everywhere. A team of decorators had to be hired to work round the clock. Ernst was too ill to attend the show and Roland almost too dispirited. More vandalism followed and more abuse for Roland, Julie and anyone connected with them.

Among the sprinkling of meaningful shows, events tended towards trashy sensationalism and some extremes of obscenity. Roland had to concede that he no longer had a place in the organisation he had created and nurtured for thirty years, so he tendered his resignation. There was a meeting at the house of the new ICA Chairman Robert Loder in an attempt at reconciliation but Roland's mind was made up. He walked home alone in the rain.

His letter of resignation concluded with dignity;

> I no longer recognise in the present situation the fundamental aspirations of the enthusiasm which have during the last thirty years caused me so willingly to give to the ICA all I could afford in time and money.[15]

1976 had probably been the worst year of Roland's life. Ernst had died on 1 April and in early November, while Roland was at Farleys still deeply depressed by his resignation, Juliet Man Ray phoned with the news that Man Ray had died.[16]

'I have just kissed him for you', she said between sobs, *'he is still warm'*. Roland and Lee's dearest friends were making their exits. Worse was to come.

Lee told me that she had cancer of the pancreas. I was not impressed. Her hypochondria had inured us all to her various ailments and no one took her seriously. But this time it was real. I returned from filming in Iran to find Lee in the sitting room at Farleys. Patsy told me she had made a special effort to come downstairs for my return. Soon nothing could move her from her bed. Roland and Patsy nursed her at Farleys with every possible care.

Lee encouraged her friends to visit and enjoy a drink with her.

'Come soon', she would say, *'I want to see you before I go'*.

Her characteristic courage gave her death as just another interesting adventure. Lee lived long enough to meet our first daughter, Ami, born in the spring before she died on 21 July 1977. We scattered her ashes in the garden on the eve of Suzanna's birthday.

Roland was overwhelmed by a flood-tide of anguish. Those of us who knew the harshness with which he and Lee treated each other on occasion were amazed. For weeks he walked a tightrope between dignity and inconsolable grief, then he became withdrawn, like a brutalised child. Slowly he emerged again, limping along like a sailing ship that has lost half its spars and canvas in a tempest. He wrote;

> For me death had ploughed its furrow in my bed and was now to sit at my table. I was to swallow my wine in silence. Its dark presence in Lee's absence was overshadowing all and its clutches inescapable. Yet life continued to demand its imperative renewal with powerful seduction.[17]

Valentine had been staying at Farleys for long periods. She was suffering from a form of leukaemia that left her ever more debilitated, but it failed to dull the brightness of her mind. With Roland's encouragement, she had assembled an anthology of her poems, which were translated by Roy Edwards.

As a schoolboy, Edwards had sent some of his poems to Roland in the days of the London Gallery and, aged seventeen, had been hired as an assistant, working with George Melly. At first, Mesens regarded Edwards as Roland's spy, but soon realised he was incapable of malice. Literature was his life's passion and he was an authority on Surrealist poetry. He and Valentine worked together for months, Roy, a poet and collagist in his own right being the only person who translated Valentine's poems to her satisfaction.

Back in 1974, Roland was on the point of selling the Ernst painting *Elephant of Célèbes* to bail out the ICA once more. The painting, which Roland bought as part of the Eluard collection, marked Ernst's evolution from Dada to Surrealism and was considered one of his key works. It hung in the dining room at Farleys for many years, a brooding, menacing presence.

Fortunately, Roland listened when Julie Lawson pointed out that his noble sacrifice of the painting would be futile as the ICA would consume infinite funds without trace. He formed The Elephant Trust to which he gave the painting. The trust then sold the painting and invested the proceeds to provide money for the kind of projects that lay outside the usual sources of funding. 'The Elephants', as the trustees, past and present are affectionately known, have had the satisfaction of enabling a wide variety of art and literature projects to happen over the years, although the occasional applications from zoo-keepers and others concerned with the welfare of pachyderms meet with disappointment.

Another cause for satisfaction was the *Dada and Surrealism Reviewed* exhibition in London at the Hayward Gallery from 11 January to 27 March 1978, which had among the committee members friends such as David Sylvester, Elizabeth Cowling, Dawn Ades, Roy Edwards and John Golding. The show was organised by Joanna Drew and Richard Francis of the Arts Council. Roland's memory was beginning to fail and he could not recall if Richard Francis's name was Francis Richard or Richard Francis. He solved it by referring to him as 'Republique Français', joking his way out of a condition that was to increase in its affliction.

A hip problem had also beset Roland and under protest, he allowed himself to contribute to the hang from a wheelchair. It was probably the most comprehensive show on the subject, tracing the early movements of Dada in Zurich, Paris and America. The catalogue remains a definitive document, its excellent essays encompassing so much of the spectrum of the movement. Roland was delighted to lend many works and to see *Elephant of Célèbes* join the menagerie of dream creatures adorning the walls. It was the anthem of his life.

'How does it feel to see the relics of your revolution laid out in the glass cases of the establishment?' I asked unkindly as we left the hanging of the show late one evening.

'It is no longer the same establishment – the revolution changed it', he replied.

'But in so doing, it has been eaten by the beast it fought. Where is your revolution now, or is there nothing left that needs changing?' I countered.

'Change is part of life. Revolution will always exist where frontiers need pushing back', he replied.

'So where is the battle now?'

'That', he said, *'is for you to find out for yourself'*.

With Franco dead, the cultural life of Spain had undergone a marvellous transformation, acutely felt by another great Catalan painter Antoni Tàpies. Tàpies is often quoted as saying *Art is life and life is transformation,* a view Roland clearly shared. When Tàpies, who was considered Spain's leading abstract painter, asked Roland to write a monograph on his life and work, he jumped at the chance. Roland's usual lack of enthusiasm for abstract painting was more than overcome by the strong influence of Surrealism and Eastern philosophy he found in Tàpies's work. A man of profound, religious-like conviction, Tàpies had been fined and imprisoned without trial by the police who considered him a threat to the Franco regime. His name in Catalan means 'a wall' and many of his works grew to be like the surfaces of walls in the old parts of his city, bearing mysterious scars and graffiti. He invites us to decode the marks and enquire what lies within and behind these walls,

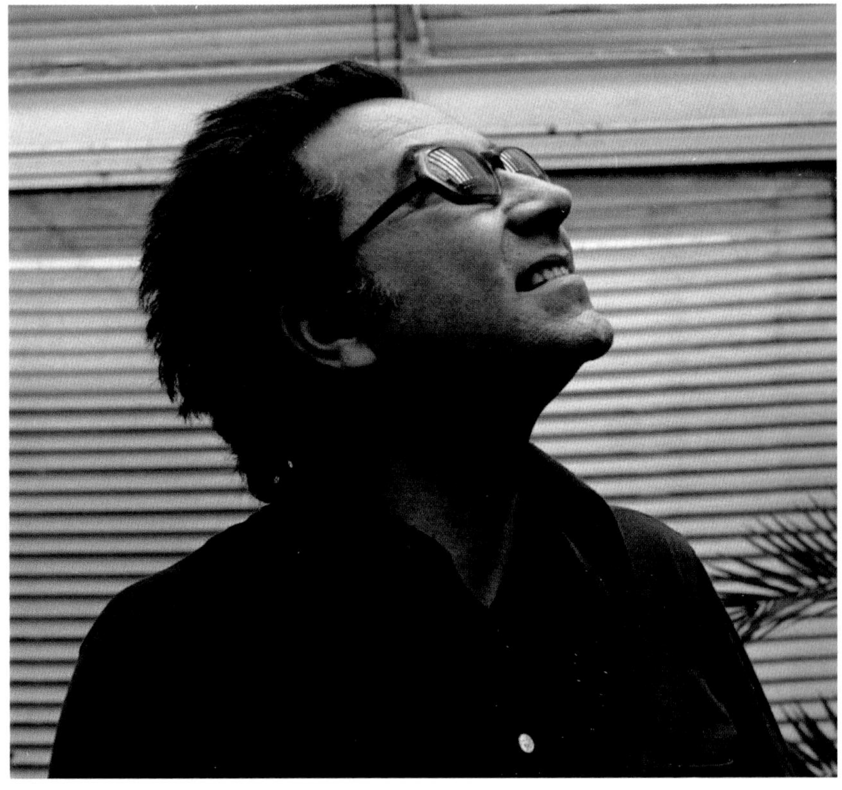

Antoni Tapies, Barcelona, Spain 1972, by Lee Miller

hidden from the gaze of the police and others who lack the receptivity needed to penetrate beyond the superficial.

Roland dedicated the book to Valentine who shared his passion for Tàpies's work.[18] At Farleys I found her studying a set of lithographs.

'This is marvellous', she said, *'It is nothing and yet it is everything'*.

A fitting tribute to the artist who it was said could see the whole universe in an insignificant piece of clay.

Valentine was fading. Patsy made her as comfortable as possible at Farleys; friends like Roy Edwards visited regularly and Roland, Suzanna and I did all we could. By the summer of 1978 she was bedridden for weeks, waiting for the moment when the door into the next world would open. *'Oh, it is so hard to die'*, she sighed one evening, in a tone that ached with weariness. The door opened enough for Valentine to slip through on 2 August. Her brother, Gilbert, her niece Martha and Roland scattered her ashes in part of the garden she particularly loved. Here the buttress roots of an oak tree sheltered an abundance of wild cyclamen that Valentine had introduced, the delicate pink flowers reminiscent of her native Gascony and Le Pouy.

> Le Pouy is sleeping in the cold, with its hard-barked chestnut tree and all its charms abandoned there with the threads of old needlework lost in the grass.[19]

Roland had lost both Lee and Valentine in just over a year. He and Daniella had sadly parted company and now his own health was deteriorating. A hip operation had gone badly wrong and had not restored the mobility he longed for.

Suzanna and I had our second daughter Eliza the following year. Roland was never very keen on small children, but as soon as the girls started producing art, he was delighted and proudly displayed several of their 'gluings' as part of his collection. Occasionally he invited them to his studio and they all made collages together.

In the summer of 1980, we loaded our small girls into a camping van and set off on tour with Roland. 'Roland's Roadies' we jokingly called ourselves and our first stop was the Fermoy Gallery in Kings Lynn, for the opening of the *Roland Penrose Retrospective Exhibition.* A selection of seventy-four paintings, frottages and collages formed the exhibition with *The Last Voyage of Captain Cook* as the centrepiece, affirming Roland's connection back to the 1936 International Surrealist Exhibition.

Roland selected the works and the six-venue tour that, to his intense pleasure, ended at the Fundació Joan Miró in Barcelona, was organised by Joanna Drew and Richard Francis for The Arts Council.[20] They printed a facsimile edition of *The Road is Wider Than Long* to accompany the show. It was thirty-one years since Roland's last one-man exhibition and his first ever retrospective. Joanna wrote an affectionate foreword to the catalogue and Norbert Lynton provided the first essay on Roland's life and work. After all the years of writing essays for other people's catalogues, Roland had at last received a perceptive and appreciative tribute worthy of his own work.

Earlier in 1980 Cob Stenham the Chairman of the ICA and Bill McAlister, the director[21] invited Roland to return as the Honorary President. We were horrified, expecting more exploitation and abuse, but he would not be dissuaded and we dreaded the outcome. The next venue of the tour was the ICA and we waited for the paint daubers to strike, but it went without a hitch. In September the ICA held a party celebrating Roland's eightieth birthday and paid a genuine homage to his work and his support for the organisation. The reviews were quite the opposite of the show at the Mayor Gallery in 1939. The *Evening Standard* wrote; 'The grand old man who introduced Surrealism to the British in 1936 has finally been given a show to commemorate his 80th Birthday'.[22]

Roland's public recognition was gratifying, but did nothing to alleviate the loneliness of his spirit. *'I cannot live without a woman in my life'*, he told me. Again he begged Diane to marry him. Sadly for him, she valued her independence too much and was repelled by his possessiveness. Although she had affection for him, she disliked his fondness for whisky and the frayed appearance of his clothes. Above all, the cats at Farleys dangerously aggravated Diane's asthma. Roland renovated his studio in a lovely old malt house in the garden with the hope she might live there, but it was not to her taste. She missed her life in Paris and staying in London suited neither of them.

Diane did persuade Roland to take some holidays. He seldom travelled for pleasure, but went with her to Trouville for sea-water therapy and then to Malindi on the Kenyan coast. He found it excessively hot and the surf was too strong for him to swim. The gentleness of Sri Lanka and its Indian culture was more to his liking. After the trips, he would return to Farleys without Diane, more conscious than ever of his loneliness. He would stay indoors forlornly waiting for her phone calls that seldom came, ignoring the pleas of Tina the Labrador to be taken for a walk.

Suzanna adored Roland and he frequented our house with his guests. The Surrealist painter Matta, Juan Martin, the Flamenco guitarist, his wife Helen and the painter David Dennison were among our visitors, with old friends such as Davie Scherman. In turn, Roland enjoyed the lively company of our travelling friends who filled the house and Suzanna's passion for modern dance added many dancers from the London Contemporary Dance Theatre who would come and stay when performing locally.

Roy Edwards was suffering from cancer and Roland was glad to

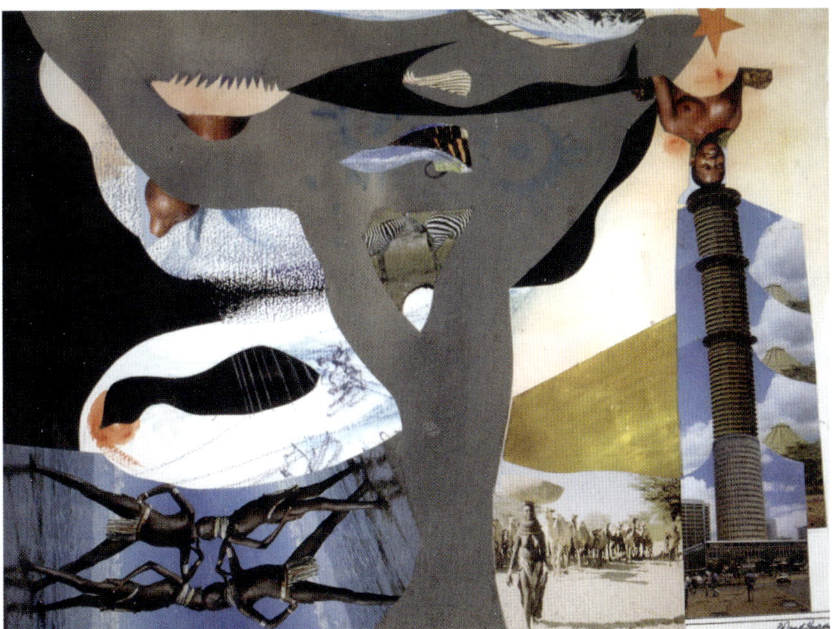

Fertillity II, Kenya, 1983, Collage

make him and his friend Geoffrey Lawson comfortable at Farleys amid the books and paintings he loved. George Melly came to visit him. John Banting had appointed both George Melly and Roland as his executors and when they met to settle the estate they forgot their old differences and forged a friendship that Roland treasured. By now there were very few with whom he could share memories of the early days, but more important he found George Melly's outrageous zest for life a great boost for his own spirits.

Roy Edwards did not allow his condition to prevent him from working with Roland on his next book. The bold, spacious design of the Tàpies book with its plentiful illustrations had provided both a model and publishers for Roland's autobiography. The Victorian habit of keeping a scrap-book had never left Roland. In a sense *The Road Is Wider Than Long* is a kind of scrap-book with its random assemblage of words and images and during the war he made his *War Time Scrap Book*, full of unrelated collages and other images. Now he accumulated folders of what literally amounted to scraps of his life; his memories of friends and autobiographical notes that became *Scrap Book 1900–1981*.[23] Disappointments, quarrels and betrayals are treated lightly. The man who so enthusiastically invited chance into his life does not permit the hypocrisy of complaining about reversals of fortune. His relentless optimism keeps him dwelling on the pleasant things in life. With habitual generosity, he gives credit to others for things he did himself and attributes his own successes to luck, that female characterisation of chance that he prized as if she were one of his lovers. But he gives himself no credit for the courage it takes to woo such a fickle and dangerous mistress.

A minor stroke affected Roland's short-term memory and complications arose with his eyesight that effectively precluded him from writing. He was utterly miserable until Diane persuaded him to redirect his energies into collage-making. When they travelled he would make small collages in his hotel room, but most were made in his studio with the mass of postcards he brought home. People would give him cards with striking images, but this was not what he wanted. He chose them for the coloured pattern and the way they could be used in a rhythm. Coral fans, palm trees, Sri Lankan elephants in ceremonial dress, or banal images of the Changing of the Guard would await their turn to become fused into agglomerations in the company of morsels of print, scraps of rubbish, fragments of trees, or

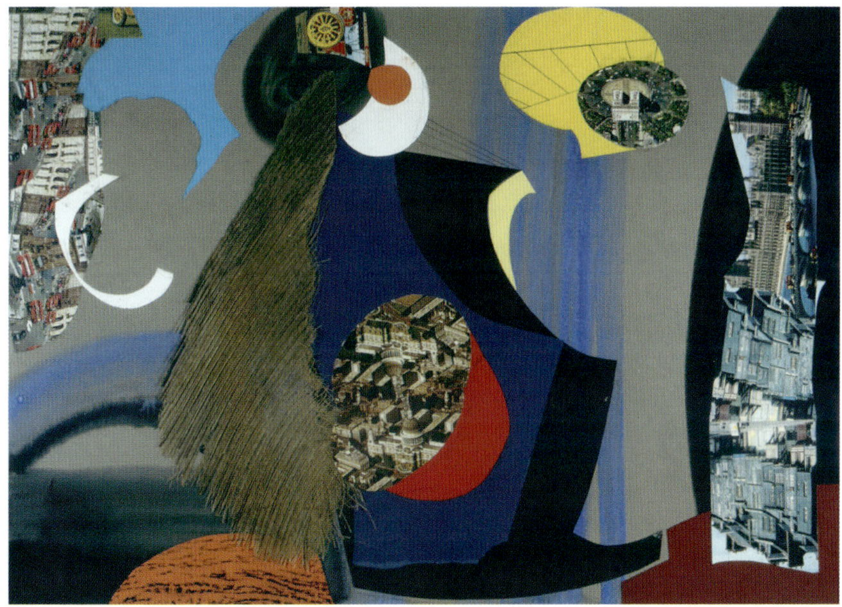

Orient Occident (East-West), 1983, Collage Mixed Media, Collection Fundacion Miró Barcelona

anything else that he might lay hands on. Working on large sheets of card, he would make sensual backgrounds of gouache for the shapes and scenes created by the repeated patterns of the snipped-up postcards.

An exhibition of recent work is an achievement at any age, but when it falls in the artist's eighty-second year, it has more than the usual poignancy. Roland was charmingly nervous about his exhibition *Roland Penrose, Collages Récents* at the Galerie Henriette Gomis in Paris.[24] He need not have been. Many red spots had appeared before the end of

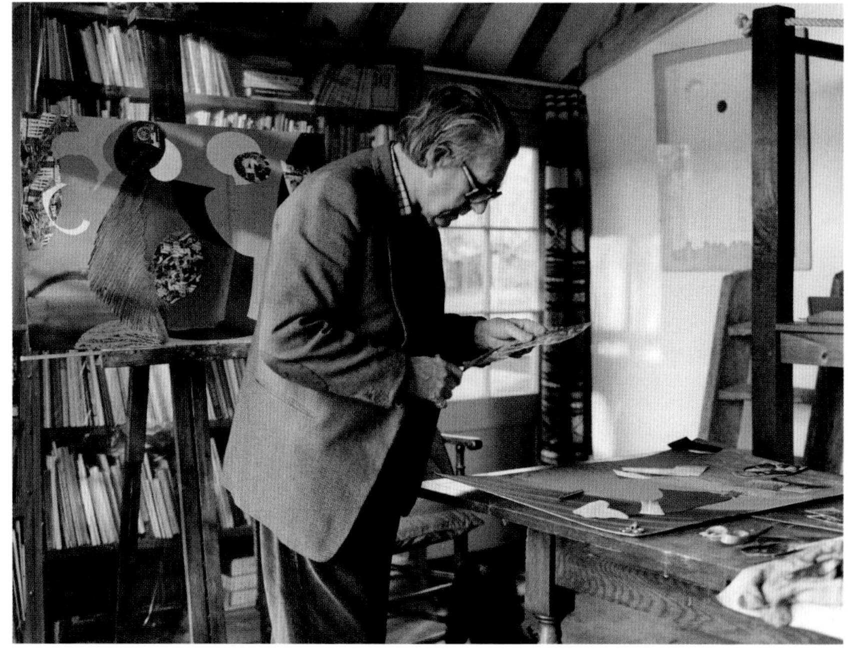

Roland Penrose in his studio at Farleys, Muddles Green Sussex, England 1983, by Antony Penrose

the private view that packed the little gallery in the Rue du Cirque. In November of the following year the show opened in the Mayor Gallery,[25] now run by Freddy's son James.

Gascoyne, who had retained his poetry and perception despite the most dreadful vicissitudes, wrote in the essay for the catalogue;

> The transmutation process of which Penrose holds the secret is that by means of which the apparently banal and commonplace material provided by picture postcards is transformed into the magic element of an enchanting visual experience. ... We should not expect to find any particular predetermined meaning in pictures such as those which Penrose presents to us; rather we should experience them as allowing them to happen to us.

Gascoyne ends his piece with this acronym;

P	Peinture	*Pictures*
E	Elargit	*Enlarge*
N	Nôtre	*Normal*
R	Realité	*Reality*
O	Ou bien	*Or else*
S	Semble	*Seem*
E	Eventrée	*Eviscerated* [26]

During Lee's lifetime, there were only three examples of her work hung among the collection at Farleys and she always maintained she had done nothing worthwhile. It astonished me when Suzanna found many boxes in the attic crammed with photographs, negatives and manuscripts going back through Lee's whole career. In an incredible act of faith, Thames and Hudson gave me a contract to write her biography and with David E. Scherman as my guide I began researching.

Roland and I were about to embark on a voyage of discovery. I would return to Farleys from my research trips to America and share my finds with Roland. He did not know that as a child of seven Lee had been raped and infected with venereal disease. He did not know that as a teenager she had witnessed her first love drowning. He did not know of her bravery under fire, her compassion or the sheer tenacity that kept her going. She had not told him. Perhaps she thought it would interfere with his perception of her. Or perhaps she just kept secrets. He had been in love with her for forty years, yet he knew nearly nothing of her past. It was a revelation for both of us. When *The Lives of Lee Miller* was finished, I had completely re-evaluated my perception of Lee. I passed through the old enmities and understood how misunderstood Lee had been. I was so sad we had wasted so many precious years in fighting.

When in the Seychelles with Diane in 1983, Roland had a stroke which was later followed by a more severe event severely afflicting his speech and mobility. Suzanna and Patsy rallied to take care of him and made him as comfortable as possible, ensuring he was never left alone. The Gardner Arts Centre in Brighton wanted to mount a show of Roland's collages in tandem with Lee's newly discovered photographs. We gathered his works and enquired of their titles. Roland was having difficulty with his speech, but he managed to caption some; *It Was Raining* or *The Sun Was Shining* were comments about the weather on the trip. There was one with a thrice-repeated image of a white bird flying serenely in a clear blue sky. I asked what the title was. *'The Last One,'* he mumbled. I thought I had heard incorrectly. *'The Last One,'* he repeated, then with a great effort, *'The Last One I made'*.

It was indeed the last collage he made. The white bird flew freely, soaring through the calm air of a golden sunset, breaking away from the sheltering images of trees, beaches and beautiful girls below on the earth. A shape like Man Ray's painting of Lee's lips floats up-ended in a distant part of the same sky. An image of serenity, of love and appreciation, it remains titled *The Last One.*

Roland deteriorated rapidly. When we were alone together, he told me of things he wanted taken care of. The words, mostly about the farm, stumbled out. In conclusion, he said;

'Look after your Suzanna, take good care of her and your little girls. Take care of Patsy and Diane'. He grasped my arm and leaned forward. *'You are honest, that's good. Be honest. It's the most important thing'*. Suzanna came in and he turned to include her. *'And now'*, he said, *'I am going to die'*.

'Oh no', we pleaded, *'We will look after you, one of us will always be with you, it's no trouble, we love you and we want to make you comfortable'*.

He fixed us both with his one good eye and said; *'I want to go'*.

It took him about five days. It was Easter and the weather was clear and bright. We carried him downstairs and into the garden in a wheelchair. He could no longer speak, but his one eye drank in the colour of the spring flowers and the tender, emergent foliage, the shade of which I felt evoked his line from *The Road is Wider Than Long; 'The Green Memories of Desire'*.

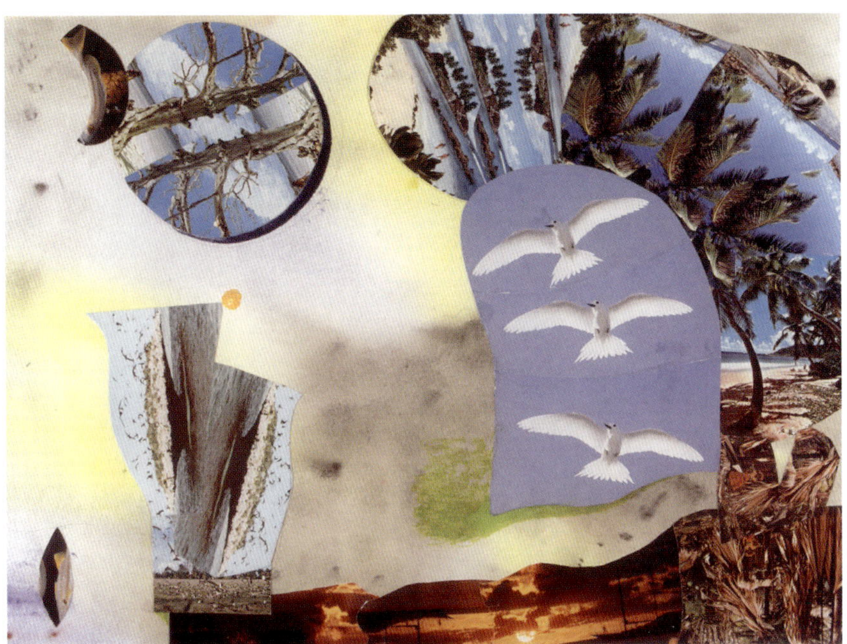

The Last One (Seychelles) 1984, collage

Diane and Beacus were there, but it was clear he drew the most comfort from Patsy. We cared for him together, assisted at night by Jan Welfare, a nurse whose Madonna-like beauty he clearly enjoyed. He drifted further and the gulf between him and us on the earth widened. Occasionally, like the soft flutter of an alighting bird, he returned for a moment with a gesture of affection.

Pneumonia settled on him – 'the old man's friend' I have heard it called for the release it brings. In the early hours of the morning his breathing slowed and all but stopped. I held his hand. The insistent beat of his pulse remorselessly held him against his will. The heart he strengthened six decades before by cross-country running and maintained by his long walks on the farm would not let him cross the last divide. The pulse flickered, steadied, beat arhythmically and then after one, lonely isolated beat like a full stop, was no more.

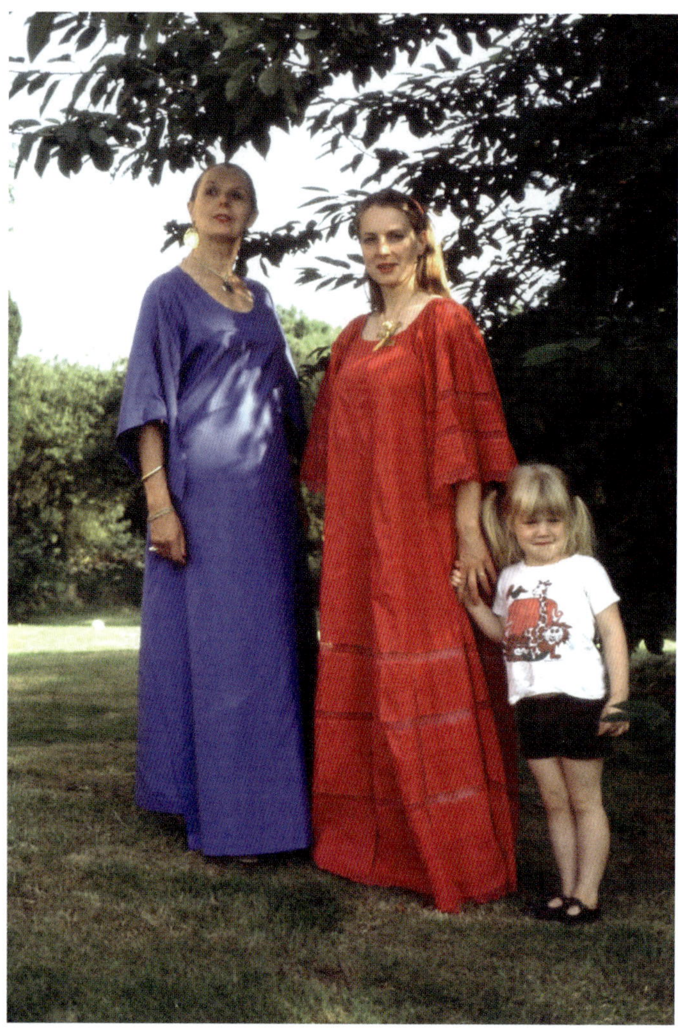

Diane De Riaz, Suzanna Penrose and Ami Bouhassane (nee Penrose) at Burgh Hill House, Chiddingly, East Sussex, England *c.*1980, by Antony Penrose

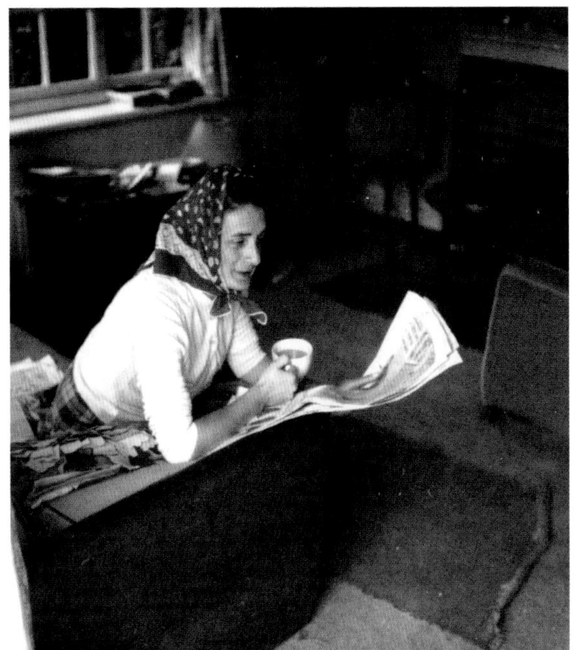

Patsy Murray reading [in the parlour], Farleys House, East Sussex, England 1960, by Lee Miller

'He's gone', whispered Jan.

We were both in tears. I phoned Suzanna and a few moments later she was walking towards me across the dew-soaked grass. We clung together like two shipwreck survivors, Moore's *Mother and Child* bestowing a benediction on us in our anguish. I touched the lichen covered surface. I wanted some of the mystic strength she held within the permanence of her stone. The sun rose, a giant disc of mellow orange, held in the branches of the apple trees.

'It's a new day for everyone except Roland', I managed to say.

'You know, I was wondering what he was waiting for', said Suzanna. *'I have just realised it is Lee's birthday. She will be so pleased to see him again'*.

It was 23 April 1984.

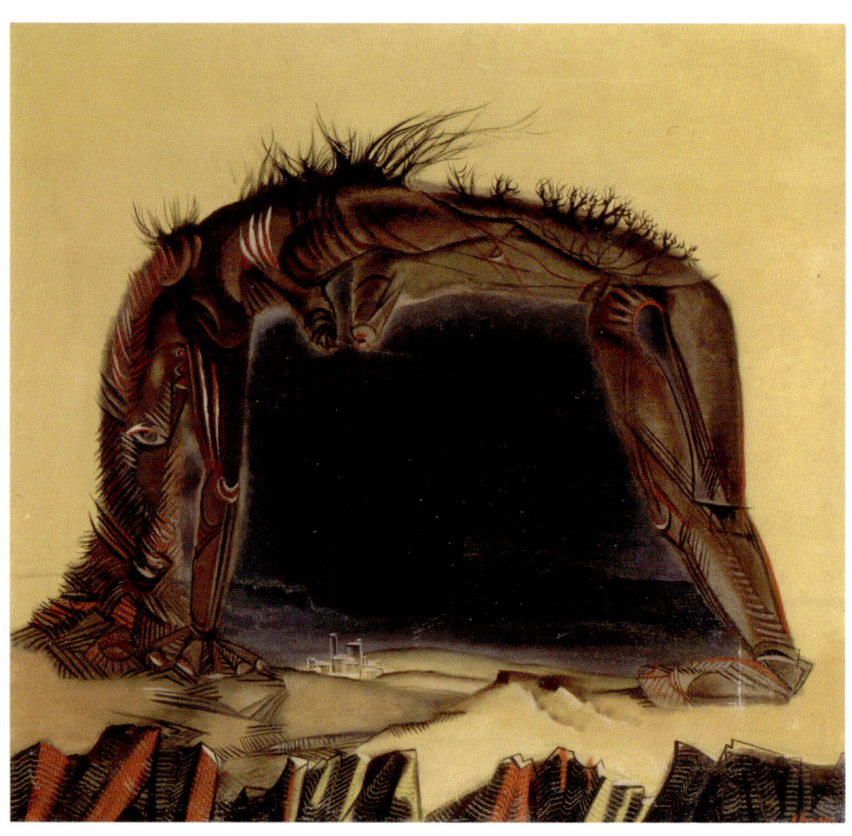

Egypt, Oil on Canvas, 1939

EPILOGUE

Suzanna died of cancer in 1992, four years after the birth of our son, Joshua Roland Erik Penrose. I was subsequently blessed with the good fortune of meeting and falling in love with my present wife, Roz. We married in 1994 and I thus gained a stepdaughter Genevieve. My daughter Ami is now co-director of Farleys House and Gallery Ltd which manages the Lee Miller Archives and The Penrose Collection. Eliza is head of conservation at Christchurch Art Gallery in New Zealand. They are both artists in their own right producing work of a strength and originality that would have delighted Roland and Lee. Patsy remained a much loved central figure for me and my family and was active in the running of Farleys House until she died suddenly 20 February 2008. Farleys House now houses the Lee Miller Archives and The Penrose Collection, sending loans and exhibitions all over the world.

David E. Scherman became one of the most important people in my life and after helping me with my biography of Lee, *The Lives of Lee Miller,* we worked closely together on the book *Lee Miller's War* and two documentary films about Lee. He died in 1996.

It took ten years for Michael Sweeney to catalogue Roland's books and papers. Thanks to the generosity of the National Heritage Memorial Fund and the National Art Collections Fund, they now form the Roland Penrose Archive at the Scottish National Gallery of Modern Art in Edinburgh, which together with the Tate Modern, owns most of the key paintings from Roland's collection.

The ashes of Lee, Roland, Valentine, Patsy and Roy Edwards are scattered in the garden at Farleys House.

NOTES

PROLOGUE

1 Roland Penrose in conversation with Dominique Bozo. Art Forum September 1980. Translated from the French by Lisa Liebman.

2 Letter from S.W. Hayter to the author, May 1984. Col. Roland Penrose Archive, Scottish National Gallery of Modern Art.

3 *Lee Miller in Sussex, & Roland Penrose, Recent Collages*. Gardner Arts Centre, Brighton. 3 to 31 May 1984.

CHAPTER 1

1 A giant prehistoric figure on the English South Downs of a man holding two staffs, originally created by incising into the turf to expose the white chalk.

2 *Born 1900*. Interview with Julian Jebb, BBC TV filmed June 1975.

3 *The Road Is Wider Than Long*. Roland Penrose interviewed by Edward Lucie-Smith. BBC Radio 3 October 1980.

4 Roland Penrose, *Scrap Book*, 1900–1981 Thames & Hudson 1981, p. 16.

5 Ibid, p. 21.

6 Ibid, p. 20.

7 Ibid, p. 22.

8 Ibid, p. 24.

9 Ibid, p. 24.

10 Ibid, p. 24.

CHAPTER 2

1 Prof. Oliver Penrose, *Lionel S. Penrose F.R.S, Human Geneticist and Human Being*. Talk given to the Wisbech Society, 11 May 1998.

2 Roland Penrose, *Scrap Book*, p. 26.

3 R. Skidelsky, *John Maynard Keynes, the Economist as Saviour 1920–1937*, London; Macmillan, 1992.

4 Roland Penrose, *Scrap Book*, p. 26.

5 F. Spalding, *Duncan Grant, A Biography*, London; Chatto & Windus, 1997, p. 232.

6 Roland Penrose interviewed by Edward Lucie-Smith for *The Road Is Wider Than Long*, BBC-Radio 3 programme, 14 October 1980.

7 R. Shone, *Bloomsbury Portraits*, London; Phaidon, 1993, p. 59.

8 Clive Bell, *Old Friends; Personal Recollections*, London; Chatto & Windus, 1956, p. 68.

9 Roland Penrose, *Scrap Book*, p. 25.

10 R. Skidelsky, *John Maynard Keynes* and MacKillop, I. F. R. *Leavis; A Life in Criticism*. L. Allen Lane,1995)

11 Dr Rylands interviewed by Michael Sweeney at King's College, 22 January 1997.
12 Valerie Grosvenor Myer, Obituary of Dr George Rylands in *The Guardian* 19 January 1999.
13 Roland Penrose, *Scrap Book*, p. 27.
14 Peter Parker, *A Life of J. R. Ackerley*. Farrar, Straus, Giroux, NY 1989.
15 Letter from Alec to Maynard Keynes, 15 or 23 August 1920 and interview with Frances Partridge by Michael Sweeney 10 March 1997.
16 Roland Penrose, *Scrap Book*, p. 27.
17 Ibid, p. 28.
18 Ibid, p. 28.
19 E. Smart, *Necessary Secrets*, London; Grafton, 1991.
20 Roland Penrose, *Scrap Book*, p. 29.
21 Ibid, p. 28.
22 Roland Penrose interviewed by Edward Lucie-Smith for *The Road Is Wider Than Long*, BBC-Radio 3 programme, 14 October 1980.

CHAPTER 3

1 *Letters of Virginia Woolf*, London; Hogarth Press, 1978. Virginia Woolf to M. Llewelyn Davies, 6 June 1929.
2 Roland Penrose, *Scrap Book*, p. 31.
3 Roland Penrose, unpublished manuscript dated 22 August 1978, thought to have been intended for use in *Scrap Book*. Coll. Scottish National Gallery of Modern Art, Roland Penrose Archive.
4 Henri Faget de Cassaigne in conversation with the author, 17 October 1999.
5 Bertha Penrose, letter to Clive Bell from Oxhey Grange, 3 September 1927.
6 Prof. Oliver Penrose, *Lionel S. Penrose F.R..S, Human Geneticist and Human Being*. Talk given to the Wisbech Society, 11 May 1998.
7 Terence O'Brien, notes for an unpublished memoir.
8 Roland Penrose, *Scrap Book*, p. 40.
9 A. Watt, 'Art Dealers of Paris; 1' in *Studio*, May 1958.
10 Interview with Julian Jebb for BBC-TV documentary *Artists Today – Born 1900*, filmed June 1975, transmitted 11 October 1975.
11 Man Ray on the occasion of his retrospective exhibition organised by Roland at the ICA in 1975.
12 Roland Penrose interviewed by Edward Lucie-Smith for *The Road Is Wider Than Long*, BBC-Radio 3 programme, 14 October 1980.
13 Valentine Penrose, *Poems & Narrations*, translated by Roy Edwards, London; Carcanet Press & Elephant Trust, 1977, p. 3.
14 André Thirion, *Revolutionaries without Revolution*, Macmillan Publishing Co., Inc NY, 1975 p. 194 and M Secrest, *Salvador Dali*, Dutton, NY 1986 p. 121.

15 Roland Penrose. *Scrap Book* p. 42.

CHAPTER 4

1 Letter from Roland Penrose to Alec Penrose from Bombay, 28 November 1932. Coll. Scottish National Gallery of Modern Art, Roland Penrose Archive.
2 Ibid.
3 Ibid, from Goa, 1 December 1932.
4 Ibid.
5 Ibid, from Ujjain, 4 January 1933.
6 Ibid.
7 Ibid, from Udaipur 12(?) January 1933.
8 Ibid, from Jaipur, 13 January 1933.
9 Ibid, from Calcutta 19 January 1933.
10 Ibid, from Calcutta 10 February 1933.
11 Ibid, from Benares, 18 March 1933.
12 Ibid, from Calcutta 18 February 1933.
13 Ibid.
14 Ibid, from Genoa 18 April 1933.
15 Unpublished manuscript thought to have been intended for *Scrap Book*, *c.*1978. Coll. Scottish National Gallery of Modern Art, Roland Penrose Archive.
16 Letters between Roland, Jung and Valentine, October 1934. Coll. Scottish National Gallery of Modern Art, Roland Penrose Archive.
17 Roland Penrose, *Scrap Book*, p. 56.
18 Letter from Roland in Colchester to Valentine at Le Pouy, 8 November 1934. Coll. Scottish National Gallery of Modern Art, Roland Penrose Archive.
19 Letter from Valentine at Le Pouy to Roland at 26 Norfolk Square, London, 16 November 1934. Coll. Scottish National Gallery of Modern Art, Roland Penrose Archive. Trans. Gwendolyn M. Wells.
20 Letter from Valentine to Roland, 11 December 1934. Coll. Scottish National Gallery of Modern Art, Roland Penrose Archive.
21 *Axis* No. 4, last quarter of 1935.
22 Visits to Rogi Andrés studio recorded on 26 and 27 October 1935. Roland Penrose appointment diaries. Roland Penrose Archive, Scottish National Gallery of Modern Art.
23 Telegram from Valentine on Strathmore to Roland in London, 12 November 1935. Coll. Scottish National Gallery of Modern Art, Roland Penrose Archive.
24 Letter from Roland in London to Valentine in Bombay, 13 November 1935. Coll. Scottish National Gallery of Modern Art, Roland Penrose Archive. Trans. by the author.
25 Lautréamont *Les Chants de Maldoror*. 1874.
26 Roland Penrose interviewed by Edward Lucie-Smith for *The Road Is Wider Than Long*, BBC-Radio 3 programme, 14 October 1980.

CHAPTER 5

1 The first recorded meeting between Roland, Herbert Read and Henry Moore is in October 1935 in Roland's appointment diaries. Coll. Scottish National Gallery of Modern Art, Edinburgh, Roland Penrose Archive.

2 Michel Remy, *Surrealism in Britain*, Aldershot; Ashgate Publishing, 1999, p. 36.

3 Informal meetings began in January 1936, and included Man Ray, McKnight Kauffer, Henry Moore, Hugh Sykes Davies, Julian Trevelyan, Ruthven Todd, Francis Bacon, Ben Nicholson, Rupert Lee and Iqbal Singh.

4 *Cahiers d'Art*, vol. 10, nos. 7–10, 1935.

5 Roland Penrose, *Scrap Book*, p. 68.

6 Roland Penrose, *Picasso, His Life and Work*, London; Gollancz, 1958, p. 254.

7 Published accounts give varying dates in 1935 and 1936 for this meeting, but 22–24 February 1936 seems the most likely, especially since *Cahiers d'Art* was not published until January 1936.

8 Eluard's daughter from his previous marriage to Gala.

9 Some years later Picasso told Roland the dealer Paul Rosenberg refused to take the painting, saying 'Non, je refuse d'avoir des trous de cul dans ma galerie' [I refuse to have arse-holes in my gallery].

10 *A Look At My Life*, Eileen Agar. Methuen 1988, p. 115.

11 Conroy Maddox interviewed by Michael Sweeney, London 19 8 1997.

12 Ibid.

13 *Paul Eluard, Lettres à Gala 1924-48* edited by P. Dreyfus. Gallimard, Paris 1984. Letter dated 23 5 36, Paris (L220).

14 *Surrealism in Britain* Michel Remy Ashgate Publishing 1999, p. 96.

15 *For Roland.* A contribution by Robert Melville to a page of obituaries in Art Monthly, May 1984. The letter has unfortunately disappeared, although the point it made has in retrospect been proved to have some justification. Maddox joined the group a year later.

16 *Exhibition of Dreams and Nightmares,* Betjamin and *They Paint Dreams*, Connolly. *Evening Standard* 11 6 36.

17 Accounts of who saved Dali and with what vary. This is the author's interpretation of the facts as understood.

18 *Journal 1936–37* 13 10 1936 David Gascoyne. Enitharmon Press, 1980.

19 *Alice Rahon Portfolio* Vanina Deler and Nancy Deffebach. *On The Bus* Double Issue 8 & 9 Bombshelter Press, Los Angeles 1991.
Through an Hourglass Lightly; Valentine Penrose and Alice Paalen Georgiana Colvile. University of Nottingham 1996.

20 'Penumatique' from Julian Levy to Lee Miller dated 20 6 37. Col. Lee Miller Archives.

21 Roland Penrose letter to Lee Miller 25 6 37. Lee Miller Archive.

22 *A Look at my Life* Eileen Agar. Methuen 1988, p. 133.

23 Pencil on paper, c. 18x12ins Fondation Eluard, Musée de Saint Denise. Inscribed à Paul et Nusch. 10 Juillet '37 Lamb Creek. Roland Penrose.

24 *L'Arlésienne*, a story by Alphonse Daudet first published in *Lettres de mon moulin* 1869.

25 *London Bulletin.* No 17, June 1939. Translated from the French by Iqbal Singh.

26 Collection Tate Modern.

27 Letter from Lee Miller in Marseilles to Roland Penrose in London, 5 October 1937. Lee Miller Archive.

28 Letter from Roland Penrose in London to Lee Miller in Cairo 6 10 37. Lee Miller Archive.

CHAPTER 6

1 Probably Thea Struve, who later worked at the Bucholz Gallery, New York, and was possibly the nude model in an untitled painting by Roland of this period. She photographed Roland making the *Dew Machine.*

2 Letter from Roland Penrose in London to Lee Miller in Cairo, 14 10 37. Lee Miller Archive.

3 Letter from Lee Miller in Cairo to Roland Penrose in London, 22 10 37. Lee Miller Archive.

4 Letter from Roland Penrose in London to Lee Miller in Cairo, 14 10 37. Lee Miller Archive.

5 Schedules and accounts compiled by Mesens. Roland Penrose Archive, Scottish National Gallery of Modern Art, Edinburgh.

6 Roland Penrose – overs from BBC Southern Life film, 1983.

7 Letter from Roland Penrose in London to Lee Milleer in Cairo, 6 11 37. Lee Miller Archive.

8 Letter from Roland Penrose in London to Lee Miller in Cairo, 3 11 37. Lee Miller Archives.

9 Letter from Lee Miller in Cairo to Roland Penrose in London, circa 7 11 37. Lee Miller Archives.

10 Letter from Roland Penrose in London to Lee Miller in Cario, 21 11 37. Lee Miller Archives.

11 Typescript titled 'Opening Speech by Mr Herbert Read'. Roland Penrose Archive, Scottish National Gallery of Modern Art, Edinburgh.

12 *Surrealism in Britain.* Michel Remy. Ashgate Publishing Ltd 1999, p. 112.

13 Letter from Roland Penrose in London to Lee Miller in Cairo, 11 1 38. Lee Miller Archives.

14 *Scrap Book* Roland Penrose Thames & Hudson 1981, p. 88.

15 Letter dated 7 4 38. Roland Penrose Archive, Scottish National Gallery of Modern Art.

16 *Surrealism in Britain.* Michel Remy. Ashgate Publishing Ltd 1999, p. 149.

17 Subtitled *An Image Diary from the Balkans*, and published by the London Gallery June 1939.

18 *Refugee Artists in Great Britain.* David Brown. Art and Artists, April 1984.

19 *Max Ernst* December 1938 and *Living Art in England*, January 1939.
20 Diana Uhlman in an interview tape recorded by her daughter September 1999.
21 Grossner Sonja. 'The Remarkable Story of Margarete Klopfleisch', *Revolutionary Socialism in the 21st Century*, 8 September 2017
22 Letter from Lee Miller in Cairo to Roland Penrose in London describing a previous visit to Siwa. 15 10 37. Lee Miller Archives.

CHAPTER 7

1 Col. Roland Penrose Archive, Scottish National Gallery of Modern Art.
2 *Surrealism in Britain.* Michel Remy. Ashgate Publishing Ltd, 1999. Page 185 and in conversation with the author, Nice, 21 10 99.
3 BBC TV, *Artists of Today – Born 1900.* Directed by Julian Jebb. Filmed June 1975
4 Related by Andrew Murray in a note to the author. 26 01 00.
5 London Bulletin. No. 3 June 1938, pp. 22–27
6 Letter from Roland Penrose in London to Lee Miller in Cairo, 15 4 39. Lee Miller Archives.
7 Letter from Miro to Roland Penrose dated 12 5 39. Private. Col. Andrew Murray.
8 Letter from Roland Penrose in London to Lee Miller in Cairo, 13 4 39.
9 *Artists of Today – Born 1900.* Roland Penrose talking to Julian Jebb. Director Julian Jebb, Producer Ann James BBV TV 1975.
10 Conroy Maddox in conversation with Michael Sweeney. 19 8 97.
11 *Surrealism Today.* Catalogue of the exhibition held at The Zwemmer Gallery 26 Litchfield Street, WC2 June 12 to July 3 1940. Col. Scottish National Gallery of Modern Art, Roland Penrose Archive.
12 *Scrap Book*, Roland Penrose, p. 134.
13 The government were supposed to settle war damage claims on insurance valuation at 2 shillings in the pound, being 10 per cent. In practice many claims went unsettled.
14 *Home Guard Manual of Camouflage.* Roland Penrose. George Routledge & Sons, Ltd. October 1941, p. 17.
15 Following his Victory in North Africa, Montgomery was in England from 16 May before returning to Tripoli on 5 June to plan the invasion of Sicily. Roland's commission did not become effective until 10 7 43, but a delay of this nature would have been usual.
16 *Lee Miller's War.* Edited by Antony Penrose with foreword by David E. Scherman. Condé Nast Books, Random Century Group Ltd, 1992, p. 8.
17 Lee attained full accreditation as a war correspondent for *Vogue* magazine as Elizabeth Miller Eloui on 30 12 42.
18 *Wrens In Camera.* Lee Miller. Hollis and Carter London 1945.
19 Letter from Roland Penrose from the School of Military Intelligence, Matlock, Derbyshire, to Lee in Hampstead. 28 5 44. Col. Lee Miller Archive.
20 Letter from Roland Penrose in Norwich to Lee Miller. 11 8 44. Col. Roland Penrose Estate.

21 *Lee Miller's War.* Edited by Antony Penrose with foreword by David E. Scherman. Condé Nast Books, Random Century Group Ltd, 1992, p. 73.

22 Writer and publisher of *Cahiers d'Art* and the Picasso *Catalogue Raisonné.*

23 *The Women Who Wrote the War.* Nancy Caldwell Sorel, Arcade Publishing, Inc., New York. 1999, p. 266.

24 *French Intellectuals and the Resistance.* Roland Penrose. Thought to be the text for a talk on BBC Radio 16 10 44. Col. Scottish National Gallery of Modern Art. Roland Penrose Archive.

25 *In the Service of the People.* Roland Penrose. William Heinemann 1945. Col. Scottish National Gallery of Modern Art. Roland Penrose Archive.

26 Ibid, p. 12.

27 Ibid, p. 54.

28 *Was There an English Surrealist Group in the Forties?* Dennis-J. Jean. Twentieth Century Literature, February 1975, pp. 81–89.

29 Letter from Jacques Brunius to Edouard Mesens, 23 2 45. Col Pennsylvania State University Library. Reproduced by kind permission. Translation by Michael Sweeney.

30 A letter from Roland Penrose to Lee Miller written when he returned from Paris states 'Mesens has delivered Paul's jacket'. Also Mesens had a particular flair for typography and usually was entrusted with the designs for publications.

CHAPTER 8

1 Lee Miller, unpublished cable ms., Vienna. Col. Lee Miller Archive.

2 Letter from Lee Miller to Roland Penrose, thought to be from Budapest. January 1946. Col. Lee Miller Archive.

3 Her real name is withheld by request.

4 Roland Penrose in Hampstead to Lee Miller in Europe or the Balkans 15 1 1946. Col. Lee Miller Archive

5 Minutes of the 2nd meeting, 20 2 46. ICA Archive at the Tate Gallery Archive.

6 Minutes of the 4th meeting, 19 3 46. ICA Archive at the Tate Gallery Archive.

7 Lee Miller. Entry in notebook whilst awaiting Caesarean section, 9 9 47. Unpublished. Col. Lee Miller Archive.

8 Trans. *Please Touch.* Col. Roland Penrose Archive, Scottish National Gallery of Modern Art.

9 Letter from Lee Miller in St Moriz to Roland Penrose in London, January 1947. Col. Lee Miller Archives.

10 Lee Miller's notebook, September 1947. Col Lee Miller Archives.

11 Roland Penrose Appointment Diary 9 9 47. Col Scottish National Gallery of Modern Art, Roland Penrose Archive.

12 '*For our friend Lee and her new born little boy, who Nusch would have so loved, she truly loved you, Lee darling*'. Col. A & R Penrose.

13 *'The beauty of Lee today. Anthony, It is sunlight on your bed.'* Col. A & R Penrose.

14 Letter from Roland Penrose to Theodore and Florence Miller, 11 September 1947.

15 Letter from Lee Miller to her parents, 2 5 47. Col. Lee Miller Archive.
16 Tate Gallery Catalogue, p 472. According to a letter from Roland to Mesens of 1939, the exhibition may have been from 14 Oct to 31 Dec. Col. The Getty Research Institute, Los Angeles.
17 Letter from Geoffry Grigson to Ivro Jarosy, Hoellering's stepson who was involved in running the Academy Cinema. 4 4 48. ICA Archive, Tate Gallery Archive.
18 William Turnbull interviewed by Michael Sweeney 19 8 98.
19 *Don't Tell Sybil.* George Melly. William Heinemann 1997, p. 129.

CHAPTER 9

1 *My Last Breath.* Luis Buñuel, Alfred A. Knopf, Inc. 1984, p. 114.
2 John Thompson was journalist on the *Evening Standard* and latterly the editor of the *Sunday Telegraph.* Cynthia worked for *Life* magazine in London.
3 Peter Braden interviewed by the author 8 12 98.
4 *The Independent Group.* Anne Massey. Manchester University Press 1995, p. 28.
5 *Picasso, His Life and Work.* Roland Penrose. Victor Gollancz. 1958, p. 367.
6 *Picasso Himself.* Lee Miller. First draft of m.s., published in Vogue November 1951. Col. Lee Miller Archives.
7 'Pensez, c'est le premier Anglais que j'ai jamais mordu!' Lee Miller, unpublished ms. Trans. the author.
8 *Artists of Today – Born 1900.* Roland Penrose interviewed and directed by Julian Jebb. BBC TV filmed June 1975.
9 *Picasso Himself.* Lee Miller. First draft of m.s., published in Vogue November 1951. Col. Lee Miller Archives.
10 The Góngora drawing and the ICA Visitors Book entry are dated 15 11 50 and they both share a similar style and medium. Lee's account in *Vogue* November 1951 states the ICA Visitors Book drawing was done at Farley Farm and although the Góngora dedication reads 'London' I feel certain it was done at Farleys at the same time.
11 *The Independent Group.* Anne Massey. Manchester University Press 1995, p.2.
12 Alec Penrose died 23 8 50.
13 Picasso's 70th Birthday was 25 10 1951. The show, *Drawings and Watercolours since 1893* opened 11 10 51.
14 *The Independent Group.* Anne Massey. Manchester University Press 1995, p. 66.
15 *The Wonder and Horror of the Human Head.* Roland Penrose, with a foreword by Herbert Read. Lund Humphries. 1953. Col. Roland Penrose Estate.
16 16 9 54, Perpignan. Roland Penrose notes on visiting Picasso, edited by Michael Sweeney. Col. Roland Penrose estate.
17 *The Sorcerer's Apprentice.* John Richardson. Alfred A. Knopf. 1999, p. 170. A car accident had left Cooper with a damaged eye.
18 9 11 55, Cannes. Roland Penrose notes on visiting Picasso, edited by Michael Sweeney.

Col. Roland Penrose estate. *Il ne faut pas croire toujours ce que je dis, les questions vous tentent à dire sont des mensonges parcequ' il n' y a pas de reponse.* (Trans. the author)

19 *Portrait of Picasso.* Roland Penrose. Lund Humphries. 1956. Second enlarged edition 1971.

20 *Scrap Book 1900–1981.* Roland Penrose. Thames & Hudson 1981, p. 223.

21 Kenneth Armitage interviewed by Michael Sweeny, 10 3 98.

CHAPTER 10

1 Arts Council Art Panel minutes, 26 2 58. Col. Arts Council Archives.

2 Arts Council Art Panel minutes, 6 10 58. Col. Arts Council Archives.

3 Letter from Roland in Cannes to Gabriel White in London. 10 2 60. Col. Arts Council Archives.

4 *Artist Unknown.* Richard Witts. Little, Brown and Co. 1998. P 288.

5 *Scrap Book 1900–1981.* Roland Penrose. Thames and Hudson 1981, p. 249.

6 Letter from George Melly in London to Roland. 23 6 60. Col. Roland Penrose Archive, Scottish National Gallery of Modern Art, Edinburgh.

7 Dawn Ades interviewed by Michael Sweeny. 2 6 1998.

8 *Sunday Times 9 10 61.*

9 *The Times,* 7 9 61.

10 *Out of This Century.* Peggy Guggenheim. The Dial Press, New York. 1946, p. 221.

11 Roland's notes on visiting Picasso, 18 June 1964. Col. Roland.

12 *Life With Picasso.* Françoise Gilot. McGraw Hill, New York 1964.

13 *This Time of Day*, BBC Home Service, 4 3 65.

14 *Long Live Picasso.* Roland Penrose. ICA Bulletin. Nov 1966.

15 Joanna Drew interviewed by Michael Sweeny, 8 10 97.

16 Mike Kustow. *Tank, An Autobiographical Fiction.* Johnathan Cape Ltd, 1975, p. 46.

17 *Scrap Book 1900–1981.* Roland Penrose. Thames and Hudson 1981, p. 263.

18 Letter from Roland to Picasso 9 4 69. Roland Penrose Archive, Scottish National Gallery of Modern Art, Edinburgh. Trans. the author.

19 8 4 69 20.30 Lime Grove Studios.

CHAPTER 11

1 17 10 73 to 16 12 73, then toured Scotland and the USA in 1974.

2 R.L. Gregory, Professor of Neuropsychology and Director of the Brain and Perception Laboratory, University of Bristol. Colin Blakemore, Lecturer in Physiology, Univ. of Cambridge, Fellow of Downing College, Cambridge. Jan Deregowski, Lecturer in Psycology, Univ Aberdeen. Sir Ernst Gombrich, F.B.A. Dir. Warburg Inst. Univ. London. H. E. Hinton, F.R.S. Prof. of Zoology, Univ. of Bristol.

3 *Illusion; In Nature and Art.* Edited by R. L. Gregory and E. H. Gombrich. Gerald Duckworth. 1973, p. 246.

4 *Miró.* Roland Penrose. Thames and Hudson. 1970, p. 60.

5 *Man Ray.* Roland Penrose. Thames and Hudson. 1975.
6 *Man Ray, American Artist.* Neil Baldwin. Clarkson N. Potter Inc. New York, p. 3.
7 *Self Portrait.* Man Ray. Andre Deutsch. 1963.
8 *Picasso, His Life and Work.* Roland Penrose. University of California Press. 1981, p. 479.
9 *Picasso's Picassos,* Hayward Gallery, July–October 1981.
10 Minutes of the ICA Council Meeting, 26 6 75. Tate Gallery Archives DM Box CL 1.
11 Sotheby Advice of Purchase note. Roland Penrose Archive. Scottish National Gallery of Modern Art, Edinburgh.
12 Cheque book stubs dated 26 9 (75) and 6 8 (75) respectively. Roland Penrose Estate.
13 *Once a Jolly Bagman.* Alistair McAlpine. Phoenix 1998, p. 185.
14 ICA Council Minutes, 14 May 1975. Tate Gallery Archive, DM Box CL 1.
15 Resignation letter dated 1 11 76. Roland Penrose Archive. Scottish National Gallery of Modern Art, Edinburgh.
16 Roland attended Man Ray's funeral in Paris 18 11 76.
17 *Scrap Book, 1900–1981.* Roland Penrose. Thames & Hudson. 1981, p. 205.
18 *Tàpies.* Roland Penrose. Thames & Hudson, 1978.
19 Valentine Penrose in Pondicherry, India to Roland. Christmas 1935.
20 Fermoy Centre, Kings Lynn 25 7 – 9 8 80. ICA London 23 8 – 28 9 80. Arnolfini Gallery Bristol 4 10 – 1 11 80. Harris Museum and Art Gallery, Preston 8 11 – 6 12 80. Ferens Art Gallery Hull, 13 12 80 – 18 1 81. Fundació Joan Miró Barcelona 26 2 – 29 3 81.
21 McAlister was appointed 13 6 77by Cob Stenham who succeeded Robert Loder as Chairman in 1977.
22 Carine Maurice. *Evening Standard* 29 8 80.
23 Commissioned and edited by Poligrafa, Barcelona 1981. English Edition by Thames and Hudson 1981. French edition by Éditions Cercle D'Art 1983.
24 12 11 to 30 12 1982.
25 *Roland Penrose Recent Collage.* 28 11 – 21 12 83.
26 *Roland Penrose.* David Gascoyne. Catalogue for *Roland Penrose, Collages récents.* Galerie Henriette Gomès, 1982.

ROLAND PENROSE: CHRONOLOGY

1900 Born 14 October St John's Wood, London

1903 Third brother Bernard (Beacus) born

1908 Family move to Oxhey Grange

1918 Joins Red Cross Ambulance Unit in Italy

1919 18 January enrols at Queens' College Cambridge to study architecture

1920 Meets Maynard Keynes and Roger Fry at Cambridge

1922 17 June Graduates from Cambridge, B.A., 1st in Architecture
Goes to Paris to study painting with André Lhote
Becomes interested in Surrealist movement
Meets Georges Braque
Meets Yanko Varda

1923 Goes to Cassis sur Mer with Yanko Varda and buys Villa les Mimosas
Builds studio with Yanko Varda
Parents visit for 1 week in October
Returns to England for Christmas at Oxhey Grange

1924 Becomes interested in Surrealism
Meets Valentine Boué
Returns to England for Christmas

1925 Parents visit in May and again in August
Goes to England with Valentine Boué in October.
Marries Valentine Boué 21 December at Jordans Meeting House

1926 Three of Valentine Boue's poems published in August edition of *Les Cahiers du Sud*, Edited by Jean Ballard
Christmas at Oxhey Grange

1927 First visit to Egypt over Christmas with Bonamy Dobrée
Meets Count Galarza

1928 They return from Egypt and go to Paris
Buys apartment in Paris, 8,rue des Sts.Pères.
Roland meets Max Ernst and Joan Miró
Roland's first one man show at Galerie Van Leer, Montparnasse, 14 – 29 June.
Summer holidays with Max Ernst at La Noblesse, La Cadière d'Azur
Second visit to Egypt to meet Count Galarza

1929 Return to Paris from Egypt via Middle East and Greece
Roland becomes friends with Paul Eluard, André Breton and other Surrealists

1930 Small role in Bunuel's film *L'Age d'Or*
Death of Roland's mother
Buys Chateau Le Pouy 26 November

1931 Alec (older brother) and Frances Penrose visit Le Pouy

1932 Roland's father dies 2 Jan 1932
Valentine studies art at the Sorbonne
Roland and Valentine visit India

1933 Walking trips in the Pyrenees
Roland plans visit to Carl Jung with Valentine

1934 Roland sponsors publication of Max Ernst's *Une Semaine de Bonté*
Roland finances Andre Bresson's film *Les Affaires Publiques*
Roland's goes to England to seek medical attention for stomach ulcer
Valentine ill with headaches and respiratory condition
Roland and Valentine separate

1935 Sells Chateau Le Pouy 30/7/35
Rents flat in Rossmore Court, London
Valentine goes to India
Meets David Gascoyne: they decide to bring Surrealism to London

1936 Moves to 21 Downshire Hill, London
Paul Eluard introduces Roland to Picasso – acquires *Nu sur la Plage*
Organises International Surrealist Exhibition in London with David Gascoyne, Herbert Read and others
Visits Mougins with Valentine
Visits Republican Spain with Valentine, Zervos, and Gascoyne
Valentine goes to India with Alice Paalen

1937 Meets Lee Miller, and goes with her to Cornwall and Mougins
Picasso paints portrait of *Lee Miller a L'Arlesienne*, later acquired by Roland
Roland makes first postcard collages
Acquires Gaffé collection
Acquires Henry Moore, *Mother and Child*
Exhibits at Surrealist Objects and Poems exhibition, London Gallery

1938 Acquires *Weeping Woman*
Exhibits at Exposition Internationale du Surréalisme at the Galerie Beaux-Arts, Paris
Buys London Gallery. Opens 1 April with Rene Magritte exhibition
Acquires Paul Eluard collection
Trip to Balkans with Lee Miller – *The Road is Wider Than Long*
Organises exhibition of Picasso's Guernica
12 December files for divorce from Valentine

1939 Goes to Egypt to visit Lee Miller

1939 *The Road is Wider than Long* published by the London Gallery in June.
19 June 1939 divorce from Valentine becomes absolute.
Lee Miller moves in to Downshire Hill
Exhibition at Mayor Gallery with Ithell Colquhoun
London Gallery closes
Last visit to France to see Max Ernst, Leonora Carrington and Picasso.
War breaks out
Contributes two works to 'United Artists' exhibition at the Royal Academy
Roland joins The Industrial Camouflage Research Unit
Lee goes to work for *Vogue* magazine as a photographer

1940 Exhibition 'Surrealism Today' at the Zwemmer Gallery, in June
Blitz – Roland works as Air Raid Warden
Valentine moves in to 21 Downshire Hill

1941 David E. Scherman arrives in England
Roland enlists in Home Guard, September

1942 Lee accredited as War Correspondent for *Vogue* magazine

1943 Roland given commission as Captain in Regular Army, runs Eastern Command School of Camouflage, July.

1944 Lee goes to Europe as a War Correspondent
Roland goes to Paris after liberation, meets Picasso, Paul Eluard and other survivors, gathers material for *In The Service of the People*

1945 Lee and David E. Scherman photograph Nazi death camps

1946 Roland demobilised from Army
Creates organisation with Herbert Read that will become the ICA
Lee returns to Roland after reporting from Eastern Europe
Roland and Lee visit New York, Arizona and California
London Gallery re-opened

1947 Move to 36 Downshire Hill
Roland and Lee marry
Contributes to 'Exposition Internationale du Surréalisme' in Paris
Son Antony Penrose born

1948 ICA first exhibition '40 Years of Modern Art'
Acquires *Kneeling Woman* commissioned from F. E. McWilliam

1949 ICA exhibition '40,000 Years of Modern Art'
Buys Farley Farm
Sells 36 Downshire Hill and moves to 11A Hornton Street
Roland one man show at London Gallery

1950 London Gallery closes

1950 ICA opens at Dover Street
Alec Penrose dies at Bradenham 22 August 1950
Picasso's visit to England

1951 Patsy Murray comes to Farleys
Visit to St Tropez for wedding of Paul and Dominique Eluard
ICA exhibition 'Picasso. Drawings and Watercolours since 1893'

1952 Paul Eluard dies

1953 Roland meets Diane Deriaz

1954 Commissioned by Gollancz to write 'Picasso, His Life and Work'

1956 ICA exhibition 'Picasso Himself'
Portrait of Picasso published
Roland becomes Fine Arts officer in Paris for British Council

1958 *Picasso, His Life and Work* published

1959 Appointed Trustee of Tate Gallery

1960 'Picasso' Arts Council exhibition at the Tate Gallery
Awarded C.B.E. for services to contemporary art

1961 'Max Ernst' Arts Council exhibition at the Tate Gallery
Roland successfully negotiates for the purchase of Picasso's *Three Dancers* by the Tate Gallery

1964 'Miro' Arts Council exhibition at the Tate Gallery

1965 Roland is made senior fellow, Royal College of Art

1966 Roland knighted
ICA begins move to Carlton House Terrace. First Sotheby's fund raising auction
Buys Burgh Hill farm, adjoining Farley Farm

1967 'Picasso Sculpture' Arts Council exhibition at the Tate Gallery
Second Sotheby's auction

1968 ICA opens in Carlton House Terrace

1969 Paintings stolen from 11A Hornton Street
Becomes President of the ICA

1970 'Miro' monograph published

1971 Antony and friends leave on Muddles Overland Trek

1973 Picasso dies
'Illusion in Nature and Art' exhibition at the ICA
Antony and Suzanna marry in New Zealand, October

1974 Roland creates The Elephant Trust
Roland and Lee go to New York for Man Ray and Max Ernst exhibition
Muddles Overland Trek returns

1975	'Man Ray. Inventor, Painter, Poet' exhibition at the ICA 'Man Ray' published in London
1976	'Max Ernst. Prints, Collages and Drawings 1919–1972' exhibition at the ICA Roland resigns from the ICA Man Ray dies
1977	Roland on selection committee for Picasso's dation Granddaughter Ami Valentine born *Tapiès* published in Barcelona Lee dies
1978	'Dada and Surrealism Reviewed' exhibition at the Hayward Gallery *Tapiès* published in London Valentine dies
1979	Bomarzo, Italy with Diane De Riaz Grand daughter Eliza born
1980	'Roland Penrose' Arts Council Retrospective *The Road is Wider Than Long* reprinted Roland returns to ICA as 'Honorary President'
1980	Honorary doctorate conferred by the University of Sussex
1981	Siri Lanka with Diane De Riaz *Scrap Book 1900–1981,* Roland's autobiography published 'Picasso's Picassos' exhibition at the Tate Visits Barcelona for his show at the Fondacio Joan Miro
1982	Visits Trouville, France with Diane Deriaz 'Roland Penrose, Collages Récents' exhibition at the Galerie Henriette Gomis Paris
1983	Visits Malindi, Kenya, with Diane Deriaz 'Roland Penrose, Recent Collages' at the Mayor Gallery
1984	Visits Seychelles with Diane Deriaz January Dies at Farley Farm 23 April. 'Roland Penrose Recent Collages and Lee Miller in Sussex' exhibition Gardner Arts Centre, Brighton

ROLAND PENROSE: THE MAJOR WORKS

Works by Roland Penrose mentioned in the text, in national collections or featuring in major exhibitions.

Date	Title	Medium
*c.*1924	*The Road to Cassis*	Oil on canvas
*c.*1925	*Boat Bath*	Oil on canvas
1928	*Conversation between Rock and Flower*	Oil on canvas
1929	*Composition with Spheres*	Frottage
	Col. Victoria & Albert Museum	
1932	*Valentine with Cat*	Oil on canvas
	Beauty Prize	
	Collage	
	Exhibited at International Surrealist Exhibition 1936	
1933	*Ox Cart*	Watercolour
1934	*Portrait of a Leaf*	Oil on board
	Abstract composition	Oil on canvas
1935	*Running Mask*	Oil on canvas
	Armed Man	Oil on canvas
1936	*The Freedom of the Seas*	Oil on canvas
	Exhibited at International Surrealist Exhibition 1936	
	Col. Estate of Eileen Agar	
	The Scales	Oil on canvas
	Col. The Israel Museum, Jerusalem	
	Le Paradis des Alouettes	Mixed media object
	Captain Cook's Last Voyage	Mixed media object
	Col. Tate Modern	
1937	*Night and Day*	Oil on canvas
	Seeing is Believing (L'Île Invisible)	Oil on canvas
	The Human Frame or *Nude in Window*	Oil on canvas
	Man Wrestling with his Thoughts	Oil on canvas
	Beacus Penrose or *Nautical Composition*	Oil on canvas
	La Promenade	Oil on canvas
	Nourishment from Heaven	Drawing
	Soleil de Mougins	Collage
1937	*The Real Woman*	Collage
	Col. National Trust	
	La Méditerranée. Étude Artistique	Collage

Date	Title	Medium
1937	*Venus of Monte Carlo*	Collage
	Dew Machine	Mixed media object
	Guaranteed Fine Weather Suitcase	Mixed media object
	The Survivor	Mixed media object
	Condensation of Games	Mixed media object
1938	*Winged Domino*	Oil on canvas
	Enemy the Sun	Oil on canvas
	Untitled Painting (Hair Boat)	Oil on canvas
	The Junction	Oil on canvas
	Col. The Israel Museum, Jerusalem	
	The Revolving Statue	Oil on canvas
	The Veteran	Oil on canvas
	Col. New Orleans Museum of Art	
	Magnetic Moths	Collage
	Col. Tate Modern	
	Le Grand Jour	Mixed media
	Col. Tate Modern	
	Elephant Bird	Collage
	Col. Victoria and Albert Museum	
1939	*Octavia* (Also entitled *Aurelia*)	Oil on canvas
	Col. Ferens Art Gallery, Hull	
	Good shooting (Also entitled *Bien Vise*)	Oil on canvas
	Col. Southampton Art Gallery	
	The Conquest of the Air	Oil on canvas
	Col. Southampton Art Gallery	
	Egypt	Oil on canvas
	Portrait	Oil on canvas
	Col. Tate Modern	
	My Windows Look Sideways …	Oil on canvas
	Col. Scottish National Gallery of Modern Art	
	The Road Is Wider Than Long	Book – London Gallery
	From the Housetops	Monotype
1940	*Black Music*	Oil on board
	Night Music	Oil on canvas
1940	*Night Orchestra*	Oil on canvas
	Nightfall	Oil on canvas
	The Dance	Oil on canvas
	Cryptic Coincidence II	Oil on canvas
	The Home Guard Manual of Camouflage	Book – Routledge
1945	*In The Service of the People*	Oil on canvas
	Col. Dr Jeffrey & Ruth Sherwin	

Date	Title	Medium
1945	*The Duchess*	Oil on canvas
	Jacobite Jacobin	Unknown
	Moon Tiger Night	Unknown
1947	*First View*	Oil on canvas
	Faites Vos Jeux	Oil on canvas
	Getting up and Going Out	Oil on canvas
	RP's First Letter to Mrs Penrose 3rd May	Decalcomania
	Self Portrait	Watercolour
	Col. National Portrait Gallery	
1948	*Une Chevelure Blonde Dans Une Barque*	Drawing
1949	*Don't You Hate Having Two Heads?*	Oil on canvas
	The Flight of Flies	Oil on canvas
1950	*The Third Eye* or *The Eye of The Storm*	Oil on canvas
	Fireplace in Farley's dinning room	Mural Oil
1951	Tree trunk at Farleys	Sculpture, acacia wood
1953	*The Tête Gallery*	Sculpture painted plaster
	Exhibited in Two Private Eyes,	
	Guggenheim New York 1999	
1956	*Portrait of Picasso*	Book – Lund Humphries
1958	*Picasso, His Life and Work*	Book – Gollancz
1960	Christmas Card for Lee Miller	Collage
1965	*Fountain*	Sculpture, copper
1968	*Hommage to Appolinaire*	Watercolour
1970	*Miró*	Book – Thames & Hudson
1975	*Hommage à Man Ray*	Mixed media
	Hommage à Max Ernst	Aquatint
	Man Ray	Book – Thames & Hudson
1978	*Hommage à Miró*	Collage
	Tàpies	Book – Thames & Hudson
1980	Poster for RP Retro Exhibition	Watercolour
1981	*How do you Like Sri Lanka Sir?*	Collage
	House the Light House?	Collage
	Col. Tate Modern	
	Scrap Book, 1900 – 1981	Book – Thames & Hudson
1982	*Reclining Target*	Collage
	No Top No Bottom	Collage
1983	*Fertility I Kenya*	Collage
	Birth of an Island	Collage
1984	*Seychelles No 1 The Sun Was Shinning*	Collage
	Seychelles No 7 It Was Raining	Collage
	The Last One (Seychelles)	Collage

SELECT BIBLIOGRAPHY

Ades, Dawn. *Dada and Surrealism Reviewed.* Arts Council of Great Britain, 1978.

Agar, Eileen. *A Look At My Life.* Methuen, 1988.

Bouhassane, Ami. *Lee Miller, A Life With Food Friends and Recipes.* Grapefruckt Forlag and Farleys House and Gallery Ltd, 2017.

Buñuel, Luis. *My Last Breath.* Knopf, *1984.*

Chadwick, Whitney. *Women Artists and the Surrealist Movement.* Thames & Hudson, 1985.

Deffebach, Nancy. *Alice Rahon Portfolio.* On The Bus Vol. III, No. 2 & Vol. IV. No. 1, Bombshelter Press, Los Angeles, 1991.

Ernst, Jimmy. *A Not So Still Life.* Pushcart Press, New York, 1984.

Gascoyne, David. *Journal 1937-1939.* Enitharmon Press, 1978.

Gilot, François. *Life With Picasso.* McGraw Hill, New York, 1964.

Gonzales, Sylvie (Editor). *Paul, Max et les Autres.* Éditions de l'Albaron, 1993.

Guggenheim, Peggy. *Out of This Century.* The Dial Press, New York, 1946.

Hartley, Keith. *Roland Penrose, private passions for the public good.* Catalogue essay in *Roland Penrose and Lee Miller, The Surrealist and the Photographer*. Scottish National Gallery of Modern Art, 2001.

Huffington, Ariana. *Picasso Creator and Destroyer.* Avon Books, New York, 1989.

Hubert, Renée Riese. *Magnifying Mirrors.* University of Nebraska Press, 1994.

King, James. Roland Penrose: *The Life of a Surrealist.* Edinburgh University Press, 2016

Massey, Anne. *The Independent Group.* Manchester University Press, 1995.

Melly, George. Photographs by Michael Woods. *Paris and the Surrealists.* Thames & Hudson, 1991.

Melly, George. *Its All Writ Out For You – The Life and work of Scottie Wilson.* Thames and Hudson, 1986.

Melly, George. *Don't Tell Sybil: an Intimate Memoir of E.L.T. Mesens.* Random House UK Ltd, 1997.

Morris, Desmond. *Animal Days.* Cape, 1979.

Newark, Timothy. *Camouflage – Camouflaging a natio*n. Pages 92, 93, 96, 97 & 117. Thames and Hudson and The Imperial War museum, March 2007

Penrose, Antony. *The Lives of Lee Miller.* Thames & Hudson, 1985.

Penrose, Antony. *The Home of The Surrealists.* Farleys House and Gallery Ltd, 2017.

Penrose, Roland. *The Road is Wider Than Long.* London Gallery Editions, 1939.

Penrose, Roland. *The Home Guard Manual of Camouflage.* Butler and Tanner, 1941.

Penrose, Roland. *Picasso His Life and Work.* Gollancz, 1958.

Penrose, Roland. *Portrait of Picasso.* Lund Humphries, 1956.

Penrose, Roland. *Miro.* Thames & Hudson, 1970.

Penrose, Roland. *Man Ray.* Thames & Hudson, 1975.

Penrose, Roland. *Tàpies.* Thames & Hudson, 1978.

Penrose, Roland. *Scrap Book 1900-1981.* Thames & Hudson, 1981.

Penrose, Valentine. *Poems and Narations.* Translation and Foreword by Roy Edwards. Carcanet Press and Elephant Trust, 1976

Remy, Michel. *Surrealism in Britain.* Ashgate, 1999.

Read, Herbert. *Surrealism.* Faber & Faber, 1936.

Richardson, John. *The Sorcerer's Apprentice.* Knopf, New York. 1999.

Sorel, Nancy Caldwell. *The Women Who Wrote the War.* Arcade, New York. 1999.

Spalding, Frances. *The Tate, A History.* Tate Gallery Publishing, 1998.

Surrealism in England in 1936 and After. Catalogue of Exhibition at the Herbert Read Gallery, Canterbury College of Art, 1986.

Smith, Michael. *Lionel Sharples Penrose: A Biography.* Michael Smith, 1999.

Tacou-Rumney, Laurence. *Peggy Guggenheim. A Collector's Album.* Flammarion, Paris – New York, 1996.

Trevelyan, Julian. *Indigo Days.* Scolar Press, 1957.

INDEX

Locators in *italics* refer to works illustrations.

D

E

H

M

N

O